Fodor's

RIO DE JANEIRO
& SÃO PAULO

RUA
DO
COMÉRCIO

AGENCIA DE CORREIOS

WITHDRAWN

D0041227

Portions of this book appear in *Fodor's Brazil.*

WELCOME TO RIO DE JANEIRO AND SÃO PAULO

Visitors to Rio de Janeiro and São Paulo should prepare to have their senses engaged to the fullest. Rio enthralls with its scenic mountains, colorful Carnival celebrations, and vibrant beaches. Sway to a bossa nova tune in glamorous Ipanema before staking out a spot at popular Copacabana beach. Brazil's most cosmopolitan city, São Paulo beguiles with top-notch nightlife and restaurants—not to mention a chic shopping scene that attracts fashionistas from around the globe. Need a break from city life? Glitzy Búzios and serene Ilhabela beckon nearby.

TOP REASONS TO GO

★ **Beaches:** White sand and stylish sunbathers await at Copacabana, Ipanema, and Búzios.

★ **Nightlife:** From Rio's Carnival to São Paulo's club scene, the options are endless.

★ **Rio's Hills:** The views from the iconic Christ the Redeemer Statue are breathtaking.

★ **Dining:** Brazilian flavors and cutting-edge fusion cuisine are here for the tasting.

★ **Shopping:** São Paulo's boutiques hold treasures for all budgets.

★ **Soccer:** Cheering with fans at the cities' iconic stadiums is a memorable experience.

12

TOP EXPERIENCES

Rio de Janeiro and São Paulo offer terrific experiences that should be on every traveler's list. Here are Fodor's top picks for a memorable trip.

1 Copacabana and Ipanema Beaches

Slip into your beachwear for a day of sunbathing and people-watching on Copacabana and Ipanema, Brazil's most iconic beaches. *(Ch. 2)*

2 Carnival in Rio

Brazilians can throw a party like no one else, and Rio's Carnival is the biggest party of the year—a raucous bacchanal of music, drink, and flesh. *(Ch. 2)*

3 Museu de Arte de São Paulo

In a city renowned for its thriving arts scene, the Museu de Arte holds São Paulo's premier fine-arts collection. *(Ch. 4)*

4 Brazilian Beats

Music is woven into the fabric of Brazilian life, and no trip here is complete without catching a live show, whether samba, bossa nova, axé, or forró. *(Ch. 1)*

5 Ilhabela

Residents and tourists alike flock to the "beautiful island" of Ilhabela, near São Paulo, for its postcard-perfect beaches and water sports. *(Ch. 5)*

6 Food and Drink

From spit-roasted meats to black bean stews, the cuisines in Rio and São Paulo pair well with a *caipirinha*, the national cocktail. *(Ch. 1)*

7 São Paulo Nightlife

São Paulo's nightlife options are seemingly endless and prove worthy venues for even the feistiest nighthawk. *(Ch. 4)*

8 Sugar Loaf Mountain

Brave the dizzying cable car ride up to the peak of Sugar Loaf mountain in Rio de Janeiro. Try to make the ascent in the late afternoon to catch breathtaking sunset views. *(Ch. 2)*

9 Búzios

Less than three hours from Rio, this former fishing village counts pristine beaches, calm waters, lively nightlife, and sophisticated shopping among its many charms. *(Ch. 3)*

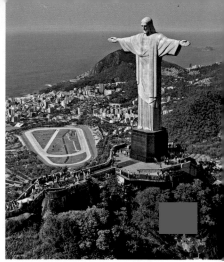

10 Soccer Matches

Soccer is a national passion and an art form in Brazil. It's a blast to sit among thousands of cheering, chanting fans in one of the country's iconic stadiums. *(Ch. 1)*

11 Christ the Redeemer Statue

Don't leave Rio without making a trip to the statue of Christ the Redeemer, arms outstretched to embrace the city from its perch on Corcovado Mountain. *(Ch. 2)*

12 Paraty

The coastal town of Paraty, southwest of Rio, is a UNESCO World Heritage Site and has one of the most perfectly preserved colonial Portuguese centers in Brazil. *(Ch. 3)*

CONTENTS

MAPS

ABOUT THIS GUIDE

Fodor's Recommendations

Everything in this guide is worth doing—we don't cover what isn't—but exceptional sights, hotels, and restaurants are recognized with additional accolades. **Fodor's Choice★** indicates our top recommendations; and **Best Bets** calls attention to notable hotels and restaurants in various categories. Care to nominate a new place? Visit Fodors.com/contact-us.

Trip Costs

We list prices wherever possible to help you budget well. Hotel and restaurant price categories from **$** to **$$$$** are noted alongside each recommendation. For hotels, we include the lowest cost of a standard double room in high season. For restaurants, we cite the average price of a main course at dinner or, if dinner isn't served, at lunch. For attractions, we always list adult admission fees; discounts are usually available for children, students, and senior citizens.

Hotels

Our local writers vet every hotel to recommend the best overnights in each price category, from budget to expensive. Unless otherwise specified, you can expect private bath, phone, and TV in your room. For expanded hotel reviews, facilities, and deals, visit Fodors.com.

Top Picks	Hotels & Restaurants
★ **Fodor's** Choice	🏨 Hotel
Listings	🛏 Number of rooms
✉ Address	🍽 Meal plans
✉ Branch address	✕ Restaurant
☎ Telephone	⌖ Reservations
🖷 Fax	👔 Dress code
⊕ Website	▭ No credit cards
✉ E-mail	$ Price
✉ Admission fee	**Other**
☉ Open/closed times	⇨ See also
Ⓜ Subway	☞ Take note
✛ Directions or Map coordinates	🏌 Golf facilities

Restaurants

Unless we state otherwise, restaurants are open for lunch and dinner daily. We mention dress code only when there's a specific requirement and reservations only when they're essential or not accepted. To make restaurant reservations, visit Fodors.com.

Credit Cards

The hotels and restaurants in this guide typically accept credit cards. If not, we'll say so.

EUGENE FODOR

Hungarian-born Eugene Fodor (1905–91) began his travel career as an interpreter on a French cruise ship. The experience inspired him to write *On the Continent* (1936), the first guidebook to receive annual updates and discuss a country's way of life as well as its sights. Fodor later joined the U.S. Army and worked for the OSS in World War II. After the war, he kept up his intelligence work while expanding his guidebook series. During the Cold War, many guides were written by fellow agents who understood the value of insider information. Today's guides continue Fodor's legacy by providing travelers with timely coverage, insider tips, and cultural context.

1

EXPERIENCE
RIO DE JANEIRO
& SÃO PAULO

BRAZIL TODAY

Brazil is immensely diverse—socially, culturally, racially, economically—and rife with profound contradictions that are not always evident at first. All this makes for a complex nation that eludes easy definitions—but is fascinating to discover.

Culture

Brazil's contrasts are everywhere. Take a look around when you land. Dense forests that are home to pint-sized monkeys and birds found nowhere else brush up against gleaming high-rises, which in turn border *favelas* (shantytowns). Juxtapositions of this sort can make any experience breathtaking and shocking at once.

Brazilians are known for their warmth, their tiny bikinis, their frequent public displays of affection—it's not uncommon to see couples kissing at length on a park bench or a beach blanket—and their riotous displays of joie de vivre in annual Carnival celebrations. But the country is also home to the world's largest Catholic population, and conservative sexual mores shape the culture more than visitors might imagine.

A stroll through any Brazilian town will show you this is one of the most racially mixed populations anywhere. The country was shaped not only by the Portuguese, who brought their religion and language, but also by millions of enslaved Africans, the native indigenous, and waves of European, Arabic, and Japanese immigrants. Most Brazilians include elements from several of these backgrounds in their cultural and ethnic heritage.

Brazil never had the institutionalized discrimination that marked the United States, yet it is far from being a color-blind society. In spite of the recent economic boom, blacks and the indigenous still face stiff discrimination and underrepresentation in government. They also far outweigh whites at the broad base of Brazil's economic pyramid.

Politics

Brazil's current president, Dilma Rouseff, is an example of how Brazil defies stereotypes. The fact that she is a woman—and twice divorced at that, currently living without a husband—was scarcely discussed during her 2010 and 2014 campaigns for president, even though this is a country were *machismo* (male chauvinism) still thrives.

Of far greater importance to voters during her first presidential campaign was that she is a member of the *Partido dos Trabalhadores* (PT), or Workers Party, and had the support of the immensely popular outgoing president, Luiz Inácio Lula da Silva, who had towered over the political landscape for the previous decade. Lula's story is fascinating. Born into poverty in the country's Northeast, he rose to prominence in São Paulo as a union leader while the country was still under the rule of a military dictatorship that had seized power in 1964. Buoyed by his charisma and his appeal to poor Brazilians, Lula was elected to the presidency twice. His popularity played a large part in securing victory for Rousseff in her initial election campaign.

During Rousseff's first term, the country slipped into recession, and many took to the streets to demand better public services. Rousseff has divided the country by keeping in place transfer-of-wealth policies that have helped alleviate poverty, but which many wealthier Brazilians see as spoon-feeding the poor in return for votes. She is widely popular in the North and Northeast but has less support in São Paulo and the South.

Economy

After punishing years of economic instability and hyperinflation in the 1980s and '90s, Brazil's GDP began to grow along with prices and demand for the commodities that make up the base of its economy, including soybeans, sugar, iron ore, and oil.

The last decade of social progress has created real improvement in the quality of life for Brazil's new middle class. About 35 million Brazilians have hoisted themselves out of poverty in that time. More than half of the country's 194 million people now officially belong to the middle class. However, many still hover perilously close to the bottom, and many more live in neighborhoods that still don't have such services as trash collection, sewage treatment, and safety. Even though the improvements have been real and visible, there have been increasing protests recently over issues such as public health care and education.

Religion

Brazil has the world's largest Catholic population, although Roman Catholicism has been losing worshippers to Evangelical churches. These churches are booming, especially in poorer communities where it is not uncommon to see several modest storefront churches on a single street.

In religion, like in so many other aspects of Brazil, the reality is more complex than it first appears. The country's rich ethnic and cultural heritage means that the dominant Christianity is often blended with other sects and religions, creating fascinating local variants that are unique to Brazil.

The most widespread examples of this blending happen within Afro-Brazilian religious practices. Forbidden from worshipping the deities they brought with them from Africa, enslaved men and women established connections between their *orixas,* or gods, and saints from the Catholic faith of their masters. This way, they could pay homage to their own gods while keeping up appearances by seeming to pray to Catholic saints.

Although freedom of religion is enshrined in the constitution, Brazil's many contradictions surface in attitudes toward Afro-Brazilian faiths such as Candomble, the more orthodox of the variations, and Umbanda, an even more syncretic religion incorporating elements of French-based spiritualism. Although some Afro-Brazilian practices are popular, including wearing white on New Year's Eve and leaving gifts of flowers and fruit on the beach to honor Iemanja, the orixa of oceans and seas, serious practitioners can be frequent targets of discrimination.

Sports

Even before the 2014 FIFA World Cup, the world knew that soccer—or *futebol*—was king here. The country's mad about it, and there's good reason: Brazil has produced some of the world's best players, and it is the only nation to have won five World Cups. The displays of passion seen during major games make them worthy of a visit. Although there is criticism over the way soccer is run, love for the "jogo bonito," or beautiful game, is unabated.

Volleyball is also a favorite. Beaches are often settings for spectacular displays of beach volleyball, and of a Brazilian combination of the two: *futevolei*, where the players can use only their feet, chest, and head to touch the volleyball.

WHAT'S WHERE

RIO DE JANEIRO

1 Centro. Until the government moved to Brasília, this was the center of power, and plenty of impressive monuments, parks, and colonial buildings remain. On weekdays streets are swollen with rushing businesspeople, but on weekends most restaurants and cafés are closed and streets can be eerily deserted.

2 Copacabana. Facing the world's most famous crescent of beach, this neighborhood actually runs only about five blocks between the hills and the sea. Crammed inside this tight space are many of the city's hotels as well as towering apartment blocks, restaurants, and souvenir shops.

3 Ipanema. Immortalized by the bossa nova song and frequented by the rich and beautiful, this is one of Rio's most upscale neighborhoods. The treelined streets are packed with trendy stores and swanky restaurants. The beach here is a bit cleaner and less crowded than its neighbor Copacabana.

4 Catete and Glória. Historic Catete and Glória are well worth an afternoon's sightseeing. The national government formerly operated out of Catete, which still has its beautiful palaces and old residences, and Glória is famous for its beautiful hilltop church.

5 Leblon. Stretching west along the same beachfront as Ipanema, Leblon is Rio's most sophisticated neighborhood. Foodies flock to the neighborhood's hip restaurants, while shoppers browse for designer gear at chic boutiques and upmarket malls. The beach itself is a little quieter than its famous neighbor, and is popular with families.

6 Santa Teresa. Often referred to as the Montmartre of South America, historic Santa Teresa is, like the Parisian neighborhood, an arsty enclave perched high on a hillside. Santa Teresa's steep cobblestone streets are lined with well-preserved and brightly painted colonial houses, some of which double as bed-and-breakfasts.

7 São Conrado and Barra da Tijuca. While the urban landscape of shopping malls and traffic jams can be a little searing in these western suburbs, fortunately the waterfront makes up for it. There are 18 km (11 miles) of some of the most beautiful beaches in the city, with stretches for surfers, kids, and even hang gliders.

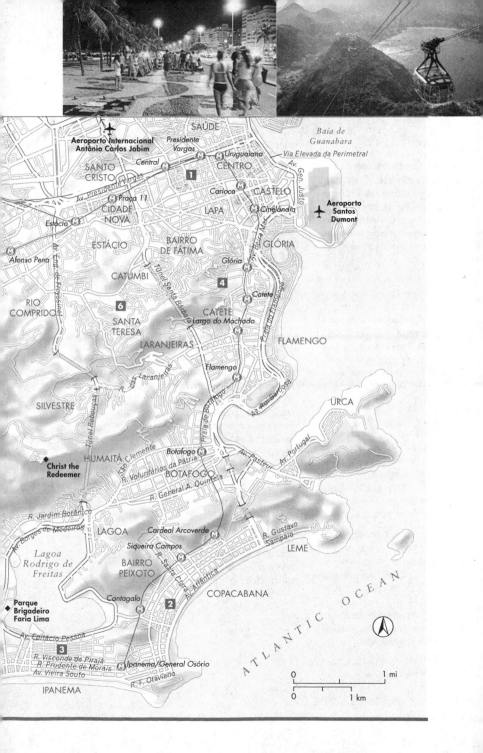

WHAT'S WHERE

SÃO PAULO

1 Centro. Though more gritty than pretty, Centro still teems with life and has the city's best architecture. Keep your eyes peeled for striking, colorful street art, often with a powerful political message.

2 Liberdade. This area is the hub of the city's Chinese and and Korean neighborhoods, and home to the largest Japanese community outside of Japan itself. On Sunday the Praça Liberdade hosts an Asian food and crafts fair, and the lantern-lined streets are pedestrian-friendly.

3 Avenida Paulista. If a city as big as São Paulo could have a principal street, Paulista, with its hotels, banks, and cultural institutions, would be it. Running along a hilltop, its north side is often called the Bela Vista side and the south side Jardins.

4 Bixiga. Officially called Bela Vista, this area is considered the old Italian heart of the city. Cozy bars and restaurants called *cantinas* run along Rua 13 de Maio. You'll find diamonds in the rough hidden among this working-class neighborhood.

5 Jardins. Its streets lined with big mossy trees and million-dollar apartments, Jardins offers Brazil's poshest shops, restaurants, and nightspots. Shade during the day and safety at night make this neighborhood a good bet for exploring by foot.

6 Itaim Bibi. As the city stretches south, the small streets of Jardins give way to the avenues of Itaim, known for boutiques, nightclubs, and gourmet restaurants. It's a good bet for those who need to do business in the south zone but still want to be close to downtown culture.

7 Pinheiros. Pinheiros. A quiet neighborhood where houses outnumber apartment buildings, Pinheiros's weekend cultural life centers on the Saturday antiques fair at Praça Benedito Calixto. The 'hood is also the center of bohemian nightlife.

8 Vila Madalena. The bohemian rep of this neighborhood comes from the time when journalists and artists gathered here to criticize the military dictatorship. Now its bars and restaurants are well-established nightspots.

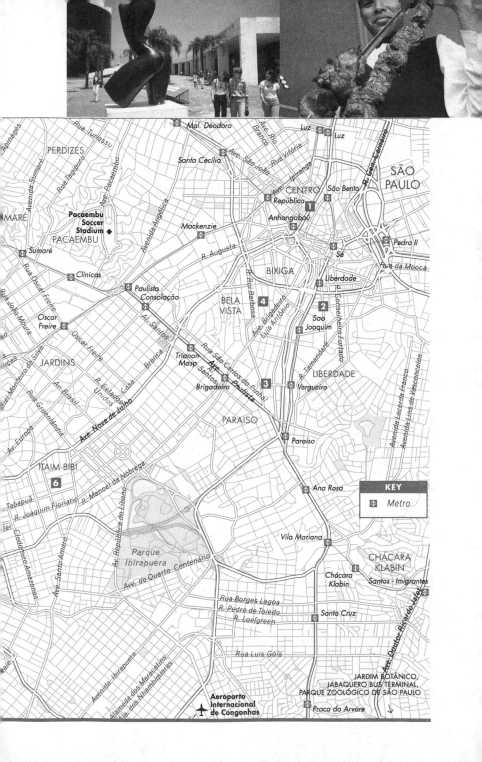

RIO DE JANEIRO AND SÃO PAULO PLANNER

Visitor Information

Although you can enjoy Rio de Janeiro and São Paulo on your own, a guide can help facilitate multiday trips through them. Official municipal tour offices offer basic information, from public transit maps to bank hours.

Rio de Janeiro Riotur, ⊕ *www.rio. rj.gov.br* ☎ *55–21/2542–8080 or 55–21/2542–8004.*

São Paulo Turismo ⊕ *www. cidadedesaopaulo.com/sp* ☎ *55–11/2226–0400.*

Festivals and Events

Festa Junina: Throughout June, Brazilians celebrate country culture, dressing their kids in blooming dresses and painting freckles on their cheeks. Enjoy rustic music while sipping *quentãos,* cocktails with wine, ginger, clove, and cinnamon.

Réveillon: Brazilians take New Year's Eve seriously—it doesn't hurt that it takes place in the middle of the hot summer. Rio's Copacabana Beach overflows with more than a million revelers each year for a fireworks and live-music show. Traditionalists wear all white in a nod to the customs of the Afro-Brazilian Candomble religion, and flowers are placed in the waters as gifts to *Yemanja,* the Candomble goddess of the sea.

Getting Here and Around

Getting Here: International flights largely arrive in Rio de Janeiro's Galeão airport or São Paulo's Guarulhos. Some nationalities, Americans and Canadians included, require a visa issued from a consulate abroad to enter Brazil. Visas are not granted on arrival. Tourist visas are generally valid for three months and can be extended for another three months by visiting the Federal Police and paying a fee.

Getting Around: Bus trips are a good option for short trips, such as exploring Rio de Janeiro's coastal beaches or traveling from São Paulo to Rio. Brazil does not have a developed intermunicipal train system, though a bullet train from São Paulo to Rio is predicted to be ready by 2020. Both Rio and São Paulo have affordable metro systems that cover most of the areas of the cities that tourists would hope to see. Expect to walk several blocks even when you get off at the station closest to your destination. Take advantage of the metro during rush hour to avoid heavy traffic. Taxis are plentiful in Rio and São Paulo, and in most parts of these cities you can easily flag one down on the street.

When to Go

Prices in beach resorts are higher during the Brazilian summer season (December–February) and in July (school-break month). If you're looking for a bargain, stick to May–June and August–October, when the weather tends to be mild. Rio suffers from oppressive heat November through April, with searing temperatures in January and February.

Climate: Seasons below the equator are the reverse of the north—summer in Brazil runs from December to March and winter from June to September. The rainy season in Brazil occurs during the summer months. Showers can be torrential but usually last no more than an hour or two.

Rio de Janeiro is on the Tropic of Capricorn, and its climate is just that—tropical. Summers are hot and humid. Be extra careful with sun exposure and use a high SPF sunscreen. In São Paulo, winter temperatures can fall to the low 40s (5°C–8°C).

Staying Safe in Rio and São Paulo

Throngs of tourists have perfectly safe vacations in Brazil each year. Still, crime and violence are sad realities in Rio de Janeiro and São Paulo. A few common-sense tips can help you have a safe trip:

Petty crime. Keep your belongings close to you and be aware of what you do and do not need as you go out each day. Stashing some cash and a credit card in a money belt is wise, as is keeping your camera in a small *pochette* (as Brazilians affectionately call fanny packs). This will make for a worry-free, hands-off day.

Carry with you only a copy of your passport as an ID—you won't need the actual document, except when making large purchases like airline tickets. In the case of a mugging, do not resist, and give up all belongings immediately. Should you be the victim of a crime, both cities have specialized tourist police stations, where police are bilingual and take extra care with your case. São Paulo's stations, for example, called the Delegacia Especializada em Atendimento ao Turista, can be found in the Guarulhos and Congonhas airports, as well as next to the Mercado Municipal and in the Parque Anhembi.

Walking. In both cities, stick to areas with high pedestrian traffic. In touristy areas, avoid walking in alleyways and closed-off areas that are empty. At night, walk only if you are in a well-lighted area with heavy pedestrian traffic.

Public Transportation. Taxis in Rio and São Paulo are regulated, safe, fairly priced, and obediently run on the meter. The subway is also a safe and fast way to get around. Buses are a widely used form of transport both within and between cities, but are occasionally the target of robberies. Avoid the informal vans that locals commonly use. After dark, take only cabs.

Money and Credit Cards. Watch your bank account after using debit cards in ATMs, since card cloning is common. Making payments with credit cards is generally fine, but keep an eye on your account.

Lodging: The Basics

Rio de Janeiro and São Paulo have a variety of lodging options, ranging from luxurious to no-frills budget hotels and bed-and-breakfasts. Beachside hotels in Ipanema or Leblon offer superlative rooms and services, as do São Paulo lodgings in posh neighborhoods like Jardins. In Rio, expect to pay a premium for a room with a view, while in São Paulo make sure to ask about noise and request a room far above the city's crowded streets. If you're traveling to either city during peak periods—from December to March—make reservations as far ahead of your visit as possible. Avoid hotels in Copacabana's backstreets, as backed-up traffic means air quality is terrible.

Rio and São Paulo's coasts offer several high-end resorts, but also a variety of casual sand-and-surf inns, called *pousadas* in Portuguese. Expect swelling crowds in the summer and book in advance.

FREE AND ALMOST FREE

RIO DE JANEIRO

Outdoor Attractions

It may be a cliché to say that the best things in life are free, but the sentiment rings true in Rio de Janeiro. For proof of this, just take a stroll along the beaches of Ipanema, Copacabana, and Leblon or around the beautiful city lake, Lagoa, soaking up the sun and admiring the stunning views. Entrance to the vast Parque Nacional da Tijuca is also free, although it is wise to stick to the main paths and go in a group if you can't afford a guide.

There are some impressive man-made attractions that are free to visit, too. Hop on the metro to the Carioca stop to admire the colorful stairwell known as the Escadaria Selarón. Nearby, check out the Lapa Aqueduct before turning your attention to some of the city's best colonial architecture in Lapa and Santa Teresa.

Museums, Galleries, and Cultural Centers

For a city known for its partying and beach culture, Rio boasts a surprisingly high number of excellent options for culture vultures on a budget. The imposing Centro Cultural Banco do Brasil and Caixa Cultural host impressive visiting art exhibitions and free film screenings. Most attractions that do charge an entry fee (including Palácio do Catete and the Museu Nacional de Belas Artes) are free to enter on Sunday. At the eye-catching Museu de Arte do Rio, a new arts center at the heart of Rio's regenerated port zone, the R$8 entry fee is waived on Tuesday.

Economical Eats

Budget visitors to Rio can eat well for very little, provided they avoid formal dining. At lunchtime, head to the Centro area for some well-priced buffet spots, where you pay by weight for anything from sushi and bean salads to steak and sausages. While similar spots in the Zona Sul charge upward of R$5 per 100 grams, in the Centro you can chow down for less than half that price.

All you need to do is stroll along the side streets that branch off Carioca and Uruguaiana squares, and look for the best prices. The cost per 100 grams is usually displayed in restaurant windows. When you enter, you will be given a piece of paper that you hand over to the staff member who will weigh your plate. Extras such as drinks will be marked at your table, and the paper is handed to the cashier when you're ready to leave. You're not obliged to eat: if you enter and don't like the look of the buffet, simply head for the exit and hand your paper back to the door staff.

■ TIP→ **Most restaurants are open from 11 am to 3:30 pm and charge less before noon and after 2 pm.**

Street Treats

Street eats are another great bet. Meat eaters can bite into burgers and hot dogs piled high with everything from matchstick potatoes to olives and quail eggs for less than R$2. Tapioca (a savory pancake made from tapioca flour) filled with cheese and tomato is a great veggie and gluten-free option that typically costs under R$7.

SÃO PAULO

Take the Stroll Road

Avenida Paulista features São Paulo's most expensive real estate but also its most popular sidewalks. Cultural centers, parks, bookstores, and iconic buildings are only some of the free attractions that line the 3-km (2-mile) road. The historic center holds great strolls as well. English-speaking guides lead free walking tours on Wednesday and Saturday afternoons. The architectural highlights include the Copan Building, Municipal Theater, and São Bento Monastery.

Default Browsers

Shopping is as much a staple of *paulistanos'* pastimes as rice and beans are of their diets. Retail ranges from Ara Vartanian and Burberry stores to the stockyards of knockoffs around Rua 25 de Março. For those looking to scrimp rather than splurge, window-gazing is a fun option. Luxury malls, such as JK Iguatemi, and trendy thoroughfares, like Oscar Freire, have beguiling display cases.

From the Windows to the Walls

Fernando Pessoa, Portinari, and Pele—São Paulo museums celebrate Brazilian masters of art forms, from fine art to futebol. Most of the leading museums charge admittance but also comp visitors at least once a week. These include Museu de Arte de São Paulo (MASP) on Tuesday; Museu do Futebol on Thursday; Pinacoteca do Estado on Saturday; Catavento Cultural on Saturday; and Museu de Arte Contemporânea on Sunday.

São Paulo also assumes a top pedestal on the street-art circuit. Walls around the metropolis are covered with top-notch work from roving *grafiteiros* (graffiti artists). Revered hot spots include Museu Aberto de Arte Urbano; Beco Aprendiz das Letras; Beco do Batman; and Túnel da Paulista.

Unstopped Programming

For one weekend each May, the Virada Cultural brings a 24-hour spree of free cultural programming. São Paulo's city government erects stages throughout the downtown area, where international and domestic musical acts headline the agenda.

Free entertainment remains available on the other 364 days. The annual English Cultural Festival features indie rock from across the Atlantic. The Bourbon Street Fest brings jazz and blues. Social Service of Commerce (SESC) cultural centers sponsor shows at little or no cost nearly every week.

Sala São Paulo, Brazil's premier classical music venue, gives away tickets to its Sunday matinees a week in advance. Competition is fierce and space can disappear only a few hours after becoming available. Seating is easier to attain for Sunday concerts at Auditório Ibirapuera. Brazilian pop, jazz, and soul predominate from a stage overlooking one of the park's lawns.

Galeria Olido promotes samba on Tuesday and samba rock on Thursday. Leading up to Carnival, Brazil's rhythmic trademark seizes the spotlight in São Paulo, with free *blocos* (mini-parade troupes) and samba school presentations.

RIO DE JANEIRO AND SÃO PAULO LIKE A LOCAL

RIO DE JANEIRO

The locals in Rio de Janeiro revel in their good fortune at being surrounded by such dazzling beauty. At the same time, many locals' personal hangouts are not those that they will enthuse about. They may consider their local bars, restaurants, or shops a little modest for tourists' tastes, but these less-celebrated spots are often among the liveliest and most laid-back in the city.

Shopping

With the high prices in Rio's shopping malls, it can be hard to understand just how *cariocas* can afford to look so good. For an answer, take the metro to the Uruguaiana stop. The vast indoor market here is a hotbed of bargain beauty buys, while the maze of shopping streets nearby, known as Saara, is the place to find affordable clothing that will have you looking like a local. From the denim shorts and tank tops that are virtually a cradle-to-grave uniform for female cariocas (the male counterpart being Bermuda shorts and loose T-shirts) to spangly Carnival costumes, Saara and Uruguaiana offer it all in abundance. Take the time to sample the fare at the Middle Eastern food stands here. The name *Saara* (Sahara) was given in honor of the many Arab settlers who have set up shop in the area.

Lunch Like a Local

Formal dining in Rio is so expensive that only the most affluent locals can afford to indulge, but even budget visitors can enjoy a hearty Brazilian repast at one of the city's ubiquitous *comida a kilo* lunch restaurants. Here, diners load up their plates with salads, pasta and rice dishes, pies, tarts, and treats such as stuffed olives and quail eggs. Food is paid for by weight, so hold off on the rice and beans and go for the sushi and the steak if you want to get your money's worth. Prices are usually cheaper before noon and after 2 pm.

Happy Hour Drinks

Cariocas have adopted the English phrase "happy hour" and applied it to their tradition of enjoying after-work drinks. With few exceptions, there aren't many two-for-one drink offers or similar promotions, but happy hour is always a good time to relax with a beer and watch the locals unwind. The business district is a top spot for happy-hour drinks, with Amarelinho a popular bar where drinkers extend happy hour well past midnight. It's handily located for city-center sightseeing, too.

For after-hours weekend drinking, every carioca night owl knows that Rio's real party action is in Lapa. Although the ongoing gentrification of the neighborhood has led to the opening of numerous chain bars that are almost carbon copies of those in the Zona Sul, there is still plenty of opportunity to find a more "authentic" style of Rio nightlife.

Head here on a Friday night to discover Rio's real Dionysian spirit, as revelers drink, dance, and flirt until sunrise at clubs close to the Lapa Arches. On Monday nights, meanwhile, the legendary *roda de samba* at Pedra do Sal (Largo João da Baiana) in a working-class district close to Centro, is a favorite among fleet-footed locals, who gather here for an informal outdoor samba party.

SÃO PAULO

Game On

São Paulo has three of Brazil's most powerful soccer clubs—Corinthians, Palmeiras, and São Paulo—with a fourth titan in neighboring Santos, where all-time and current kings of the national sport, Pelé and Neymar, came to fame. Games normally occur on weekends and Wednesday night, when kickoff happens only after the prime-time Brazilian soaps have concluded.

Parks and Recreation

São Paulo has plenty of public space for amateur athletes and outdoor enthusiasts. Paulistanos convene at the city's plentiful parks to play sports, walk, jog, bike, skate, and sunbathe.

Centrally located Ibirapuera Park—with its ponds, monuments, and Oscar Niemeyer–designed buildings—features many of São Paulo's most recognizable cityscapes. The sprawling lawns and network of pathways attract leisure-seeking locals from all walks of life. The grounds' museums, theaters, and planetarium speak to those seeking mental stimulation.

Outside of Ibirapuera, there's Burle Marx and the botanical gardens in the south, Villa Lobos and the campus of University of São Paulo to the west, Tietê Ecological Park in Guarulhos, and Parque do Juventude up north.

Shopping Till You Drop

If soccer is São Paulo's principal sport, then shopping is surely its second. JK Iguatemi and Cidade Jardim are the city's most opulent malls. With stunning skyline views and greenhouse lushness, both demand as much attention as their encased stores, which feature brands like Animale and Valentino.

São Paulo's streets offer excellent browsing as well. In the Jardins neighborhood, Oscar Freire lures shoppers at the highest end of the market, as does João Cachoeira in Itaim Bibi. Bom Retiro's José Paulino focuses on women's clothing, especially evening wear. The boutiques of Vila Madalena specialize in artwork, apparel, and household ornaments. The vendors of weekend flea markets at plazas Benedito Calixto (Saturday) and Dom Orione (Sunday) sell antiques.

Food Shopping

For food, find the nearest *feira* (farmers' market), where locals purchase much of their produce and chow down on *pasteis* (fried pastries with savory or sweet fillings). These markets change location depending on the day of the week. One of the biggest occurs Saturday in Vila Madalena (Rua Mourato Coelho).

Padarias (bakeries) resemble American-style diners, and are favored locally for their menu diversity. Bella Paulista (near Avenida Paulista) and Santa Etienne (Alto de Pinheiros) top the list.

Nightlife

With its party atmosphere, São Paulo never idles entirely. Paulistanos catch meals and drinks nightly at gastropubs in the Vila Madalena, Pinheiros, Itaim, and Jardins neighborhoods. Bar do Juarez (Itaim) and Boteco São Bento (Vila Madalena) are fashionable choices. Music and dance clubs ensure the celebrations continue into the early hours. Nightlife starts during the afternoon on Saturday, when locals gather to dance samba and pagode, and eat *feijoada* (black bean and pork stew). Try Traço de União (Pinheiros) or Você Vai Se Quiser (Centro).

BEACHGOING IN BRAZIL

Close your eyes, say the word "Brazil," and one of the first images to float up in your mind most likely will be of a tropical beach: white sands, azure water, and a fringe of palm trees. There's good reason for that. The country boasts 8,000 kilometers (5,000 miles) of coastline, and most of the population is concentrated along the coast, where the ocean's moderating influence tempers the tropical sun.

Beaches are often the center of social life, and there is one to suit every taste: kitsch paradises where you can sip juice cocktails under brightly colored umbrellas, chichi playgrounds for the rich, windswept gems, hard-to-reach fishing villages, and surfer havens with pounding waves.

In short, beaches are places to tan, strut, eat, drink, play sports, catch up with friends, and chat with strangers. Beaches are also worth a visit for people-watching and experiencing this quintessential aspect of Brazilian culture.

What to Expect

Brazilians are well known for being comfortable wearing very little. This goes for all ages and body types. Men often wear *sungas,* Speedo-style swimming trunks, though they avoid high-cut models that show too much leg. In recent years, the popular *sungao,* a wider model, has taken over as the outfit of choice. Surfers wear board shorts, and these are acceptable on and off the beach.

Women generally wear two-piece bathing suits, although stylish one-pieces have increasingly become a part of Brazilian beach fashion. Since details such as size, print, and design vary, fashionistas will buy several bikinis to alternate during the summer. Window-shop if you want to get a sense of this year's models. Although the infamous string bikini can still be found, it is no longer common.

Men and women will generally wear light, easy-to-remove clothes over their bathing suits so that they can undress easily at the beach and then compose themselves enough at the end of the day to make a stop at a beachside restaurant. *Havaianas,* rubber flip-flops that come in a rainbow of colors, are ubiquitous.

Finally, *kangas* (sarongs) are a must. The large rectangles of cloth come in a variety of prints and can be used to sit on the sand and to drape over your lounge chair or around your shoulders. Bringing a bulky towel to the beach is something a Brazilian generally wouldn't do.

Forget your kanga at the hotel? Never fear, Brazil's inventive beach vendors will happily sell you one, along with everything from sunblock, light summer dresses, bikinis, and even grilled shrimp. Usually, you can rent lounge chairs, sun umbrellas, and even children's paddling pools from them as well.

Food vendors offer cheese grilled over live coals, popsicles, savory pastries stuffed with spinach, meat, or cheese, frozen açaí slushies, and fresh fruit. Drinks range from the conventional—water, beer, sodas—to the uniquely Brazilian, such as green coconuts, sweet maté tea, and caipirinhas.

While beaches in Brazil are relatively free of hazards—no sharks or jellyfish—conditions vary. Always heed local warnings about riptides. When in Rio, check the newspaper section next to the weather to see if the beach you're planning to go to is clean. Heavy rain showers often wash sewage and trash into the ocean, rendering otherwise beautiful beaches unfit for bathing for at least 24 hours.

FLAVORS OF BRAZIL

Food, for Brazilians, is a social affair—portions are often heaping and, rather than coming individually on one plate, arrive in a series of platters meant to be shared among diners.

Meat and Carbs

Perhaps the most well-known Brazilian staple is meat, especially those that come from *churrascarias* (grills): sizzling cuts of beef, some lined generously with fat, served on skewers by men in aprons and boots called *gaúchos*. (The name refers to the southern state of Rio Grande do Sul, with which the style is associated, though churrascarias are found throughout Brazil.) Brazilians also love their carbs. White rice is served with virtually every meal, often alongside potato fries or *aipim* (cassava), which is usually served fried or baked in butter.

Churrascarias also serve up sausages (*linguiça*), chicken (*frango*), and various types of fish. Expect little in the way of spice—just salt and garlic. The natural flavors of the meat are meant to carry the meal. In a rodízio-style churrascaria, you get all the meat and side dishes you can eat at a fixed price. *Rodízio* means "going around," which explains the gaúchos who constantly circle the restaurant, only resting their skewers to slice another strip of meat onto your plate.

Feijoada, black beans stewed with fatty pork parts, is a popular party food synonymous with carefree weekend afternoons spent digesting the heavy dish. The dish is often topped with *farofa* (toasted manioc root) and served with *couve* (collard greens) and rice. The dish is traditionally served with orange slices, which are said to aid digestion and stop cholesterol levels from soaring.

Native Fruits and Vegetables

Beyond the meat-and-carbs crowd-pleasers, Brazil's tropical expanse allows for a diversity of fruits and vegetables. Visitors will find these on display in colorful *feiras* (fresh-food fairs) throughout the country. Tropical fruits include *maracujá* (passion fruit), *abacaxi* (pineapple), *mamão* (papaya), *caqui* (persimmon), and *acerola* a sour berry with vitamin C levels that are said to be 100 times higher than the orange. When in season, Brazilian fruits crop up as alternatives to lime in *caipirinhas*, Brazil's national drink made with *cachaça*, a sugarcane-based liquor.

Visitors should make a point to sample some of the unique flavors of the Amazon, such as *cupuaçú*, a fragrant yellow fruit, or *mangaba*, something of a cross between a honeydew and a durian. At *lanchonetes*, no-frills snack bars that consist of metal chairs lined along a bar, you'll often find bowls of a purple, sorbet-style concoction made with açai, a purple Amazonian berry that is touted for its health benefits. For an extra energy boost, they may be mixed with *guaraná*, an energy-packed red berry.

Bahian Specialties

Bahian food from Brazil's Northeast revolves around seafood and is normally spicy and hot. Specialties include *moqueca*, a seafood stew cooked quickly in a clay pot over a high flame, and *acarajé*, a bean-meal patty deep-fried in *dendê* oil and filled with sun-dried shrimp and hot-pepper sauce. Brazilians from around the country lick their chops at the mention of *pirão de peixe*, a thick blended stew often made with fish heads and manioc flour.

CARNIVAL IN RIO DE JANEIRO AND SÃO PAULO

Brazilians can throw a party like no one else, and Carnival is the biggest party of the year. This is a time of transgression, when excesses are encouraged and lines are crossed: men dress as women, the poor dress as kings, strangers kiss in the streets, and rules are bent, if only for a few days.

Like Mardi Gras, Carnival has its origins in pagan festivals of spring. Carnival is supposed to last five days, from the Friday until the Tuesday before Ash Wednesday. But the reality is that pre-Carnival parties begin to stoke the wild atmosphere for a few weeks before the official opening ceremony. This is when the mayor gives the keys of the city to the rotund King Momo, a jester-like figure who presides over the chaos and debauchery.

The fun often continues for days after Ash Wednesday. Be prepared for days and nights fueled by light Brazilian beer and potent *caipirinhas* (sugarcane liquor mashed up with fruit), and streets jammed with partiers following sound floats playing old-fashioned samba songs morning to night.

RIO DE JANEIRO

Carnival finds its fullest expression in Rio, where streets are taken over by revelers. The city also hosts the fabulously lavish culmination of the festival: the Carnival parades, in which samba groups (*escolas de samba*) compete for the top prize with elaborate, mechanized floats, sequined dancers, and huge percussion sections.

Safety

The crowds in Rio de Janeiro are surprisingly peaceful, but keep your wits about you. This is generally the hottest time of the year, so drink plenty of water and bring sunblock. Since pickpockets work the masses, carry only cash you plan to spend that day and leave home any nice watches, jewelry, or sunglasses. Groping can be a real hassle for women. Travel in groups and avoid wearing a skirt—hands might get up there.

Some of the most traditional *blocos*—the Bola Preta, for example—draw millions, so if you go, be prepared for a crush of sweat-soaked humanity. If you want a calmer experience, choose a smaller bloco away from Ipanema or Copacabana, in neighborhoods like Laranjeiras, Flamengo, or Humaita. Since it is easy to lose members of your party, establish meeting points beforehand. Avoid traveling through the city, because traffic can turn nightmarish.

Planning

Plan your Carnival visit well in advance. Hotels fill up and prices can be steep. Also, it is important to do your research. The party takes on various flavors. Finding the best fit is important to enjoying the experience.

During the season, Rio's neighborhoods are also taken over by *blocos*—brass bands or sound trucks that parade through the streets, dragging behind them throngs of faithful revelers in a variety of costumes. There are nearly 500 of these spread around town. For many Rio residents, they are the heart of Carnival.

Most attract a mixed crowd, but some target a particular audience or have special characteristics: the traditional Banda de Ipanema draws a plethora of drag queens; among the Carmelitas, in the Santa Teresa neighborhood, you'll see many partygoers dressed as nuns. There are blocos for children, for journalists, for Michael Jackson lovers—you name it. Street blocos are impossible to miss. In fact, if you are not

interested in full-immersion Carnival, avoid Rio during the time period, because the party is unavoidable.

Carnival balls are good options for those who prefer an enclosed, less chaotic setting. These are massive parties of mostly costumed revelers with live music, and can range from more staid, black-tie affairs like the famous (and pricey) Copacabana Palace ball, to LGBT balls, balls for children, and smaller ones in samba joints like Rio Scenarium.

A great place to browse for ready-made costumes or beads and baubles for a DIY Carnival getup is Saara. Worth a visit in its own right, this outdoor maze of more than 1,200 stores and stalls was originally established by Middle Eastern and Jewish immigrants and has been operating since the 17th century. Just about anything can be found for sale within its jam-packed, labyrinthine streets: fabric, toys, jewelry, furnishings, costumes, masks, glitter, confetti, and other seasonal essentials.

To learn more about Carnival, from the schedules of the parading escolas de samba to where to find the street bloco of your dreams, visit the Riotur website (⊕ *www.rioguiaoficial.com.br*), or pick up their free Carnaval de Rua (street Carnival) guide. *Veja* magazine, sold at all newsstands, also has a Rio insert, *Veja Rio*, with a lot of good information about events during Carnival.

For tickets to see the Carnival parade, go to ⊕ *liesa.globo.com*. They go on sale as early as December. Alternatively, you can check in with travel agencies. They snap up most of the tickets, and resell them at a higher cost in the months preceding Carnival.

SÃO PAULO

São Paulo's Carnival may not have the fame of its rival city Rio, but taking part in the festivities here provides a different Brazilian experience. Brazilians themselves often rotate where they spend the holiday each year, from big cities to small, traditional celebrations in Brazil's interiors, asking one another, "So where are you doing Carnival this year?"

Similar to Rio de Janeiro, São Paulo's Carnival divides into two main parts. The first is the much-hyped *desfiles* (parades) of the samba schools, who compete against each other in the Sambódromo do Anhembi designed by the late Oscar Niemeyer. The second is the *carnaval de rua* (street carnival) block parties that mushroom around the city in the weeks leading up to Carnival proper.

Blocos are concentrated in bohemian-chic Vila Madalena and in the Centro, though other neighborhoods also host their own. Expect a good time and enjoy a true rarity—dancing in São Paulo's usually traffic-clogged streets.

Tickets to the desfiles in the Sambódromo are available at counters around the city; check the website ⊕ *www.cidadedesaopaulo.com/carnaval* for the most up-to-date information. The same site includes a link to online ticket purchases and a list of Carnival party blocks, which are also routinely published in local newspapers. For a more local experience, catch a free rehearsal of a samba school, which happens in the weeks leading up to Carnival. Die-hard fans of a school, often those who can't afford the pricey tickets of the Carnival competition, show up with a beer in hand and brimming over with enthusiasm.

QUINTESSENTIAL RIO DE JANEIRO & SÃO PAULO

RIO DE JANEIRO

Outdoor Rio

In Rio de Janeiro, great granite boulders plunge into the azure Atlantic, and palm trees sway along the sweeps of white sand that ribbon the city. But there is a lot more to nature in Rio than beaches. There is the Lagoa Rodrigo de Freitas, a lagoon beloved by local joggers, bikers, and strolling families. It stands between Ipanema Beach and the forested mountains that have, at their peak, the famous statue of Christ the Redeemer. The Botanical Garden is one of the most beautiful green areas in the city. Its quiet, shaded walkways meander past more than 6,000 species. Also nearby is Parque Lage, a green area that has an early-20th-century mansion now housing an art school, and a café with good weekend brunches. If you're in the mood for a strenuous hike, a steep trail leads to the Christ the Redeemer statue.

People-Watching

The beaches of Rio provide some of the most interesting people-watching on the continent. If Copacabana is Rio distilled to a 3-km (2-mile) curl of white sand and a wide sidewalk, then Sunday on the beachfront Avenida Atlântica is a real slice of city life. The Avenida closes down to cars and opens up to human traffic of all shapes and sizes. Kiosks hawk everything from crafts to coco water, but most people are, shall we say, "just looking" at passersby with a frank yet relaxed gaze (a trademark of carioca self-assuredness). Don't be surprised to find, walking among lithe bodies designed for teeny bikinis or Speedos, plenty of folks shaped like the rest of us and wearing the same infamously skimpy suits. And why not?

SÃO PAULO

Sidewalk Happy Hour

Beach-bum cariocas snicker that paulistanos are workaholics—12-hour days at the office are commonplace. Unsurprisingly, locals relish their happy hour as a chance to kick back for a few hours before going home. On weekday evenings workers flock to the prized outdoor tables until the rush-hour traffic tapers off. A three-piece brass band might wander by, hoping that you're feeling generous enough to drop something in the hat. The epicenter for all this is the corner of Avenida Paulista and Joaquim Eugênio Lima, where a long line of bars multiplies the noise into a delightful cacophony of sizzling plates of meat and back-slapping colleagues. Grab a table early and enjoy the merrymaking.

Markets

From glorious tropical flowers to cheap toys, expect a lot of fun and color when exploring São Paulo's vast markets. The Mercado Municipal offers diverse food options, from gourmet food stalls to butchers; you can have a stylish lunch at one of its many empórios. Downtown 25 de Março is a chaos of outdoor stalls and stores on both sides of the street. Experience Christmas shopping unlike a Northern Hemisphere resident ever has as you huddle with bargain-hunting Brazilians on a hot December day. The most intrepid travelers should make their way to the CEAGESP—it is open to individual buyers, though you'll have to squeeze your way among the industrial trucks that crowd this giant retail fruit, vegetable, flower, and fish market.

IF YOU LIKE

RIO DE JANEIRO

Music

Finding music in Rio is as about as hard as finding the ocean. There is plenty of *sertaneja*, *forró*, MPB (translated literally as Brazilian Popular Music), bossa nova, *choro*, and irreverent funk carioca. Lapa is where you can get closest to the true pulse of the samba revival. Upscale bars in nicer neighborhoods offer classic bossa nova.

Bip Bip. One of the most traditional spots in the city for samba, this tiny Copacabana bar lets amateurs mix with the pros in impromptu jam sessions, while photos of various samba legends look on from the wall. *Rua Almirante Gonçalves 50, Copacabana.*

Plataforma. For better or worse, this Leblon music hall turns samba and other traditional music forms into an extravaganza approaching the size and glamour of Las Vegas. Be prepared to pay a hefty ticket price, and don't even ask how much it is for a beer. *Rua Adalberto Ferreira 32, Leblon.*

Rio Scenarium. The grande dame of downtown, and located a few shakes away from the Lapa aqueduct, the Scenarium's interior—a cross between an antiques store and movie set—is certainly worth a look. The nightly shows feature different acts playing any of the above-mentioned styles. *Rua do Lavradio 20, Lapa.*

Toca do Vinicius. Named after Vinicius de Moraes, poet, singer, and one of the founding fathers of the form, this bar is sure to scratch that bossa nova itch. *Rua Vinicius de Moraes 129, Ipanema.*

Outdoor Sports

Rio de Janeiro has been blessed with a varied geographical landscape—exuberant flora, miles of beaches, rugged mountains, and lush jungles—within its city limits. The more active and adventurous travelers can easily fill their days and nights with a multitude of adrenaline-pumping activities.

Biking. Rio has miles of bike paths around the city, a nice way of getting exercise while seeing the city from a different perspective. A citywide bike rental system makes it easy and cheap to hire a bike—look for the bright orange bikes parked at strategic locations across the south zone and downtown. Passes for the bikes can be bought at ⊕ *www.movesamba.com.br/bikerio.* A great route runs along the beach from Leblon all the way to Parque do Flamengo.

Hang Gliding. There are a number of companies that can take you from mountaintop to beachside in what may be the most exciting (and longest) 30 minutes of your life. Watch them land at the Praia do São Conrado.

Hiking. Given the changeable weather and the harsh terrain, guides are recommended for all major walks and climbs in Rio. Our favorite hikes include the trail up Corcovado from Parque Lage and the trip through Tijuca Forest to Pico da Tijuca.

Surfing. If you're keen on not merely wearing all manner of surfing attire filling nearly every shop window but actually riding some waves, Praia do Arpoador is the most popular surf spot and has great breaks. Praia do Diabo, between Ipanema and Copacabana, is smaller, but the view and the waves are hard to beat.

Sidewalk Cafés

Much of Rio's famed easygoing nature can be found in its sidewalk bars and cafés, where you can chat the night away while sipping smooth, foamy draft beer or seemingly subzero bottled beers poured into tiny glasses. Called *botequim*, or simply *botecos*, these small, casual bars offer the aforementioned beer and plentiful appetizers, but more than anything, a taste of what makes this city by the sea so eminently livable.

Bar Garota de Ipanema. If you want to tell your friends that you sat where Tom Jobim and Vinicius de Moraes wrote "The Girl from Ipanema," go to the bar that was renamed after their song. *Rua Vinicius de Moraes 39, Ipanema.*

Bar Luiz. Since 1927, locals have flocked to this bar for the best *chopp* (draft beer) in town. The chopp comes in light and dark varieties, both served incredibly cold. Nosh on sausages and other German specialties as you imbibe. *Rua da Carioca 39, Centro.*

Bracarense. Relaxed and straightforward, this place spreads its tables haphazardly around the surrounding sidewalk, leaving plenty of room for the folks milling in between. Popular with cariocas, it's not too far away from the gigantic Estadio Maracanã. *Rua Jose Linhares 85, Leblon.*

Overwhelming Spectacle

Without changing seasons to measure the passing of time, the orbit of the Brazilian year swings heavily around two events stuck at one end of the calendar, and between which nothing seems to happen at all. New Year's (called *Réveillon*, from the French) serves to close the business of the old year, and Carnival allows everyone to max out on fun (or rest) in order to get in the proper mind-set to start it all over again. Rio's version of both these events is the shiniest, most produced, and in many ways, the center of national attention while the celebration rages. A lot of the city's natives flee during these dates, but none will deny that you have to experience the full glory of each holiday at least once—and each event has one spot where everybody wants to be.

New Year's Eve on the Beach. In a tradition borrowed from the Candomblé religion, Brazilians wear white and jump seven waves at the turning of the year, sending flowers off into the waters. That means that when the 31st comes, everyone wants to be on the beach, and everyone flocks to Rio.

Sambódromo at Carnival. Though the party is citywide, this Oscar Niemayer–designed hybrid of stadium and street holds hordes of revelers who are willing to endure crushing crowds and sky-high ticket prices to see the glitz and feel the pounding power of the samba schools up close.

SÃO PAULO

Soccer

São Paulo is home to three of the biggest teams in the country, four if you count nearby Santos of Pelé fame. There are two different seasons: the Brasileirão, a countrywide competition spanning the winter months, and the summer Paulistão, a state tourney that allows teams from lower divisions to take on the big guys. For those looking to see a game, the classicos in which the big teams clash are high stakes—you can see fans at their most spirited, which can make for enthusiastic camaraderie or violent brawls. Choosing a game where the visiting team won't stir up the rabble-rousers will make for a smoother trip.

Arena Corinthians. The modern home of Corinthians, the team of the masses and second-most popular in all of Brazil, this stadium, with a seating capacity of 47,600, is a howling bowl of energy from kickoff to final whistle. This is the team of Brazil's most dedicated die-hards.

Allianz Parque. Home of Palmeiras, the green, white, and red team whose faithful come from the large Italian presence in the city, the stadium was completely rebuilt ahead of the 2014 World Cup. The Palmeiras-Corinthians rivalry is the biggest in the city.

Estádio Morumbi. This is the biggest stadium in the state and where the classicos are played. Otherwise it's the home turf of the wealthy and successful São Paulo Football Club. It's difficult to get to without a car and it lacks the intimacy of the smaller venues. These days the club is tops, winning state, national, and even an international championship in recent years.

Coffee

Coffee is what started São Paulo's transformation from sleepy town to teeming metropolis, and the drink forms an integral part of city life. Espresso is the drink of choice at most of the city's many cafés, so expect a small hot cup that packs a big punch. It's designed to be gulped in the moment rather than to be slowly sipped. In fact, any conversation with a local about coffee is sure to bring up a disparaging remark about the weak, undrinkable U.S. version. If you take yours with milk, ask for *pingado*, meaning a "drop." Coffee shop culture here is a little faster paced, though the comfy chairs and long chats of the American-style cafés are beginning to make an impact.

Chains. Chain cafés like Fran's Café and Café do Ponto serve up a powerful espresso at innumerable outlets around the city, ranging from sit-down cafés to stand-up bars. Resisting the dessert display might be one of the hardest parts of your day.

Lanchonetes. If espresso is not your thing, street-corner *lanchonetes* (snack bars) serve a slightly weaker brew—just look for the large silver urn on the counter. This coffee might already have sugar, and if so, it's probably sweetened beyond your taste.

Starbucks. Have you no shame? If your addiction to certain multinamed concoctions is strong enough to stomach the idea of buying American coffee in the land of the bean, take a look inside most upperclass malls and you will find what you need.

Shopping

São Paulo is where Brazil earns its money, and those who have it aren't afraid to flaunt it. In Brazil's richest state—the gross domestic product of the city of São Paulo rivals that of entire neighboring countries—there is no lack of places to consume conspicuously, or drive a hard bargain.

Malls. Called *shoppings*, these are gems of high commerce, and hordes of Brazilians are content to spend a whole day wandering in and out of the shops. Food courts are expansive and go well beyond fast food. Shopping Morumbi and Shopping Cidade Jardim allow you to gaze at the life of São Paulo's newly wealthy.

Paulista Mini-Malls. For those with a taste for expensive-looking goods of questionable authenticity, the Chinatown of São Paulo, just one block east of Trianon, might be right up your alley. Two mini-malls face each other, their merchants crammed into tiny booths, selling diverse trinkets from watches and statues to shiny handbags.

Rua 25 de Março. Near metro São Bento, this bazaar of street vendors is only for the brave. Here, shop owners from all over the state come to buy in bulk, so the prices are unbeatable and up for bargaining. If you know a willing Brazilian, take them with you to help with the haggling.

Rua Oscar Freire. Drawing frequent comparisons to L.A.'s Rodeo Drive, this boulevard is lined with boutiques both international and Brazilian. The stores are packed on Saturday and closed on Sunday.

Four-Wheeled Fantasies

Though they do celebrate Carnival, it seems as if the citizenry of São Paulo prefers fast cars to quick-stepping women. Their love of cars shows itself daily in deep conversations about ownership and the daredevil acts performed in city traffic, but it is when the spring rolls around that the passion for all things auto comes on display in two events. On everybody's lips are the newest innovations of the big carmakers, as well as the names of the country's latest racing hopefuls, though none can ever hope to touch Ayrton Senna. His 1994 death elevated the already-famous racer to a legendary status in the national consciousness equaled only by Pelé.

Autódromo de Interlagos—Grand Prix do Brasil. Located on the southern edge of the city, this used to be open to the public during practice runs and time trials of the Grand Prix. Those good old days have been replaced by a mandatory three-day ticket that rivals the golden one of chocolate-factory fame in terms of supply-versus-demand ratios. For those stuck on the outside, TV offers the solace of public channels single-mindedly dedicated to every nuance of the race.

International Auto Show. In a city where stoplight robberies and traffic discourage those who can afford a sports car from showing it off on the streets, the Salão Internacional do Automóvel gives the rest of Brazil a chance to see their dream wheels up close. The 10-day festive show, thanks to the 600,000 people who pass through its gates, provides an unmistakable boost to city hotels, restaurants, and traffic every October.

GREAT ITINERARIES

INTRODUCTION TO RIO, 4 DAYS

Rio de Janeiro is a city like no other on Earth—prepare to have your senses dazzled by the sheer beauty of the place. With so many unmissable attractions, good planning is key to making the most of your time in the *Cidade Maravilhosa.*

Day 1: Explore the Beaches and the Bars

Shake off your jet lag and satisfy your curiosity for the iconic Rio you've heard about in songs by heading straight to **Ipanema Beach**. Before hitting the beach, order a tasty, blended glass of açaí from any of the nearby juice bars. Fortified by the Amazonian berry's many vitamins and antioxidants, take a stroll and watch the show; on the city's beaches, you'll find the most spectacularly proportioned bodies and equally spectacular views.

When you've had enough sun, surf, and sightseeing, make your way to Leblon for a tasty bite of *bolinho de bacalhau* (small cod cake)—or any other seafood dish on the menu at one of the restaurants that we recommend. A sunset visit to **Pão de Açucar** is a lovely way to end your first day.

Logistics: Be careful with Rio's strong undertow and waves. Bring only the bare minimum of belongings to the beach, and make sure someone from your group keeps an eye on them if you take a dip.

Day 2: Enjoy Bird's-Eye Views from Corcovada

Regardless of how you chose to end your first night, an early wake-up on Day 2 is advisable if you want to see gorgeous views of the city from **Corcovado**. It's also a good idea if you want to avoid both the haze and throngs of sightseers who set upon the peak as the day wears on.

Next, spend the afternoon in Santa Teresa, leisurely walking the narrow, cobblestone streets lined with beautiful, Portuguese-style homes. Stop by **Bar do Arnaudo** for a hearty late lunch, or **Cafecito** for a fortifying coffee and a light snack. If you still have enough energy, make a night of it in Lapa.

Logistics: Check the weather to make sure the Christ statue will not be above the clouds. Wear comfortable shoes for hiking.

Day 3: The City as It Lives and Breathes

Wandering around Centro is a lovely way to spend your third day, stopping by the **Theatro Municipal** and exploring the various plazas and churches. The ornate **Confeitaria Colombo** is one of the oldest eateries in Rio and a nice place for a tea break. Order the lavish afternoon tea if you really want to treat yourself.

If you missed Lapa by night, see it by day by taking a stroll down here—be sure to check out the colorful *Escadaria Selaron* and the gigantic, whitewashed *Arcos da Lapa* (Lapa Arches). Alternatively, if you have an itch for sand between your toes, head down to Copacabana, where you can either sunbathe or simply walk its 4-km (2½-mile) promenade.

Day 4: Shop Till You Drop

If your final day falls on a weekend, Ipanema's **Feira Hippie** takes place on Sunday and is well worth a gander. Local arts and crafts, handmade clothes, and accessories are on offer alongside mass-produced tourist knickknacks. There is more outdoor shopping along Avenida Atlântica and at the Feira Nordestina, also known as the Feira de São Cristóvão, which runs from Friday at 10 am through Sunday at 8 pm. The fair, which celebrates

Northeastern Brazilian food and culture, features live forró music and feels like a vast nightclub after midnight on Saturday. If it is raining, popping into the Rio Sul mall is a good option. Dining at the Porcão Rio, which serves the finest Brazilian churrasco in the city, will round out your Rio experience.

Option 1 for Days 5–6: Brigitte Bardot's Búzios

Just over two hours from Rio, the old fishing village of **Búzios** has some wonderful beaches (Azeda and Azedinha are particularly quiet and perfect for a romantic afternoon). If you can swing the sometimes hefty price tag, stay at the **Casas Brancas**—it's a delicious spot for doing absolutely nothing and feeling wonderful about it. For those with a little less money to burn, the **Galápagos Inn** has a lovely view of the sea and sunset, and even has bar service at the beach.

When hunger strikes, **Cigalon** is one of the finest restaurants in town; make sure to have a meal on its seductive veranda that overlooks the beach. If you're on a budget, just off the Rua das Pedras is the pay-per-kilo restaurant **Buzin,** which also serves churrasco. Its casual, welcoming atmosphere is perfect for those who want to keep their weekend away from Rio as unpretentious as possible. There are plenty of activities to keep you busy in Búzios, such as surfing lessons or windsurfing. For those who want to be on the water but don't want to paddle, take a three-hour catamaran around the peninsula from Orla Bardot. Don't miss the statue of Brigitte Bardot on the Orla Bardot along the water near downtown.

Logistics: Búzios is about 175 km (110 miles) northeast of Rio. The trip is much more pleasant if you rent a car. Driving in Rio de Janeiro State isn't difficult but do be mindful of other drivers. You'll be thankful you have a car if you want to find some of the more idyllic beaches in the area.

Days 5–6 (Option 2): The Unspoiled Island of Ilha Grande

Ilha Grande once provided refuge for pirates, and was the first point of entry for many slaves brought here from Africa. Now, it's known for its lovely, somewhat unspoiled beaches.

The island is a nature lover's dream, and getting there is simpler than it once was thanks to collective transfer services, which include hotel pickup, minibus, and schooner boat from Coneicao de Jacare, near Angra dos Reis. Once there, we recommend using **Vila do Abraão**—the island's only real town—as a starting point for your beach explorations. There are no roads and no private cars on the island, so try to travel light, bring comfortable shoes, and expect to walk a lot.

Hire a local boatman who can take you to a quiet, pristine beach or an even more remote islet. Don't miss the shockingly clear waters of Abraãozinho Beach, accessible only by foot (about 25 minutes from Vila do Abraão) or by boat.

Logistics: The quickest and most cost-effective way to reach the island is by organized transfer. Whiz along in a comfy minivan to the small town of Conceicao de Jacare, around two hours' drive from Rio, before taking a schooner boat (around 45 minutes) to the island's main settlement. The island has bountiful trekking opportunities, although taxi boats are on hand to whisk less energetic visitors to the best beaches.

INTRODUCTION TO SÃO PAULO, 4 DAYS

Those who set out to explore this vast, packed Brazilian metropolis will be well rewarded for their efforts. Top-notch restaurants, hip nightclubs, and excellent museums and galleries make São Paulo Brazil's cultural reference point. Architecture buffs can marvel at some impressive examples of grand colonial buildings.

Day 1: Getting to Know the City

International flights will bring you in through Guarulhos, which is actually a sister city to megacity São Paulo. Budget at least an hour of travel time—double that if it's rush hour—to get to your lodgings in the center of São Paulo.

Once you get yourself somewhat situated—always difficult in this sprawling megalopolis—find your way to the top of **Avenida Paulista** (where it meets Consolação) and begin a walk down the long blocks of this busy business artery. You'll pass one international bank after another, interspersed with the occasional multinational corporation, until you reach the inimitable and easily identifiable **Museu de Arte de São Paulo (MASP)**, designed by the late Oscar Niemeyer. Right across the street is **Trianon Park**, a surprisingly peaceful jungle in the midst of all the traffic and concrete of Paulista. If you continue down Paulista to Brigadeiro, you can either walk or catch a bus into Bixiga and lunch at one of the charming Italian cantinas on 13 de Maio.

Day 2: The Architecture of São Paulo

São Paulo is the financial heart of the country, and architecturally, it shows. Try exploring the city's structures by starting with the old: search for the elegant **Theatro Municipal** first. From there, the iconic **Edifício Martinelli** shouldn't be hard to pick out of the modernist skyline. The spectacular view over the valley on Anhangabaú makes for a great photo opportunity. Another treasure is the **Centro Cultural Banco do Brasil**. The building itself is a small marvel and it often has world-class exhibits within its marbled walls.

From there, the **Praça da Sé** is not far, and the massive Cathedral is certainly worth a peek inside. Take a seat on one of the Praça's benches to watch a veritable cross section of paulistano life go by. Just two metro stops away at República, you can see perhaps the most iconic São Paulo skyscraper, Niemeyer's **Edifício Copan**. It's just down the street from the Edifício Itália, which was once the city's tallest building.

In the waning daylight hours, make your way to the vaulted roofs of São Paulo **Estação da Luz**, a bustling train station. Finish the day by walking to the nearby top-notch **Pinacoteca** art museum and resting in its elegant tree-lined grounds.

Day 3: São Paulo's Boutiques

Fashionistas flock to São Paulo for the clothes, shoes, fashion shows, and accessories. In fact, shopping is a tourist attraction in its own right. Rub elbows with São Paulo's rich and fabulously dressed by doing a little clothing shopping at the western end of **Rua Oscar Freire** (where it meets Rebouças). Here you can find some of Brazil's most famous designer collections, as well as a good sampling of international names.

With your new outfits, you may want to sample São Paulo's famous nightlife. Make your way to **Vila Madalena** or **Pinheiros**, both lively nighttime neighborhoods lined with bars and restaurants. Catch a live performance of bossa nova or samba at happy hour at Grazie a Dio.

Day 4: A Jungle Within the City

When you need a break from the urban jungle, surround yourself with lush greens at **Parque Ibirapuera**. It's crowded on the weekends—great for people-watching—and doesn't see too much foot traffic during the week. Follow the path to Marquise Ibirapuera, which connects several buildings, including the **Museu de Arte Moderna (MAM)** and the **Pavilhão da Bienal**, the site of São Paulo Fashion Week.

Also worth visiting is the polygonal **Oca**, built by Oscar Niemeyer, who along with Roberto Burle Marx, helped design the park itself. The nursery in Ibirapuera is a charming visit, and the staff will be able to point you to the park's most exotic trees, such as glorious wide-limbed banyans. Take some time to explore the outskirts of the city—around Parque Ibirapuera are some of the most expensive mansions and apartment buildings in Latin America. Make your way to the lively **Liberdade** neighborhood to catch the Saturday street food festival or to dine at its many sushi and yakisoba restaurants.

Day 5–6 (Option 1): Embu das Artes

Embu is a small Portuguese colonial-era town of churches and antiques shops, handicrafts fairs, and furniture makers. It makes a relaxing alternative to the nonstop urban pulse of cosmopolitan São Paulo. Visit the **Igreja Nossa Senhora do Rosario**, built in 1690, then check out the **Canto das Artes** for mosaics and furniture. If you need a break, relax at Os Girassóis Restaurante e Choperia over a nice frosty beer.

Devote some of your visit to understanding why Embu is also called Land of the Arts. Explore the Open Arts fair, which occupies all the central areas of the city and specializes in historical and colonial art. It is open Saturday, Sunday, and holidays. Be aware that the Embu is a popular destination and can get crowded.

Logistics: Embu is a mere 27 km (17 miles) west of São Paulo. You can catch a bus at the Terminal Bandeira close to metro Anhangabaú or at Tietê bus station. Once there, it's easily navigable by foot.

Day 5–6 (Option 2): Ilhabela

Ilhabela is the largest sea island in the country and will hit the spot if you're in the mood for pure relaxation. There are two small towns on the island. One is where the locals live; the other is where most of the hotels, restaurants, and stores are located and, hence, the tourists as well. Be aware that during the winter months most businesses that cater to travelers, including restaurants, are open only on weekends.

When you arrive, head straight for **Praia Grande** for your first taste of the shore, and at night, **Praia do Curral** will satisfy all your restaurant and bar needs. Ilhabela is a sportsman's paradise; there is plenty of boating, sailing, hiking, scuba diving, and surfing (both of the board and wind variety) available. Scuba divers have several 19th- and early-20th-century wrecks to explore—this region has the most wrecks of any area off Brazil's coast—and hikers can set off on the numerous inland trails, many of which lead to a waterfall (the island has more than 300). Be aware that not all sport options are available on all parts of the island.

Logistics: Ilhabela is a 7-km (5-mile) boat ride from São Sebastião. The boat leaves every 30 minutes from 6 am to midnight and hourly during the night. It should take about 15 minutes. The coastal town São Sebastião itself is easily reached by bus from the Tietê bus station.

SOUNDS OF BRAZIL

Music is woven into the fabric of Brazilian life and is the art form that most completely translates this diverse nation's creativity and richness. Travelers will be exposed to it throughout their visit, whether it is an upbeat *forro* playing on the radio of your taxi or a traditional samba coming from a local bar where musicians have gathered for an afternoon jam session. You'll learn much about the country and the region you're in from music, since local rhythms usually say much about the place's unique ethnic makeup and history.

Samba

Samba, the music most associated with Brazil, was born in the mostly black neighborhoods near Rio de Janeiro's docks among stevedores and other laborers in the early 20th century. There are many varieties of it, generally all fast-paced and driven by percussion instruments including the deep bass *bumbo* and the smaller *atabaque*, tambourines, and complemented by stringed instruments like the *cavaquinho*, which looks like a tiny guitar.

There are great venues to see traditional samba in Rio's bohemian Lapa neighborhood, among them Semente and Carioca da Gema. Trapiche Gamboa, in the port-side neighborhood of Saude, has great bands in a beautifully restored old warehouse.

One of the real delights of Rio is to see samba played outdoors in samba circles much as it was over a century ago. These circles often spring up without notice, but there are parts of town where musicians traditionally gather. These include Ouvidor Street in downtown, which generally has music on Wednesdays and Saturdays, and Pedra do Sal, an outdoor space in Saude that hosts hugely popular samba circles on Monday and Friday evenings.

Bossa Nova

Bossa nova, which means "new trend," is a fresh, jazzy take on percussion-heavy samba. Where samba is cathartic and communal and built on drums and powerful voices, bossa nova is intimate and contemplative, with the melody up front and percussion in the background, often played with brushes for a softer texture.

Bossa nova was born in the bars of Rio's posh south side neighborhoods like Ipanema in the 1950s. It became famous worldwide with the song "The Girl from Ipanema." A good place to hear bossa nova is Rio's Vinicius Piano Bar, across the street from the Ipanema bar where the song's authors watched their muse saunter by.

Forro

Brazil's Northeast has the country's richest musical tradition. From these arid backlands sprung *coco, xaxado, baiao, xote, axe,* and *frevo,* among many others. The best known across Brazil is the *forro,* a fast, syncopated rhythm driven by the accordion and the *zabumba,* a rustic drum. It was brought to wealthier São Paulo and Rio de Janeiro by Northeastern migrants who left their impoverished hometowns in search of work.

Derided for years as the "music of maids and doormen," forro has gained a mainstream following. Good places to check it out are São Paulo's Canto da Ema or Feira Moderna, a charming little bar with Northeastern fare and music. In Rio de Janeiro, the Feira de Sao Cristovao—a huge indoor fair with about 700 stands selling Northeastern food, arts, and crafts—is the place to go.

RIO DE JANEIRO

Updated By
Lucy Bryson

Welcome to the Cidade Maravilhosa, or the Marvelous City, as Rio is known in Brazil. Synonymous with the girl from Ipanema, the dramatic views from Christ the Redeemer atop Corcovado mountain, and fabulously flamboyant Carnival celebrations, Rio is a city of stunning architecture, abundant museums, and marvelous food. Rio is also home to 23 beaches, an almost continuous 73-km (45-mile) ribbon of sand.

As you leave the airport and head to Rio's beautiful *Zona Sul* (the touristic South Zone), you'll drive for about 40 minutes on a highway from where you'll begin to get a sense of the dramatic contrast between beautiful landscape and devastating poverty. In this teeming metropolis of 12 million people (6.2 million of whom live in Rio proper), the very rich and the very poor live in uneasy proximity. You'll drive past seemingly endless cinder-block *favela*, but by the time you reach Copacabana's breezy, sunny Avenida Atlântica—flanked on one side by white beach and azure sea and on the other by condominiums and hotels—your heart will leap with expectation as you begin to recognize the postcard-famous sights. Now you're truly in Rio, where *cariocas* (Rio residents) and tourists live life to its fullest.

Enthusiasm is contagious in Rio. Prepare to have your senses engaged and your inhibitions untied. Rio seduces with a host of images: the joyous bustle of vendors at Sunday's Feira Hippie (Hippie Fair); the tipsy babble at sidewalk cafés as patrons sip their last glass of icy beer under the stars; the blanket of lights beneath the Pão de Açúcar (Sugarloaf Mountain); the bikers, joggers, strollers, and power walkers who parade along the beach each morning. Borrow the carioca spirit for your stay; you may find yourself reluctant to give it back.

ORIENTATION AND PLANNING

GETTING ORIENTED

Cariocas divide their city into four main sections: the suburban Zona Norte (North Zone), the chic Zona Sul (South Zone), the sprawling Zona Oeste (West Zone), and the urban Centro.

Most tourist activity takes place in the Zona Sul, with its mix of residential areas, office buildings, shops, restaurants, bars, hotels, and beaches. This is the city's most affluent section, with fancy condos housing Rio's middle and upper class, and dozens of theaters and music halls.

Centro and neighboring Lapa and Santa Teresa are filled with the remnants of the old Portuguese colony, including some impressive neoclassical structures housing churches, museums, and art galleries. The vast

TOP REASONS TO GO

Stunning Beaches: Unpack your Speedo or thong bikini and join the masses at Rio's miles of gorgeous beaches.

Carnival: Head to the streets or the Sambódromo, and revel in the celebration of Rio's biggest party.

Brazilian Beats: Tap your feet to the uniquely Brazilian styles of music such as samba, bossa nova, funk, and pagode that echo from the myriad clubs and live-music venues.

Scrumptious Meals: Tickle your taste buds with delicious dining experiences—there's a lot to like for meat lovers and vegetarians at Rio's diverse restaurants.

Breathtaking Landscapes: Bask in the beauty of the endlessly breathtaking landscapes that unfold between mountain and ocean.

Zona Norte is primarily residential and lower class, but the international airport and the legendary Maracanã soccer stadium are here. Zona Oeste is the "up and coming" part of Rio, occupied largely by the newly rich, and replete with malls, superstores, and untouched beaches. As the center of operations for the 2016 Rio Olympics, the West Zone is set to benefit from improved transport links to the rest of the city as well as a boost in hotel numbers.

Centro. Architectural gems left behind from the days of Portuguese colonialism share space with modern high-rises in Rio's financial district. Ornately decorated churches, museums, and palaces are just some of the highlights.

Catete and Glória. Historic Catete and Glória, two largely residential neighborhoods close to Centro, are well worth an afternoon's sightseeing. The national government formerly operated out of Catete, which still has its lovely palaces and old residences; the playground in Catete Palace grounds is one of the nicest spots in the city to bring young children. Glória is famous for its beautiful hilltop church.

Santa Teresa and Lapa. One of Rio's first residential neighborhoods, Santa Teresa is worth a visit to explore its narrow, cobblestone streets. Many of the beautiful colonial mansions lining them have been converted into stylish guesthouses and boutique hotels.

Adjacent to Centro, the Lapa neighborhood has some of the best music halls and dance clubs in the city. If you've come to Rio to explore its nightlife, you'll become intimately familiar with Lapa.

Flamengo and Botafogo. The middle-class neighborhoods of Flamengo and Botafogo, both good places to find value lodgings, are famed for their rival soccer teams, two of Brazil's biggest teams. Sports rivalry aside, the Parque de Flamengo, designed by the world-famous landscape architect Roberto Burle Marx, is an oasis of calm and a popular spot for walkers and joggers, while Botafogo is home to some of Rio's best independent bars and restaurants.

Urca. East of Botafogo is tiny, mainly residential Urca, where you can ascend the huge morro Sugarloaf by cable car. Praia Vermelha, a small, sheltered beach beneath Sugarloaf, is a wonderful spot for sunbathing, and on the easy walking trail nearby there's a good chance you'll see marmoset monkeys at play.

Copacabana and Leme. Copacabana Beach is the main attraction in the city's most tourist-packed neighborhood. It's the perfect place to sunbathe, stroll, people-watch, buy souvenirs at the open-air night market, sip a caipirinha at a beach kiosk, or gaze in awe at the giant apartment buildings and hotels (including the Copacabana Palace) that line the Avenida Atlântica. At its eastern end, Copacabana Beach becomes Leme, and this quieter spot is popular with families.

> **WHAT'S A CARIOCA?**
>
> The term *carioca* was an indigenous word meaning "white man's house" and was used in the city's early history to describe the Portuguese colonizers. Today the word is used more broadly, to identify residents of the city of Rio. But the word defines much more than birthplace, race, or residence: it represents an ethos of pride, a sensuality, and a passion for life. Poor or rich, cariocas share a common identity and a distinct local accent, considered by many foreigners and Brazilians alike to be the most beautiful within the Portuguese language.

Ipanema and Leblon. Famously the place where "The Girl from Ipanema" caught the eye of bossa nova songwriters Tom Jobim and Vinicius de Moraes in the 1960s, this affluent neighborhood is a collection of tree-lined streets harboring smart condos, fabulous restaurants, and trendy boutiques. The gorgeous beach, framed by the towering Dois Irmaos (Two Brothers) mountains, is the sunbathing spot of choice for Rio's young and beautiful. Extending west from Ipanema, affluent, intimate Leblon borrows some of its neighbor's trendy charms and is home to many of Rio's hippest restaurants.

São Conrado and Barra da Tijuca. West of Leblon, the well-heeled neighborhoods of São Conrado and Barra da Tijuca have long stretches of unspoiled beach. São Conrado contains some striking mansions, while towering condos and vast shopping malls have earned Barra da Tijuca the nickname Estados Unidos da Barra (United States of Barra). Rio's metro system is set to reach Barra da Tijuca in time for the Rio 2016 Olympics, which will be based here. Barra's beach is the longest in the city and tends to be much quieter than Copacabana and Ipanema.

Inland Zona Sul. The middle-class residential neighborhoods of Jardim Botânico, Gávea, Lagoa, Laranjeiras, and Cosme Velho are worth visiting for their stunning scenery and opportunities for peaceful strolls and nature-spotting rambles. The highlights here include the botanical garden in Jardim Botânico, the cable-car ride to the Christ the Redeemer statue in Cosme Velho, Gávea's planetarium, Laranjeiras's street fairs, and the massive city lake in Lagoa, which is good for a brisk stroll, run, or bike ride.

PLANNING

WHEN TO GO

Rio is a year-round destination, but Carnival, which usually takes place in February, is the best time to soak up the city's party spirit. Arrive a few days before the celebrations begin, or stay a few days after they end to enjoy the museums and other sights that close for the four days of revelry. Prices rise substantially during Carnival season, and accommodations need to be booked several months in advance.

Temperatures in Rio tend to be highest from January to March, when they often soar above 100 degrees. The city generally sees the most rain during December, when it might pour for days at a time. To tour the city at a quieter time with gentler temperatures and at lower prices, come in the off-season, from May to October (Brazil's winter). The temperature in the winter tends to be in the upper 70s during the day and rarely falls below 50 degrees at night.

PLANNING YOUR TIME

Rio has more than its fair share of stellar attractions—both natural and man-made—and good planning is key to fitting it all in. It is possible to visit the beaches of Copacabana, Ipanema, and Leblon in one day on foot. From Leblon it's just a short stroll down to Lagoa, home to the city's vast lake set against the mountains.

Set aside another full day to see the historic heart of the city in Lapa, Santa Teresa, Glória, and Catete. All are within close walking distance of each other, but the steep hills up to Santa Teresa can be a challenge in the heat, so grab a taxi or bus instead. Key attractions such as the Christ statue and Sugarloaf Mountain can be visited as part of a full-day or half-day city tour, which will make whistle-stop visits to other key locations in the city, too.

GETTING HERE AND AROUND

Rio's shuttle system currently extends from the Zona Norte to Ipanema, with shuttles to areas west of the final stop. By 2016 the metro should extend as far as Barra da Tijuca. Within Ipanema and Copacabana, it's easy to get around on foot, but some attractions are far apart, so a taxi might be in order. After dark you should always take a taxi if you're venturing into unexplored territory. Cabs are yellow and easy to hail on every main street. Public buses are cheap and cover every inch of the city, but can be difficult to figure out if you don't speak Portuguese.

AIR TRAVEL

Nearly three-dozen airlines regularly serve Rio, but most flights from North America stop first in São Paulo. Several international carriers offer Rio–São Paulo flights.

AIRPORTS All international flights and most domestic flights arrive and depart from the Aeroporto Internacional Antônio Carlos Jobim, also known as Galeão (GIG). The airport is about 40 minutes northwest of the beach area and most of Rio's hotels. Taxis are plentiful and operate on a fixed-fare basis (those outside the arrivals area are cheaper than those from kiosks inside), and comfortable, spacious air-conditioned buses leave the airport for Centro, the Zona Sul, and Barra da Tijuca.

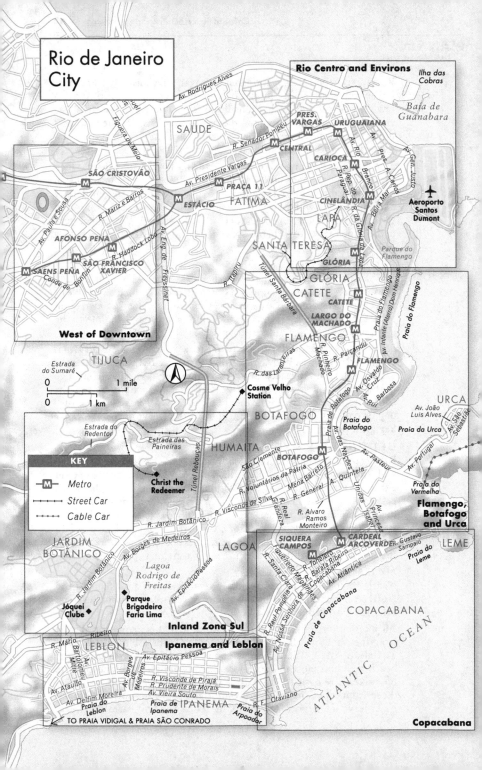

2

Aeroporto Santos Dumont (SDU), 20 minutes from the beaches and within walking distance of Centro, is served by the Rio–São Paulo air shuttle and other domestic flights.

Airport Information Aeroporto Internacional Antônio Carlos Jobim (*Galeão, GIG*). ✉ *Av. 20 de Janeiro s/n, Ilha do Governador* ☎ *021/3004–6050* ⊕ *www. riogaleao.com.* **Aeroporto Santos Dumont** (*SDU*). ✉ *Praça Senador Salgado Filho s/n, Centro* ☎ *021/3814–7070* ⊕ *www.aeroportosantosdumont.net.*

AIRPORT TRANSFERS: BUSES AND TAXIS

Most visitors arrive at Rio International Airport, about a 40-minute car ride from the tourist destinations. The speediest way to reach Centro and the Zona Sul is to take a taxi. Prices are steep, however. Expect to pay up to R$90 to reach Copacabana, and slightly more to Ipanema and Leblon. There are taxi booths in the arrivals area, and passengers pay a set fare in advance, though drivers may charge extra if you have lots of luggage. Also trustworthy are the white radio taxis parked in front of arrivals; these metered vehicles cost an average of 20% less than the airport taxis.

Comfortable, air-conditioned buses run by Real (marked Real Premium) park curbside outside the arrivals lounge; there is plenty of luggage storage space, and staff will safely stow your luggage beneath the bus. The buses (R$14) make the hour-long trip from Galeão to the Zona Sul, following the beachfront drives and stopping at major hotels along the way. If your hotel is inland, the driver will let you off at the nearest corner. Buses operate from 5:30 am to 11:45 pm (*See Bus Travel, below, for contact information*).

BUS TRAVEL

ARRIVING AND DEPARTING

Long-distance and international buses leave from and arrive at the Rodoviária Novo Rio. Any local bus marked "rodoviária" will take you to the station. You can buy tickets at the depot or, for some destinations, from travel agents. To buy online you will need a CPF (Brazilian Social Security) number. A staff member at your hotel may be able to help you with online purchases.

Bus Stations Rodoviária Novo Rio. ✉ *Av. Francisco Bicalho 1, Santo Cristo* ☎ *021/3213–1800, 021/3213–1800* ⊕ *www.novorio.com.br.*

TRAVEL WITHIN RIO DE JANEIRO

Rio's urban buses are cheap, frequent, and generally safe to use, but do not show cameras or wallets, and do not wear expensive-looking clothes or jewelry. Wear backpacks on your front, and avoid getting on or off the bus in deserted areas. Local buses have a fixed price (R$3), and can take you anywhere you want to go. Route maps aren't available, but local tourist offices (*See Visitor Information, below*) have route lists for the most popular sights. Enter buses at the front, pay the attendant, and pass through a turnstile. Have your fare in hand when you board to avoid flashing bills or your wallet. When you want to get off, pull the overhead cord and the driver will pause at the next designated stop. Exit from the rear of the bus.

The comfortable, privately run, and air-conditioned Real Premium buses serve the beaches, downtown, and Rio's two airports. These vehicles, which look like highway buses, stop at regular bus stops but also may be flagged down wherever you see them. Expect to pay around three times the price of the regular bus.

Bus Contacts Real Auto Onibus. *☎ 021/3035–6700, 021/3035–6700 ⊕ www. realautoonibus.com.br.*

CAR TRAVEL

The carioca style of driving is passionate to the point of abandon: speeding is de rigueur, traffic jams are common, the streets aren't well marked, and red lights are often ignored by drivers. Although there are parking areas along the beachfront boulevards, finding a spot can be a real problem. If you do choose to drive, exercise extreme caution, wear seat belts at all times, and keep the doors locked.

Car rentals can be arranged through hotels or agencies and at this writing cost between R$1200 and R$200 a day for standard models. Major agencies include Avis, Hertz, and Unidas. Localiza is a local agency. Hertz and Unidas have desks at the international and domestic airports.

Turismo Clássico Travel can arrange for a driver to get you around the city, with or without an English-speaking guide (US$50 per hour). Clássico's owners, Liliana and Vera, speak English, and each has more than 20 years of experience in organizing transportation. They also lead sightseeing tours.

Car Rental Contacts Unidas. *☎ 021/4001–2222 ⊕ www.unidas.com.br.*

SUBWAY TRAVEL

Metrô Rio, the subway system, is clean, relatively safe, and efficient, but it's not comprehensive. The system has two lines. Line 1 covers the Zona Sul, with 19 stops between Tijuca and Ipanema, along with integrated metro-bus services going to Barra da Tijuca, Gávea and Botafogo. Line 1 is being extended ahead of the 2016 Rio Olympics, with six more stations being added between Ipanema and Barra da Tijuca. Line 2 goes from the Zona Norte neighborhood of Pavuna to Cidade Nova in Rio's City Center (*Centro*). Reaching sights distant from metro stations can be a challenge, especially in summer, when beach traffic increases. Tourism offices and some metro stations have maps.

Trains operate daily between 5 am and midnight except on Sundays and holidays, when they run between 7 am and 11 pm. A single metro ticket costs R$3.50, but it is quicker and easier to use a pre-pay card. Machines at each metro station allow passengers to buy and load up cards from R$5 to the value of their choice, and although there are no financial savings, you'll avoid queues and hassle each time you take the subway.

Subway Information Metrô Rio. *⊠ Centro ☎ 0800/595–1111 information line ⊕ www.metrorio.com.br.*

TAXI TRAVEL

Taxis are plentiful in Rio, and in most parts of the city you can easily flag one down on the street. Yellow taxis have meters that start at a set price and have two rates. The "1" rate applies to fares before 8 pm, and the "2" rate applies to fares after 8 pm, on Sunday, on holidays, throughout December, in the neighborhoods of São Conrado and

Barra da Tijuca, and when climbing steep hills, such as those in Santa Teresa. Drivers are required to post a chart noting the current fares on the inside of the left rear window. CentralTaxi has a fare calculator on its website that will give you a general idea of what the fare from one destination to another might be. ■TIP➜ **Taxi drivers may be reluctant to make the steep climb to Santa Teresa, so if you are heading here wait until you are already inside the taxi before stating your destination, and stand your ground—by law drivers cannot refuse to take you here.**

Radio taxis and several companies that routinely serve hotels (and whose drivers often speak English) are also options. They charge 30% more than other taxis but are reliable and usually air-conditioned. Other cabs working with the hotels also charge more, normally a fixed fee that you should agree on before you leave. Reliable radio-cab companies include Coopacarioca and Coopatur.

Most carioca cabbies are pleasant, but there are exceptions. If flagging down a taxi on the street, check to see that an official phone number is displayed on the side and that the driver's official identity card is displayed. Remain alert and trust your instincts. Unless you've negotiated a flat fee with the driver, be sure the meter is turned on. ■TIP➜ **Few cab drivers speak English, so it's a good idea to have your destination written down to show the driver, in case there's a communication gap.**

Taxi Companies CentralTaxi. ☎ *021/2195–1000* ⊕ *www.centraltaxi.com.br.* **Coopacarioca.** ☎ *021/2518–3857, 021/2158–1818* ⊕ *www.cooparioca.com.br.* **Coopatur.** ☎ *021/3885–1000.*

RESTAURANTS

With nearly a thousand restaurants, Rio's dining choices are broad, from low-key Middle Eastern cafés to elegant contemporary eateries with award-winning kitchens and first-class service. The succulent offerings in the *churrascarias* (restaurants specializing in grilled meats) can be mesmerizing for meat lovers—especially the places that serve *rodízio*-style (grilled meat on skewers is continually brought to your table—until you can eat no more). Hotel restaurants often serve the national dish, *feijoada* (a hearty stew of black beans and pork), on Saturday—sometimes on Friday, too. Wash it down with a *chopp* (the local draft beer; pronounced "shop") or a caipirinha (sugarcane rum, lime, and sugar).

HOTELS

Lodgings in Rio de Janeiro are among the most expensive in the world, though the price-to-quality ratio often disappoints. That said, there are some wonderful accommodation options in all price ranges if you know where to look. Copacabana and Ipanema are awash with lodgings and are the best bet for sun seekers, but expect to get more bang for your buck the farther you travel from the famous beaches. Leafy Santa Teresa contains many charming guesthouses and chic boutique hotels, while Centro, Flamengo, and Botafogo have solid options for business travelers. ■TIP➜ **Note that "motels" are not aimed at tourists. They attract couples looking for privacy and usually rent by the hour.**

Expect to pay a premium for a room with a view. Most hotels include breakfast in the rate, and Brazilian breakfasts are usually a lavish affair involving everything from fresh fruit and juices to cakes, cold meats, and cheeses. If you're traveling during peak periods—from December to March—make reservations as far ahead of your visit as possible. *Hotel reviews have been shortened. For full information, visit Fodors.com.*

VISITOR INFORMATION

The Rio de Janeiro city tourism department, Riotur, operates a tourist information website in English and Portuguese ⊕ *www.rioguiaoficial. com.br* as well as a monthly free magazine with key tourist information and listings. The magazine, and city maps, can be picked up at Riotur booths at the bus station and airports, in Barra, Copacabana, Leblon, Gavea, at Sugarloaf, Lapa, and by Candelaria church in Centro. You can also try contacting Brazil's national tourism board, Embatur, via its Visit Brasil website.

Information **Riotur information booth.** ⊠ *Kiosk 15, Av. Atlantica, in front of Rua Hilário Gouveia, Copacabana* ☎ *021/2547-7522* ⊕ *www.rioguiaoficial.com. br* Ⓜ *Siqueira Campos.* **Turisrio.** ⊠ *Praça Pio X 119, Centro* ☎ *021/2271-7000* ⊕ *www.turisrio.rj.gov.br* Ⓜ *Cinelandia.* **Visit Brasil.** ⊕ *www.visitbrasil.com.*

TOURS

CITY TOURS

Be a Local. This well-established outfit conducts walking tours of Rocinha that make various stops inside the community, as well as trips to soccer matches, speedy city tours, and lively nocturnal visits to samba school rehearsals. On Sunday night, the fun favela funk-party tour (R$65) includes transport, entrance, and admission to a VIP area—be prepared to be the focus of locals' amorous attentions, and to head home just before daybreak. ⊠ *Rua Barata Ribeiro 111* ☎ *021/7816-9581* ⊕ *www. bealocal.com* ✉ *From R$65.*

Brazil Expedition. This reliable tour company runs a hugely popular city tour–known as the Big Dude tour–which takes a scenic route through Tijuca National Park to the Christ statue before visiting other key Rio landmarks such as Santa Teresa and the Lapa Steps, with an optional visit to Sugarloaf Mountain. Other recommended excursions include trips to samba school rehearsals (August–February) and an interesting street-art tour. The English-speaking guides are knowledgeable and friendly. ☎ *021/9998-2907, 021/9376-2839* ⊕ *www.brazilexpedition. com* ✉ *From R$200.*

Favela Tour. If you're interested in learning more about the favelas that cling to Rio's mountainsides, Favela Tour is the way to do it. Led by Marcelo Armstrong, this highly respected outfit conducts tours twice daily through Rocinha and Vila Canoas. Marcelo pioneered favela tourism in Rio and offers tours in English, Spanish, French, and Portuguese. Tours are informative but not voyeuristic, and there are opportunities to buy locally produced arts and crafts as you tour the communities. Hotel pickup and drop-off are included in the price. ☎ *021/3322-2727, 021/9989-0074* ⊕ *www.favelatour.com.br* ✉ *From R$90.*

FAMILY
Fodor's Choice
★

Rio Cultural Secrets. This quality outfit has enthusiastic, knowledgeable English-speaking private guides who whisk visitors around the city in comfortable air-conditioned cars. Popular trips include visits to Tijuca National Park and Rio's Botanical Gardens, soccer games, and city tours that take in major attractions such as Sugar Loaf and the Christ statue. Rio Cultural Secrets can also take visitors up to the imperial city of Petropolis, around an hour's drive from Rio. ☎ *21/98031–2692* ⊕ *www.rioculturalsecrets.com* ✉ *From R$140.*

Rio Free Walking Tour. Expert English-speaking guides lead free tours through Centro each weekday. Rain or shine, the guides will take you on a three-hour morning stroll, explaining the history of downtown Rio's major buildings, streets, statues, and monuments. The walk is followed by lunch at a pay-by-weight buffet restaurant. Tours leave from in front of the Theatro Municipal at 9:30 am Monday through Friday. There's no need to book in advance, just look out for the yellow-shirted guides. Although there's no charge, tips are welcomed. ☎ *021/97214–5095* ⊕ *www.riofreewalkingtour.com* ✉ *Free.*

Rio Hiking. This professional outfit leads hiking and climbing trips in Rio and the wider Rio de Janeiro state. All equipment is provided, guides are bilingual, and there are treks, tours, and adventure trips to suit all levels of experience. ✉ *Laranjeiras* ☎ *021/2552–9204* ⊕ *www. riohiking.com.br* ✉ *From R$210.*

HELICOPTER TOURS

Helisight. With landing pads at Morro da Urca (the smaller peak next to Sugarloaf), Lagoa, and Dona Marta view point in Tijuca National Park, Helisight conducts helicopter tours that pass over the Christ the Redeemer statue, the beaches of the Zona Sul, and other iconic sights. Prices start at R$260 for a seven-minute flight, while hour-long trips over this majestic city will set you back more than R$1,500. ✉ *Conde de Bernadotte 26, Leblon* ☎ *021/2259–6995 Lagoa, 021/2542–7935 Morro da Urca, 021/9602–1224 Dona Marta* ⊕ *www.helisight.com. br* ✉ *From R$260.*

SAFETY AND PRECAUTIONS
IN THE CITY

As with any city its size, crime occurs in Rio, but taking a few basic precautions should keep you from becoming a victim of it. Crimes involving visitors generally occur in crowded public areas: beaches, busy

---

THE COPS

Once known as the murder capital of the world, Rio is now much less dangerous than it was a decade ago. Simple changes such as installing lights on the beaches have improved safety. An increased police presence has also helped. In Rio there are three types of police: the gray-uniformed Military Police, the beige-uniformed Municipal Guard, and the black-uniformed special forces called the BOPE (pronounced "boppy"). For a glimpse at Rio's SWAT team, the BOPE, check out the film *Tropa de Elite (Elite Squad)* (2007) and its Oscar-nominated sequel, *Tropa de Elite 2* (2010).

2

sidewalks, intersections, and city buses. Pickpockets, usually children, work in groups. One will distract you while another grabs a wallet, bag, or camera. Be particularly wary of children who thrust themselves in front of you and ask for money or offer to shine your shoes. Another member of the gang may strike from behind, grabbing your valuables and disappearing into the crowd. Another tactic is for criminals to approach your car at intersections. Always keep doors locked and windows partially closed. Leave valuables in your hotel safe, don't wear expensive jewelry or watches, and keep cameras hidden except when snapping shots. Avoid walking around after dark, and avoid deserted areas even in broad daylight. ■ TIP→ Keep large bills and cards in a hidden money belt, carry an inexpensive phone, and have a few notes ready to hand over just in case.

ON THE BEACH
Don't shun the beaches because of reports of crime, but *do* take precautions. Leave jewelry, passports, and large sums of cash at your hotel; don't stroll the beaches at night; and be alert if groups of seemingly friendly youths attempt to engage you in conversation. They may be trying to distract you while one of their cohorts snatches your belongings. A big danger is actually the sun. From 10 am to 3 pm the rays are merciless, making heavy-duty sunscreen, hats, cover-ups, and plenty of liquids essential; you can also rent a beach umbrella from vendors on the beach or your hotel.

EXPLORING

When in Rio, don't be afraid to follow the tourist trail—the major attractions really are "must-sees." Contrary to tourist-board images, the sun doesn't always shine on the city, so when it does, make the most of it. If the skies are clear, waste no time in heading for Cosme Velho to visit the Christ the Redeemer statue atop Corcovado mountain, or to Urca to make the cable car ascent to the peak of Sugar Loaf. Time-pressed travelers will find that whistle-stop city tours are a good way to see many attractions in one day, while those lucky enough to spend a week or more here can afford to take a more leisurely approach. Cloudy days are a good time to visit the attractions of leafy Lagoa and Jardim Botânico and the breezily bohemian hilltop neighborhood of Santa Teresa. The historic buildings, museums, and cultural centers of Centro, Catete, Glória, and Lapa are ideal rainy-day options.

CENTRO

What locals generally refer to as Centro is actually several sprawling districts containing the city's oldest neighborhoods, churches, and most enchanting cafés. Rio's beaches, broad boulevards, and modern architecture may be impressive; but its colonial structures, old narrow streets, and alleyways in leafy inland neighborhoods are no less so. The metro stations that serve Centro are Cinelândia, Carioca, Uruguaiana, Presidente Vargas, Central, and Praça Onze.

Rio's settlement dates back to 1555. You can experience much of the city's rich history by visiting churches, government buildings, and villas in and around Centro. The metro is a good way to get downtown, but head here early, wear comfortable shoes, and be ready to walk multiple blocks as you explore this historic City Center. There are also daily free walking tours with English-speaking guides. If you're not up for a long walk, consider taking an organized bus tour.

TOP ATTRACTIONS

Biblioteca Nacional. Corinthian columns adorn the neoclassical National Library (built between 1905 and 1908), the first such establishment in Latin America. Its original archives were brought to Brazil by King João VI in 1808. The library contains roughly 13 million books, including two 15th-century printed Bibles, manuscript New Testaments from the 11th and 12th centuries, and volumes that belonged to Empress Teresa Christina. Also here are first-edition Mozart scores, as well as scores by Carlos Gomes, who adapted the José de Alencar novel about Brazil's Indians, *O Guarani,* into an opera of the same name. The library is accessible by guided tour only; tours are available in English. ⊠ *Av. Rio Branco 219, Centro* ☎ *021/3095–3879* ⊕ *www.bn.br* ✉ *Tours R$4* ☉ *Tours on the hr weekdays 10–5, weekends 12:30–4* Ⓜ *Cinelândia.*

Catedral de São Sebastião do Rio de Janeiro (*Catedral Metropolitana*). The exterior of this circa-1960 metropolitan cathedral, which looks like a concrete beehive, divides opinion. The daring modern design stands in sharp contrast to the baroque style of other churches in Rio, but don't judge until you've stepped inside. When light floods through the colorful stained-glass windows, it transforms the interior—which is 80 meters (263 feet) high and 96 meters (315 feet) in diameter—into a warm, serious place of worship that accommodates up to 20,000 people. An 8½-ton granite rock lends considerable weight to the concept of an altar. ⊠ *Av. República do Chile 245, Centro* ☎ *021/2240–2669* ⊕ *www.catedral.com.br* ✉ *Free* ☉ *Daily 7–6* Ⓜ *Carioca or Cinelândia.*

Convento do Santo Antônio. The Convent of St. Anthony was completed in 1780, but some parts date from 1615, making it one of Rio's oldest structures. Its baroque interior contains priceless colonial art, including wood carvings and wall paintings. The sacristy is covered with traditional Portuguese *azulejos* (ceramic tiles). The church has no bell tower: its bells hang from a double arch on the monastery ceiling. An exterior mausoleum contains the tombs of the offspring of Dom Pedro I and Dom Pedro II. ⊠ *Largo da Carioca 5, Centro* ☎ *021/2262–0129* ⊕ *www.conventosantoantonio.org.br* ✉ *Free* ☉ *By appointment only, call ahead or email conventorj@franciscanos.org.br to set up a visit* Ⓜ *Carioca.*

Igreja de São Francisco da Penitência. This baroque church was completed in 1737, nearly four decades after construction began. Today it's famed for its wooden sculptures and its rich gold-leaf interior. The nave contains a painting of St. Francis, the patron of the church—reportedly the first painting in Brazil done in perspective. ⊠ *Largo da Carioca 5, Centro* ☎ *021/2262–0197* ✉ *R$2* ☉ *Tues.–Fri. 9–noon and 1–4* Ⓜ *Carioca.*

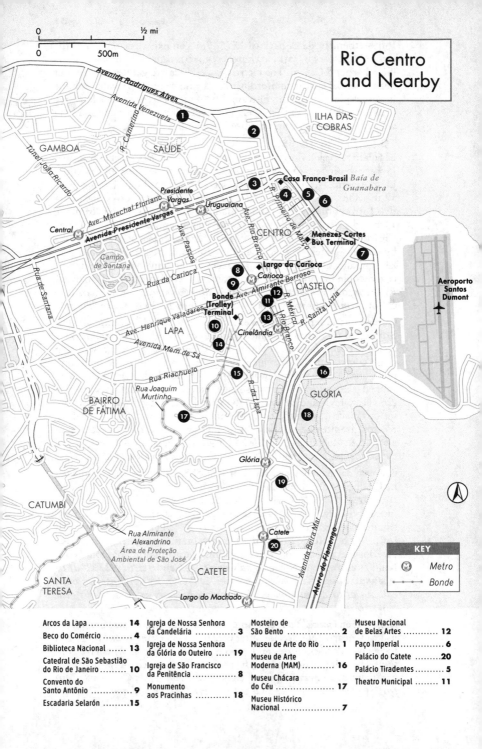

Rio Centro
and Nearby

½ mi

500m

GAMBOA

SAÚDE

ILHA DAS
COBRAS

Avenida Rodrigues Alves

Avenida Venezuela

R. Camerino

Túnel João Ricardo

Presidente
Vargas

Casa França-Brasil *Baía de
Guanabara*

Central

Ave. Marechal Floriano

Avenida Presidente Vargas

Uruguaiana

CENTRO

Menezes Cortes
Bus Terminal

Ave. Passos

Ave. Rio Branco

R. Primeiro de Março

Aeroporto
Santos
Dumont

Campo
de Santana

Rua da Carioca

Largo da Carioca

Carioca

Ave. Almirante Barroso

CASTELO

Bonde
(Trolley)
Terminal

Ave. Henrique Valadares

LAPA

Cinelândia

R. México

R. da Lapa

R. Santa Luzia

Rio Branco

Avenida Mém de Sá

Rua Riachuelo

Rua Joaquim
Murtinho

BAIRRO
DE FÁTIMA

GLÓRIA

CATUMBI

Glória

Rua Almirante
Alexandrino
Área de Proteção
Ambiental de São José

Catete

Avenida Beira Mar

Aterro do Flamengo

SANTA
TERESA

CATETE

Largo do Machado

KEY

Ⓜ *Metro*

•—•—• *Bonde*

Arcos da Lapa **14**
Beco do Comércio **4**
Biblioteca Nacional **13**
Catedral de São Sebastião
do Rio de Janeiro **10**
Convento do
Santo Antônio **9**
Escadaria Selarón **15**

Igreja de Nossa Senhora
da Candelária **3**
Igreja de Nossa Senhora
da Glória do Outeiro **19**
Igreja de São Francisco
da Penitência **8**
Monumento
aos Pracinhas **18**

Mosteiro de
São Bento **2**
Museu de Arte do Rio **1**
Museu de Arte
Moderna (MAM) **16**
Museu Chácara
do Céu **17**
Museu Histórico
Nacional **7**

Museu Nacional
de Belas Artes **12**
Paço Imperial **6**
Palácio do Catete **20**
Palácio Tiradentes **5**
Theatro Municipal **11**

Mosteiro de São Bento. Just a glimpse of the Monastery of St. Benedict's main altar can fill you with awe. Layer upon layer of curvaceous wood carvings coated in gold lend the space an opulent air, while spiral columns whirl upward to capitals topped by the chubbiest of cherubs and angels that appear lost in divine thought. Although the Benedictine monks arrived in 1586, work didn't begin on this church and monastery until 1617. It was completed in 1641, but artisans including Mestre Valentim (who designed the silver chandeliers) continued to add details almost to the 19th century. Sunday Mass at 10 am is accompanied by Gregorian chants. ⊠ *Rua Dom Gerardo 68, Centro* 🕾 *021/2206–8100* ⊕ *www.osb.org.br* ⊠ *Free* 🕙 *Daily 7–6.*

Museu de Arte do Rio. Rio's once run-down port zone is now the focus of a major investment and regeneration program, and the 2013 opening of the Museu de Arte do Rio (MAR) has provided a compelling reason for visitors to head to this part of town. The attention-grabbing museum structures—a colonial palace and a modernist former bus station, united visually by a wavelike postmodern form that floats on stilts above them—represent an impressive feat of architectural reimagination. The gallery celebrates depictions of Rio throughout the ages, and the eight gallery spaces inside the buildings contain permanent collections of surrealist, modernist, and *naif* artworks. Visiting exhibitions tend to be good, and the views from the top floor—looking out to sea and across Rio's port—are impressive. ⊠ *Praça Mauá 5, Centro* 🕾 *021/2203–1235* ⊕ *www.museudeartedorio.org.br* ⊠ *R$8, free on Tues.* 🕙 *Tues. 10–7, Wed.–Sun. 10–5* Ⓜ *Uruguiana.*

Museu de Arte Moderna (MAM). A great place to take the pulse of the vibrant Brazilian visual-arts scene, the Museum of Modern Art occupies a striking concrete-and-glass modernist building. Augmenting the permanent collection of about 6,400 works by Brazilian and international artists is the slightly larger Gilberto Chateaubriand Collection of modern and contemporary Brazilian art. MAM has earned respect over the years for its bold, often thought-provoking exhibitions, including a vibrant annual street-art festival. The venue also hosts events such as music performances and DJ sessions. Its theater screens Brazilian and international independent and art-house films. ⊠ *Av. Infante Dom Henrique 85, Centro* 🕾 *021/2240–4944* ⊕ *www.mamrio.com.br* ⊠ *R$8* 🕙 *Tues.–Fri. noon–6, weekends and holidays noon–7* Ⓜ *Cinelândia.*

Museu Histórico Nacional. The building that houses the National History Museum dates from 1762, though some sections—such as the battlements—were erected as early as 1603. It seems appropriate that this colonial structure should exhibit relics that document Brazil's history. Among its treasures are rare papers, Latin American coins, carriages, cannons, and religious art. ⊠ *Praça Marechal Ancora, Praça 15 de Novembro, Centro* 🕾 *021/2550–9224, 021/2220–2328* ⊕ *www.museuhistoriconacional.com.br* ⊠ *R$8, free Sun.* 🕙 *Tues.–Fri. 10–6, weekends noon–7* Ⓜ *Carioca or Cinelândia.*

Museu Nacional de Belas Artes. Works by Brazil's leading 19th- and 20th-century artists fill the space at the National Museum of Fine Arts. The most notable canvases are those by the country's best-known modernist,

Cândido Portinari, but be on the lookout for such gems as Leandro Joaquim's heartwarming 18th-century painting of Rio (a window to a time when fishermen still cast nets in the waters below the landmark Igreja de Nossa Senhora da Glória do Outeiro). After wandering the picture galleries, tour the extensive collections of folk and African art. ⊠ *Av. Rio Branco 199, Centro* ☎ *021/2262–6067* ⊕ *www.mnba.gov.br/ abertura/abertura.htm* ⊠ *R$8, free Sun.* ☉ *Tues.–Fri. 10–6, weekends noon–5* Ⓜ *Carioca or Cinelândia.*

Fodor'sChoice   **Theatro Municipal.** If you visit one place in Centro, make it the Munici-
★   pal Theater, modeled after the Paris Opera House and opened in 1909. Now restored to its sparkling best, the theater boasts Carrara marble, stunning mosaics, glittering chandeliers, bronze and onyx statues, gilded mirrors, German stained-glass windows, and brazilwood inlay floors. Murals by Brazilian artists Eliseu Visconti and Rodolfo Amoedo further enhance the opulent feel. The main entrance and first two galleries are particularly ornate. As you climb to the upper floors, the decor becomes simpler, a reflection of a time when different classes entered through different doors and sat in separate sections, but also due in part to the exhaustion of funds toward the end of the project. The theater seats 2,357—with outstanding sight lines—for its dance performances and classical music concerts. English-speaking guides are available. ⊠ *Rua Marechal Floriano s/n, Centro* ☎ *021/2332-9195* ⊕ *www.theatro municipal.rj.gov.br* ⊠ *Tours R$10* ☉ *Guided tours Tues.–Fri. on the hr noon–4, Sat. at 11, 1, and 9* Ⓜ *Cinelândia or Carioca.*

WORTH NOTING

Beco do Comércio. A network of narrow streets and alleys centers on this pedestrian thoroughfare, also called the Travessa do Comércio, whose name translates to Alley of Commerce. The area is flanked by restored 18th-century homes, now converted to offices, shops, and galleries. The best-known sight here is the Arco de Teles, a picturesque archway named in honor of the wealthy Teles de Menezes family, who built many of the street's most handsome buildings. Beco do Comércio is a good place to stop for lunch—the street is lined with everything from simple pay-by-weight buffet spots and casual bars to more upmarket restaurants and cafés. ⊠ *Praça 15 de Novembro, Centro* Ⓜ *Uruguaiana/ Carioca.*

Igreja de Nossa Senhora da Candelária. The classic symmetry of Cande-lária's white dome and bell towers casts an unexpected air of tranquil-lity over the chaos of downtown traffic. The church was built on the site of a chapel founded in 1610. Construction on the present church began in 1775, and although the emperor formally dedicated it in 1811, work on the dome wasn't completed until 1877. The sculpted bronze doors were exhibited at the 1889 World's Fair in Paris. ⊠ *Praça Pio X, Centro* ☎ *021/2233-2324* ⊠ *Free* ☉ *Weekdays 7:30–4* Ⓜ *Uruguaiana.*

Paço Imperial. This two-story building with thick stone walls and an ornate entrance was built in 1743, and for the next 60 years was the headquarters for Brazil's captains (viceroys), appointed by the Portu-guese court in Lisbon. When King João VI arrived, he made it his royal palace. After Brazil's declaration of independence, emperors Dom Pedro

I and II called the palace home, and when the monarchy was over-thrown, the building became Rio's central post office. Restoration work in the 1980s transformed the palace into a cultural center and concert hall. The building houses a restaurant, a bistro, and a bit of shopping. The square on which the palace sits, Praça 15 de Novembro, known in colonial days as Largo do Paço, has witnessed some of Brazil's most significant historic moments: here two emperors were crowned, slavery was abolished, and Emperor Pedro II was deposed. The square's mod-ern name is a reference to the date of the declaration of the Republic of Brazil: November 15, 1889. Praça 15, as it is widely known, sits in front of Rio's ferry terminal and is at the heart of a major regeneration project aiming to transform Rio's run-down docklands. ⊠ *Praça 15 de Novembro 48, Centro* ☎ *021/2533–4359* ⊕ *www.pacoimperial.com.br* ⊠ *Free* ☉ *Tues.–Sun. noon–6.*

Palácio Tiradentes. The Tiradentes Palace contains a permanent exhibit describing its history as the seat of the Brazilian parliament before Brasília was built in the late 1950s. Getúlio Vargas, Brazil's president for almost 20 years and by far the biggest force in 20th-century Brazil-ian politics, used the palace in the 1940s as a nucleus for disseminat-ing propaganda. Free half-hour tours are given in Portuguese, English, and Spanish. ⊠ *Rua Primeiro de Março s/n, Centro* ☎ *021/2588–1000* ⊕ *www.alerj.rj.gov.br* ⊠ *Free* ☉ *Mon.–Sat. 10–7, Sun. noon–5.*

CATETE AND GLÓRIA

Though a little run-down, historic, residential Catete and Glória are well worth an afternoon's sightseeing. The Palácio do Catete, the presi-dential palace until the government moved to Brasília, itself warrants at least two hours. In addition to its hilltop church, Glória has a lovely marina that's perfect for a picnic or stroll, especially on a Sunday, when the main road is closed to traffic.

Handily located on the metro line between the Zona Sul and Centro, the two neighborhoods' subway stations are just a few minutes' walk from each other. From Ipanema or Copacabana take the 10-minute ride to Catete, and you'll emerge right in front of the Museum of the Republic. Set aside a couple of hours to see the exhibits and enjoy a coffee in the gardens before taking a stroll down to Glória's marina, taking in the monument to fallen soldiers. The surrounding area can be a little rough, so jump on a metro to Centro or the Zona Sul when you're done sightseeing.

TOP ATTRACTIONS

Igreja de Nossa Senhora da Glória do Outeiro. The aptly named Church of Our Lady of the Glory of the Knoll (Church of Glory for short) sits on top of a hill and is visible from many spots in the city, making it a landmark that's truly cherished by the cariocas. Its location was a stra-tegic point in the city's early days, and the views from church grounds are impressive. Estácio da Sá took this hill from the French in the 1560s and then went on to expand the first settlement and to found a city for the Portuguese. The baroque church, which wasn't built until 1739, is notable for its octagonal floor plan, large dome, ornamental stonework, and vivid tile work. Tours are given by appointment only. As opening hours are sporadic, visitors might choose to arrive shortly before 9 am or 11 am on Sundays, when a Mass takes place and the church is open to the public. ✉ *Praça Nossa Senhora da Glória 135, Glória* ☎ *021/2225–2869* ⊕ *www.outeirodagloria.org.br* Ⓜ *Glória.*

FAMILY
Fodor'sChoice
★

Palácio do Catete. Once the villa of a German baron, this elegant, 19th-century granite-and-marble palace became the presidential residence after the 1889 coup overthrew the monarchy and established the Republic of Brazil. Eighteen presidents lived here. Gaze at the palace's gleaming parquet floors and intricate bas-relief ceilings as you wander through its **Museu da República** (Museum of the Republic). The permanent exhibits include a shroud-draped view of the bedroom where President Getúlio Vargas committed suicide in 1954 after the military threatened to overthrow his government. Presidential memorabilia, furniture, and paintings that date from the proclamation of the republic to the end of Brazil's military regime in 1985 are also displayed. The palace gardens are free, and worth a visit in themselves. With their imperial palm trees, water features, chattering monkeys, and strolling geese they are among the most pleasant—and safest, thanks to patrolling guards—parks in the city, and there's a well-equipped children's playground at the far end, A small contemporary art gallery, a movie theater, a café, and a bistro operate within the grounds, and there's free live music around 6 pm each weekday, courtesy of a group of senior local *sambistas.* ✉ *Rua do Catete 153, Catete* ☎ *021/3235–3693* ⊕ *www.museus. gov.br/os-museus* ✆ *Tues. and Thurs.–Sat. R$6, Wed. and Sun. free* ◷ *Tues., Thurs., and Fri. noon–5, Wed. 2–5, weekends 2–6* Ⓜ *Catete.*

WORTH NOTING

Monumento aos Pracinhas. The Monument to the Brazilian Dead of World War II—the nation sided with the Allies during the conflict—is actually a combination museum and monument. The museum houses military uniforms, medals, stamps, and documents belonging to soldiers, and two soaring columns flank the tomb of an unknown soldier. The best time to visit is on a Sunday, when the road in front of the monument is closed to traffic, and joggers, dog-walkers, and strolling families fill the area. ✉ *Parque Brigadeiro Eduardo Gomes, Glória* ☎ *021/2240–1283* ⊕ *www.mnmsgm.ensino.eb.br* ✆ *Free* ◷ *Tues.–Sun. 10–5* Ⓜ *Glória.*

SANTA TERESA AND LAPA

With its cobblestone streets and bohemian atmosphere, Santa Teresa is a delightfully eccentric neighborhood. Gabled Victorian mansions sit beside alpine-style chalets as well as more prosaic dwellings—many hanging at unbelievable angles from the flower-encrusted hills. Cafés, galleries, and antiques shops have nudged their way into nooks and crannies between the colorful homes, many of which house artists and their studios. Downhill from Santa Teresa, Lapa has some of the oldest buildings in the city and is home to the imposing Arcos da Lapa (Lapa Aqueduct) and the colorful Escadaria Selarón, also called the Lapa Steps, as well as the city's oldest street, the café-paved Rua do Lavradio.

By night, Lapa is transformed into the party heart of Rio, with countless bars and clubs and a notoriously wild weekend street party.

Santa Teresa and Lapa merit a full day's exploring, and Santa Teresa is at its bohemian best from Thursday through Saturday—many bars and restaurants don't open early in the week. Take the metro to Carioca metro station and stroll past the towering cubic Petrobras building to Rua do Lavradio to browse the antiques stores and sidewalk cafés. From here, the Lapa Steps and Lapa Aqueduct are a quick stroll, or take the bone-rattling cab ride up the cobbled steps. Jump off at Largo do Guimaraes and prepare to spend a few hours admiring the architecture, galleries, and museums and enjoying the café culture here; the area is best seen on foot but avoid deserted streets. If it's a weekend or holiday, make a night of it by starting with drinks in one of Santa Teresa's many lively bars before taking a cab or bus down to the Lapa street party around midnight.

TOP ATTRACTIONS

Arcos da Lapa. Formerly the Aqueduto da Carioca (Carioca Aqueduct), this structure with 42 massive stone arches was built between 1744 and 1750 to carry water from the Carioca River in the hillside neighborhood of Santa Teresa to Centro. In 1896 the city transportation company converted the aqueduct, by then abandoned, into a viaduct, laying trolley tracks along it. For decades, Santa Teresa's rattling yellow street cars (the "bonde" or "bondinho") passed over the aqueduct as they carried passengers from Centro up to the hillside neighborhood of Santa Teresa. After an accident in 2011, however, when the tram's brakes failed and six passengers were killed, the bonde was shut down pending major upgrades. Many of Santa Teresa's main roads are currently being ripped up as new tramlines are laid down, and as of this writing new trams were being tested on the first section of track. The trams are expected to be in service before the 2016 Rio Olympics, although the same was said of the 2014 FIFA World Cup, a target that proved wildly optimistic. ⊠ *Estação Carioca, Rua Professor Lélio Gama, Lapa* Ⓜ *Carioca or Cinelândia.*

Fodor's Choice
★
Escadaria Selarón (*Selarón's Staircase*). After traveling the world and living in more than 50 countries, Chilean painter Selarón began working in 1990 on the iconic tile staircase that is now one of the highlights of Lapa. With tiles from around the world, Selarón's staircase is the product of years of dedication, artistic vision, and donations of tiles from places far and near. Sadly, in 2013 Selarón was found murdered at his nearby home. The colorful stairs provide a great photo opportunity— Snoop Dogg and Pharell Williams shot the video for their song "Beautiful" here. ⊠ *Escadaria Selarón 24, Lapa.*

Museu Chácara do Céu (*Museum of the Small Farm of the Sky*). The collection of mostly modern works at this museum was left—along with the hilltop house that contains it—by one of Rio's greatest arts patrons, Raymundo de Castro Maya. Included are originals by 20th-century masters Picasso, Braque, Dalí, Degas, Matisse, Modigliani, and Monet. The Brazilian holdings include priceless 17th- and 18th-century maps and works by leading modernists. The views of the aqueduct, Centro, and the bay are splendid from the museum's grounds. The adjoining Parque das Ruinas (Ruins Park, free) is well worth a visit, too, and has some spectacular views from the top floor of a once-abandoned colonial mansion. ⊠ *Rua Murtinho Nobre 93, Santa Teresa* ☎ *021/3970–1126* ⊕ *www.museuscastromaya.com.br/chacara.htm* ⊠ *R$5, free Wed.* ⊙ *Wed.–Mon. 11–5.*

WORTH NOTING

Largo do Guimarães (*Guimarães Square*). Much of the activity in close-knit Santa Teresa takes place around its village-like squares, among them Largo do Guimarães, a social hub that frequently hosts street parties. The informal restaurant Bar do Arnaudo is a popular hangout for local artistic types; the neighborhood's main drinking and dining strip spans out from here. On weekends, live music spills out from bars opening onto the square, and street vendors sell beer and caipirinhas. If you follow the tram track 1.2 km (¾ mile) northwest from here you'll come to **Largo das Neves** (Neves Square), with its picturesque white-washed church. Families and other locals gather in this square until late at night. ⊠ *Rua Paschoal Carlos Magno, Ladeira do Castro, and Rua Almirante Alexandrino, Santa Teresa.*

FLAMENGO AND BOTAFOGO

These largely residential neighborhoods connect the southern beach districts and Centro via a series of highways that intersect here. It's easy to reach these neighborhoods by metro. Apartment buildings dominate, but Rio Sul—one of the city's most popular shopping centers—is here, as are some of the city's best museums and public spaces.

The eponymous beach at Flamengo no longer draws swimmers (its gentle waters look appealing but are polluted; the people you see are sunning, not swimming). A marina sits on a bay at one end of the beach, which is connected via a busy boulevard to the smaller beach (also pol-luted), at Botafogo. The city's yacht club is here, and when Rio was Brazil's capital, it was also the site of the city's glittering embassy row. The embassies relocated to Brasília long ago, but the mansions that housed them remain. Among Botafogo's more interesting mansion- and tree-lined streets are Mariana, Sorocaba, Matriz, and Visconde e Silva.

TOP ATTRACTIONS

FAMILY
Fodor's Choice
★

Casa Daros. A grand 19th-century neoclassical building has been lov-ingly restored in conjunction with the acclaimed Swiss art institute Daros to create one of Rio's most impressive exhibition spaces. As well as housing the city's most comprehensive collections of South American art—including paintings, photos, videos, and installations—the center hosts interesting visiting exhibitions and film screenings. Even the res-taurant—run by the team behind culinary hot spot Miam Miam—is a cut above your average gallery café, and the vast grounds are a great place for visiting children to burn off some energy. ⊠ *Rua General Seve-riano 159, Botafogo* ☎ *21/2138–0850* ⊕ *www.casadaros.net* ⊠ *R$14, free Wed.* Ⓜ *Botafogo.*

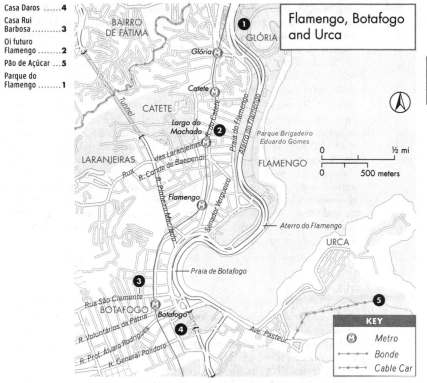

Flamengo, Botafogo and Urca

FAMILY **Oi Futuro Flamengo** (*Hi, Future*). This slick, ultramodern exhibition space also houses Rio's Telecommunications Museum. The museum itself delivers a unique multimedia adventure—lots of monitors, blinking lights, and media artifacts. After you've been oriented in the use of the MP3 headsets, a light- and mirror-filled airlock-like room awaits. The sights in this tiny exhibit space will likely mesmerize you, and if you don't speak Portuguese, the English guide will explain what you can't figure out from the visual cues. The other floors of the Oi Futuro building house cultural spaces devoted to theater performances, film screenings, and art exhibits. There's also a café whose rooftop terrace is a pleasant place to enjoy an iced cappuccino on a balmy day. ⊠ *Rua Dois de Dezembro 63, Flamengo* ☎ *021/3131–3060* ⊕ *www.oifuturo. org.br/en* ⊠ *Free* ☉ *Weekdays 11–5* Ⓜ *Largo do Machado or Catete.*

WORTH NOTING

FAMILY **Casa Rui Barbosa.** Steps away from Botafogo metro station is a museum in the former home of the 19th-century Brazilian statesman, writer, and scholar Rui Barbosa, a liberal from Bahia State who drafted one of Brazil's early constitutions. The pink mansion, which dates from 1849, is itself worth a visit. Stepping inside instantly transports you to the period when writers and other intellectuals inhabited this street's grand houses. Among the memorabilia and artifacts on display are Barbosa's 1913 car and legal, political, and journalistic works. The extensive libraries are testament to Rui Barbosa's love for literature. The well-tended gardens stretch for 9,000 meters and are filled with small pools and fountains, making them a pleasant place to take respite from the rush and crush of the city. There's a good children's library, regular kids' workshops and events, and free live music performances. ⊠ *Rua São Clemente 134, Botafogo* ☎ *021/3289–4600* ⊕ *www.casaruibarbosa.gov.br* ⚊ *R$2, free Sun.* ◷ *Gardens daily 8–6, library Wed.–Fri. 10–5:30* Ⓜ *Botafogo.*

FAMILY **Parque do Flamengo.** The landscape architect Roberto Burle Marx designed this waterfront park that flanks the Baía de Guanabara from the Glória neighborhood to Flamengo. Frequently referred to as "Aterro do Flamengo," it gets its nickname from its location atop an *atêrro* (landfill). The park contains playgrounds and public tennis and basketball courts, and paths used for jogging, walking, and biking wind through it. On weekends the freeway beside the park is closed to traffic and the entire area becomes one enormous public space. For safety reasons, avoid wandering the park after dark. ⊠ *Inland of beach from Glória to Botafogo,* ⚊ *Free* Ⓜ *Glória or Flamengo.*

URCA

Tiny, sheltered Urca is home to one of Rio's most famous attractions, the Pão de Açúcar morro. As tranquil and bucolic as the rest of Rio is fast-paced and frenetic, Urca is a wonderful place for an afternoon's wandering. Fishing boats bob on a bay set against a spectacular view of Christ the Redeemer on his mountaintop perch, and the neighborhood contains some wonderful colonial architecture. The Pão de Açúcar separates Urca's tree-lined streets from Praia Vermelha, its small, coarse-sand beach. This beach is, in turn, blocked by the Urubu and Leme mountains from the 1-km (½-mile) Leme Beach at the start of the Zona Sul.

Urca is a little tricky to reach by public transport, so take a cab from Botafogo metro station. Come here in the morning and spend some time on the beaches. Take the pleasant 30-minute nature walk around the base of Sugar Loaf, and aim to be at the cable car station late afternoon to appreciate the stunning sunset views from the peak. Round off a perfect day by sipping a caipirinha by the harbor wall at Bar e Restaurante Urca.

TOP ATTRACTIONS

FAMILY
Fodor's Choice
★
Pão de Açúcar (*Sugarloaf Mountain*). The indigenous Tupi people originally called the soaring 396-meter (1,300-foot) granite block at the mouth of Baía de Guanabara *pau-nh-acugua* (high, pointed peak). To the Portuguese the phrase seemed similar to *pão de açúcar,* itself fitting because the rock's shape reminded them of the conical loaves in which refined sugar was sold. Italian-made bubble cars holding 75 passengers each move up the mountain in two stages. The first stop is at Morro da Urca, a smaller, 212-meter (705-foot) mountain; the second is at the summit of Pão de Açúcar itself. The trip to each level takes three minutes. In high season long lines form for the cable car; the rest of the year the wait is seldom more than 30 minutes. Consider visiting Pão

de Açúcar before climbing the considerably higher Corcovado, as the view here may seem anticlimactic if experienced second. ⊠ *Av. Pasteur 520, near Praia Vermelha, Urca* ☎ *021/2546–8400* ⊕ *www.bondinho. com.br* ⬚ *R$62* ⊘ *Daily 8–7:50.*

COPACABANA

Copacabana is Rio's most famous tourist neighborhood thanks to its fabulous beach and grande-dame hotels such as the Copacabana Palace. The main thoroughfare is Avenida Nossa Senhora de Copacabana, two blocks inland from the beach. The commercial street is filled with shops, restaurants, and sidewalks crowded with colorful characters. Despite having some of the best hotels in Rio, Copacabana's heyday is over, and the neighborhood is grittier than Ipanema or Leblon. It's no secret to thieves that tourists congregate here, so keep your eyes peeled for shady types when walking around after dark. *For a description of Copacabana Beach, see Beaches, below.*

Copacabana is Rio's most iconic neighborhood, and it's home to the city's largest concentration of hotels. The beach is the main attraction and is served by three metro stations. Cardeal Arcoverde is the closest to Leme, the quieter, family-oriented end of the beach, Siqueira Campos is right at the center, and Cantagalo is within walking distance of Ipanema. Plan to spend the best part of a day here, buying food and drink from beach vendors or the many kiosks that line the sidewalk.

TOP ATTRACTIONS

FAMILY **Forte de Copacabana and Museu Histórico do Exército.** Copacabana Fort was built in 1914 as part of Rio's first line of defense, and many original features, such as the thick brick fortification and old Krupp cannons, are still visible. In the '60s and '70s, during Brazil's military dictatorship, political prisoners were kept here. The fort is impressive in itself, and the entrance archway perfectly frames a postcard view of Sugar Loaf. The best views, however, follow the path to its end and climb the steep stairs to the cannon roof, which juts right out into the ocean and takes in sweeping vistas over the Zona Sul beaches. The on-site military-history museum is worth a stop, and there are two good cafés here as well as a gift shop. During the Brazilian summer, violin recitals, classical music performances, and outdoor cinema screenings are held here, many free of charge. ⊠ *Praça Coronel Eugênio Franco 1, Copacabana* ☎ *021/2287–3781* ⊕ *www.fortedecopacabana.com* ⬚ *R$6* ⊘ *Tues.–Sun. 10–6.*

IPANEMA AND LEBLON

Ipanema, Leblon, and the blocks surrounding Lagoa Rodrigo de Freitas are part of Rio's money belt. For an up-close look at the posh apartment buildings, stroll down beachfront Avenida Vieira Souto and its extension, Avenida Delfim Moreira, or drive around the lagoon on Avenida Epitácio Pessoa. The tree-lined streets between Ipanema Beach and the lagoon are as peaceful as they are attractive. The boutiques along Rua Garcia D'Ávila make window-shopping a sophisticated endeavor. Other

Gay Rio

Gay Rio rocks almost every night with a whole menu of entertainment options. During the day, dedicated areas of the beach in Copacabana (Posto 6) and Ipanema (in front of Rua Farme de Amoedo, near Posto 8) are gay and lesbian havens. After dark, the nightlife is welcoming and inclusive. Kick off the evening taking a walk along Farme do Amoeda in Ipanema, which is lined with GLS (Gay/Lesbian/Sympathiser) bars and restaurants. Close to the famous street, be sure to check out **Galeria Café**, also in Ipanema, or **Rainbow Kiosk**, right on the sands in front of the Copacabana Palace. As the night nudges 1 am, head toward **Le Boy** or the quieter **La Cueva**, one of Copacabana's longest-running gay venues, which attracts a more mature male. Most of the livelier underground clubs, such as **Casa Rosa** and **Fosfobox**, run GLS nights during the week. The downtown party district of Lapa, previously lacking in appealing GLS options, was given a boost with the opening of **Sinônimo**, a three-story club incorporating live music, DJs, and a cocktail lounge. The sporadic circuit party B.I.T.C.H (Barbies in Total Control ⊕ *www.bitch.com.br*) has been one of the biggest events on the gay calendar since the 1980s. Many gay-focused parties and parades take place during carnival, while the annual Gay Pride parade along Copacabana Beach is one of the biggest and most colorful events on the international gay calendar.

chic areas near the beach include Praça Nossa Senhora da Paz, which is lined with wonderful restaurants and bars; Rua Vinicius de Moraes; and Rua Farme de Amoedo. Gourmands should make a beeline for Leblon's Rua Dias Ferreira, where top-notch restaurants thrill diners daily. The lively bar scene here encompasses everything from exclusive lounges and wine bars to relaxed post-beach watering holes. *For descriptions of Ipanema Beach and Leblon Beach, see Beaches, below.*

Ipanema is famous for its beach, beautiful people, and boutiques, so sun-seekers and shopaholics will want to spend at least a day here. There's a metro station a couple of blocks from the beach. Arrive at the beach early to bag a prime people-watching position and spend a few hours here—beach vendors will keep you refreshed with coconut water, soft drinks, beer, and snacks. In the afternoon head to Visconde de Piraja for shopping, before stopping at one of the many upscale restaurants for early evening food and drinks. Should you choose to make a night of it, there are plenty of lively bars here.

TOP ATTRACTIONS

Museu H.Stern. Hans Stern started his gem empire in 1945 with an initial investment of about $200. Today his company's interests include mining and production operations, as well as stores in Europe, the Americas, and the Middle East. The world headquarters of H.Stern contains a small museum that exhibits rare gems. On the self-guided workshop tour, you'll learn about the entire process of cutting, polishing, and setting stones. Afterward, you get a personal consultation with a salesperson, although you should not feel obliged to buy. The museum can arrange free transport to and from your hotel. ✉ *Rua Garcia D'Avila 113, Ipanema* ☎ *021/2106–0000* ⊕ *www.hsterninrio. com* ✉ *Free* ☉ *Tours by appointment only; booking form on website* Ⓜ *Ipanema/General Osorio.*

SÃO CONRADO AND BARRA DA TIJUCA

West of the Zona Sul lie the largely residential (and considerably affluent) neighborhoods of São Conrado and Barra da Tijuca. If you're accustomed to the shop-lined and restaurant-filled streets of Copacabana and Ipanema, you're in for a shock if you head to these neighborhoods, dominated mainly by towering, modern apartment buildings. São Conrado's main attractions are the beach, which serves as a landing point for hang gliders and paragliders, and the chic Fashion Mall. Barra da Tijuca, often likened to Miami because of its wide avenues, towering condos, and sprawling malls, offers ample high-end dining opportunities as well as a white-sand beach that stretches for a staggering 15 km (9 miles).

Barra da Tijuca is not known as a cultural hot spot, but if you are looking for serious shopping it is the place to go. It's also home to Rio's largest beach, so set aside a day for both beachgoing and retail therapy. A metro station is set to open here ahead of the 2016 Olympics, but until that happens it is best reached by cab; ask the driver to stop at São Conrado so you can snap a few photos of the hang gliders, or alternatively visit this beach hangout as part of a group tour—until the metro arrives it is a little difficult to reach by public transport.

TOP ATTRACTIONS

FAMILY
Fodor's Choice
★

Sítio Roberto Burle Marx (*Roberto Burle Marx Farm*). It's a cab ride out of town and visits need to be booked in advance, but nature lovers and architecture buffs will find it worth the effort to visit this plantation-turned-museum honoring Roberto Burle Marx, Brazil's legendary landscape architect. Marx, the mind behind Rio's swirling mosaic beachfront walkways and the Atêrro do Flamengo, was said to have "painted with plants," and he was the first designer to use Brazilian flora in his projects. More than 3,500 species—including some discovered by and named for Marx, as well as many on the endangered list—flourish at this 100-acre estate. Marx grouped his plants not only according to their soil and light needs but also according to their shape and texture. He also liked to mix the modern with the traditional—a recurring theme throughout the property. The results are both whimsical and elegant. In 1985 he bequeathed the farm to the Brazilian government, though he remained here until his death in 1994. His house is now a cultural center full of his belongings, including collections of folk art, and the beautiful gardens are a tribute to his talents. The grounds also contain his ultramodern studio (he was a painter, too) and a small, restored colonial chapel dedicated to St. Anthony. ✉ *Estrada Roberto Burle Marx 2019, Pedra da Guaratiba* ✛ *At far end of Barra da Tijuca* ☎ *021/ 2410–1412* ⊕ *sitioburlemarx.blogspot.com.br* ✉ *R$10* ☉ *Tues.–Sun. by appointment only; tours at 9:30 am and 1:30 pm.*

FAMILY **Museu Casa do Pontal.** If you're heading toward the beaches of Prainha or Grumari, consider taking a detour to Brazil's largest folk-art museum. One room houses a wonderful mechanical sculpture that represents all of the *escolas de samba* (samba schools) that march in the Carnival parades. Another mechanical "scene" depicts a circus in action. This is the private collection of French expatriate Jacques Van de Beuque, who collected Brazilian treasures—including religious pieces—from his arrival in the country in 1946 until his death in 2000. ⊠ *Estrada do Pontal 3295, Grumari* ☎ *021/2490–3278* ⊕ *www.museucasadopontal. com.br* ⊠ *R$10* ☉ *Tues.–Sun. 9:30–5.*

WORTH NOTING

São Conrado. The juxtaposition of the "haves" and "have nots" couldn't be more stark, or more startling, than it is in São Conrado, where mansions and expensive condos sit right next to sprawling favelas. As you approach the neighborhood heading west from Ipanema, Avenida Niemeyer, blocked by the imposing Dois Irmãos Mountain, snakes along rugged cliffs that offer spectacular sea views on the left. The road returns to sea level again in São Conrado, a natural amphitheater surrounded by forested mountains and the ocean. Development of this upper-class residential area began in the late 1960s with an eye on Rio's high society. A short stretch along the beach includes the condominiums of a former president, the ex-wife of another former president, an ex-governor of Rio de Janeiro State, and a onetime Central Bank president. The towering Pedra da Gávea, a huge flattop granite boulder, marks the western edge of São Conrado. North of the boulder lies Pedra Bonita, the mountain from which gliders depart. ⊠ *Just west of Leblon, .*

INLAND ZONA SUL

In the western portion of the city north of Leblon, trees and hills dominate the landscape in the neighborhoods of Jardim Botânico, Lagoa, Cosme Velho, and Laranjeiras. In addition to their parks and gardens, these primarily residential neighborhoods have marvelous museums, seductive architecture, and tantalizing restaurants. The architecture is a blend of modern condominiums and colonial houses. These neighborhoods tend to be quieter during the day because they're not on the beachfront, but they do have some of the hippest nightclubs in Rio. You can't say you've seen Rio until you've taken in the view from Corcovado and then strolled through its forested areas or beside its inland Lagoa (Lagoon) Rodrigo de Freitas—hanging out just like a true carioca.

These picturesque inland neighborhoods lack metro stops, so the best way to visit them all in one day is as part of an organized tour or with a private guide. If you have time to spare, each neighborhood warrants at least half a day's exploring. Be sure to visit Lagoa, which can be reached on foot from Leblon, Ipanema, and Copacabana, and the nearby Botanical Gardens. Cosme Velho is home to impressive mansions as well as the station for trains up to the Christ statue, and it's a pleasant stroll along the main road from here to Laranjeiras, which has some good bars and restaurants as well as pleasant squares and street markets.

CLOSE UP

Favelas

A BIT OF HISTORY
Named after the flowers that grow on the hills of Rio, the first favela began as a squatter town for homeless soldiers at the end of the 19th century. Later, freed slaves illegally made their homes on these undeveloped government lands. The favelas flourished and expanded in the 1940s as the population in Brazil shifted from a rural-based to an urban-based one. In the 1970s, during the military dictatorship, the government moved favela dwellers into public housing projects.

RIO'S LARGEST FAVELA
Rocinha is Rio's largest and most developed favela. Between 150,000 and 300,000 people reside in this well-developed community (there are three banks, a nightclub, and many shops and small markets). Brace yourself for a variety of smells, both good and bad: you'll find savory-smelling, grilled *churrasquinho* (meat skewers) sold in the street, and any number of delicious aromas drifting out of nearby restaurants. On the flip side, residents dump their trash on the side of the road (in designated areas) and in some places, raw sewage flows in open canals.

EXPLORING
The main thoroughfare, the Estrada da Gávea, begins in São Conrado and ends on the other side of Rocinha, in Gávea. Anyone can take a stroll up this street, and visitors are likely to hear English being spoken. If you're feeling intrepid and want to explore Rocinha on foot without a guide, be aware of the following: In 2012 police wrested control of Rocinha from the drug faction Amigos dos Amigos (ADA) as part of an ongoing citywide pacification project. Though UPPs (Police Pacification Units) have largely kept the peace since then, shoot-outs between police and faction members are not unheard of. Crime against tourists in the favela is rare, but unguided visitors stand a real chance of getting lost in the maze of streets. By far the safest way to visit Rocinha or other favelas is to take an organized tour. *For information about favela tours, see Tours, in Rio de Janeiro Planning, above.*

TOP ATTRACTIONS

FAMILY
Fodor's Choice
★

Corcovado and Christ the Redeemer. Rio's iconic *Cristo Redentor* (Christ the Redeemer) statue stands arms outstretched atop 690-meter-high (2,300-foot-high) Corcovado mountain. There's an eternal argument about which city view is better, the one from Pão de Açúcar (Sugarloaf) or the one from here. In our opinion, it's best to visit Sugarloaf *before* you visit Corcovado, or you may experience Sugarloaf only as an anticlimax. Corcovado has two advantages: it's nearly twice as high, and it offers an excellent view of Pão de Açúcar itself. The sheer 300-meter (1,000-foot) granite face of Corcovado (the name means "hunchback" and refers to the mountain's shape) has always been a difficult undertaking for climbers.

It wasn't until 1921, the centennial of Brazil's independence from Portugal, that someone had the idea of placing a statue atop Corcovado. A team of French artisans headed by sculptor Paul Landowski was assigned the task of erecting a statue of Christ with his arms apart as if embracing the city. (Nowadays, mischievous cariocas say Christ is getting ready to clap for his favorite escola de samba.) It took 10 years, but on October 12, 1931, Christ the Redeemer was inaugurated by then-president Getúlio Vargas, Brazil's FDR. The sleek, modern figure rises more than 30 meters (100 feet) from a 6-meter (20-foot) pedestal and weighs 700 tons. In the evening a powerful lighting system transforms it into an even more dramatic icon.

There are three ways to reach the top: by funicular railway, by official van, or on foot (not recommended without a guide for safety reasons). The train, built in 1885, provides delightful views of Ipanema and Leblon from an absurd angle of ascent, as well as a close look at thick vegetation and butterflies. (You may wonder what those oblong medicine balls hanging from the trees are, the ones that look like spiked watermelons tied to ropes—they're *jaca*, or jackfruit.) Trains leave the Cosme Velho station (*Rua Cosme Velho 513, Cosme Velho, 021/2558–1329, www.corcovado.com.br*) for the steep, 5-km (3-mile), 17-minute ascent. Late-afternoon trains are the most popular; on weekends be prepared for a long wait. Buy tickets online to avoid queueing twice: once to buy tickets and once to board the train. Official vans are slightly cheaper but not as much fun as the railway. There are boarding points for the vans in Copacabana and Largo do Machado, and at Paineiras inside the national park. Tickets can be bought online (*www.paineirascorcovado.com.br*). After disembarking you can climb up 220 steep, zigzagging steps to the summit, or take an escalator or a panoramic elevator. If you choose the stairs, you pass little cafés and shops selling souvenirs along the way. Save your money for Copacabana's night market; you'll pay at least double atop Corcovado. Once at the top, all of Rio stretches out before you. Visit Corcovado on a clear day; clouds often obscure the Christ statue and the view of the city. Go as early in the morning as possible, before people start pouring out of tour buses, and before the haze sets in. ⊠ *Estrada da Redentor, Cosme Velho* ⊕ *www.corcovado. com.br* 🚋 *R$62 by train, R$55 by minibus, R$30 on foot with guide* ⊙ *Daily 8–7; trains run every 30 minutes, vans 8–6 daily.*

FAMILY **Fundação Planetário.** Rio's planetarium is a great escape if your vacation gets rained on, or if you simply have a passion for astronomy. The adjoining interactive Museu do Universo (Museum of the Universe) illustrates the history of space exploration and travel in a futuristic exhibition area with lots of hands-on activities for kids. The planetarium frequently updates its programming, which consists of a mixture of fictitious adventures in space (recommended for kids) and nonfiction shows about the constellations and our solar system. If your aim is stargazing without the voice-over and music, the Praça dos Telescópios is open for sky observation from Tuesday to Friday, between 7:30 pm and 9:30 pm. ⊠ *Rua Vice-Governador Ruben Bernardo 100, Gávea* 🕾 *021/2274–0046* ⊕ *www.planetariodorio.com.br* 🚋 *Museum R$4; museum and planetarium session R$16; weekends half price* ⊙ *Tues.– Fri. 9–5, weekends and holidays 2:30–5.*

FAMILY
Fodor'sChoice
★ **Jardim Botânico.** The 340-acre Botanical Garden contains more than 5,000 species of tropical and subtropical plants and trees, including 900 varieties of palms (some more than a century old) and more than 140

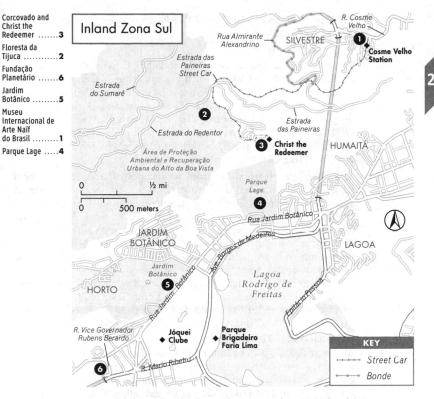

species of birds. The shady garden, created in 1808 by the Portuguese king João VI during his exile in Brazil, offers respite from Rio's sticky heat. In 1842 the garden gained its most impressive adornment, the Avenue of the Royal Palms, a 720-meter (800-yard) double row of 134 soaring royal palms. Elsewhere, the Casa dos Pilões, an old gunpowder factory, has been restored and displays objects pertaining to the nobility and their slaves. Also on the grounds are a museum dedicated to enviromental concerns, a library, two small cafés, and a gift shop. ⊠ *Rua Jardim Botânico 1008, Jardim Botânico* ☎ *021/3874–1808, 021/3874–1214* ⊕ *www.jbrj.gov.br* ⊠ *R$7* ⊗ *Mon. noon–7, Tues.–Sun. 8–5.*

FAMILY **Parque Lage.** This lush green space down the road from Jardim Botânico was acquired by Antônio Martins Lage Jr., whose grandson, Henrique Lage, fell head-over-heels in love with the Italian singer Gabriela Bezanzoni. The magnificent palace he had constructed for her was completed in 1922; the impressive mansion and grounds were turned into a public park in 1960. A visual-arts school and a café occupy the mansion. On the grounds are small aquariums and a few caves that have stalactites and stalagmites. If you want to tackle Corcovado on foot to make your pilgrimage to see Christ the Redeemer, start in Parque Lage; trails are clearly marked, though you shouldn't go alone. ⊠ *Rua Jardim Botânico*

414, Jardim Botânico ☎ *021/3257–1800* ⊕ *www.eavparquelage.rj.gov. br* 🖃 *Free* ⊙ *Daily 8–5.*

WORTH NOTING

FAMILY **Floresta da Tijuca** (*Tijuca Forest*). Surrounding Corcovado is the dense, tropical Tijuca Forest, also known as the Parque Nacional da Tijuca. Once part of a Brazilian nobleman's estate, it's studded with exotic trees and thick jungle vines and has several waterfalls, including the delightful Cascatinha de Taunay (Taunay Waterfall). About 180 meters (200 yards) beyond the waterfall is the small pink-and-purple Capela Mayrink (Mayrink Chapel), with painted panels by the 20th-century Brazilian artist Cândido Portinari.

The views are breathtaking from several points along this national park's 96 km (60 miles) of narrow winding roads. Some of the most spectacular are from Dona Marta, on the way up Corcovado; the Emperor's Table, supposedly where Brazil's last emperor, Pedro II, took his court for picnics; and, farther down the road, the Chinese View, the area where Portuguese king João VI allegedly settled the first Chinese immigrants to Brazil, who came in the early 19th century to develop tea plantations. A great way to see the forest is by Jeep or van; you can arrange tours through several agencies, among them Brazil Expedition (*www.brazilexpedition.com*) and Jeep Tour (*021/2108–5800, www.jeeptour.com.br*). ✉ *Estrada da Cascatinha 850, Alta da Boa Vista* ☎ *021/2492–2252* ⊕ *www.parquedatijuca.com.br* 🖃 *Free* ⊙ *Daily 8–5.*

FAMILY **Museu Internacional De Arte Naïf do Brasil** (*International Museum of Naïve Art from Brazil*). More than 6,000 works by Brazil's best self-taught painters, along with some by their counterparts from around the world, grace the walls of a colonial mansion that was once the studio of painter Eliseu Visconti. The museum is a few steps uphill from the station for the train to Corcovado, and entrance is half price for those with a train ticket for the same day. The works on display date from the 15th century to the present. Don't miss the colorful, colossal 7×4–meter (22×13–foot) canvas that depicts the city of Rio; it reportedly took five years to complete. There's a pleasant, kid-friendly organic café on the grounds. ✉ *Rua Cosme Velho 561, Cosme Velho* ☎ *021/2205–8612* ⊕ *www.museunaif.com/en* 🖃 *R$12* ⊙ *Tues.–Fri. 10–6, weekends and holidays noon–6.*

WEST OF DOWNTOWN

Neighborhoods west of downtown are mainly residential. Some are middle-class and some are poor. Unless you're a local, it's hard to know which areas are safe and which are not, so you should avoid wandering around. One exception is pleasant Quinta da Boa Vista, which is fine to wander. You can easily get here by metro, but avoid coming after dark.

Few visitors will make their base in the area west of downtown, but one compelling reason to visit is the mighty Maracana soccer stadium, which is open for tours on non–match days. If you want to catch a game it is easiest to go as part of a group trip. Nearby, the city zoo, national museum, and scenic gardens at Quinta da Boa Vista are worth a visit if you have the time.

TOP ATTRACTIONS

FAMILY
Fodor's Choice
★
Maracanã. Fans have witnessed many historic sports moments at this stadium that hosted the finals of the 1950 and 2014 FIFA World Cups and was the venue where the soccer star Pelé scored his 1,000th goal. Now seating 78,838 fans after a major makeover in anticipation of the 2014 World Cup, the stadium will host key matches during the 2016 Rio Olympics, and big local games are also held here during the seemingly never-ending Brazilian soccer season. The stadium is officially called Estádio Mário Filho, after a famous journalist, but it's best known as Maracanã, the name of the surrounding neighborhood and a nearby river. Guided and non-guided stadium tours can be booked on the official website. ⊠ *Rua Professor Eurico Rabelo, Gate 16,* ☎ *0800/ 062-7222* ⊕ *www.maracana.com* ✉ *Match tickets R$30–R$100, non-guided tours from R$26, guided tours from R$40* Ⓜ *Maracanã.*

FAMILY
Museu Nacional. A little off Rio's main tourist track, the National Museum is well worth the metro ride to view its exhibits of botanical, anthropological, and animal specimens. With a permanent collection of 20 million objects (give or take a few), the supply is nearly endless. Temporary exhibitions focus on subjects such as meteorites, tribal art, and animal evolution. The opulent museum building—a former imperial palace—itself merits a visit, and the vast grounds are home to Rio's city zoo. ⊠ *Quinta da Boa Vista, São Cristóvão* ☎ *021/2562–6900* ⊕ *www.museunacional.ufrj.br* ✉ *R$6* ◷ *Tues.–Fri. 10–5, Mon. noon–5* Ⓜ *Estação São Cristóvão.*

FAMILY
Quinta da Boa Vista. Complete with lakes and marble statuary, this vast public park on a former royal estate's landscaped grounds is a popular spot for family picnics. You can rent boats to pedal on the water, and bicycles to pedal on land. The former imperial palace now houses the Museu Nacional. The city zoo sits adjacent to the park, which often hosts live-music events. ⊠ *Av. Paulo e Silva at Av. Bartolomeu de Gusmão, São Cristóvão* ✉ *Free* ◷ *Daily 10–6* Ⓜ *São Cristóvão.*

WORTH NOTING

FAMILY
Jardim Zoológico. For children and others with an interest in seeing birds and beasts up close, Rio's city zoo makes for a diverting day out. Colorful native birds and a variety of South American monkeys are among the attractions; the "nursery" for baby animals and the reptile house are always popular with younger visitors. The zoo has received criticism for the somewhat small enclosures the larger animals—including lions and bears—endure, but conditions overall have improved in recent years. ⊠ *Quinta da Boa Vista, São Cristóvão* ☎ *021/3878–4200* ⊕ *www.rio. rj.gov.br/web/riozoo* ✉ *R$6* ◷ *Wed.–Sun. 9–4:30* Ⓜ *São Cristovão.*

BEACHES

Rio's circuit of *praias* (beaches) begins in the north with Flamengo, on Guanabara Bay, but the best strands are farther south. Beaches are the city's pulse points: exercise centers, gathering places, lovers' lanes.

Although cariocas wander into the water to cool off, most spend their time sunning and socializing, not swimming. Copacabana and Ipanema are the most active areas. As you head west from Barra da Tijuca the beaches become increasingly isolated and have little tourist infrastructure. Ruggedly beautiful, they are popular with surfers.

Zona Sul beaches can be easily reached by metro, but for the farther-flung strands, consider taking a taxi. City buses and chartered minivans drop you off along the shore, but they can be confusing if you don't speak Portuguese. Turismo Clássico can arrange for drivers and guides.

Beaches are listed geographically from north to south.

FLAMENGO AND BOTAFOGA

Praia do Flamengo. This small curved beach with a terrific view of Sugar Loaf is much busier from 5 to 7 in the morning than on a sunny afternoon. That's because Flamengo Beach is a great place to go for a walk, jog, run, or stroll, but not such a great place for a dip in the (usually brown) water. Vying with the beach for the attention of locals is Porcão Rio's, a not-to-be-missed churrascaria. **Amenities:** food and drink. **Best for:** walking. ⊠ *Rua Praia do Flamengo, Flamengo* Ⓜ *Flamengo.*

Praia do Botafogo. Though very much a strand, the Zona Sul's most polluted beach doesn't attract swimmers and sunbathers. Locals joke that the fish here come ready-coated in oil for frying, but don't let that stop you from jogging along the sidewalk if you're staying nearby. Early risers are often rewarded with a stunning sunrise from this shore. **Amenities:** none. **Best for:** sunrise. ⊠ *Between Praça Praia Nova and Praça Marinha do Brasil, Botafogo* Ⓜ *Botafogo.*

URCA

FAMILY **Praia Vermelha.** Right at the foot of Sugar Loaf, this sheltered, rough-sand beach (the name means "red beach," a reference to the distinctive coarse sand here) is one of the safest places in the city for sunbathing thanks to its location next to a military base. Frequented more by local families than by tourists, and with only a few vendors, Vermelha is a tranquil spot to catch some rays. The water here is calm, but it's often too dirty for swimming. **Amenities:** food and drink. **Best for:** sunset. ⊠ *Praça General Tibúrcio, Urca.*

COPACABANA

FAMILY **Praia do Leme.** Leme Beach is a natural extension of Copacabana Beach to the northeast, toward Pão de Açúcar. A rock formation juts into the water here, forming a quiet cove that's less crowded than the rest of the beach. This is a top spot for families, and small wading pools can be rented along with the usual beach chairs and sun umbrellas at the many *barracas* (beach tents selling food and drink). Along a sidewalk, at the side of the mountain overlooking Leme, anglers stand elbow to elbow with their lines dangling into the sea. Many locals swim here, but be wary of the strong undertow, and never head into the water when the

2

red flag is displayed on the beach. **Amenities:** food and drink; toilets; showers; lifeguards. **Best for:** walking; sunset. ✉ *From Av. Princesa Isabel to Morro do Leme, Leme* Ⓜ *Cardeal Arcoverde.*

Fodor's Choice ★ **Praia de Copacabana.** Maddening traffic, noise, packed apartment blocks, and a world-famous beach—this is Copacabana, or, Manhattan with bikinis. Walk along the neighborhood's classic crescent to dive headfirst into Rio's beach culture, a cradle-to-grave lifestyle that begins with toddlers accompanying their parents to the water and ends with silver-haired seniors walking hand in hand along the sidewalk. Copacabana hums with activity: you're likely to see athletic men playing volleyball using only their feet and heads, not their hands—a sport Brazilians have dubbed *futevôlei.* As you can tell by all the goal nets, soccer is also popular, and Copacabana has been a frequent host to the annual world beach soccer championships. You can swim here, although pollution levels and a strong undertow can sometimes be discouraging. Pollution levels change daily and are well publicized; someone at your hotel should be able to get you the information.

Copacabana's privileged live on beachfront Avenida Atlântica, famed for its wide mosaic sidewalks designed by Roberto Burle Marx, and for its grand hotels—including the Copacabana Palace Hotel—and cafés with sidewalk seating. On Sunday two of the avenue's lanes are closed to traffic and are taken over by joggers, rollerbladers, cyclists, and pedestrians. **Amenities:** food and drink; lifeguards; showers; toilets. **Best for:** sunset; walking. ✉ *Av. Princesa Isabel to Rua Francisco Otaviano, Copacabana* Ⓜ *Cardeal Arcoverde, Siqueira Campos, and Cantagalo.*

NEED A BREAK?

Manoel & Juaquim. For a cooling early evening drink after a walk along the beach, drop by this air-conditioned *boteco* (casual bar-restaurant) whose windows face the sand. Part of a chain whose branches you'll find elsewhere in Copacabana and in Ipanema, this is a fine place to settle in with a cold draft beer, order a few *empadas* (little pies filled with shrimp, chicken, or cheese), and watch carioca life unfold. ✉ *Av. Atlântica 1936, Copacabana* ☎ *021/2547–8192* ⊕ *manoelejuaquim.com.br/copacabanaposto3* ⊗ *Closed Sun.* Ⓜ *Siqueira Campos.*

Praia do Diabo. A barely noticeable stretch of sand tucked away between Arpoador and a natural rock wall that extends to Copacabana's fort, Praia do Diabo is popular with local *surfistas* (surfers) but the dangerous waves, which can smash an unskilled surfer into the nearby rocks,

---

NEW YEAR'S EVE IN RIO

Rio's New Year's celebration, or *Réveillon* as it's known in Brazil, is a whirling dervish of a party in which an estimated 3 million people truck over to Copacabana for drinks, dancing, and a spectacular fireworks show in Guanabara Bay. A word of warning: stay away from the stage. The area immediately surrounding the temporary stage on the beach becomes packed with people, and you run the risk of getting pickpocketed. Plan your hotel stay months in advance, and be prepared to pay more. Prices at least double, and rooms fill quickly.

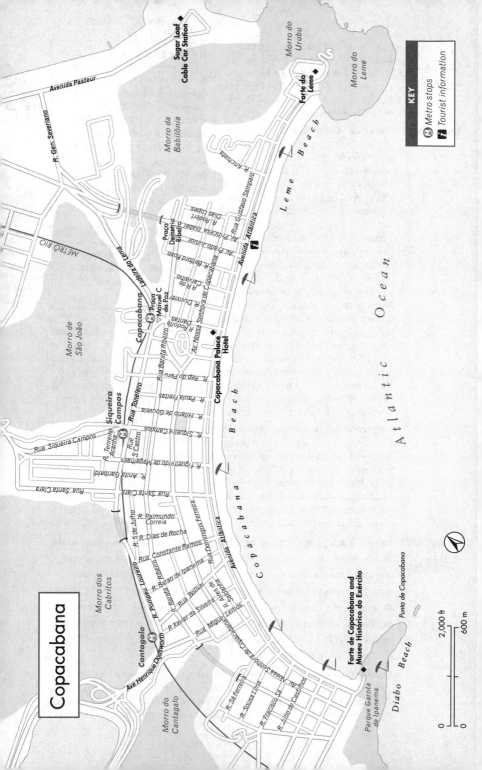

Copacabana

Sugar Loaf Cable Car Station

Avenida Pasteur

R. Gen. Severiano

R. Santa Clara

Rua Santa Clara

Rua Siqueira Campos

Siqueira Campos

Rua Tonelero

R. Tenente Marsh

R. Anita Garibaldi

R. Figueiredo de Magalhães

R. Hilário de Gouvêa

R. Siqueira Campos

Rua S. Castro

R. Raimundo Correia

R. Dias de Rocha

R. 5 de Julho

Rua Constante Ramos

R. Pompeu Loureiro

R. Ribeiro

R. Barata Ribeiro

Rua Barão de Ipanema

R. Bolívar

R. Xavier da Silveira

R. Alves de Saldanha

R. Miguel Lemos

R. Sá Ferreira

R. Souza Lima

R. Francisco

R. Xilha de Castilhos

Av. Nossa Senhora de Copacabana

Cantagalo

Ave Henrique Dodsworth

Morro do Cantagalo

Morro dos Cabritos

Parque Garota de Ipanema

Punta de Copacabana

Forte de Copacabana and Museu Histórico do Exército

Diabo Beach

Copacabana Beach

Atlantic Ocean

Avenida Atlântica

Av. Nossa Senhora de Copacabana

Copacabana Palace Hotel

R. Barata Ribeiro

R. Rep. do Peru

R. Paula Freitas

Rua Domingos Ferreira

R. Rodolfo Dantas

R. Figueiredo

Av. N. Sra. de Copacabana

R. Duvivier

R. de Carvalho

R. Belford Roxo

Av. Princesa Isabel

R. Robert Dias Lopes

Praça Demétrio Ribeiro

Copacabana

Praça Manuel C da Paz

Ladeira do Leme

METRO RIO

Morro de São João

Morro da Babilônia

Av. Gustavo Sampaio

R. Anchieta

Avenida Atlântica

Leme Beach

Forte do Leme

Morro do Urubu

Morro do Leme

0   2,000 ft

0   600 m

leave no mystery as to why this beach is called the Devil's Beach in Portuguese. Take advantage of the exercise bars, but stay out of the water unless you are a very experienced surfer. Toilets and showers can be found at nearby Arpoador and Copacabana. **Amenities:** none. **Best for:** surfing. ✉ *Between Arpoador rock and Copacabana Fort, Copacabana* Ⓜ *Ipanema/General Osório.*

IPANEMA AND LEBLON

Praia do Arpoador. At the point where Ipanema Beach meets Copacabana, Praia do Arpoador has great waves for surfing. They're so great that nonsurfers tend to avoid the water for fear of getting hit by boards. A giant rock jutting out into the waves provides panoramic views over the beaches and out to sea. Not surprisingly, the rock is a favorite haunt of romantic couples looking to catch the sunset. With more elbow room and fewer vendors than Ipanema, this beach is a prime spot for a relaxed sunbathing session. **Amenities:** food and drink; toilets; showers; lifeguards. **Best for:** sunset; surfing. ✉ *Rua Francisco Otaviano, Arpoador* Ⓜ *Ipanema/General Osório or Cantagalo.*

FAMILY

Fodor's Choice

★

Praia de Ipanema. As you stroll this world-famous beach you'll encounter a cross section of the city's residents, each favoring a particular stretch. Families predominate in the area near Posto (Post) 10, for instance, and the gay community clusters near Posto 8 by a giant rainbow flag. Throughout the day you'll see groups playing beach volleyball and soccer, and if you're lucky you might even come across the Brazilian Olympic volleyball team practicing here. At kiosks all along the boardwalk, you can sample all sorts of food and drink, from the typical coconut water to fried shrimp and turnovers. **Amenities:** food and drink; lifeguards; showers; toilets. **Best for:** walking; sunset. ✉ *Avenida Viera Souto to Praça do Arpoador, Ipanema* Ⓜ *Ipanema/General Osório.*

FAMILY

Praia do Leblon. At the far end of Ipanema lies Praia do Leblon, a stretch of beach usually occupied by families and generally less lively as far as beach sports are concerned. The water tends to be rough and a strong undertow makes swimming unwise, but this a nice place for a paddle and a splash. Vendors pass by selling everything from ice-cold beer and coconut water to bikinis and sarongs, so come with a few reals to spend. As you stroll along the beautifully tiled sidewalk, take note of the sprawling Vidigal favela, which perches on the hillside overlooking the area. Continue up the road a bit to one of Leblon's *mirantes,* boardwalk-like areas that offer a great view of the entire beach from Leblon to Arpoador. **Amenities:** food and drink; lifeguards; toilets; showers. **Best for:** walking; sunset. ✉ *Av. Epitácio Pessoa to Praça Escritor Antônio Callado, Leblon* Ⓜ *Ipanema/General Osorio.*

Praia do Vidigal. Quiet Vidigal Beach is next to the Sheraton hotel. The small stretch of sand was the playground of residents of the nearby Vidigal favela until the hotel was built in the 1970s. These days it's practically a private beach for hotel guests. The water is calm enough for swimming, but like others in Rio can be dirty after heavy rainfall. **Amenities:** food and drink. **Best for:** swimming. ✉ *Av. Niemeyer at Sheraton, Vidigal.*

What's Your Beach Style?

To cariocas, where you hang out on the beach says a lot about you. Each of Rio's beaches has its own style, and the longer stretches of sand are themselves informally divided according to social groupings and lifestyles. There are sections of beach for singles, families, sporty types, and those looking for a quiet time. Cariocas who choose to bronze their bodies at Ipanema are generally considered to be more chic than those who catch their rays at Copacabana, with Ipanema's Posto Nove (lifeguard post 9) the hangout of choice for a young, fashionable crowd. Nearby, a vast rainbow flag in front of Rua Farme do Amoeda marks Ipanema Beach's gay and lesbian section. Families and beachgoers who prefer working on their tans to making new friends, on the other hand, largely populate Leblon Beach.

Wherever you choose to make your beach base, note that bringing along a beach towel constitutes a social faux pas. Women should equip themselves with a colorful sarong, and men are expected to remain either standing or engaged in sporting activity.

SÃO CONRADO AND BARRA DA TIJUCA

FAMILY **Praia da Barra.** Some cariocas consider the beach at Barra da Tijuca to be Rio's best, and the 18-km-long (11-mile-long) sweep of sand and jostling waves certainly is dramatic. Pollution isn't generally a problem, and in many spots neither are crowds. Barra's water is cooler and its breezes more refreshing than those at other beaches. The strong waves in some sections attract surfers, windsurfers, and jet-skiers, so you should swim with caution. The beach is set slightly below a sidewalk, where cafés and restaurants beckon. Condos have also sprung up here, and the city's largest shopping centers and supermarkets have made inland Barra their home. **Amenities:** food and drink; toilets; showers. **Best for:** walking; surfing. ⊠ *Av. Sernambetiba to Av. Lúcio Costa, Barra da Tijuca.*

FAMILY **Praia de Grumari.** A bit beyond Prainha, off Estrada de Guaratiba, is Grumari, a beach that seems a preview of paradise. What it lacks in amenities—it has only a couple of groupings of thatch-roof huts selling drinks and snacks—it makes up for in natural beauty: the glorious red sands of its quiet cove are backed by low, lush hills. Weekends are extremely crowded—arrive early. Take a lunch break at Restaurante Point de Grumari, which serves excellent fish dishes. If you've ventured this far, you might as well take a slight detour to the Museu Casa do Pontal, Brazil's largest folk-art museum, and, for an in-depth look at one of the world's greatest landscape artists, the Sítio Roberto Burle Marx. **Amenities:** food and drink. **Best for:** surfing; sunset. ⊠ *Av. Estado de Guanabara, Grumari.*

Praia de São Conrado. West of Leblon, Praia de São Conrado sits empty during the week but is often packed on weekends and holidays. The strand of soft sand attracts both wealthy locals and residents of the nearby Rocinha favela, and it provides a soft landing for hang gliders

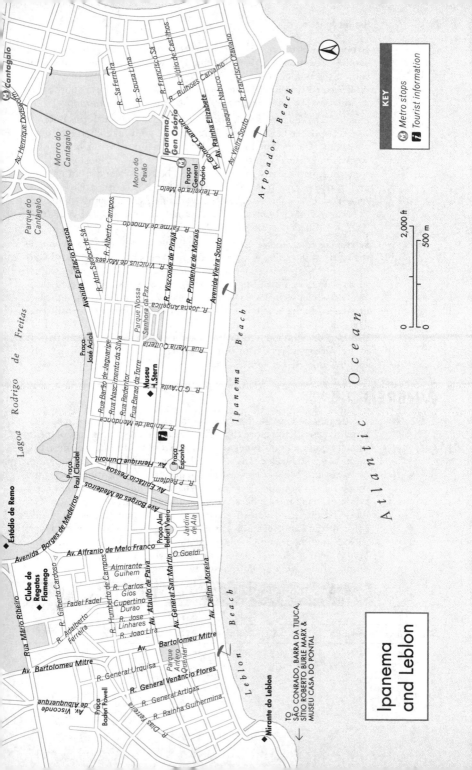

Ipanema
and Leblon

KEY
Ⓜ Metro stops
ⓘ Tourist information

Atlantic Ocean

Ipanema Beach

Arpoador Beach

Leblon Beach

Lagoa Rodrigo de Freitas

Parque do Cantagalo

Morro do Cantagalo

Morro do Pavão

Ⓜ Cantagalo

Ⓜ Ipanema/ Gen Osório

Praça General Osório

Av. Henrique Dodsworth

R. Sá Ferreira
R. Sousa Lima
R. Francisco Sá
R. Júlio de Castilhos
R. Bulhões Carvalho
R. Gomes Carneiro
Av. Rainha Elizabete
R. Joaquim Nabuco
R. Francisco Otaviano
Av. Vieira Souto

R. Teixeira de Melo
R. Farme de Amoedo
R. Alm Saddock de Sá
R. Alberto Campos
Avenida Epitácio Pessoa
R. Vinícius de Moraes
R. Visconde de Pirajá
R. Prudente de Moraes
R. Joana Angélica
Avenida Vieira Souto

Parque Nossa Senhora da Paz

Rua Maria Quitéria

R. G C D'Avila

Museu H.Stern

Rua Barão de Jaguaripe
Rua Nascimento da Silva
Rua Redentor
Rua Barão da Torre
R. Aníbal de Mendonça
Av. Henrique Dumont

Praça Nossa
Praça José Aciolí
Praça Espinho
R. Redem
Av. Epitácio Pessoa
Ave. Borges de Medeiros
Praça Paul Claudel
Praça Alm. Belfort Vieira
Jardim de Ala

Av. Alfranio de Melo Franco

O Goeldi

Almirante Guihem
R. Carlos Gios
Cupertino Durão
R. José Linhares
R. Joao Lira
Humberto de Campos
Av. Ataulfo de Paiva
Av. General San Martin
Av. Delfim Moreira

Fadel Fadel
R. Gilberto Cardoso
R. Adalberto Ferreira
Rua Mário Ribeiro

Av. Bartolomeu Mitre

Av. Bartolomeu Mitre

R. General Urquisa
R. General Venâncio Flores
R. General Artigas
R. Rainha Guihermina
R. Dias Ferreira
Av. Visconde de Albuquerque
Praça Baden Powell
Parque Antero Quental

◆ Estádio de Remo

◆ Clube de Regatas Flamengo

◆ Mirante do Leblon

TO:
SÃO CONRADO, BARRA DA TIJUCA,
SÍTIO ROBERTO BURLE MARX &
MUSEU CASA DO PONTAL

0   2,000 ft
0   500 m

swooping over the city. Surfers love the crashing waves, but swimmers should be cautious because of the undertow. It's worth remaining until sunset; the pumpkin sun often performs a dazzling show over Pedra da Gávea (Gávea Rock). **Amenities:** food and drink; water sports; lifeguards. **Best for:** sunset; surfing. ⊠ *Av. Niemeyer, São Conrado.*

Prainha. The length of two football fields, Prainha ("Little Beach") is a vest-pocket beach favored by surfers, who take charge of it on weekends. The swimming is good, but watch out for surfboards. On weekdays, especially in the off-season, the beach is almost empty; on weekends, particularly in peak season, the road to and from Prainha and nearby Grumari is so crowded it almost becomes a parking lot. **Amenities:** toilets; showers. **Best for:** swimming; surfing; sunset. ⊠ *35 km (22 miles) west of Ipanema on coast road; accessible only by car from Av. Lúcio Costa (Av. Sernambetiba), Grumari.*

FAMILY **Recreio dos Bandeirantes.** At the far end of Barra's beachfront avenue—the name of the street was changed a few years back to Avenida Lúcio Costa, but locals still call it Sernambetiba—is this 1-km (½-mile) stretch of sand anchored by a huge rock that creates a small, protected cove. Recreio's quiet seclusion makes it popular with families. Although busy on weekends, the beach here is wonderfully quiet during the workweek. The calm, pollution-free water, with no waves or currents, is good for bathing, but don't try to swim around the rock—it's bigger than it looks. **Amenities:** food and drink. **Best for:** swimming; walking. ⊠ *Av. Lúcio Costa, Recreio dos Bandeirantes.*

WHERE TO EAT

Rio de Janeiro is world famous for its *churrascarias* (grilled-meat restaurants) but there's more to its dining scene than sizzling cuts of meat: the city embraces all types of cuisine, from traditional set meals of meat, rice, and black beans to upscale French cuisine. Unlike the states of Bahia and Minas Gerais, Rio doesn't have an identifiable cuisine, though its coastal location ensures that fish and seafood dishes are a staple of many menus here. Vegetarian cuisine has become more visible in recent years. Non-carnivores can feast on a vast range of vividly colored fruits and vegetables at a number of health-food spots. Don't leave Rio without enjoying a relaxed meal and drinks at a traditional *boteco* (casual bar-restaurant), or taking your pick from the heaping buffets at a *comida-a-kilo* (pay-by-weight) restaurant.

WHAT IT COSTS IN REALS			
	$	**$$**	**$$$**	**$$$$**
AT DINNER	under R$31	R$31–R$45	R$46–R$60	over R$60

Restaurant prices are the average cost of a main course at dinner or, if dinner is not served, at lunch.

CENTRO

$$$$ SEAFOOD

🍴 **Albamar Restaurante.** Open since 1933, the Albamar is not hard to spot: this outstanding seafood house is inside a distinctive green octagonal building with 360-degree views of Guanabara Bay. Chef Luiz Incao arrived here from Copacabana Palace in 2009 with a major reputation—he's cooked for Princess Diana, Bill Clinton, and Mick Jagger, among others—and he works wonders with dishes such as sautéed lobster with asparagus and saffron risotto. The attentive staff are happy to advise on wine pairings. Most main dishes are large enough for two people to share. If you're just looking to nibble, order a cocktail and some classic codfish balls, sit back, and take in the spectacular view across the bay. [$] *Average main: R$90* ✉ *Praça Marechal Âncora 186, Centro* ☎ *021/2240–8378* 🌐 *albamar.com.br* 🕒 *No dinner Sun.* [M] *Carioca* ✥ *1:F1.*

$$ BRAZILIAN

🍴 **Amarelinho.** The best spot for city-center people-watching, this vast pavement *boteco* (bar) sits directly in front of the Biblioteco Nacional, and to the side of the Theatro Nacional. An institution that's been around since 1921, the bar attracts hordes of lunchtime and after-work diners, competing for the tables and chairs that sit directly on the flagstones of the busy Praça do Floriano. Waitstaffers in bright yellow waistcoats and bow ties flit among the tables delivering simple Brazilian dishes such as the mixed grill served with rice and fries. Pizzas are also popular here, as is the ice-cold draft beer, and the fresh fruit salad is a nice option on a hot day. Given the prime location, prices are surprisingly reasonable. Don't confuse Amerelinho with the adjoining bar, Vermelhino. Both have yellow roof canopies and yellow plastic chairs, but Amerelinho serves superior food. [$] *Average main: R$40* ✉ *Praça Floriano 55B, Cinelândia, Centro* ☎ *021/2240–8434* 🌐 *www.amarelinhodacinelandia.com.br* 🕒 *Closed Sun.* [M] *Cinelândia* ✥ *1:F2.*

$$ GERMAN

🍴 **Bar Luiz.** It's been well over a century since Bar Luiz first opened its doors—it's been at this location since 1927—and you could be excused for thinking that little has changed since, including the affable waiters. Claiming the best *chopp* (draft beer) in the city would arouse controversy from a lesser venue, but few in Rio would bother to argue. Tasty sausages and other German favorites are the culinary specialty; locals pop in for simple meals such as white bratwurst with potato salad dressed in a singular homemade mayonnaise. The chopp comes in light and dark varieties, both served *estupidamente gelado* (stupidly cold). The wooden tables, tiled floor, and wall-mounted photographs of old Rio combine to create a pleasingly nostalgic ambience. [$] *Average main: R$45* ✉ *Rua da Carioca 39, Centro* ☎ *021/2262–6900* 🌐 *www.barluiz.com.br* 🕒 *Closed Sun. No dinner* [M] *Carioca* ✥ *1:F1.*

$$ INTERNATIONAL

🍴 **Bistrô do Paço.** this is a good option for a light lunch and well placed for Centro sightseers. European influences abound, and the vegetarian-friendly menu includes salads, quiches, and grilled fish. Daily set plates include a soup or salad and a main. There are some tempting desserts, too, such as a popular apple strudel. [$] *Average main: R$38* ✉ *Praça Quinze de Novembro 48, Centro* ☎ *021/2262–3613* 🌐 *www.bistro.com.br* 🕒 *No dinner.* [M] *Uruguaiana* ✥ *1:F1.*

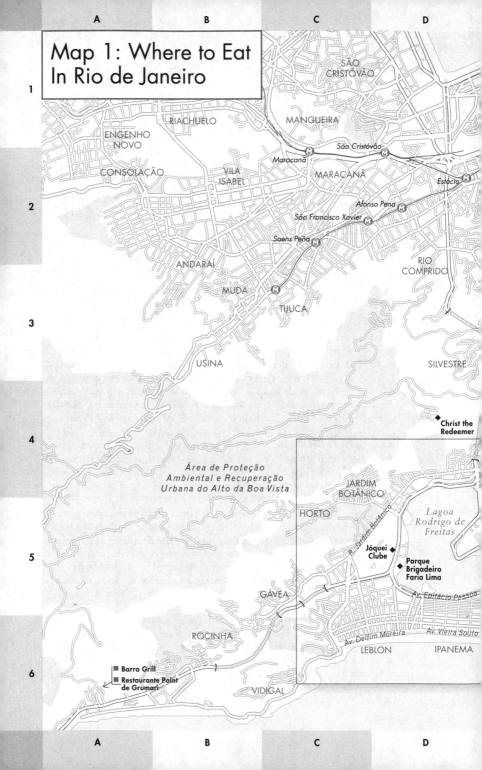

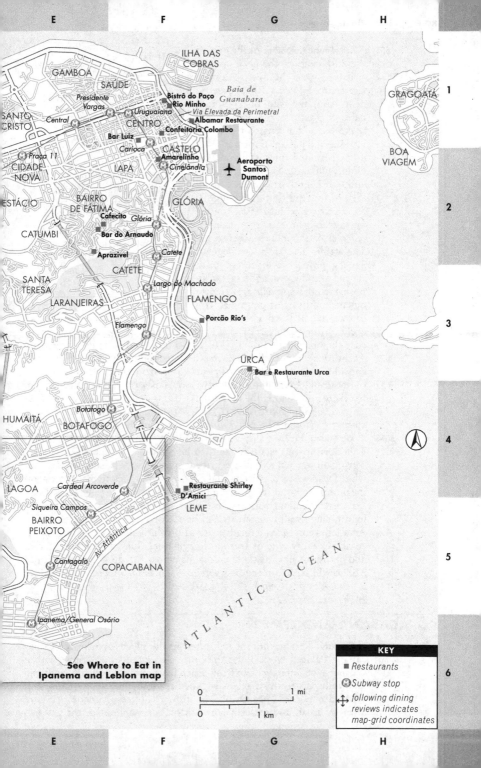

E F G H

1

ILHA DAS
COBRAS

GRAGOATÁ

GAMBOA
SAÚDE

Baía de
Guanabara

Bistrô do Paço
Rio Minho

Presidente
Vargas

SANTO
CRISTO

Central

Uruguaiana

Via Elevada da Perimetral

Albamar Restaurante

BOA
VIAGEM

CENTRO

Confeitaria Colombo

Bar Luiz

Carioca

Praça 11

CASTELO

CIDADE
NOVA

LAPA

Amarelinho

Cinelândia

Aeroporto
Santos
Dumont

2

ESTÁCIO

BAIRRO
DE FÁTIMA

GLÓRIA

Cafecito

Glória

CATUMBI

Bar do Arnaudo

Aprazível

Catete

SANTA
TERESA

CATETE

LARANJEIRAS

Largo do Machado

FLAMENGO

3

Flamengo

Porcão Rio's

URCA

Bar e Restaurante Urca

4

Botafogo

HUMAITÁ

BOTAFOGO

LAGOA

Cardeal Arcoverde

Restaurante Shirley

D'Amici

Siqueira Campos

LEME

BAIRRO
PEIXOTO

5

Cantagalo

COPACABANA

ATLANTIC OCEAN

Ipanema/General Osório

**See Where to Eat in
Ipanema and Leblon map**

0   1 mi

0   1 km

KEY

■ Restaurants

Ⓜ Subway stop

✛ following dining
reviews indicates
map-grid coordinates

6

E F G H

$$$
CAFÉ
Fodor's Choice
★

✕ Confeitaria Colombo. At the turn of the 20th century, the belle epoque structure that houses Colombo Confectionery was Rio's preeminent café, the site of elaborate balls, afternoon teas for upper-class *senhoras,* and a center of political intrigue and gossip. Enormous jacaranda-framed mirrors from Belgium, stained glass from France, and tiles from Portugal are among the art nouveau decor's highlights. Diners come to nibble on above-average *salgados* (savory snacks) and melt-in-the-mouth sweet treats. The waffles here are a local legend. Savory pastries are stuffed with shrimp and chicken, and vegetarian nosh includes spinach and ricotta quiche and heart-of-palm pie. You can wash it all down with a creamy coffee, a European lager, or a fruity cocktail (served virgin or laced with alcohol). If you want to experience the opulent side of city life, do so the way Rio's high society did a century ago: with *chá da tarde,* or afternoon tea. R$46 buys a lavish spread of cakes, sandwiches, breads, jams, fruit salad, and your choice of hot drink. Confeitaria Colombo now has a branch in Copacabana, but there's no beating the original. $ *Average main: R$46* ⊠ *Rua Gonçalves Dias 32, Centro* ☎ *021/2505–1500* ⊕ *www.confeitariacolombo. com.br* ⊗ *Closed Sun. No dinner* Ⓜ *Carioca* ✛ *1:F1.*

> ### DINING TIPS
>
> Some restaurants in Rio serve a *couvert* (a little something to nibble), usually bread, olives, or another type of munchie. The couvert is not free. If you don't want to pay for it, just hand it to your waiter. An "artistic" cover charge of around R$20 is usually applied when there's live music. Also, restaurants will include a 10% service charge, only half of which is distributed among the restaurant staff. Feel free to leave a little extra on the table for your server, but this is by no means obligatory.

$$$$
SEAFOOD

✕ Rio Minho. Enjoy a slice of history along with your afternoon snack. This downtown restaurant said to be the oldest in the city has been serving up seafood to hungry cariocas since 1884. The simple blue-and-white facade of its pretty colonial building harks back to that time, as do the uniforms of the attentive waiters who show you to your seats. For a real taste of culinary history, order the Sopa Leáo Veloso—this fortifying Brazilian soup was created in honor of the Brazilian ambassador. An adaptation of the French seafood broth, *bouillabaisse marselhesa*—combines every type of seafood imaginable, along with onion, garlic, and herbs. It's now a staple on menus across Rio de Janeiro State, but Minho still serves up the best version. $ *Average main: R$122* ⊠ *Rua do Ouvidor 10, Centro* ☎ *021/2509–2338* ⊗ *Closed Sun. No dinner* Ⓜ *Uruguaiana* ✛ *1:F1.*

COPACABANA AND LEME

$$$$
ITALIAN

✕ Cipriani. This restaurant is housed in the plush environs of Copacabana Palace, overlooking the hotel's enormous pool. Start with a Cipriani—champagne with fresh peach juice (really a Bellini)—and then take your pick from an extensive Northern Italian menu prepared with great care by chef Luca Orini. The dishes with freshly made pasta are always a treat, and gnocchi with lobster is a standout. Meat and fish entrées, such as wild boar, are appropriate to their lavish surroundings. Service, as one would expect, is excellent. The degustation menu costs R$228, or R$360 with wine. [$] *Average main: R$85* ✉ *Copacabana Palace Hotel, Av. Atlântica 1702, Copacabana* ☎ *021/2545–8747* 🌐 *www.copacabanapalace.com.br* ✍ *Reservations essential* [M] *Cardeal Arcoverde* ✣ *2:B6.*

$$$$ ITALIAN 🍴 **D'Amici.** A world away from the touristy restaurants that line Copacabana's beachfront, this refined Italian restaurant is easily overlooked but well worth seeking out. The menu celebrates Italy's diverse regional cuisines. The fish-stuffed ravioli with saffron and shrimp sauce stands out among many wonderful pastas, and the meat cuts are uniformly top-quality. Finish with that classic Italian dessert, tiramisu. The knowledgeable staff can advise you about appropriate wine pairings—helpful, as the list is extensive. [$] *Average main: R$76* ✉ *Rua Antônio Vieira 18, Leme* ☎ *021/2541–4477* 🌐 *www.damiciristorante.com.br* ✍ *Reservations essential* [M] *Cardeal Arcoverde* ✣ *1:F4.*

$$$$ FRENCH 🍴 **Le Pré-Catalan.** In an elegant space overlooking Copacabana Beach, this carioca version of the same-named Parisian restaurant serves some of Rio's best haute cuisine. Swarovski chandeliers illuminate the dining room, and chef Roland Villard, who's won numerous awards acknowledging his culinary skills, offers two prix-fixe menus. For the first he creates dazzling dishes using ingredients from the Amazon region; for the second he puts a chic French spin on traditional Brazilian cuisine. Each meal consists of a staggering 10 courses and costs R$290. You can also order à la carte and feast on sophisticated plates such as steak tartare with tomato and olive paste. Among some seriously tempting desserts, the dark chocolate mousse with raspberry sorbet and vanilla ice cream is a standout. [$] *Average main: R$90* ✉ *Sofitel Rio, Av. Atlântica 4240, Copacabana* ☎ *021/2525–1160* 🌐 *gastronomiasofitel.com.br* ⏲ *No lunch* ✍ *Reservations essential* [M] *Cantagalo* ✣ *2:D5.*

$$$$ SEAFOOD 🍴 **Nomangue.** Seafood fans will be in their element at this well-located restaurant specializing in Northeastern Brazilian fish dishes. The atmosphere is relaxed, the service attentive, and the food excellent. The *bolinjho de bobo de camarao* (fried balls of shrimp with potato) served with spicy tomato sauce are an excellent place to begin your culinary adventure. Don't miss the oysters au gratin or the *moqueca*—the classic Northeastern dish with seafood in a tomato, coconut, and palm oil sauce is made here with your choice of crab or octopus. [$] *Average main: R$90* ✉ *Rua Sa Ferreira 25, Copacabana* ☎ *021/2521–3237* 🌐 *www.nomangue.com.br* [M] *Cantagalo* ✣ *2:C5.*

$$$$ SPANISH 🍴 **Restaurante Shirley.** Traditional Spanish seafood casseroles are a strong suit at this small restaurant on a shady street, which has been attracting locals for more than 70 years. A line snakes around the block at peak hours, but it's worth the wait to find a table: the food is terrific. Seafood paella is among the most popular of the generously portioned traditional dishes. The waiters, clad in white suits, add to the old-time atmosphere. [$] *Average main: R$86* ✉ *Rua Gustavo Sampaio 610, Loja A, Leme* ☎ *021/2275–1398* ✍ *Reservations not accepted* [M] *Cardeal Arcoverde* ✣ *1:F4.*

$$$$ BRAZILIAN

🍴 **Siri Mole & Cia.** This restaurant takes its name from a soft-shell crab native to Brazil, and the signature dish here is *moqueca*—a Bahian stew that combines palm oil and coconut milk with seafood. For your stew, you can choose from squid, lobster, fish, or, of course, siri mole crab. Another delicious dish is *acaraje,* for which bean-flour patties are deep fried, split in two, and filled with shrimp, an okra paste, chili, and tomato. Vegetarians can opt for a shrimp-free version. This is one of Rio's best places for seafood served Bahia-style. [$] *Average main: R$120* ✉ *Rua Francisco Otaviano 50, Copacabana* ☎ *021/2267–0894* 🌐 *www.sirimole.com.br* 🕒 *No lunch Mon.* [M] *Ipanema/General Osório* ✥ *2:D5.*

FLAMENGO AND BOTAFOGO

$$$ ECLECTIC Fodor's Choice ★

🍴 **Miam Miam.** Blink and you could miss this hip Botafogo eatery housed in a tiny white colonial building and furnished entirely with pieces from the 1950s to the 1970s. The French–Brazilian owners have created a relaxed, casual dining space where they prepare hearty portions of tasty comfort food. The lentil ragu with sautéed mushrooooms, spiced okra, and roasted garlic is a treat for vegetarians, and the fish and meat dishes are unfailingly good. Leave room for dessert: the mini churros with *doce de leite* are an indulgent treat and a long-standing favorite on the menu. The relaxed vibe and kitsch decor ensures Miam Miam's popularity with Rio's bohemian crowd, and the award-winning cocktail list includes the *basel julep,* a vivacious concoction of rum, tangerine juice, and basil. [$] *Average main: R$55* ✉ *Rua General Góes Monteiro 34, Botafogo* ☎ *021/2244–0125* 🌐 *www.miammiam.com.br* 🕒 *Closed Sun. and Mon. No lunch* ✍ *Reservations essential* [M] *Botafogo* ✥ *2:A6.*

$$$$ BRAZILIAN FAMILY Fodor's Choice ★

🍴 **Porcão Rio's.** At lively Porcão, the ultimate in Brazilian churrascaria experiences, bow-tied waiters wielding giant skewers slip nimbly between linen-draped tables, slicing off portions of sizzling barbecued beef, pork, and chicken until you can eat no more. The buffet is huge, with salads, sushi, and pasta and rice dishes, and enough meat-free sides to keep the staunchest of vegetarians happy. Porcão is a chain, with three restaurants in Rio—including one in Ipanema—but the nearly floor-to-ceiling windows with a view over Guanabara Bay to the Sugar Loaf make the Flamengo branch, known as Porcão Rio's, the top choice. At all branches, children up to 6 eat free, while those aged 6–11 eat for half price. In the unlikely event you have room for dessert, these are charged separately. [$] *Average main: R$112* ✉ *Parque do Flamengo, Av. Infante Dom Henrique s/n, Flamengo* ☎ *021/3461–9020* 🌐 *www.porcao.com.br* [M] *Flamengo* ✥ *1:F3.*

IPANEMA AND LEBLON

$$$$ PORTUGUESE Fodor's Choice ★

🍴 **Antiquarius.** This pricey but much-loved establishment is famous for its flawless rendering of Portuguese classics, including many cod and lobster dishes. The couvert (R$29) includes tasty cod-and-potato balls, seafood rissoles, and imported cheeses. Seafood dishes are by far the best options. The chef prepares the shrimp cocktail simply but elegantly, and the vast seafood risotto is a knockout. The wine list is impressive, if predictably expensive, and the knowledgeable sommelier is always on hand to give tips on food and wine pairings; service is top-notch. [$] *Average main: R$145* ✉ *Rua Aristides Espínola 19, Leblon* ☎ *021/2294–1049* ✍ *Reservations essential* ⊕ *2:D1.*

$$$ SEAFOOD

🍴 **Azul Marinho.** You'll catch superb sunsets from the beachside tables at this spot in Arpoador that serves high-quality seafood and pasta dishes for lunch and dinner. Across from the beach on the Arpoador Inn's ground floor, the restaurant has a giant window with panoramic views. *Moqueca* is the house specialty, made with shrimp, cod, lobster, crab, or octopus—or a mix of them all. The service at Azul Marinho is excellent and the seafood is ultrafresh, but an even better reason to come here is to sit at one of the outdoor tables next to the sand and enjoy early-evening appetizers, drinks, and a marvelous sunset. [$] *Average main: R$60* ✉ *Arpoador Inn, Av. Francisco Bhering s/n, Arpoador* ☎ *021/2513–5014* [M] *Ipanema/General Osório* ⊕ *2:D5.*

$ VEGETARIAN

🍴 **Blyss Holy Foods.** Hidden away in a small arcade off Ipanema's main square, Blyss Holy Foods provides culinary delights for vegetarians, vegans, and anyone who fancies a break from the meat-centric Brazilian diet. The restaurant's organic lunch buffet is laden with fresh vegetable soups, colorful salads, fish-free sushi, savory pies and tarts, and a host of other dishes that are as tasty as they are nourishing. For a guilt-free feast after marveling at the parade of perfect beach bodies on Ipanema Beach, look no further. The friendly owners run yoga groups in the neighborhood and welcome out-of-towners to join the classes. [$] *Average main: R$23* ✉ *Rua Visconde de Pirajá 180, Loja H, Ipanema* ☎ *021/9218–5511* ⏲ *Closed weekends. No dinner* [M] *Ipanema/General Osório* ⊕ *2:D3.*

$$$$ ECLECTIC Fodor's Choice ★

🍴 **Brigite's.** Leblon's Rua Dias Ferreira is a real go-to street for foodies, and the upmarket bar-restaurant Brigite's is a major reason why. As one might expect in body-conscious Leblon, there's an emphasis on fresh, organic ingredients, and vegetarians fare well here thanks to the emphasis on seasonal vegetables. The menu changes frequently, but seafood and pasta dishes are reliably good. The wine choices are extensive, and delicious, if pricey, cocktails can be enjoyed at the long balcony bar. Floor-to-ceiling plate-glass windows allow sunlight to flood Brigite's by day, and dim lighting creates a more atmospheric mood for after-dark drinking and dining. [$] *Average main: R$85* ✉ *Rua Dias Ferreira 247 A, Leblon* ☎ *021/2274–5590* 🌐 *www.brigites.com.br* ⏲ *No lunch Mon.* ⊕ *2:D1.*

$$ MEXICAN Fodor's Choice ★

🍴 **La Calaca.** A labor of love from a Californian expat couple passionate about Mexican food, this casual-chic restaurant at the heart of Leblon sets culinary standards way above sour cream–heavy Tex Mex fare. Deliciously *picante* dishes are prepared according to traditional recipes and immaculately presented—the trio of tacos is a house specialty and looks (almost) too good to eat. The cocktails are a strong suit, with the frozen margaritas deliciously cooling on a balmy Rio evening, when the pavement tables are fiercely contested. The decor is modern and colorful with a nod toward kitsch, prices are more than reasonable, and the service is first-rate. Serious tequila fans will find plenty to keep them happy here, too—there's a wealth of imported varieties on offer. [$] *Average main: R$40* ✉ *Av. Ataulfo de Paiva 1240, Leblon* ☎ *021/3264–2217* ⊕ *2:D2.*

$$$$ ITALIAN 🍴 **Capricciosa.** Rio fairly bursts with pizza places, but this upmarket chain's Ipanema branch emerges at the top of the list. Wood-fired, thin-crust pizzas are made with imported Italian flour, and the toppings—from wild mushrooms and handmade buffalo mozzarella to wafer-thin Parma ham and fresh tuna—are of the highest quality. Capricciosa has branches in Jardim Botânico, Barra da Tijuca, Copacabana, and the beach resort of Búzios, but the Ipanema venue stands out for its location and tall glass windows that are perfect for people-watching. [$] *Average main: R$65* ✉ *Rua Vinicius de Moraes 134, Ipanema* ☎ *021/2523–3394* 🌐 *www.capricciosa.com.br* 🕒 *No lunch* [M] *Ipanema/General Osório* ⊕ *2:D4.*

PIZZA RIO STYLE

Cariocas love pizza, and they've added some touches of their own to the established formula. As well as sharing the pan-Brazilian penchant for pizza bases covered in chocolate, Rio residents are also known to indulge in unusual topping combinations such as cheese with pepperoni, banana, and cinnamon. In one last break with tradition, many cariocas eschew the idea of tomato sauce *beneath* the cheese, in favor of squirting ketchup on the surface.

$$$$ BRAZILIAN FAMILY 🍴 **Casa da Feijoada.** Restaurants traditionally serve *feijoada*, Brazil's savory national dish, on Saturday, but here the huge pots of the stew simmer every day. You can choose which of the nine types of meat you want in your stew, but if it's your first time, waiters will bring you a "safe" version with sausage, beef, and pork—sans feet and ears. The feijoada comes with the traditional side dishes of rice, collard greens, *farofa* (toasted and seasoned manioc flour), *aipim* (cassava), *torresminho* (pork rinds), and orange slices. The set meal price includes an appetizer portion of black-bean soup and sausage, a choice of dessert, and a lime or passion-fruit *batida* (creamy cachaça cocktail). The menu also features options such as baked chicken, shrimp in coconut milk, grilled trout, and filet mignon. Desserts include *quindim* (a yolk-and-sugar pudding with coconut crust) and Romeo and Juliet (guava compote with fresh cheese). The caipirinhas are made not only with lime but also with tangerine, passion fruit, pineapple, strawberry, or kiwi. Be careful—they're strong. [$] *Average main: R$78* ✉ *Rua Prudente de Morais 10, Ipanema* ☎ *021/2247–2776* [M] *Ipanema/General Osório* ⊕ *2:D4.*

$$ VEGETARIAN 🍴 **Celeiro.** One of an increasing number of organic eateries in Rio, Celeiro is a combination café and health-food store that's popular with models and other body-conscious locals. The restaurant operates on a pay-by-weight system, and the buffet features a staggering 50 types of salad, as well as oven-baked pies, wholemeal pastries, fish and chicken dishes, and low-calorie desserts. The homemade breads are delicious. [$] *Average main: R$40* ✉ *Rua Dias Ferreira 199, Leblon* ☎ *021/2274–7843* 🌐 *www.celeiroculinaria.com.br* 🕒 *Closed Sun. No dinner* ⊕ *2:D1.*

$ BRAZILIAN 🍴 **Colher de Pau.** Sweet-toothed visitors should make a beeline for this little Leblon spot, which serves some of the most tempting cakes, pastries, and tarts in the city. If you try just one thing here, make it the *brigadeiro*, a much-loved traditional Brazilian treat made of condensed milk, butter, and chocolate. Colher de Pau's version is arguably the best in the city. [$] *Average main: R$8* ✉ *Rua Rita Ludolf 90, Loja A, Leblon* ☎ *021/2523–3018* 🌐 *www.colherdepaurio.com.br* ⏲ *No dinner* ✍ *Reservations not accepted* ✥ *2:D1.*

2

$$$$ FRENCH 🍴**CT Boucherie.** The city's most celebrated chef—Claude Troisgros—has changed the face of the all-you-can-eat churrascaria with this chic bistro. Unlike at traditional rodizios, where waiters deliver cut after cut of meat, here they dash from table to table with steaming plates of roasted palm hearts, stuffed tomatoes, creamy mashed potatoes, and other meat-free sides to accompany meaty mains. Among the top picks are a substantial prime rib and the more accessibly priced house burger. As tempting as they are, consider skipping the entrées to save room for the never-ending flow of vegetable plates. [$] *Average main: R$90* ✉ *Rua Dias Ferreira 636, Leblon* ☎ *021/2529–2329* 🌐 *www.ctboucherie.com.br* 💳 *No credit cards* ✥ *2:D1.*

$$$$ BRAZILIAN 🍴**Esplanada Grill.** This churrascaria is famed for the quality of its meats, among them T-bone steak and *picanha,* a tasty Brazilian cut of beef marbled with a little fat. All the grilled dishes come with fried palm hearts, seasoned rice, and a choice of fried, baked, or sautéed potatoes. [$] *Average main: R$86* ✉ *Rua Barão da Torre 600, Ipanema* ☎ *021/2512–2970* 🌐 *www.esplanadagrill.com.br* [M] *Ipanema/General Osório* ✥ *2:C3.*

$$$$ ITALIAN 🍴**Gero.** This award-strewn and beautifully appointed restaurant is frequently cited as the best Italian in Rio. Choose from among wonderful pastas and risottos, as well as excellent fish and meat dishes. Vegetarian options are plentiful, and the tiramisu is a perfect blend of creamy, espresso-laced mascarpone. Owned by the Italian Fasano chain, the high-ceilinged, wooden-floor building exhibits the clean, contemporary design that is the Fasano hallmark. A second Rio branch operates in Barra da Tijuca, but the Ipanema location is a better option for Zona Sul–based visitors. [$] *Average main: R$90* ✉ *Rua Anibal de Mendonca 157, Ipanema* ☎ *021/2239–8158* 🌐 *www.fasano.com.br* ✍ *Reservations essential* ✥ *2:C3.*

$$ CAFÉ 🍴**Gula Gula.** The salads at the upscale café chain Gula Gula are anything but boring. Beyond classics such as Caesar and chicken pesto, fresh local fruits and veggies are mixed into curried quinoa with tomatoes and marinated eggplant and bean sprouts, and the organic palm-heart salad comes with tomatoes, watercress, and raisins. Grilled fish or steak, baked potatoes, and soups are good nonsalad options, and there are some very fine desserts. A carioca favorite for over 30 years, Gula Gula operates a dozen restaurants in Rio, plus one in Niterói, but its location a few blocks from the beach makes the Ipanema branch an excellent choice. [$] *Average main: R$35* ✉ *Rua Henrique Dumont 57, Ipanema* ☎ *021/2259–3084* 🌐 *www.gulagula.com.br* [M] *Ipanema/General Osório* ✥ *2:D3.*

$$ BRAZILIAN Fodor's Choice ★ 🍴**Jobi.** The post-beach hangout of choice for neighborhood locals since 1956, Jobi serves good coffee, super-chilled draft beer, and lip-smackingly delicious seafood. The bar's *bolinhos de bacalhau* (cod and potato balls) may well be the best in town. Because the restaurant is so small

and unassuming, it's only after you step inside and see the many awards hanging on the walls that you realize just how special Jobi is. This Leblon institution is open from 9 am to 4 am, so you should be able to squeeze it into your schedule. A cocktail favorite here is the *caipitequila*, a variation on the classic caipirinha that's made with tequila instead of sugarcane rum. [$] *Average main: R$35* ✉ *Rua Ataulfo de Paiva 1166, Leblon* ☎ *021/2274–0547* ✥ *2:D1.*

$$$$ ITALIAN 🍴 **Margutta.** A block from Ipanema Beach, Margutta has a reputation for outstanding Mediterranean-style seafood, such as shrimp panfried in olive oil, white wine, and garlic and lobster baked with butter and saffron rice. There's a handful of vegetarian options including mixed-vegetable risotto with truffle oil. [$] *Average main: R$62* ✉ *Av. Henrique Dumont 62, Ipanema* ☎ *021/2259–3887* 🌐 *www.margutta.com.br* 🕒 *No lunch weekdays* [M] *Ipanema/General Osório* ✥ *2:D3.*

$$ BRAZILIAN 🍴 **New Natural.** One of many buffet restaurants in Rio where you pay per 100 grams of food, this one stands out for its use of natural and organic products and its delicious fruit juices. The food is mainly vegetarian, with many soy-based dishes, but there are fish and chicken options. On hot days seek out the somewhat hidden upstairs dining room, which is air-conditioned. Attached to the restaurant is Emporia Natural—a health-food shop that sells oven-baked pastries to go. The palm heart with soft and creamy *catupiry* cheese is a winning combination. [$] *Average main: R$32* ✉ *Rua Barão da Torre 169, Ipanema* ☎ *021/2247–1335* [M] *Ipanema/General Osório* ✥ *2:D4.*

$$ BRAZILIAN 🍴 **Pipo.** The latest Rio venture from the high-profile Brazilian chef Felipe Bronze sees him apply his culinary wizardry to traditional boteco cuisine. The down-to-earth design features white walls and standard-issue boteco tables and chairs. But the food that emerges from the open kitchen is anything but standard. Neat tricks include a version of the traditional thick bean soup that here comes topped with a luminous green froth of *couve* (collard greens). Don't miss the chunky *aipim* (manioc) fries that come coated with coalho cheese foam for dipping. [$] *Average main: R$45* ✉ *Rua Dias Ferreira 64, Leblon* ☎ *021/ 2239–9322* 🌐 *www.piporestaurante.com* 🕒 *Closed Mon. No lunch Tues.–Sat.* ✥ *2:D1.*

$$$$ SEAFOOD Fodor's Choice ★ 🍴 **Satyricon.** Some of the best seafood in town is served at this smart restaurant that has impressed A-list visitors including Madonna and Jared Leto. A tank of snapping lobsters at the entrance gives diners an indication of the freshness of the fare served here, and the decor is low-key with plenty of exposed wood and sparkling white walls. The carpaccio entrée is a specialty—it and the daily specials, such as red snapper baked in red wine and herbs, are rendered beautifully, while sides such as rice with lemon are suitably simple companions to the main event. Grilled swordfish and sea bass are other popular orders, and the homemade Italian-style ice cream is a sweet way indeed to round off a meal. [$] *Average main: R$115* ✉ *Rua Barão da Torre 192, Ipanema* ☎ *021/2521–0627* 🌐 *www.satyricon.com.br* [M] *Ipanema/General Osório* ✥ *2:C4.*

$$$ ITALIAN 🍴 **Stuzzi.** Bringing the concept of Italian *stuzzichini* (tapas-style small plates of food for sharing), Stuzzi has evolved into a star of Leblon's

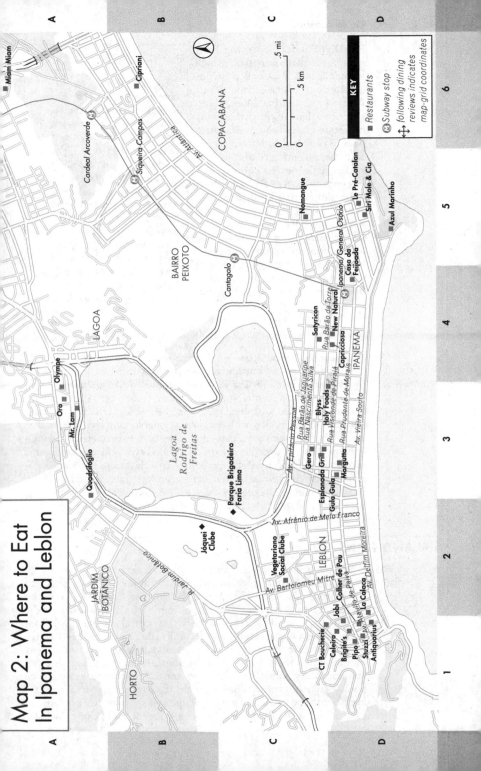

Map 2: Where to Eat
In Ipanema and Leblon

JARDIM BOTÂNICO

HORTO

LAGOA

Lagoa Rodrigo de Freitas

BAIRRO PEIXOTO

COPACABANA

LEBLON

IPANEMA

R. Jardim Botânico

Av. Bartolomeu Mitre

Av. Afrânio de Melo Franco

Av. Epitácio Pessoa

Av. Atlântica

Rua Barão de Jaguaripe
Rua Nascimento Silva
Rua Visconde de Pirajá
Rua Prudente de Morais
Av. Vieira Souto
Rua Barão da Torre

Av. Delfim Moreira
Av. Ataulfo de Paiva

Miam Miam

Cipriani

Cardeal Arcoverde

Siqueira Campos

Nomangue

Le Pré-Catalan
Sirí Mole & Cia
Azul Marinho

Casa da Feijoada
Ipanema/General Osório

Cantagalo

New Natural
Capricciosa

Satyricon

Olympe
Oro
Mr. Lam
Quadrifoglio

Gero
Esplanada Grill
Gula Gula
Blyss
Holy Foods
Morguta

Parque Brigadeiro Faria Lima

Jóquei Clube

Vegetariano Social Clube

CT Boucherie
Celeiro
Brigite's
Pipo
Stuzzi
Antiquarius
Jobi Colher de Pau
Kotobuki
La Calaca

KEY

■ Restaurants
Ⓜ Subway stop
↔ following dining reviews indicates map-grid coordinates

0   .5 km
0   .5 mi

Rua Dias Ferreira foodie strip. Start with the mixed antipastos, which include a basket of baked breads and authentic Grana Padano cheese, Parma ham, marinated eggplant, and other light bites. Among the other don't-miss dishes are the fried balls of rice filled with meat ragout and the polenta *grissini* (breadsticks) with tomato chutney and Gorgonzola sauce. For something more substantial, head here on a Sunday for the Buffet da Mamma, a serve-yourself comfort-food feast. Arrive early to get a table on the leafy patio, and take your pick from the impressive cocktail menu; standouts include the *perfetto limone*—a sense-stimulating mix of bourbon, limoncello, lemon, passion fruit, and chili pepper. [$] *Average main: R$58* ✉ *Rua Dias Ferreira 48, Leblon* ☎ *021/2274–4017* 🌐 *www.stuzzibar.com.br* 🕒 *No lunch Mon.–Sat.* ✥ *2:D1.*

> **FOOD ON THE GO**
>
> There's a street snack for every taste in Rio—from low-cal treats such as corn on the cob and chilled pineapple slices to less virtuous, but absolutely delicious, barbecued sticks of grilled cheese served with or without herbs. Tasty bags of roasted and salted peanuts and cashews are found everywhere, as are giant hot dogs, served on a stick and covered in manioc flour. Barbecued chicken heart (*coraçao*) is not for the fainthearted, and the grilled shrimp at the beach is best avoided unless you want a side order of food poisoning.

$$ VEGETARIAN 🍴 **Vegetariano Social Clube.** Vegan restaurants are a growing trend in body-conscious Rio, but few are as established and well loved as the Vegetarian Social Club. The serve-yourself organic lunch buffet (R$28) includes tasty and wholesome soups, whole-grain rice, colorful salads, and many soy-based dishes. Dining in the evening is à la carte, with options such as quinoa with seasonal vegetables and tofu cream. The tempeh burgers with soya mayonnaise are a post-beach treat. Detoxifying juices and smoothies are on the drinks menu, along with organic wines and cachaças for those less in need of a cleansing. The Sunday feijoada, made with smoked tofu instead of pork, attracts vegetarians from across the city. [$] *Average main: R$32* ✉ *Rua Conde de Bernadotte 26, Loja L, Leblon* ☎ *021/2294–5200* 🌐 *www.vegetarianosocialclube.com.br* ✥ *2:C2.*

INLAND ZONA SUL

$$$$ CHINESE 🍴 **Mr. Lam.** In a city where Chinese food has long been associated with low-budget dining, this restaurant tossed out the rule book, attracting a discerning clientele with top-quality Peking-style cuisine. The menu is created by the famous Mr. Lam, formerly of Mr Chow, first at the London branch and then in New York City, and chef Chui Kwok Kam executes them to perfection. The decor is rather ostentatious—fixtures include a terra-cotta warrior, and a speedboat motor serves as support for one of the tables. The downstairs dining room is spacious and well illuminated by enormous windows, but for the ultimate experience book a table on the top floor. At night the roof retracts to allow dining beneath the stars, and you can request a spot directly beneath the gaze of Christ the Redeemer. The satay chicken and Peking duck are two of the signature dishes. You can dine à la carte, but most patrons choose from one of the set menus (from R$139 to R$169 per person). $ *Average main: R$98* ⊠ *Av. Maria Angélica 21, Lagoa* ☎ *021/2286–6661* ⊕ *www.mrlam.com.br* ☉ *No lunch Mon.–Sat.* ⌂ *Reservations essential* ✛ *2:A3.*

$$$$ ✕ **Olympe.** Claude Troisgros, of the celebrated Michelin-starred Trois-
FRENCH   gros family of France, today runs something of an empire of upscale
Fodor'sChoice   restaurants in Rio, and this is his original and most celebrated ven-
★   ture. Troisgros creates the menu together with his equally talented son Thomas, applying nouvelle-cooking techniques to meals with all-Brazilian ingredients. Cases in point include quail stuffed with raisin and onion *farofa* (seasoned manioc flour) served with a kale confit, and duck with passion-fruit *jus*.At lunch on weekdays (1–4), there's a three-course set menu for R$115. $ *Average main: R$130* ⊠ *Rua Custódio Serrão 62, Jardim Botânico* ☎ *021/2539–4542* ⊕ *olympe.com.br* ☉ *Closed Sun. No lunch Sat.* ⌂ *Reservations essential* ✛ *2:A3.*

$$$$ ✕ **Oro.** Food as theater is the theme of the acclaimed restaurant of
CONTEMPORARY   celebrity chef Felipe Bronze, who has created an avant-garde dining
Fodor'sChoice   experience like no other in the city. A pink-hued glass wall allows din-
★   ers to watch his culinary team prepare ultracontemporary dishes, many using traditional Brazilian ingredients. There are à-la-carte dishes, but most diners here choose one of the tasting menus (from R$180 for four courses to R$295 for nine). The "mains" are really a series of small, elaborately prepared dishes, including a tiny burger made of duck confit and foie-gras powder and served with guava "ketchup." Don't miss the *Brasilidades* dessert, which features no fewer than 10 tiny but perfectly rendered modern takes on classic Brazilian sweets. Clever tricks such as using liquid nitrogen to "freeze" chocolate mousse add to the stylish-yet-playful atmosphere, as do the waitstaff's uniforms, designed by Lenny Niemeyer, famous for her high-fashion bikinis. $ *Average main: R$160* ⊠ *Rua Frei Leandro 20, Jardim Botânico* ☎ *021/2266–7591* ⊕ *www.ororestaurante.com* ☉ *Closed Sun. No lunch* ⌂ *Reservations essential* ✛ *2:A3.*

$$$$ ✕ **Quadrifoglio.** Many locals consider cozy Quadrifoglio to be Rio's best
ITALIAN   Italian restaurant. The restaurant has been around since 1991, and the
Fodor'sChoice   service and the food are impeccable, the former perhaps because much
★   of the original waitstaff still works here. Standout starters include a comforting white bean soup with shrimp, and a salad of arugula, goat cheese, walnuts, and pear in a balsamic reduction, while the potato gnocchi with steak and porcini mushrooms is one of many stellar mains. Ice cream with baked figs is among the justly famous desserts. $ *Average main: R$78* ⊠ *Rua J.J. Seabra 19, Jardim Botânico* ☎ *021/2294–1433* ⊕ *www.quadrifogliorestaurante.com.br* ☉ *No dinner Sun* ✛ *2:A3.*

SANTA TERESA

$$$$ ✕ **Aprazível.** A tropical garden filled with exotic plants, monkeys, and
BRAZILIAN   birds is the spectacular setting for this family restaurant serving pan-
ECLECTIC   Brazilian dishes. The owner and chef, Ana Castilha, hails from Minas
FAMILY   Gerais but received her formal training at New York City's French Culinary Institute. As a delightful consequence, there's a French twist

to dishes she has created with native ingredients, among them baked palm heart with pesto, basil, and cashews. The award-winning wine list includes many artisan Brazilian bottles, and their high quality may surprise those who have dismissed the country's wines. Dine in one of the straw-roofed gazebos to enjoy excellent views of downtown and Guanabara Bay, keeping an eye out for toucans overhead. By night hanging lanterns and twinkling fairy lights create a magical atmosphere in the garden. Call ahead to reserve, as opening hours can be erratic. [$] *Average main: R$65* ✉ *Rua Aprazível 62, Santa Teresa* ☎ *021/2508–9174* 🌐 *www.aprazivel.com.br* ⏲ *Closed Mon. No dinner Sun.* ✍ *Reservations essential* ✥ *1:E2.*

$$$ BRAZILIAN Fodor's Choice ★

🍴 **Bar do Arnaudo.** A neighborhood favorite for more than three decades, this informal tavern in the heart of Santa Teresa serves excellent Northeastern cuisine in more than ample portions. Sun-dried beef is a popular choice among carnivores, and vegetarians will love the set meal of *queijo coalho* (grilled white cheese, similar to halloumi) with brown beans, rice, and seasoned farofa. Reservations aren't necessary, but the restaurant is always packed on weekend evenings. It's quieter at lunchtime, when you may be able to occupy one of the two tables that have views down to Guanabara Bay. Though the friendly staffers are speedy, the service never feels rushed. Wine isn't sold here, but your waiter will happily uncork any bottle you bring. [$] *Average main: R$48* ✉ *Rua Almirante Alexandrino 316B, Santa Teresa* ☎ *021/2252–7246* ⏲ *Closed Mon.* ✥ *1:E2.*

$ CAFÉ Fodor's Choice ★

🍴 **Cafecito.** Coffee culture is beginning to take off in Rio, and Argentine-owned Cafecito is one of just a few places so far to capture the essence of "café society." A leafy terrace overlooking Santa Teresa's main eating, drinking, and shopping strip provides a relaxed setting for brunches, lunches, and early-evening nibbles and cocktails. Chef Felipe Alves has previously worked at Copacabana Palace, and the dishes here are immaculately presented. The knickknack-strewn café serves what's arguably the city's best cappuccino—with a dusting of cinnamon and a morsel of gooey chocolate brownie—but the food menu also has plenty to recommend it. The standouts include the toasted ciabatta sandwiches (the Brie with artichoke hearts is delicious) and some pleasingly rustic baked mushrooms with melted Gorgonzola. [$] *Average main: R$26* ✉ *Rua Pashcoal Carlos Magno 121, Santa Teresa* ☎ *021/2221–9439* 💳 *No credit cards* ⏲ *Closed Wed.* ✥ *1:E2.*

SÃO CONRADO AND BARRA DA TIJUCA

$$$$ BRAZILIAN

🍴 **Barra Grill.** A nice place to stop after a long day at Barra Beach, this informal and popular steak house serves more than 30 cuts of top-quality meat. Choose from the menu or go the whole hog with the all-you-can-eat rodizio (R$109). The buffet is impressive in range and quality, with seafood and sushi as well as colorful, fresh salads. Prices for the rodízio-style feasts are slightly higher on weekends, when reservations are essential, but female diners eat for half price after 6 pm. [$] *Average main: R$65* ✉ *Av. Ministro Ivan Lins 314, Barra da Tijuca* ☎ *021/2493–6060* 🌐 *www.barragrill.com.br* ⏲ *No dinner Sun.* ✥ *1:A6.*

$$$$ SEAFOOD 🍴 **Restaurante Point de Grumari.** From Grumari Beach, Estrada de Guaratiba climbs up through dense forest, emerging atop a hill above the vast Guaratiba flatlands. Here you'll come upon this restaurant famed for its *moqueca*, the traditional seafood stew. Other standards on the seafood-focused menu are lobster and grilled beefsteak, while the passion-fruit caipirinha is nearly flawless. With its shady setting, colorful flora, and glorious vistas, this is a fine spot for an early lunch after a morning on the beach and before an afternoon visit to the Sítio Roberto Burle Marx or the Museu Casa do Pontal. Or come here in the early evening to catch the spectacular sunset. [$] *Average main: R$62* ✉ *Estrada do Grumari 710, Grumari* ☎ *021/2410–1434* 🌐 *www.pointdegrumari.com.br* 🕒 *No dinner* ✣ *1:A6.*

URCA

$$ BRAZILIAN 🍴 **Bar e Restaurante Urca.** Dine indoors in this relaxed spot, or make like the locals and enjoy a snack alfresco, propped against the harbor wall across the street: the sea wall doubles as a makeshift table, and waiters run to and fro delivering orders. You'll have a stunning backdrop to your light meal—the panorama takes in bobbing boats, framed by a clear view of Christ the Redeemer. Enjoy a cold beer and some finger food while you contemplate the menu—the *salgadinhos* (little savory snacks) are a strong suit, with the shrimp pastries a particular standout. More substantial dishes can be enjoyed upstairs in the restaurant and include some good Portuguese-influenced fare. Bar e Restaurante Urca breaks with tradition and serves feijoada on Fridays instead of Saturdays, and at a good price for what you get: R$68 for two. [$] *Average main: R$38* ✉ *Rua Cândido Gaffrée 205, Urca* ☎ *021/2295–8744* 🌐 *www.barurca.com.br* 💳 *No credit cards* 🕒 *No dinner Sun.* ✣ *1:G3.*

WHERE TO STAY

Rio's accommodations are among the most expensive in the world, with beachfront lodgings in particular charging a premium for their enviable locations. Expect hotel rates to be the most expensive during high season (from December through February), especially during Carnival and New Year's, and for special events such as the 2016 Rio Olympics. For stays during these times, it would be wise to book ahead as far as possible. The low season (from March to November) sees prices fall across the city.

As for the types of lodgings available, there are some excellent luxury options on the beachfront—most notably the Belmond Copacabana Palace and Ipanema's Fasano Rio—as well as standard chain hotels. Ipanema and neighboring Leblon are more expensive than Copacabana, but they are also safer and more pleasant to walk around at night. Rio's expanding boutique-hotel scene centers largely around the Santa Teresa and Gávea neighborhoods, while Botafogo and Flamengo offer some decent midrange options. *Hotel reviews have been shortened. For full information, visit Fodors.com.*

	WHAT IT COSTS IN REALS			
	$	$$	$$$	$$$$
FOR 2 PEOPLE	under R$251	R$251–R$375	R$376–R$500	over R$500

Hotel prices are the lowest cost of a standard double room in high season, excluding tax.

CENTRO

$$$ HOTEL

Windsor Guanabara. One of the few solid hotel choices right in Centro, the Windsor Guanabara has reasonably sized and tastefully appointed rooms (although some are beginning to show signs of age), and the contemporary rooftop pool area—with white tiles, white trellises, and white patio furnishings—offers a welcome escape from the city swelter and stunning views of Guanabara Bay. The buffet breakfast is good, too, although the evening buffet served in the restaurant is a little steep. **Pros:** good transport links—close to metro and domestic airport; close to downtown attractions and nightlife; good pool with views. **Cons:** far from beaches; Centro is nearly deserted on Sunday. [$] *Rooms from: R$438* ✉ *Av. Presidente Vargas 392, Centro* ☎ *021/2195–5000* 🌐 *www.windsorhoteis.com.br* 🛏 *539 rooms, 3 suites* 🍴 *Breakfast* [M] *Uruguaiana* ✥ *B1.*

COPACABANA AND LEME

$$$$ HOTEL Fodor's Choice ★

Belmond Copacabana Palace. Built in 1923 for the visiting king of Belgium and inspired by Nice's Negresco and Cannes's Carlton, Copacabana Palace was the first luxury hotel in South America, and it's still one of the top hotels on the continent. **Pros:** historic landmark; front-facing rooms have spectacular ocean views; great on-site restaurants. **Cons:** area is a little seedy at night; need to take taxis to best bars and restaurants; "city view" rooms have poor views of backstreets. [$] *Rooms from: R$1,490* ✉ *Av. Atlântica 1702, Copacabana* ☎ *021/2548–7070* 🌐 *www.copacabanapalace.com.br* 🛏 *129 rooms, 116 suites* 🍴 *Breakfast* [M] *Cardeal Arcoverde* ✥ *G3.*

$$$$ B&B/INN

Casa Mosquito. On a hillside between Ipanema and Copacabana, this stylish boutique guest house with just nine uniquely designed rooms has excellent service, a wonderful location, and a rooftop pool with lovely ocean views. **Pros:** boutique lodgings with character; personalized service; excellent in-house chef. **Cons:** it's a walk to beaches, nightlife, and metro. [$] *Rooms from: R$700* ✉ *Rua Saint-Roman 222, Copacabana* ☎ *21/3586–5042, 21/2523–1031* 🌐 *www.casamosquito.com* 🛏 *9 rooms* 🍴 *Breakfast* [M] *Cantagalo or Ipanema/General Osorio* ✥ *E5.*

$$$ HOTEL

Copacabana Rio Hotel. The decor at this hotel may be a little dated, but rooms are spacious and the location—one block from Copacabana and a short walk from Ipanema—is spot on. **Pros:** comfortable rooms; handy to Copacabana and Ipanema beaches; fine breakfast. **Cons:** busy and noisy street; minimum seven-day stay in high season; decor looking dated. [$] *Rooms from: R$415* ✉ *Av. Nossa Senhora de Copacabana 1256, Posto 6, Copacabana* ☎ *021/3043–1111* 🌐 *www.*

copacabanariohotel.com.br *90 rooms, 8 suites* 🍴 *Breakfast* [M] *Ipanema/General Osório* ✥ *E5.*

$$$ HOTEL **Golden Tulip Regente Hotel.** The excellent location in front of Copacabana Beach is this hotel's main draw; the rooms are spic and span and reasonably tasteful, and some have been recently refurbished. **Pros:** good location; generous breakfast; small but well-equipped gym; pool. **Cons:** south-facing rooms have poor view; Copacabana isn't the safest area. [$] *Rooms from: R$486* ✉ *Av. Atlântica 3716, Copacabana* ☎ *021/3545–5400, 021/3545–5445 reservations* 🌐 *www.goldentulipregente.com* *228 rooms, 2 suites* 🍴 *Breakfast* [M] *Cantagalo* ✥ *F5.*

$$$$ HOTEL **JW Marriott Rio de Janeiro.** You could be walking into a Marriott anywhere in the world, which is a comfort for some and a curse for others: expect spotlessly clean rooms and public areas, an efficient English-speaking staff, and modern (and expensive) services and facilities. **Pros:** close to beach; efficient service; bountiful breakfasts; modern facilities. **Cons:** extra charge for Internet access; expensive; street noise heard in some rooms. [$] *Rooms from: R$1,100* ✉ *Av. Atlântica 2600, Copacabana* ☎ *021/2545–6500* 🌐 *www.marriott.com* *229 rooms, 16 suites* 🍴 *Breakfast* [M] *Siqueira Campos* ✥ *F4.*

$$$ B&B/INN FAMILY Fodor's Choice ★ **Marta's Rio Guesthouse.** Offering a personal touch that you won't find at Copacabana's larger hotels, this penthouse inn close to Ipanema enjoys sweeping views across Copacabana Beach and out to Sugarloaf Mountain. **Pros:** close to Copacabana Beach, restaurants, and nightlife; stunning views from the balcony; excellent value for the location; walking distance to Ipanema. **Cons:** rooms lack views. [$] *Rooms from: R$380* ✉ *Rua Francisco Sá 5, at the corner of Av. Atlântica, Copacabana* ☎ *021/2521–8568* 🌐 *www.martariogguesthouse.com* *3 rooms, 3 suites* 🍴 *Breakfast* [M] *Cantagalo* ✥ *F5.*

$$$$ HOTEL **Miramar Palace by Windsor.** With a prime beachfront location, this classic Copacabana hotel underwent a complete face-lift in 2013 and is now one of the neighborhood's best hotels. **Pros:** beachfront location; great service; modern decor. **Cons:** small pool. [$] *Rooms from:* ✉ *Av. Atlântica 3668, Copacabana* ☎ *021/956–200, 0800/23–2211* 🌐 *www.windsorhoteis.com* *197 rooms, 3 suites* 🍴 *Breakfast* [M] *Cantagalo* ✥ *F5.*

$$$$ HOTEL **Pestana Rio Atlântica.** This well-located hotel offers friendly service, a great breakfast, and a good location opposite Copacabana Beach, but the real stars of the show are the rooftop pool and bar—the sunset views are incredible. **Pros:** good value for the area; rooftop pool and bar; good beachfront location. **Cons:** some rooms need revamping; can feel a little crowded. [$] *Rooms from: R$760* ✉ *Av. Atlântica 2964, Copacabana* ☎ *021/2548–6332* 🌐 *www.pestana.com* *109 rooms, 105 suites* 🍴 *No meals* [M] *Cantagalo* ✥ *F4.*

$$$$ HOTEL FAMILY **Porto Bay Rio Internacional.** All rooms at this Copacabana landmark hotel have balconies with sea views, a rarity on Avenida Atlântica. **Pros:** excellent service; good views; beachfront location. **Cons:** some rooms quite small; Copacabana not as safe as Ipanema after dark; hotel beginning to look dated. [$] *Rooms from: R$755* ✉ *Av. Atlântica 1500, Copacabana* ☎ *021/2546–8000* 🌐 *www.portobay.com* *117 rooms, 11 suites* 🍴 *Breakfast* [M] *Cardeal Arcoverde* ✥ *G3.*

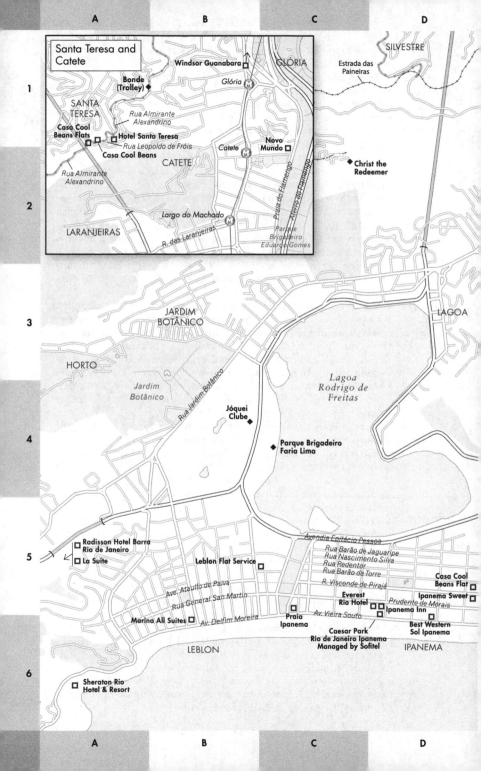

Santa Teresa and Catete

GLÓRIA

SILVESTRE

Windsor Guanabara

Glória

Estrada das Paineiras

Bonde (Trolley)

SANTA TERESA

Rua Almirante Alexandrino

Casa Cool Beans Flats

Hotel Santa Teresa

Rua Leopoldo de Fróis

Casa Cool Beans

Catete

Novo Mundo

CATETE

Christ the Redeemer

Rua Almirante Alexandrino

Largo do Machado

LARANJEIRAS

R. das Laranjeiras

Parque Brigadeiro Eduardo Gomes

Praia do Flamengo

Aterro do Flamengo

JARDIM BOTÂNICO

LAGOA

HORTO

Jardim Botânico

Rua Jardim Botânico

Jóquei Clube

Lagoa Rodrigo de Freitas

Parque Brigadeiro Faria Lima

Radisson Hotel Barra Rio de Janeiro

La Suite

Leblon Flat Service

Avenida Epitácio Pessoa

Rua Barão de Jaguaripe
Rua Nascimento Silva
Rua Redentor
Rua Barão da Torre
R. Visconde de Pirajá

Casa Cool Beans Flat

Ipanema Sweet

Everest Rio Hotel

Prudente de Morais

Ipanema Inn

Ave. Ataulfo de Paiva

Rua General San Martin

Marina All Suites

Av. Delfim Moreira

Praia Ipanema

Av. Vieira Souto

Best Western Sol Ipanema

Caesar Park Rio de Janeiro Ipanema Managed by Sofitel

IPANEMA

LEBLON

Sheraton Rio Hotel & Resort

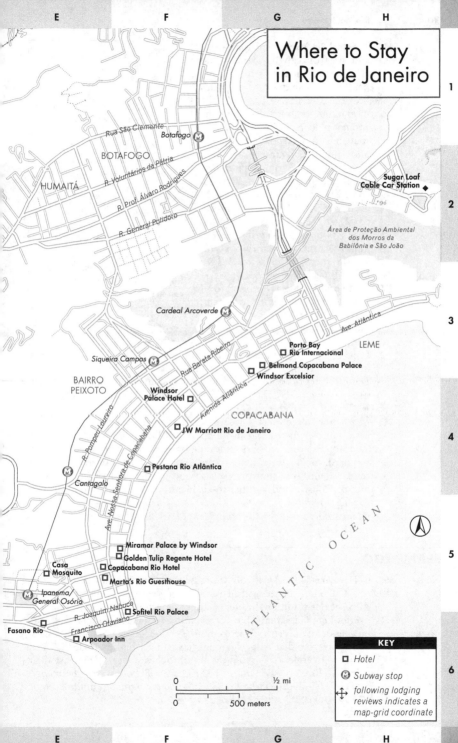

Where to Stay in Rio de Janeiro

BOTAFOGO

HUMAITÁ

Rua São Clemente

Botafogo Ⓜ

R. Voluntários da Pátria

R. Prof. Álvaro Rodrigues

R. General Polidoro

Sugar Loaf
Cable Car Station ◆

Área de Proteção Ambiental
dos Morros da
Babilônia e São João

Cardeal Arcoverde Ⓜ

Ave. Atlântica

LEME

Porto Bay
□ Rio Internacional

Siqueira Campos Ⓜ

Rua Barata Ribeiro

□ Belmond Copacabana Palace

□ Windsor Excelsior

**BAIRRO
PEIXOTO**

Windsor
Palace Hotel □

Avenida Atlântica

COPACABANA

R. Pompeu Loureiro

□ JW Marriott Rio de Janeiro

Ave. Nossa Senhora de Copacabana

Ⓜ

Cantagalo

□ Pestana Rio Atlântica

ATLANTIC OCEAN

□ Miramar Palace by Windsor
□ Golden Tulip Regente Hotel

Casa
□ Mosquito

□ Copacabana Rio Hotel

□ Marta's Rio Guesthouse

Ⓜ Ipanema/
General Osório

R. Joaquim Nabuco

□ Sofitel Rio Palace

Francisco Otaviano

□ Fasano Rio

□ Arpoador Inn

ATLANTIC OCEAN

	KEY
□	*Hotel*
Ⓜ	*Subway stop*
✛	*following lodging reviews indicates a map-grid coordinate*

0 ————— ½ mi

0 ————— 500 meters

$$$$ HOTEL 🏨 **Sofitel Rio Palace.** Anchoring one end of Copacabana Beach, and close to Ipanema, this huge hotel has an "H" shape that provides breathtaking views of the sea, the mountains, or both, from all the rooms' balconies. **Pros:** handy to Ipanema and Arpoador Beaches and nightlife; fantastic views. **Cons:** very large; somewhat impersonal; small bathrooms in some rooms. [$] *Rooms from: R$890* ✉ *Av. Atlântica 4240, Copacabana* ☎ *021/2525–1232* 🌐 *www.sofitel.com/gb/hotel-1988-sofitel-rio-de-janeiro-copacabana/index.shtml* 🛏 *388 rooms, 286 suites* 🍴 *No meals* [M] *Cantogalo* ✥ *F6.*

$$$$ HOTEL 🏨 **Windsor Excelsior.** This beachfront hotel, part of the Windsor chain, may have been built in the 1950s, but its look is sleek and contemporary—from the sparkling marble lobby to the guest-room closets paneled in gleaming Brazilian redwood. **Pros:** top-notch service; rooftop pool; good breakfast. **Cons:** slightly impersonal chain feel; busy street can be dangerous at night. [$] *Rooms from: R$603* ✉ *Av. Atlântica 1800, Copacabana* ☎ *021/2195–5800* 🌐 *www.windsorhoteis.com.br* 🛏 *230 rooms, 3 suites* 🍴 *Breakfast* [M] *Cardeal Arcoverde* ✥ *G3.*

ALTERNATIVE HOUSING

Rio has accommodations to suit virtually every taste and wallet. There are plenty of self-catering options for those who value their own space over hotel luxury. Agencies specialize in everything from luxury Ipanema penthouses to pokey Copacabana digs. One good one, Alex Rio Flats (🌐 *www.alexrioflats.com*), has 10 air-conditioned studios and apartments, many with beachfront locations and full sea views, that cost R$220 and up per night. Alex, the English-speaking owner, provides friendly, personalized service and can help book trips and tours.

$$$ HOTEL 🏨 **Windsor Palace Hotel.** Close to Copacabana's main shopping area, handy for the metro and just a couple of blocks from the beach, the Windsor Palace is a solid midrange option with decent services and standard, cookie-cutter hotel rooms, many of which have recently been refurbished. **Pros:** rooftop views; good amenities; two blocks from metro. **Cons:** bland rooms; so-so location. [$] *Rooms from: R$480* ✉ *Rua Domingos Ferreira 6, Copacabana* ☎ *021/2195–6600* 🌐 *www.windsorhoteis.com* 🛏 *73 rooms, 1 suite* 🍴 *Breakfast* [M] *Siqueira Campos* ✥ *F4.*

FLAMENGO

$$$ HOTEL 🏨 **Novo Mundo.** A short walk from the Catete metro station, next door to Palacio de Catete, and five minutes by car from Santos Dumont Airport, this traditional hotel occupies an attractive art deco building overlooking Guanabara Bay. Convention rooms are popular with the business crowd. **Pros:** close to metro; some rooms have great views; good playground at palace gardens next door; children under 12 free. **Cons:** metro ride away from the best beaches; some rooms past their prime. [$] *Rooms from: R$390* ✉ *Praia do Flamengo 20, Flamengo* ☎ *021/2105–7000, 0800/25–3355* 🌐 *www.hotelnovomundo.com.br* 🛏 *209 rooms, 22 suites* 🍴 *Breakfast* [M] *Catete* ✥ *C2.*

2

IPANEMA AND LEBLON

$$$ HOTEL **Arpoador Inn.** This pocket-size hotel is functional rather than luxurious, but it benefits from one of the best beachfront locations in the city at Arpoador, the point at which Ipanema meets Copacabana. **Pros:** great sunsets; right-on-the-beach location; good restaurant; reasonable prices. **Cons:** front rooms can be noisy; hotel often busy with groups of surfers. [$] *Rooms from: R$475* ✉ *Rua Francisco Otaviano 177, Ipanema* ☎ *021/2523–0060* 🌐 *www.arpoadorinn.com.br* *50 rooms, 1 suite* 🍴 *Breakfast* [M] *Ipanema/General Osório or Cantagalo* ✥ *E6.*

$$$$ HOTEL FAMILY **Best Western Sol Ipanema.** Another of Rio's tall, slender hotels, this one has a great location at the eastern end of Ipanema Beach between Rua Vinicius de Moraes and Farme de Amoedo, and though it isn't luxurious, the hotel has comfortable accommodations with crisp, clean, and modern interiors. **Pros:** great beach location; near lively Ipanema nightlife; friendly staff; decent value for Ipanema. **Cons:** standard facilities; tiny pool. [$] *Rooms from: R$780* ✉ *Av. Vieira Souto 320, Ipanema* ☎ *021/2525–2020* 🌐 *www.solipanema.com.br* *90 rooms* 🍴 *Breakfast* [M] *Ipanema/General Osório* ✥ *D6.*

$$$$ HOTEL **Caesar Park Rio de Janeiro Ipanema Managed by Sofitel.** In the heart of Ipanema, close to high-class shops and gourmet restaurants, this beachfront hotel has established itself among business travelers, celebrities, and heads of state, who appreciate its impeccable service; and while the suites are impressive, other rooms feel more functional than luxurious. **Pros:** great location; good business facilities; good views. **Cons:** no balconies; small pool; uninspired decor. [$] *Rooms from: R$780* ✉ *Av. Vieira Souto 460, Ipanema* ☎ *021/2525–2525* 🌐 *www.sofitel.com* *221 rooms, 28 suites* 🍴 *No meals* [M] *Ipanema/General Osorio* ✥ *D6.*

$$$ RENTAL Fodor's Choice ★ **Casa Cool Beans Flats.** A block from the beach in Ipanema, this lodging in a converted 1940s building has eight flats that have stylish, contemporary furnishings and artworks by popular Rio artist Paulo Freire. **Pros:** excellent value for Ipanema; close to beach, bars, restaurants, shopping, and the metro; gay-friendly. **Cons:** two-night minimum (three for major holidays and events); no guests under age 18; no elevator. [$] *Rooms from: R$460* ✉ *Rua Vinicius de Moraes 72, Ipanema* ☎ *021/2262–0552, 202/470–3548 in the U.S.* 🌐 *flats.casacoolbeans.com* *5 suites, 3 studios* 🍴 *No meals* [M] *Ipanema/General Osório* ✥ *D5.*

$$$$ HOTEL **Everest Rio Hotel.** In the heart of Ipanema's shopping and dining district, a block from the beach, this hotel has standard accommodations and in-room amenities but a great rooftop view—a postcard shot of Corcovado and the lagoon. **Pros:** rooftop views and pool; good business amenities; fine location close to beach, restaurants, and nightlife. **Cons:** noisy air-conditioning; other buildings hamper some views. [$] *Rooms from: R$530* ✉ *Rua Prudente de Morais 1117, Ipanema* ☎ *021/2525–2200, 0800/709–2220* 🌐 *www.everest.com.br* *148 rooms, 8 suites* 🍴 *Breakfast* [M] *Ipanema/General Osório* ✥ *D5.*

$$$$ HOTEL **Fasano Rio.** The Italian-owned Fasano Group is renowned for its stylish, elegant hotels and restaurants, and Fasano Rio has the added glamour of having been crafted by the French designer Philippe Starck. **Pros:** chic decor; wonderful views from pool; glamorous clientele. **Cons:**

standard rooms lack views; expensive; street noise. Ⓢ *Rooms from: R$1,600* ✉ *Av. Viera Souto 80, Ipanema* ☎ *021/3202–4000* ⊕ *www. fasano.com.br* ⌨ *82 rooms, 10 suites* ⏺ *Breakfast* Ⓜ *Ipanema/General Osório* ✛ *E6.*

$$$ ⌐ **Ipanema Inn.** If you want to stay in Ipanema and avoid the ultrahigh
HOTEL prices of beachfront accommodations, this no-frills hotel with great service is a wise choice. **Pros:** great location; good value. **Cons:** basic rooms; no views. Ⓢ *Rooms from: R$460* ✉ *Rua Maria Quitéria 27, Ipanema* ☎ *021/2523–6092, 021/2529–1000* ⊕ *www.ipanemainn.com. br* ⌨ *56 rooms* ⏺ *Breakfast* Ⓜ *Ipanema/General Osório* ✛ *D5.*

$$$ ⌐ **Ipanema Sweet.** In this smart residential building in the heart of
RENTAL Ipanema—two blocks from the beach and steps away from the neigh-
FAMILY borhood's best bars, restaurants, and shops—one- and two-bedroom apartments are rented out by the night, week, or month. **Pros:** great location; stylish public areas; more space than standard hotel rooms. **Cons:** not all apartments have safe boxes; small pool; maid service costs extra. Ⓢ *Rooms from: R$420* ✉ *Rua Visconde de Pirajá 161, Ipanema* ☎ *021/8201–1458, 021/98137–2774 Raissa Cordeiro* ⌨ *10 apartments* ⏺ *No meals* Ⓜ *Ipanema/General Osório* ✛ *D5.*

$$$ ⌐ **Leblon Flat Service.** A good option for those who want to save money
RENTAL by cooking some meals, this hotel-like complex with an excellent loca-
FAMILY tion three blocks from Leblon Beach rents simply decorated, small fur-
nished apartments with one or two bedrooms and balconies and has a small pool. **Pros:** good rate for Leblon area; kitchens; near shopping, restaurants, and nightlife. **Cons:** unattractive building; basic lodgings. Ⓢ *Rooms from: R$500* ✉ *Rua Professor Antônio Maria Teixeira 33, Leblon* ☎ *021/ 2127–7700 for information, 021/3722–5053 for reser-
vations, 021/3722–5054* ⌨ *120 apartments* ⏺ *Breakfast* ✛ *C5.*

$$$$ ⌐ **Marina All Suites.** In front of Leblon Beach and surrounded by designer
HOTEL stores and upmarket restaurants, this hotel is a favorite with chic vaca-
tioners (Gisele Bundchen and Calvin Klein are regulars). **Pros:** good location; spacious, well-equipped suites; excellent service; pool with sea views. **Cons:** expensive; Leblon Beach is not quite as pretty as Ipanema; small pool. Ⓢ *Rooms from: R$1,100* ✉ *Av. Delfim Moreira 696, Leblon* ☎ *021/2172–1001* ⊕ *www.marinaallsuites.com.br* ⌨ *37 suites* ⏺ *Breakfast* ✛ *B6.*

$$$$ ⌐ **Praia Ipanema.** This hotel between Ipanema and Leblon may not be
HOTEL deluxe, but it's across from the beach, and each room has a sea view and a private balcony. **Pros:** great views; beachfront location; close to Ipanema and Leblon shopping and nightlife. **Cons:** some furnishings a little shabby. Ⓢ *Rooms from: R$740* ✉ *Av. Vieira Souto 706, Ipanema* ☎ *021/2141–4949* ⊕ *www.praiaipanema.com* ⌨ *103 rooms* ⏺ *Break-
fast* Ⓜ *Ipanema/General Osorio* ✛ *C5.*

$$$$ ⌐ **Sheraton Rio Hotel & Resort.** Between the upmarket neighborhoods
RESORT of São Conrado and Leblon, this hotel has the most spacious leisure
FAMILY area in the city, with three pools, two tennis courts, and a children's playground; however, the leisure area is less than pristine, and the hotel's location directly in front of the sprawling favela of Vidigal may make some guests uncomfortable. **Pros:** great for families; wonder-
ful beach; good amenities. **Cons:** isolated location means taxi rides;

some furnishings past their prime; pool area is not clean. $ *Rooms from: R$690* ⊠ *Av. Niemeyer 121, Leblon* ☎ *021/2529 1122* ⊕ *www. sheraton-rio.com* ⟿ *500 rooms, 59 suites* ⟐❘ *Breakfast* ✚ *A6.*

SANTA TERESA

$$
B&B/INN
Fodor's Choice
★

⠿ **Casa Cool Beans.** American expats Lance and David opened Casa Cool Beans in 2010, determined to raise the bar for accommodations in Rio, and their guests' raves about the attentive service, chill atmosphere, and gorgeous decor testify to their success. **Pros:** excellent service; characterful building; peaceful neighborhood; breakfast alfresco. **Cons:** difficult for taxis to find; far from the beach; two-night minimum stay. $ *Rooms from: R$290* ⊠ *Rua Laurinda Santos Lobo 136, Santa Teresa* ☎ *021/2262–0552, 202/470–3548 in U.S.* ⊕ *www.casacoolbeans.com* ⟿ *10 rooms* ⟐❘ *Breakfast* ✚ *A1.*

$$$$
HOTEL
Fodor's Choice
★

⠿ **Hotel Santa Teresa.** This five-star hotel, located in the historic hilltop neighborhood of Santa Teresa, is housed in a regenerated coffee plantation mansion that pays homage to Brazil's cultures and traditions with folk art and handicrafts from across the nation. **Pros:** sense of place; highlights Brazilian artists; stylish setting; excellent restaurant; close to Santa Teresa's drinking and dining scene. **Cons:** it's a cab ride to the beach; hotel bar sometimes closed for private events. $ *Rooms from: R$1,100* ⊠ *Rua Almirante Alexandrino 660, Santa Teresa* ☎ *021/3380– 0204* ⊕ *www.santa-teresa-hotel.com* ⟿ *44 rooms* ⟐❘ *Breakfast* ✚ *A1.*

SÃO CONRADO, BARRA DA TIJUCA, AND BEYOND

$$$$
HOTEL
Fodor's Choice
★

⠿ **La Suite.** If you're looking for an extra-special place to spend a romantic night in Rio, this luxurious cliffside hideaway is the one to book: La Suite's off-the-beaten-track location amid the secluded mansions of Joatinga—often referred to as "the Beverly Hills of Rio"—gives it an ultra-exclusive feel, and the French owners have imbued their boutique hotel with real Parisian chic. **Pros:** impossibly scenic location; exclusive feel; romantic ambience. **Cons:** it's a cab ride to bars and restaurants. $ *Rooms from: R$1,300* ⊠ *Rua Jackson de Figueiredo 501, Joatinga* ☎ *021/2484–1962* ⟿ *7 rooms* ⟐❘ *Breakfast* ✚ *A5.*

$$$$
HOTEL
FAMILY

⠿ **Radisson Hotel Barra Rio de Janeiro.** Each of the spacious and comfortable rooms in this mammoth hotel has a balcony overlooking Barra Beach, and while the hotel is in need of modernization, it has a large heated pool as well as tennis courts and a fitness center. **Pros:** good facilities; Barra Beach is quieter than Zona Sul. **Cons:** traffic is bad; neighborhood is more like Miami than Rio. $ *Rooms from: R$720* ⊠ *Av. Lúcio Costa 3150, Barra da Tijuca* ☎ *021/3139–8000* ⊕ *atlantica hotels.com.br* ⟿ *264 rooms, 28 suites* ⟐❘ *Breakfast* ✚ *A5.*

NIGHTLIFE AND PERFORMING ARTS

Rio supports a rich variety of cultural activity and cutting-edge nightlife. The classic rhythms of samba can be heard in many clubs and bars, and on street corners, but it's possible to find something to suit every kind of musical taste almost every night of the week. Major theater, opera, ballet, and classical-music performances are plentiful, and smaller, more intimate events happen in most neighborhoods. Arts enthusiasts should pick up the bilingual *Guia do Rio* published by Riotur, the city's tourist board, which is available free at tourist information kiosks and hotel reception. The Portuguese-language newspapers *Jornal do Brasil* and *O Globo* publish schedules of events in the entertainment supplements of their Friday editions, which can be found online at ⊕ *www.jb.com.br* and ⊕ *www.oglobo.com.br*. Finally, *Veja Rio* is the city's most comprehensive entertainment guide, published every Saturday and available at all newsstands.

PLAYING IT SAFE

Safety after dark is a paramount concern in Rio. Be aware of your surroundings at all times. Always take a taxi after dark, and be sure it has the company name and phone number painted on the outside before you get in. Pickpockets love Copacabana and Lapa, so keep valuables either at the hotel or well hidden. If you're heading to Lapa, arrange a meeting point in case you get separated from your group, as it's easy to get lost in the crush of people.

NIGHTLIFE

It's sometimes said that cariocas would rather expend their energy on the beach and that nighttime is strictly for recharging their batteries and de-sanding their swimsuits, but witnessing the masses swarming into Lapa at 10 pm on a Friday night make this a tricky argument to endorse. New nightclubs and bars continue to sprout up with remarkable regularity, and there are cutting-edge underground rhythms and musical styles competing with samba, chorro, and Brazilian pop (MPB) for the locals' hearts.

Live music is nighttime Rio's raison d'être, with street corners regularly playing host to impromptu renditions. During Carnival the entire city can feel like one giant playground. The electronic-music scene is also very much alive, and the underground popularity of funk (the city's own X-rated genre, not to be confused with the James Brown version) is slowly seeping into the mainstream, down from the huge *bailes* or open-air parties held weekly in the city's favelas. In addition to samba and MPB, hip-hop, electronica, and rock can be heard in clubs around the city.

COPACABANA

BARS

Bip Bip. Here the *roda de samba*—where musicians sit and play instruments around a central table (in fact the *only* table in this tiny bar)—is legendary, as is the help-yourself beer policy. The gnarled old owner makes drink notations and keeps the crowd in check. The standards of the music here are as high as the bar is simple: big-name Brazilian musicians have been known to drop in for a jam session, and on weekend evenings the revelry often spills out onto the street. ⊠ *Rua Almirante Gonçalves 50, Copacabana* ☎ *021/2267–9696.*

2

Cervantes. This no-frills Copacabana institution marries great beer with great sandwiches made with fresh beef, pork, and cheese crammed into French bread (with the obligatory pineapple slice). It's closed on Monday, but merely to give the staff a chance to recover: the rest of the week everyone's up until all hours catering to the lively late night–early morning crowd. ✉ *Rua Barata Ribeiro 7, Loja B, Copacabana* ☎ *021/2275–6147* ⊕ *www.restaurantecervantes.com.br.*

BAR TALK

A few useful Portuguese words under your belt will make the bar experience even more enjoyable and help you feel like a local. *Chopp* is the ubiquitous draft beer served in small glasses, while *cerveja* is the universal word for bottled beer. A simple *mais uma* will get you "one more," and a *saideira* will get you "one for the road." Finally, ask for *a conta* or "the bill" when you want to settle your tab.

NIGHTCLUBS AND LIVE MUSIC

Fosfobox. For the more serious dance-music enthusiast, Fosfobox, in the heart of Copacabana, plays the best underground tunes, as well as rock and pop. Dancers cram onto the floor in the industrial-feeling basement, while an upstairs bar offers opportunity for conversation. It's closed on Monday and Tuesday. ✉ *Rua Siqueira Campos 143, Loja 22A, Copacabana* ☎ *021/2548–7498* ⊕ *www.fosfobox.com.br* 💲 *R$50.*

Le Boy. The focal point of Rio's gay scene, this classic club has expansive dance floors and lively DJ sets as well as outrageous stage shows. The liveliest action takes place after 1 am, and one dance floor only opens at 6 am. ✉ *Rua Paul Pompéia 102, Posto 6, Copacabana* ☎ *021/2513–4993* ⊕ *www.leboy.com.br* 💲 *R$15, men free before midnight.*

FLAMENGO AND BOTAFOGO

BARS

Belmonte. If you find yourself in need of refreshment after a stroll through the beautiful Parque do Flamengo, then your best stop is Belmonte. The original outlet of a now successful chain, it keeps the carioca spirit alive and well with its carefree air, great tapas and Brazilian snacks, and icy chopp. ✉ *Praia do Flamengo 300, Flamengo* ☎ *021/2552–3349.*

Cobal do Humaitá. Occupying a vast outdoor space under the gaze of Christ the Redeemer, this collection of bars, restaurant, and shops throngs with people after dark, when the air is filled with the tipsy chatter of locals relaxing over dinner and drinks. ✉ *Cobal do Humaitá, Rua Voluntarios Da Patria 446, Loja 3/4 A, Humaitá.*

NIGHTCLUBS AND LIVE MUSIC

Casa da Matriz. With its multiroom layout, old-school arcade games, and small junk shop, this shabby-chic venue has the look and feel of a house party. The club's youngish crowd appreciates the adventurous musical policy: don't be surprised if the DJ follows a 1960s Beatles track with down-and-dirty favela funk. It's closed Sunday to Tuesday. ✉ *Rua Henrique de Novaes 107, Botafogo* ☎ *021/2226–9691* ⊕ *casadamatriz.com.br* 💲 *R$15–R$20.*

IPANEMA AND LEBLON

BARS

Fodor's Choice ★ **Academia da Cachaça.** Not merely *the* place in Rio to try caipirinhas (made here with a variety of tropical fruits), Academia da Cachaça is a veritable temple to cachaça. The small bar sells close to 100 brands of cachaça by the glass or bottle, as well as mixing the famous sugarcane rum into dangerously drinkable concoctions such as the *cocada geladinha*—frozen coconut, coconut water, brown sugar, and cachaça. The Northeastern bar snacks here include sun-dried beef, baked palm hearts, and delicious black-bean soup. ⊠ *Rua Conde de Bernadotte 26, Leblon* ☎ *021/2239–1542* ⊕ *www. academiadacachaca.com.br.*

Bar Garota de Ipanema. This is the original Garota (there are branches all over the city), where Tom Jobim and Vinicius de Moraes penned the timeless song "The Girl from Ipanema." The place serves well-priced food and drink that no doubt originally appealed to the two songsmiths. Occasional live-music events take place in the upstairs lounge. ⊠ *Rua Vinicius de Moraes 39, Ipanema* ☎ *021/2523–3787* ⊕ *www.bargarotadeipanema.com* Ⓜ *Ipanema/General Osório.*

Bracarense. A trip to Bracarense after a hard day on the beach is what Rio is all about. Crowds spill onto the streets while parked cars double as chairs and the sandy masses gather at sunset for ice-cold chopp and some of Leblon's best pork sandwiches, fish balls, and empadas. ⊠ *Rua José Linhares 85, Leblon* ☎ *021/2294–3549* ⊕ *www. bracarense.com.br.*

Devassa. Another cross-city bar chain, Devassa is notable for its house-brand beers, including delicious pale ales and *chopp escuro* (dark beer). The bar also has a great menu of meat-related staples and lighter bites as well as a lunch buffet. This branch has a plum location a couple of blocks from Ipanema Beach and is a popular post-beach hangout for sociable locals. ⊠ *Rua Visconde de Pirajá 539, Ipanema* ☎ *021/2540– 8380* ⊕ *www.devassa.com.br* Ⓜ *Ipanema/General Osório.*

Jobi Bar. Authentically carioca and a fine place to experience Rio spirit, the bar at down-to-earth Jobi stays open on weekends until the last customer leaves. Don't be fooled by the unassuming exterior—Jobi serves some of Rio's most delicious bar snacks and is one of the best-loved bars in the Zona Sul. ⊠ *Av. Ataulfo de Paiva 1166, Loja B, Leblon* ☎ *021/2274–0547* ⊕ *jobibar.com.br/wp.*

THE REAL GIRL FROM IPANEMA

Have you ever wondered if there really *was* a girl from Ipanema? The song was inspired by schoolgirl Heloisa Pinheiro, who caught the fancy of songwriter Antônio Carlos (aka Tom) Jobim and his pal, lyricist Vinicius de Moraes, as she walked past the two bohemians sitting in their favorite bar. They then penned one of last century's classics. That was in 1962, and today the bar has been renamed **Bar Garota de Ipanema.** Its owners have further capitalized on their venue's renown, with "Garota de ... " bars across the city, with the appropriate neighborhood names appended.

NIGHTCLUBS AND LIVE MUSIC

House of Music. The fashionable nightclub and live-music venue attracts a young, photogenic crowd. There's an interesting and varied program of live music and DJs, taking in everything from *sertanejo* (Brazilian country music) and samba to hip-hop. ⊠ *Rua Rita Ludolf 47, Leblon* ☎ *021/2249–9309* ✉ *From R$25.*

Plataforma. Although Plataforma is very tourist-oriented, if you're in Rio outside of Carnival season, then seeing the shows here will give you a taste of the festival's costumes, music, and energy. Capoeira martial-arts displays complete an enjoyable if expensive look at some great Brazilian traditions. Reservations can be made on the venue's website (also for the restaurant). ⊠ *Rua Adalberto Ferreira 32, Leblon* ☎ *021/2274–4022* ⊕ *www.plataformashow.com* ✉ *R$60–R$100.*

INLAND ZONA SUL

BARS

FAMILY **Assis Garrafeira.** Just a few minutes' stroll from the station for the funicular railway that whisks tourists up to the Christ statue, this welcoming bar prides itself on its enormous selection of quality beers. In a building once occupied by the late fiction writer Machado do Assis—a giant of Brazilian literature—the walls of the lounge are occupied by well-stocked bookshelves. Staff are hugely knowledgeable about drink pairings and beer, and can help you choose from the list of almost 200 bottles, which includes many imported Belgian beers. ⊠ *Rua Cosme Velho 174* ☎ *021/2205–3598.*

Boteco D.O.C. A pleasant 10-minute walk from the Corcovado railway station, this gastrobar is run by talented young chef Gabriel Carvalho, who has worked at some of the best restuarants in the city. Food is a main focus—try the *bolinho da bacalhau 90%*, a version of the classic cod-and-potato ball that comes with more fish and less filler than standard. There are good cocktails, including one made with cashew, gin, and tonic. It's a small space, so things get full quickly—come early if you want a seat. ⊠ *Rua das Laranjeiras 486, Laranjeiras* ☎ *021/3486–2550* ⊕ *www.botecodoc.com.*

Lagoa. Rio's beautiful city lake is flanked with bars and informal kiosks. Along with the usual beers and cocktails, the food—Italian, Arabian, burgers, and other nontraditional Brazilian—may not be spectacular, but the view of surrounding water and mountains, with Christ the Redeemer lighted up in the distance, most certainly is. In November and December a giant floating Christmas tree lit by millions of twinkling lights adds to the spectacle. The kiosks close down around 1 am. ⊠ *Parque Brigadeiro Faria Lima, turnoff near BR gas station, Av. Epitácio Pessoa 1674, Lagoa* ☎.

NIGHTCLUBS AND LIVE MUSIC

Fodor'sChoice **00 (Zero Zero).** Alongside the Gávea Planetarium, 00 is at once a buzzing ★ nightclub, chic sushi restaurant, and open-air bar. Music at this enduringly popular carioca hangout ranges from modern Brazilian samba and house to drum and bass. ⊠ *Av. Padre Leonel Franca 240, Gávea* ☎ *021/2540–8041* ⊕ *www.00site.com.br* ✉ *From R$30.*

Casa Rosa. A former brothel in a bright-pink mansion on the Laranjeiras hillside is now a hot spot for live music and dancing. The Sunday-afternoon *feijoada* and samba on the terrace is a must for anyone seeking out a true carioca experience. ⊠ *Rua Alice 550, Laranjeiras* ☎ *021/2557–2562* ⊕ *www.casarosa.com.br* ⊡ *From R$20.*

SANTA TERESA AND LAPA

BARS

Fodor'sChoice

★

Bar do Gomez. Officially Armazem São Thiago, this neighborhood institution is universally referred to by its nickname, Bar do Gomez, in honor of the owner, whose family has run the business for close to 100 years. Pictures documenting the bar's history adorn the high wooden walls, and surveying the scene in the present, you get the pleasant impression that little has changed over the years. The draft beer flows like water, locals swap stories at the long wooden bar, and new friendships are forged at the outdoor drinking posts. Favorites among the bar snacks include the giant olives, a pastrami sandwich, and the shrimp plate. Early on a Friday night, this is a good place to strike up a conversation with locals before heading down the hill to Lapa. ⊠ *Rua Aurea 26, Santa Teresa* ☎ *021/2232–0822* ⊕ *www.armazemsaothiago.com.br.*

Bar do Mineiro. The liveliest of Santa Teresa's many drinking dens and the hub of much social activity, this enduringly popular *boteco* anchors one end of the neighborhood's main drinking and dining strip. Some excellent snacks are served here—the *pasteis de feijao* (fried pastries filled with black beans) being a firm favorite with locals—as well as hearty plates of meat-based *comida mineira* (cuisine from Minas Gerais State). A street-party atmosphere prevails on Sunday afternoon, when the bar is standing room only and revelers spill out onto the road outside. ⊠ *Rua Paschoal Carlos Magno 99, Santa Teresa* ☎ *021/2221–9227.*

Mangue Seco Cachaçaria. Specializing in some of Brazil's finest institutions—strong and fine-tasting cachaças (Brazilian rum), mouthwatering *moquecas* (stews), and, of course, live samba—Mangue Seco's location on the popular Rua do Lavradio makes it a perfect place to start a night out. Arrive at sundown, grab one of the sidewalk tables, and watch Lapa life unfold as you sip a caipirinha and browse the menu. ⊠ *Rua do Lavradio 23, Lapa* ☎ *021/3852–1947* ⊕ *www.manguesecocachacaria. com.br.*

NIGHTCLUBS AND LIVE MUSIC

Carioca da Gema. A favorite among local *sambistas,* Carioca da Gema is one of Lapa's liveliest spots, with talented musicians performing seven nights a week. By 11 pm, finding a place to stand can be difficult, but regulars still find a way to samba. Call ahead and book a table if you are more keen to be a spectator. There's a good pizzeria downstairs. ⊠ *Rua Mem de Sá 79, Lapa* ☎ *021/2221–0043* ⊕ *www.barcariocadagema. com.br* ⊡ *From R$23.*

Fodor'sChoice

★

Circo Voador. A great venue in an excellent location right by the Lapa arches, Circo Voador hosts club nights during the week, but it's the varied live shows that really stand out, with a big stage set under a huge open-sided circular tent and room for up to 1,500 people to dance the night away. ⊠ *Rua dos Arcos s/n, Lapa* ☎ *021/2533-0354* ⊕ *www. circovoador.com.br* ⊠ *From R$25.*

Lapa Street Party. Lapa's transformation from no-go area to must-go party district has been dramatic, and the ongoing gentrification of this formerly neglected part of downtown has extended to the weekend street parties held in the area surrounding the Arcos da Lapa (Lapa Aqueduct). On Fridays and Saturdays, smart-looking canvas kiosks sprout up, offering everything from super-strong fruit cocktails to alcohol-absorbing pizzas and burgers, and thousands of revelers come to rub shoulders. The lively scene often involves impromptu music performances, and the party doesn't wind down until the sun rises. Both men and women should be prepared for an onslaught of attention from locals. If this attention is unwanted, be polite but clear and walk away—small talk may be perceived as flirting. An increased police presence has made Lapa safer than it was, but pickpocketing remains a problem, so don't bring valuables here. ⊠ *Rua dos Arcos, Lapa* Ⓜ *Carioca.*

Leviano. Among the best of the slick modern bars to crop up as part of the ongoing gentrification of Lapa, Leviano is situated at the heart of the action. A glass frontage allows patrons to look out onto the hedonistic hordes from the comfort of an air-conditioned lounge, and the second floor features live bands—jazz nights here have been a particular success—while downstairs circus acrobats whirl and twirl from the ceiling. Should you be loathe to tear your eyes away, there's an extensive menu of light meals to accompany those ice-cold beers and caipirinhas. ⊠ *Av. Mem de Sá 49, Lapa* ☎ *021/2507–5779* ⊕ *www.levianobar.com. br* Ⓜ *Carioca or Cinelandia.*

Fodor's Choice **Rio Scenarium.** Despite the hordes of samba-seeking tourists, Rio Sce-
★ narium somehow manages to retain its authenticity and magic. This is partly due to the incredible setting—a former movie-props warehouse still crammed to the rafters with old instruments, bikes, furniture, and puppets—but also to the great bands and persevering locals who love to show off their moves and entice novices onto the dance floor. On weekends arrive before 9 pm to avoid the lines, or call ahead and book a table. It's closed on Sunday and Monday. ⊠ *Rua do Lavrádio 20, Lapa* ☎ *021/3147–9005* ⊕ *www.rioscenarium.com.br* ⊠ *From R$30* Ⓜ *Carioca or Cinelandia.*

PERFORMING ARTS

Theater, classical music (*música erudita*), and opera may be largely the preserve of the affluent upper classes in Rio, but tickets remain reasonably priced by international standards and can be purchased easily from box offices. Although understanding Portuguese may prove difficult for some visitors, musicals provide a good opportunity to catch the glitzier side of Rio, and the international language of song and dance is considerably more comprehensible. Since many of the venues are in downtown or more out-of-the-way areas, use taxis to get to and from them, as the surrounding streets can feel dangerously deserted by night.

Visual-art venues and museums are also very well endowed, with privately funded cultural centers hosting a rich variety of exhibitions,

Carnival in Rio

The four-day Carnival weekend, marked on every Brazilian's calendar, is by far the biggest event of the year, with planning and preparation starting months ahead. What began as a pre-Lent celebration has morphed into a massive affair of street parties, masquerades, and samba parades. Elaborate costumes, enormous floats, and intensive planning all unfurl magically behind the scenes as Brazilians from all walks of life save their money for the all-important *desfile* (parade) down the Sambódromo. Even though Carnival has set dates based on the lunar calendar that determine when Lent occurs, the *folia* (Carnival festivities) start at least a week before and end at least a week after the samba schools parade. Five-star hotels such as the Sheraton and Copacabana Palace have balls that are open to the public, as long as you can afford tickets (which run upward of R$3,000). A cheaper option is partying at the Carnival *blocos* (street parties), along the streets of Centro and Santa Teresa and the beaches of the Zona Sul. If you really want to get close to the action, then you'll need to buy tickets (well in advance) for a seat at the Sambódromo. Most samba schools begin their rehearsals around October; if you're in Rio from October to January, visit one of the samba schools *(see Performing Arts)* on a rehearsal day. Whether your scene is hanging out at the bars, partying in the street, parading along the beach, masked balls for the elite, or fun in a stadium, Rio's Carnival is an experience of a lifetime.

specific details of which are again best sought out in the Friday editions of the Rio press.

CLASSICAL MUSIC

FAMILY **Centro Cultural Municipal Parque das Ruinas.** With a glorious view of Guanabara Bay and downtown, the Parque das Ruinas houses the remains of a mansion building that was Rio's bohemian epicenter in the first half of the 20th century. Today live music and theater performances are held here, and the panoramic views from the top of the building are stunning. Occasional music and art events take place during the summer. ⊠ *Rua Murtinho Nobre 169, Santa Teresa* ☎ *021/2252–1039*.

Escola de Música da UFRJ. The music school auditorium, inspired by the Salle Gaveau in Paris, has 1,100 seats, and you can listen to chamber music, symphony orchestras, and opera, all free of charge. ⊠ *Rua do Passeio 98, Lapa* ☎ *021/2222–1029* Ⓜ *Cinelândia*.

Instituto Moreira Salles. Surrounded by beautiful gardens, the institute creates the perfect atmosphere for classical music. Listen to musicians performing pieces from Bach, Chopin, Debussy, and other classical composers. Outdoor cinema screenings are held here, too. ⊠ *Rua Marquês de São Vicente 476, Gávea* ☎ *021/3284–7400* ⊕ *www.ims.com.br*.

Sala Cecília Meireles. A popular concert venue for classical music in the city, the Sala hosts regular performances in a midsize hall. ⊠ *Largo da Lapa 47, Lapa* ☎ *021/2332–9223* ⊕ *www.salaceciliameireles.com.br* ▣ *From R$25* Ⓜ *Cinelândia*.

CONCERT HALLS

Cidade das Artes. This enormous cultural complex and live-music venue opened in 2013 and is now the largest concert hall in South America, seating 1,780. Designed by French architect Christian de Portzamparc, the Cidade das Artes (City of Arts) complex covers around 90,000 square meters and houses theaters and cinemas, and is home to the Brazilian Symphony Orchestra, and hosts major rock and pop shows. ⊠ *Av. das Americas 5300, Barra da Tijuca* ☏ *021/3325–0102* ⊕ *www. cidadedasartes.org.*

Citibank Hall. This huge venue hosts some of the biggest Brazilian and international names playing in Rio, such as Caetano Veloso, Adele, Smashing Pumpkins, and Lady Gaga. ⊠ *Via Parque Shopping, Av. Ayrton Senna 3000, Barra da Tijuca* ☏ *0300/789–6846* ⊕ *www. citibankhall.com.br* ☚ *From R$90.*

HSBC Arena. HSBC Arena hosts big-name rock and pop stars. ⊠ *Av. Embaixador Abelardo Bueno 3401, Barra da Tijuca* ☏ *021/3035–5200.*

FILM

Estação Net Ipanema. The charming two-screen Estação Net Ipanema cinema is part of a lively area of small restaurants and bookstores, perfect for hanging out before or after the films (the theater itself has a coffee shop). Other locations of the Estação chain of small art-house cinemas can be found on the Ipanema beachfront (Estação Net Laura Alvim), in Flamengo (Estação Paissandu), Barra da Tijuca (Estação Barra Point), and two in Botafogo (Estação Net Rio and Estação Botafogo). ⊠ *Av. Visconde de Pirajá 605, Ipanema* ☏ *021/2279–4603* ⊕ *www. grupoestacao.com.br* ☚ *From R$15.*

FAMILY **UCI New York City Center.** This 18-screen, American-style multiplex is located in a large mall that comes complete with a model of the Statue of Liberty outside. Fittingly, it shows many Hollywood blockbusters. ⊠ *Av. das Américas 5000, Loja 301, Barra da Tijuca* ☏ *021/2461–1818* ⊕ *www.ucicinemas.com.br* ☚ *From R$20.*

OPERA

Fodor's Choice **Theatro Municipal.** Built in 1909, the stunning Municipal Theater at
★ Cinelândia is the city's main performing-arts venue, hosting dance, opera, symphony concerts, and theater events for most of the year. The season officially runs from March to December, so don't be surprised to find the theater closed in January and February. The theater also has its own ballet company. ⊠ *Praça Floriano, Rua Manuel Carvalho s/n, Centro* ☏ *021/2332–9134, 021/2332–9191, 021/2262–3501, 021/2299–1717* ⊕ *www.theatromunicipal.rj.gov.br* Ⓜ *Cinelândia.*

SAMBA-SCHOOL SHOWS

Weekly public rehearsals (*ensaio*) attract crowds of samba enthusiasts and visitors alike to the *escolas de samba* (samba schools) from August through to Carnival (February or March). As the schools frantically ready themselves for the high point of the year, the atmosphere in these packed warehouses is often electric, and with Mangueira and Beija Flor, always sweaty. This may prove one of your liveliest and most chaotic nights on the town. Ticket prices range from R$15 to R$35. The tour company Brazil Expedition (*See Tours, in the Rio de Janeiro*

Planner) offers trips to samba school rehearsals, including transport and entrance, for R$75. On weekends during the run up to Carnival, technical rehearsals are held at the Sambodromo. Entrance is free, crowds are relatively small, and the spectacle is almost as exciting as the real thing. Check local listings for details.

Acadêmicos do Salgueiro. The samba school Salguiero holds its pre-Carnival rehearsals only on Saturdays, from 10 pm. The school also runs Samba Experience events from 9:30 pm, which include a limbloosening caipirinha, samba classes, and entry to the rehearsals. ⊠ *Rua Silva Teles 104, Andaraí* ☎ *021/2238-0389* ⊕ *www.salgueiro.com.br* ✉ *From R$30.*

Beija-Flor. The several-times winner of Rio's annual Samba School competition, Beija-Flor holds public rehearsals on Thursdays at 9 pm in the months leading up to Carnival. ⊠ *Pracinha Wallace Paes Leme 1025, Nilópolis* ☎ *021/2247–4800* ⊕ *www.beija-flor.com.br* ✉ *From R$30.*

Estação Primeira de Mangueira. One of the most popular schools and always a challenger for the Carnival title, Estação Primeira holds its rehearsals on Saturdays at 10 pm. ⊠ *Rua Visconde de Niterói 1072, Mangueira* ☎ *021/2567–4637* ⊕ *www.mangueira.com.br* ✉ *From R$30.*

THEATER

Fodor'sChoice **Centro Cultural Banco do Brasil.** Formerly the headquarters of the Banco
★ do Brasil, in the late 1980s this opulent six-story domed building with marble floors was transformed into a space for plays, art exhibitions, and music recitals. Today the CCBB is one of the city's most important cultural centers, with a bookstore, three theaters, a video hall, four individual video booths, a movie theater, two auditoriums, a restaurant, a coffee shop, a children's library, and a tearoom. It's open Wednesday through Sunday between 10 am and 9 pm, and there are regular children's shows on weekends. ⊠ *Rua 1° de Março 66, Centro* ☎ *021/3808-2020* ⊕ *www.bb.com.br/cultura* ☽ *Tues.–Sun 10 am–9 pm* Ⓜ *Uruguaiana.*

FAMILY **Teatro das Artes.** Located in a shopping mall in well-heeled Gavea, this theater hosts popular productions. Two smaller theaters are reserved for less commercial productions. ⊠ *Shopping Center da Gávea, Rua Marques de São Vicente 52, Loja 264, Gávea* ☎ *021/2540–6004, 021/2294–1096* ⊕ *www.teatrodasartes.com.br* ✉ *From R$40.*

Teatro João Caetano. The city's oldest theater dates to 1813, and while the building itself is less than spectacular, the 1,200-seat venue hosts some interesting productions. These tend to be accessibly priced so it's worth a look, especially since the once-seedy area around the theater has been smartened up. ⊠ *Praça Tiradentes, Centro* ☎ *021/2332–9166* ⊕ *www.cultura.rj.gov.br/espaco/teatro-joao-caetano* ✉ *From R$20* Ⓜ *Presidente Vargas.*

SPORTS AND THE OUTDOORS

Simply put, Rio de Janeiro is sports mad. Though much of the frenzy centers on soccer, other sports—among them volleyball, basketball, beach soccer, beach volleyball, and *futevolei* (a soccer-volleyball hybrid)—are taken extremely seriously. Invigorated by the success of the 2014 FIFA World Cup, it is with a sense of fevered anticipation that Rio awaits the 2016 Olympics, whose impact on the city cannot be understated. In addition to the vast sums spent to renovate existing and create new sports facilities and an Olympic village in the city's West Zone, significant investments are being made to upgrade the public-transportation system.

CYCLE RIO

With its many bike paths, Rio is a great place to explore by bicycle, and Bike Rio, a citywide bicycle-sharing system, has made it easier than ever to do so. Locals and visitors can pick up one of hundreds of bicycles at rental stations along the beachfront and at other bike-friendly locations, returning the bikes to similar stations at journey's end. Daily passes cost R$5 and can be purchased online at ⊕ *www. mobilicidade.com.br.*

BOATING AND SAILING

Dive Point. Schooner tours around the main beaches of Rio and as far afield as Búzios and Arraial do Cabo are offered here, as well as deep-sea and wreck diving. Be sure to ask if prices include all the necessary equipment and training (if required). ⊠ *Av. Ataulfo da Paiva 1174, SS 04, Leblon* ☎ *021/2239–5105, 021/2239–5105* ⊕ *www.divepoint. com.br.*

FAMILY **Saveiro's Tour.** Take a trip down the coast to Angra or catch one of the two-hour daily cruises around Guanabara Bay—views of Sugar Loaf, Botafogo Bay, and the Rio-Niterói Bridge are among the highlights. Saveiro's also hires out speedboats and sailboats by the day. ⊠ *Marina da Glória, Av. Infante Dom Henrique s/n, Lojas 13 e 14, Glória* ☎ *021/2225–6064* ⊕ *www.saveiros.com.br* ☒ *From R$55* Ⓜ *Gloria.*

GOLF

Gávea Golf and Country Club. With a stunning setting overlooking the ocean and framed by the towering Pedra da Gávea mountain, Gávea Golf and Country Club has an impeccably groomed course. It's members-only on weekends, but nonmembers can play during the week. ⊠ *Estrada da Gávea 800, São Conrado* ☎ *021/3322–4141* ⊕ *www. gaveagolfclub.com.br* ☒ *R$350 weekdays* 🏌 *18 holes, 5986 yards, par 18* Ⓜ *No metro.*

FAMILY **Golden Green Golf Club.** This small but well-maintained golf course may only have six holes, but given the exclusivity and prices of the alternatives, this could be your best option for getting in a little play in Rio. Nonmembers are welcome every day, but it's a little out of town. ⊠ *Av.*

Prefeito Dulcídio Cardoso 2901, Barra da Tijuca ☎ *021/2434–0696* ⌂ *R\$80 weekdays, R\$100 weekends* ⚑ *6 holes, 2637 yards, par 54.*

HANG GLIDING

Just Fly. This highly reputable and experienced outfit will collect you from your hotel, take you through the basics, and then run you off Pedra Bonita mountain into the sky high above Tijuca Forest. The excellent instructors can also film or photograph the experience for an extra charge. ✉ *Ipanema* ☎ *021/2268–0565, 021/9985–7540* ⊕ *justflyinrio. blogspot.co.uk* ⌂ *From R\$240.*

São Conrado Eco-Aventura. This reliable and experienced team can provide you with a bird's-eye view of Rio either by hang glider or paraglider as well as leading jungle treks and Jeep tours. It is possible to book adventure packages combining several activities for a discounted price. ✉ *São Conrado* ☎ *021/2522–5586* ⊕ *www.saoconradoecoaventuras. com.br* ⌂ *From R\$250.*

HIKING AND CLIMBING

Given the changeable weather and the harsh terrain, guides are recommended for all major walks and climbs in Rio. Of particular note within the city itself are the hikes up Corcovado from Parque Lage and the trip through Tijuca Forest to Pico da Tijuca.

Centro Excursionista Brasileiro. The largest and oldest mountaineering organization in Brazil, Centro Excursionista Brasileiro runs climbing courses and leads treks throughout Rio State and as far away as Minas Gerais, providing guides, maps, and all the gear you'll need. ✉ *Av. Almirante Barroso 2, 8th fl., Centro* ☎ *021/2252–9844* ⊕ *www.ceb.org.br.*

Rio Adventures. This professional outfit with English-speaking guides runs a range of adventure sports activities and tours, including stand-up paddleboarding, white-water rafting, jungle treks, and climbing trips. ✉ *Praça Radial Sul 25, Botafogo* ☎ *021/2705–5747, 021/9768–5221* ⊕ *rioadventures.com* Ⓜ *Botafogo.*

Rio Ecoesporte. This ecotourism outfit specializes in exploring Rio's West Zone on foot and horseback, as well as running rappel and surf excursions. The excursions set off from Vargem Grande, a rural neighborhood west of Rio, and the tour company also has its own hostel, Rio Ecoesporte Hostel. ✉ *Estrada dos Bandeirantes 24081, Vargem Grande* ☎ *021/ 96416–4930 Activities, 021/3734–0744 Hostel* ⊕ *www. rioecoesporte.com.br* Ⓜ *No metro.*

HORSE RACING

Jóquei Clube. This beautiful old racetrack conjures up a bygone era of grandeur with its impeccably preserved betting hall, 1920s grandstand, and distant beach views framed by Cristo Redentor and the Dois Irmaos mountain. When the big event of the year, the Grande Premio, comes around in August, expect the crowds to swell and everyone to be dressed to the nines. Entry is free year-round, but you need to dress smart–casual, with no shorts or flip-flops allowed in the main stand. ✉ *Praça Santos Dumont 31, Gávea* ☎ *021/2512–9988* ⊕ *www.jcb.com. br* Ⓜ *No metro.*

SOCCER

FAMILY
Fodor'sChoice
★

Estádio Maracanã. The vast stadium is nothing short of legendary, and watching a soccer game here is a must if the season (from mid-January to November) is in swing. As entertaining as some of the games are the obsessive supporters, devoted to their team colors but not afraid to trash their own players, the opposition, other fans, and of course the referee. The huge flags and fireworks are always spectacular. Tickets are available in advance and often on game day from the stadium ticket office. The *branco* or white section of the *archibancado*, or upper tier, is the safest option for the neutral fan. Expect to pay around R$35 for a ticket there, and arrive in good time to grab the best seats and soak up the atmosphere. Major refurbishments were made to prepare the 78,838-seat stadium for the FIFA 2014 World Cup, and the stadium will also host decisive soccer matches—including the final—of the 2016 Rio Olympics. On non–match days visitors can take tours of the stadium. ✉ *Rua Prof. Eurico Rabelo s/n, Maracanã* ☎ *0800/062–7222 Freephone info number* ⊕ *www.maracana.com/site* 🚇 *From R$35* Ⓜ *Maracana.*

> ### RIO SURF BUS
>
> The Surf Bus travels seven days a week from Botafogo to Prainha, which is considered to be the best surfing beach close to the city. The two-hour trip takes in the best surf breaks west of Rio, including all 12 km (7½ miles) of Barra, Recreio, and Macumba. There's no snobbery if you don't have a board and are just going along for the ride. Catch the bus from anywhere along the Copacabana, Ipanema, or Leblon beachfront for an easy route to some stunning out-of-town beaches. Check outward and return times at ⊕ *www.surfbus. com.br*, because you do not want to be left stranded.

SURFING

Surfing remains hugely popular in Rio, and stand-up paddleboarding is a current trend—kiosks offer stand-up paddleboards and classes all along the Zona Sul beaches. Kite surfing is growing rapidly, too, with several schools opening on Barra beachfront and out of town toward Cabo Frio.

Escola de Surf do Arpoador. The most consistent break in the city has its own surf school based on the beach; call up or stop by to book an early-morning appointment. ✉ *Av. Francisco Bhering s/n, in front of Posto 7, Arpoador* ☎ *021/99438–2980 surf and stand-up paddle, 021/9180–2287 stand-up paddle* ⊕ *www.surfrio.com.br* 🚇 *From R$120* Ⓜ *Cantagalo or Ipanema/General Osorio.*

Kitepoint Rio. One of several companies based in beach kiosks along Avenida do Pepê near Posto 7, Kitepoint provides all the equipment and training you'll need to master the sport of kite surfing. Wind conditions have to be just right, though, so patience is a virtue when seeking lessons. ⊠ *Av. do Pepê, Kiosk 7, next to Bombeiro, Barra da Tijuca* ☎ *021/8859–2112, 021/9200–0418* ⊕ *www.kitepointrio.com. br* ⊠ *From R$110* Ⓜ *No metro.*

SHOPPING

Rio shopping is most famous for its incomparable beachwear and gemstone jewelry, both of which are exported globally. Brazil is one of the world's largest suppliers of colored gemstones, with deposits of aquamarines, amethysts, diamonds, emeralds, rubellites, topazes, and tourmalines. If you're planning to go to Minas Gerais, do your jewelry shopping there; otherwise stick with shops that have certificates of authenticity and quality. Other good local buys include shoes, Havaianas flip-flops, arts and crafts, coffee, local music, and summer clothing in natural fibers. With lots of low-quality merchandise around, the trick to successful shopping in Rio is knowing where to find high-quality items at reasonable prices.

Ipanema is Rio's most fashionable shopping district. Its many exclusive boutiques are in arcades, with the majority along Rua Visconde de Pirajá. Leblon's shops, scattered among cafés, restaurants, and newspaper kiosks, are found mainly along Rua Ataulfo da Paiva. Copacabana has souvenir shops, bookstores, and branches of some of Rio's better shops along Avenida Nossa Senhora de Copacabana and connecting streets. For cheap fashion finds and Carnival costumes, head to the maze of shopping streets behind the Uruguaiana metro station.

CENTRO

BOOKS

Livraria Leonardo da Vinci. One of Rio's best sources for foreign-language titles, this bookstore has a wide selection of titles in English, Spanish, and French. ⊠ *Av. Rio Branco 185, Subsolo, Centro* ☎ *021/2533–2237* ⊕ *www.leonardodavinci.com.br* Ⓜ *Carioca.*

CAHAÇA

Lidador. Deli goods and more than 30 types of cachaça are sold at Lidador. ⊠ *Rua da Assembléia 65, Centro* ☎ *021/2533–4988* Ⓜ *Carioca.*

DEPARTMENT STORES

Lojas Americanas. Rio's largest chain department store sells casual clothing, toys, records, candy, cosmetics, and sporting goods. There are branches in virtually every neighborhood of the city, some of which are smaller "Express" stores. ⊠ *Rua do Passeio 42–56, Centro* ☎ *021/2524–0284* ⊕ *www.americanas.com.br* Ⓜ *Cinelândia.*

MARKETS

Feira de Antiquários da Praça 15 de Novembro. This open-air antiques fair held on Saturdays attracts more locals than tourists—it's a good place to pick up vintage clothing, sunglasses, rare vinyl, and antique furniture and jewelry. Arrive early to get the best buys, and be prepared to haggle.

Serious collectors arrive as early as 6 am, often with an eye to grabbing a bargain and reselling it a few hours later at a higher price. Sellers begin to close up shop by early afternoon. ✉ *Praça 15 de Novembro, Centro* ☉ *Sat. 7 am–2 pm.*

FAMILY
Fodor's Choice
★
Feira do Rio Antigo (*Rio Antiques Fair*). Vendors at this outdoor fair sell antiques, rare books, records, and all types of objets d'art on the first Saturday afternoon of the month. New and vintage fashion is also a strong suit. Live samba music and capoeira performances create a festival-like atmosphere, and the pavement bars and restaurants buzz with locals and visitors. ✉ *Rua do Lavradio, Centro* ☎ *021/2224–6693* ⊕ *www.polonovorioantigo.com.br* Ⓜ *Carioca or Cinelandia.*

FAMILY
Feira Nordestina (*Northeastern Fair*). The crowded, lively Feira de São Cristóvão, better known as the Feira Nordestina, is a social hub for Brazilians from the country's Northeast who live in Rio. They gather to hear their own distinctive music, eat regional foods, and buy arts, crafts, home furnishings, and clothing. With two stages for live music, the fair takes on a nightclub vibe after dark, and there are some seriously impressive displays of *forro* dancing. This fair is at its busiest and most exciting on the weekends. It's best to take a taxi here. ✉ *Campo de São Cristóvão, Pavilhão de São Cristóvão, 7 km (4½ miles) northwest of Centro, São Cristóvão* ☎ *021/2580–0501, 021/2580–5335* ⊕ *www.feiradesaocristovao.org.br* ☉ *Tues.–Thurs. 10–6, Fri. 10 am–Sun. 8 pm (continuously)* Ⓜ *São Cristóvão.*

MUSIC
Musical Carioca. A paradise for musicians and music lovers, Musical Carioca shares a street with many other music stores. Brazilian percussion instruments are also sold here. ✉ *Rua da Carioca 89, Centro* ☎ *021/2524–6029, 021/3814–3400* ⊕ *www.musicalcarioca.com.br.*

COPACABANA AND LEME

BEAUTY
Spa do Pé. If touring and shopping have left you in need of revival, stop by Spa do Pé for a massage, manicure, or a foot treatment. The Copacabana branch is one of several across the city. ✉ *Av. Nossa Senhora de Copacabana 680, Loja L, Copacabana* ☎ *021/2547–0459, 021/2523–8430* ⊕ *www.spadope.com.br* Ⓜ *Siqueira Campos.*

CENTERS AND MALLS
Shopping Center Cassino Atlântico. Antiques shops, jewelry stores, art galleries, and souvenir outlets predominate at this mall adjoining the Royal Rio Palace hotel. ✉ *Av. Nossa Senhora de Copacabana 1417, Copacabana* ☎ *021/2523–8709* Ⓜ *Ipanema/General Osorio.*

COFFEE
Pão de Açúcar. The upscale supermarket Pão de Açúcar is a good bet for coffee that's cheaper than you'd pay at a coffee shop. ✉ *Av. Nossa Senhora Copacabana 749, Copacabana* ☎ *021/2547–0372* ⊕ *www.pao deacucar.com.br* Ⓜ *Siqueira Campos.*

MARKETS

Avenida Atlântica. In the evening and on weekends along the median of Avenida Atlântica, artisans spread out their wares. You can find paintings, carvings, handicrafts, handmade clothing, and hammocks. ⊠ *Av. Atlântica, Copacabana* Ⓜ *Siqueira Campos.*

Feirarte. This street fair similar to the Sunday Feira Hippie in Ipanema takes place on weekends from 8 to 6. Handmade clothes, jewelry, and artsy knickknacks can be found here. ⊠ *Praça do Lido, Copacabana* Ⓜ *Cardeal Arcoverde.*

> ### BARGAINING IN RIO
>
> Bargaining in shops is unusual, but you can try your luck and ask if there's a discount for paying in cash, especially if it's a high-priced item. When granted, you can expect a 5% to 10% discount. Market or street-vendor shopping is a different story—bargain to your wallet's content.

SURF AND EXTREME SPORTS GEAR

Centauro. The massive Centauro store caters to the needs of all sorts of sporting enthusiasts. ⊠ *Shopping Leblon, Av. Afrânio de Melo Franco 290, Loja 106 and 107 A, Leblon* ☎ *021/2512–1246, 021/2512–1246* ⊕ *www.centauro.com.br.*

Galeria River. Stores at this youth-focused arcade sell all the clothing and equipment you'll need for a surfing or sporting vacation, as well as gear for climbing, rapelling, and other extreme sports. ⊠ *Rua Francisco Otaviano 67, Copacabana* ☎ *021/2267–1709* ⊕ *www.galeriariver.com. br* Ⓜ *Ipanema/General Osório.*

FLAMENGO AND BOTAFOGO

CENTERS AND MALLS

FAMILY **Rio Sul.** The popular Rio Sul retail complex has more than 400 stores, plus a cineplex, bars, and a giant food court where you can chow down on anything from sushi to coffee and cakes. ⊠ *Av. Lauro Müller 116, Botafogo* ☎ *021/2122–8070* ⊕ *www.riosul.com.br.*

SHOES, BAGS, AND ACCESSORIES

Mr. Cat. The stylish Mr. Cat carries handbags and leather shoes for men and women and has stores all over the city. ⊠ *Botafogo Praia Shopping, Praia de Botafogo 400, Lojas 124 and 125, Botafogo* ☎ *021/2552– 5333* ⊕ *www.mrcat.com.br* Ⓜ *Botafogo.*

Victor Hugo. A Uruguayan who began making handbags when he came to Brazil in the 1970s, Victor Hugo has become famous nationally for chic leather handbags that are similar in quality to those of more expensive brands such as Louis Vuitton, Gucci, and Prada. ⊠ *Shopping Rio Sul, Av. Lauro Müller 116, Loja B19, Botafogo* ☎ *021/2542–2999* ⊕ *www.victorhugo.com.br.*

IPANEMA AND LEBLON

ART

Gam Arte e Molduras. A good place to find high-quality modern and contemporary paintings and sculptures, this gallery, which ships items abroad for customers, also sells photographs that can be made to size. ⊠ *Rua Garcia D'Ávila 145, Loja C, Ipanema* ☎ *021/2247–8060* ⊕ *www.gamarteemolduras.com.br* Ⓜ *Ipanema/General Osório.*

BEACHWEAR

Bumbum Ipanema. Alcindo Silva Filho, better known as Cidinho, opened Bumbum in 1979 after deciding to create the smallest (and by some accounts, the sexiest) bikinis in town. Bumbum remains a solid beachwear brand, and today sells slightly more modest styles as well as the trademark teeny bikinis. ⊠ *Forum Ipanema, Rua Visconde de Pirajá 351, Loja B, Ipanema* ☎ *021/2227-4080* ⊕ *www.bumbum.com.br* Ⓜ *Ipanema/General Osório.*

Espaço Brazilian Soul. For funky T-shirts and high-quality swimsuits, go to Brazilian Soul. The two-floor department store sells pricey but hip clothes and accessories from Brazilian designers and carries international brands such as Osklen. ⊠ *Rua Prudente de Moraes 1102, Ipanema* ☎ *021/2522–3641* Ⓜ *Ipanema/General Osório.*

Garota de Ipanema Shop. Come here for killer bikinis as well as T-shirts, tanks, colorful beach bags, and everything else you'll need to look fabulous at the beach. ⊠ *Rua Vinicius de Moraes 53, Loja A, Ipanema* ☎ *021/2521–3168* ⊕ *www.garotadeipanemabrasil.com.br* Ⓜ *Ipanema/General Osório.*

Fodor'sChoice
★ **Lenny.** Upmarket swimwear store Lenny sells sophisticated, exquisitely cut pieces in a range of sizes, and lots of fashionable beach accessories. Prices are high, but the bikinis are particularly creative. ⊠ *Forum Ipanema, Rua Visconde de Pirajá 351, Loja 114/115, Ipanema* ☎ *021/ 2523–3796* ⊕ *www.lenny.com.br* Ⓜ *Ipanema/General Osório.*

Lenny Off. If you are looking for an affordably priced designer bikini and don't mind last season's models, check out Lenny Off, selling slashed-rate pieces from the celebrated bikini designer Lenny Niemeyer. ⊠ *Rua Carlos Góis 234, Loja H, Leblon* ☎ *021/2511–2739* ⊕ *www.lenny. com.br.*

BEAUTY

Farma Life. The drugstore Farma Life has a wide selection of beauty products. ⊠ *Av. Ataulfo de Paiva 285, Loja B/C, Leblon* ☎ *021/2239– 1178* ⊕ *www.farmalife.com.br.*

O Boticario. This shop carries soaps, lotions, perfumes, shampoos, and cosmetics made from native Brazilian plants and seeds. There are branches across the city, but the Ipanema branch is handy for post-beach shopping. ⊠ *Rua Visconde de Pirajá 371, Ipanema* ☎ *021/2287– 2944* ⊕ *www.oboticario.com.br* Ⓜ *Ipanema/General Osório.*

Shampoo Cosmeticos. This shop sells local and imported beauty products. ⊠ *Rua Visconde de Pirajá 581, Loja A, Ipanema* ☎ *021/2529–2518* ⊕ *www.shampoocosmeticos.com.br.*

BOOKS

Argumento. Its large selection of books in English has made this bookstore popular with expats and vacationers. There's also a CD section. The very fine Café Severino, in the back, has coffee, pastries, salads, crepes, and sandwiches. ✉ *Rua Dias Ferreira 417, Leblon* ☎ *021/2239–5294.*

CACHAÇA

Academia da Cachaça. You can buy close to 100 brands of cachaça here. The bar serves amazing caipirinhas and other cachaça-based drinks. ✉ *Rua Conde Bernadote 26, Loja G, Leblon* ☎ *021/2239–1542* ⊕ *www.academiadacachaca. com.br.*

THE BRAZILIAN BIKINI

Urban myth has it that Brazilian model Rose de Primo fashioned the Brazilian string bikini when she hurriedly sewed a bikini for a photo shoot with too little material. Whatever its history, the Tanga (string bikini) provides less than half the coverage of conventional bikinis, and makes the itsy bitsy teeny-weeny yellow polka-dot bikini look rather conservative. If you're looking to buy a Brazilian bikini but want a little more coverage, ask for a "sunkini." Happily for those reluctant to bare almost all, recent years have seen chic cariocas increasingly embrace one-piece swimwear.

Garapa Doida. At Garapa Doida you can learn how to prepare a good caipirinha and purchase everything you need to make it, including glasses, straws, barrels to conserve the alcohol, and cachaça from all over the country. ✉ *Rua Carlos Góis 234, Loja F, Leblon* ☎ *021/2274–8186.*

A Garrafeira. The charming liquor store Garrafeira sells a wide range of cachaça, including excellent versions from Minas Gerais State. ✉ *Rua Dias Ferreira 259, Loja A, Leblon* ☎ *021/2512–3336* ⊕ *www. agarrafeira.com.br.*

CENTERS AND MALLS

Shopping Leblon. International designers and chic local boutiques can be found at this upmarket fashion mall in Leblon. There is some seriously good food to be found in the food court—think fine dining rather than fast food—and the mall has free Wi-Fi and a modern four-screen cineplex. ✉ *Av. Afrânio de Melo Franco 290, Leblon* ☎ *021/2430–5122* ⊕ *www.shoppingleblon.com.br* Ⓜ *No metro.*

CLOTHING

Alessa. For fashion-forward designs, visit Alessa. Pay special attention to Alessa's fabulously fun underwear, which makes for great presents. ✉ *Rua Nascimento Silva 399, Ipanema* ☎ *021/2287–9939* ⊕ *www. alessa.com.br* Ⓜ *Ipanema/General Osorio.*

Animale. A favorite among local fashionistas, Animale carries casual wear and formal wear that's both sophisticated and sexy. If you want to make an impression in Rio's social scene, head here for slinky dresses, chic cover-ups, and showstopping shoes and accessories. ✉ *Rua Joana Angelica 116, Ipanema* ☎ *021/2227–3336* ⊕ *www.animale.com.br* Ⓜ *Ipanema/General Osório.*

Farm. Fun colors and bold patterns make Farm popular with cariocas. It's a great place to find feminine dresses and cute tops. ⊠ *Rua Visconde de Pirajá 365, Loja C–D, 202–204, Ipanema* ☎ *021/3813–3817* ⊕ *www.farmrio.com.br* Ⓜ *Ipanema/General Osório.*

Osklen. The Osklen brand is synonymous with fashionable sportswear, and all the clothes and accessories are designed to help you look good in the great outdoors. The brand is popular with sports-loving locals, and there are several stores in Rio. ⊠ *Rua Maria Quitéria 85, Ipanema* ☎ *021/2227–2911* ⊕ *www.osklen.com.br* Ⓜ *Ipanema/General Osório.*

Richards. A classic Brazilian clothing store selling tasteful, well-made pieces, Richards was originally just for men but now also carries women's clothing and children's wear. It's the place to go to for good-quality linen clothing. ⊠ *Rua Maria Quiteria 95, Ipanema* ☎ *021/2522–1245* ⊕ *www.richards.com.br* Ⓜ *Ipanema/General Osório.*

COFFEE

Armazém do Café. The "Coffee Store" chain has several branches in Rio, including ones in Ipanema and Leblon where you can enjoy a cappuccino or espresso and a pastry at the café before browsing the coffees and coffee-making devices for sale. ⊠ *Rua Visconde de Pirajá 595, Loja 101/102, Ipanema* ☎ *021/3874–2920* ⊕ *www.armazemdocafe.com.br* Ⓜ *Ipanema/General Osório.*

Zona Sul. Branches of this upscale supermarket can be found throughout Rio's South Zone, and they're good places to pick up deli goods, coffee, chocolate, and fresh fruit and vegetables. The promotional prices displayed usually apply only to those holding Zona Sul loyalty cards. ⊠ *Prudente de Morais 49, Ipanema* ☎ *021/2267–0361* Ⓜ *Ipanema/General Osório.*

JEWELRY

Amsterdam Sauer. One of Rio's top names in jewelry, this is the perfect place to pick up an elegant gift. The on-site gemstone museum is open weekdays between 10 and 6 and Saturday between 9 and 2 for free guided tours that can be booked online. ⊠ *Rua Visconde de Pirajá 484, Ipanema* ☎ *021/3539–0165, 021/2512–9878 for the museum* ⊕ *www.amsterdamsauer.com* ⊗ *Closed Sun.* Ⓜ *Ipanema/General Osório.*

Francesca Romana Diana. The store's namesake designer, who has five shops in Rio, creates great gold and silver jewelry and works with semiprecious stones. Check out the wonderful bangles featuring the famous Copacabana or Ipanema sidewalk pattern. ⊠ *Rua Visconde de Pirajá 547, Ipanema* ☎ *021/2274–8511* ⊕ *www.francescaromanadiana.com.*

H.Stern. The award-winning designers at H.Stern create distinctive contemporary pieces—the inventory runs to about 300,000 items. The shops downstairs sell more affordable pieces and folkloric items. Around the corner at the company's world headquarters, you can see exhibits of rare stones and watch craftspeople transform rough stones into sparkling jewels. ⊠ *Rua Visconde de Pirajá 490, Ipanema* ☎ *0800/227–442* ⊕ *www.hstern.com.br* Ⓜ *Ipanema/General Osorio.*

Sobral. Visit Sobral for chunky, colorful resin jewelry, accessories, and decorative items, including its signature multicolored replicas of the

THE 7 WONDERS OF RIO SHOPPING

Arts and crafts. The hills of Santa Teresa brim with arts and crafts stores selling paintings, colorful wooden animals, and other works by local artists. (R$10 and up)

Brazilian soccer shirt. You just can't leave Brazil without one of the country's most emblematic gifts. (R$35 and up)

Cachaça. While showing your friends your vacation pictures, you can impress them with a caipirinha made with genuine cachaça. (R$10 and up)

Chic swimwear. You can show off your Rio tan back home in a daringly revealing bikini—Lenny and Bumbum have some of the best designs—or a more modest, but still sexy, one-piece suit. (R$90 and up)

Gilson Martins bag. Whatever style or size you buy from the hip designer's stores will make a cool souvenir or gift. (R$30 and up)

Havaianas. The brand's stores in Ipanema and Centro sell its flip-flops at such low prices, how can you not take home a bagful? (R$17 and up)

Mini-Cristo. Sobral makes a colorful miniversion of one of the seven wonders of the modern world. (R$50)

Christ statue. Reclaimed materials are used to make the store's funky goods, and its owners invest in social projects such as jewelry-making classes for young people in disadvantaged communities. ⊠ *Forum Ipanema, Rua Visconde de Pirajá 351, Loja 105, Ipanema* 🕾 *021/2267–0009* ⊕ *www.rsobral.com.br* Ⓜ *Ipanema/General Osório.*

MARKETS

FAMILY **Feira Hippie** (*Hippie Fair*). The colorful handicrafts street fair takes place on Sundays between 9 am and 7 pm. Shop for high-quality jewelry, hand-painted dresses, paintings, wood carvings, leather bags and sandals, rag dolls, knickknacks, furniture, and samba percussion instruments, among many other items. It's fun to browse here even if you're not looking to buy anything. ⊠ *Praça General Osório, Ipanema* ⊕ *www.feirahippieipanema.net* Ⓜ *Ipanema/General Osório.*

MUSIC

Fodor's Choice **Toca do Vinicius.** Tiny Toca do Vinicius bills itself as a "cultural space
★ and bossa nova salon," and indeed the shop feels like more than just a place of business. Bossa nova aficionados from around the world gather here, and if you're one of them, there's a good chance you'll leave with the email address of at least one new pal. You'll also find sheet music, T-shirts, CDs, and books on music, including a few in English. One Sunday a month the shop hosts an intimate bossa nova concert. ⊠ *Rua Vinicius de Moraes 129, Loja C, Ipanema* 🕾 *021/2247–5227* ⊕ *www.tocadovinicius.com.br* Ⓜ *Ipanema/General Osório.*

SHOES, BAGS, AND ACCESSORIES

Constança Basto. Costly women's shoes made of crocodile and snake leather in original styles are the specialty of Constança Basto. ⊠ *Shopping Leblon, Av. Ataulfo de Paiva 290, Loja 311j, Leblon* 🕾 *021/2511–8801.*

Fodor's Choice ★ **Gilson Martins.** The shops of one of Brazil's most gifted and acclaimed designers sell his colorful Rio-inspired bags and accessories at affordable prices. ⊠ *Rua Visconde de Pirajá 462, Ipanema* ☎ *021/2227-6178* ⊕ *www.gilsonmartins.com.br* Ⓜ *Ipanema/General Osorio.*

Havaianas Store. The Ipanema Havaianas store carries the fun and funky flip-flops in all colors, styles, and sizes, for men, women, and kids. The range is staggering, from classic Brazil-flag designs to limited-edition gem-encrusted versions. The prices start at R$15 and creep over R$100. Alongside the legendary flops, the store also sells canvas deck shoes and sturdier sandals, as well as opinion-dividing "flip flop socks." Other locations around town include one in Centro. ⊠ *Rua Farme de Amoedo 76A, Ipanema* ☎ *021/2267-7395* ⊕ *br.havaianas.com* Ⓜ *Ipanema/General Osório.*

Via Mia. You'll find a large selection of reasonably priced shoes, bags, and accessories at Via Mia. ⊠ *Rua Anibal de Mendonça 55, Loja F, Ipanema* ☎ *021/2274-9996* ⊕ *www.viamia.com.br* Ⓜ *Ipanema/General Osorio.*

INLAND ZONA SUL

ART
Contorno. The gallery Contorno exhibits and sells an eclectic selection of Brazilian art. ⊠ *Gávea Trade Center, Rua Marquês de São Vicente 124, Loja 102, Gávea* ☎ *021/2274-3832* ⊕ *www.contornoartes.com.br.*

CENTERS AND MALLS
Shopping da Gávea. The brand-name stores and smaller boutiques at the fashionable Shopping da Gávea mall sell designer fashions, accessories, and swimwear, and there are several good cafés and coffee shops. ⊠ *Rua Marquês de São Vicente 52, Gávea* ☎ *021/2294-1096* ⊕ *www.shoppingdagavea.com.br.*

HANDICRAFTS
Fodor's Choice ★ **O Sol Artesanato.** Exhibiting Brazilian craftsmanship at its finest, O Sol is a nonprofit, nongovernmental shop promoting and selling the handiwork of artisans from all regions of Brazil. It's one of Rio's best handicraft stores, and well worth a visit. ⊠ *Rua Corcovado 213, Jardim Botânico* ☎ *021/2294-6198.*

Pé de Boi. A popular arts and crafts store that carries woodwork pieces, ceramics, weaving, and sculptures created by artists from around Brazil, Pé de Boi specializes in objects from the states of Pernambuco and Minas Gerais. ⊠ *Rua Ipiranga 55, Laranjeiras* ☎ *021/2285-4395* ⊕ *www.pedeboi.com.br.*

MARKETS
Babilônia Feira Hype (*Babylon Hype Fair*). This fair that takes place roughly every couple of months combines fashion, design, art, and gastronomy. It's good not only for shopping, but also for watching the parade of beautiful people. ⊠ *Clube Monte Líbano, Avenida Borges de Medeiros s/n, Leblon* ☎ *021/2267-0066* ⊕ *www.babiloniafeirahype.com.br* 🖾 *R$10.*

FAMILY
Fodor's Choice
★
Feira de General Glicério. Browse for local crafts, enjoy delicious snacks, sip a caipirinha, and listen to the delicate sounds of live *choro* at this laid-back Saturday street market in the leafy residential neighborhood of Laranjeiras. Vendors selling fruit and veggies set up stalls on the streets surrounding a small neighborhood square, but the main focus of attention are the clothing and crafts stalls on the square itself, as well as food and drink sellers and the famous Barraca do Luiz—a tent selling caipirinhas and rare music CDs as choro bands perform nearby. Come early: the market opens at 10 am and the fun is over by midafternoon. ⊠ *Rua General Glicério, Laranjeiras* Ⓜ *No metro.*

SANTA TERESA

CLOTHING

Eu Amo Vintage. Bohemian Santa Teresa is a hotbed of vintage fashions, and the style-savvy team behind I Love Vintage has put together the biggest and best collection of all. If you find yourself envying the effortless, thrift store–chic of the neighborhood's gals and guys about town, the staff here can help you join their ranks. The store sits right behind the lively Bar do Gomez, so you can slip into your new threads and instantly fit in with the bar's hipster throngs. ⊠ *Rua Monte Alegre 374, Loja R, Santa Teresa* ☎ *021/2221–2855* ⊕ *blogeuamovintage.blogspot.co.uk.*

HANDICRAFTS

La Vereda. Head to this Santa Teresa arts and crafts store for colorful ceramics, ornate mirrors, and original works by local artists. For the quality and inventiveness of the objects it sells, La Vereda warrants a lengthy browsing session. ⊠ *Rua Almirante Alexandrino 428, Santa Teresa* ☎ *021/2507–0317* ⊕ *www.lavereda.com.br.*

SÃO CONRADO AND BARRA DA TIJUCA

CENTERS AND MALLS

Barra Shopping. By far Rio's largest mall, this is the place to come for a serious shopping spree. There are some 600 stores here, ranging from high-street names such as C&A to small and seriously chic boutique fashion, jewelry, and lingerie stores. A branch of the legendary bikini store Bumbum Ipanema is here, and there's a wealth of good dining options. ⊠ *Av. das Américas 4666, Barra da Tijuca* ☎ *021/4003–4131* ⊕ *www.barrashopping.com.br.*

São Conrado Fashion Mall. The shops at Rio's least crowded and most sophisticated mall sell domestic and international fashions to a clientele that knows how to splurge. High-end Brazilian and international labels can be found here, and there are some very decent restaurants as well as a four-screen movie theater. ⊠ *Estrada da Gávea 899, São Conrado* ☎ *021/2111–4444* ⊕ *www.fashionmall.com.br/contato.asp.*

SIDE TRIPS FROM RIO

Updated By
Lucy Bryson

Rio's frenetic pace can be as exhausting as it is exhilarating, so it's handy that the city is surrounded by idyllic beaches and peaceful historic towns that are perfect for recharging the batteries. Just a couple of hours' drive east is the chic beach resort of Búzios, with its 23 beaches, boutiques and lively nightlife, while to the west is the unspoiled, untamed beauty of Ilha Grande. Nearby lies Paraty, Brazil's best preserved colonial town.

The Costa do Sol (Sun Coast), famed for its beautiful beaches, enjoys more sunny days than anywhere else in Rio de Janeiro State. Here, the hip resort town of Búzios is a playground for Rio de Janeiro's *gente bonita* (beautiful people), who come to relax on the beaches by day and socialize in the stylish bars and clubs by night. En route to Búzios is the quieter beach resort of Arraial do Cabo, an unpretentious fishing town known as the "Caribbean of Brazil" because of its crystal clear waters and white-sand beaches.

Sitting west of the city on the verdant Costa Verde (Green Coast), pretty Paraty's pedestrianized historical center has changed little since the 18th century. The vast nature-reserve island of Ilha Grande, just off the Green Coast, provides virtually unlimited opportunities for beach hopping, hiking on nature trails, and just relaxing.

Heading inland from Rio, the stifling temperatures drop a little as steep mountain roads deliver you to the imperial city of Petrópolis, summer residence of Emperor Pedro II.

ORIENTATION AND PLANNING

GETTING ORIENTED

The Sun Coast. En-route to the gorgeous beaches and scorched mountains of the Costa do Sol is the small city of Niterói, whose ancient forts stand in stark contrast to its contemporary Museu de Arte Contemporânea. Farther east is the coastal town of Cabo Frio, one of the country's oldest settlements, and the small village of Arraial do Cabo, whose clear turquoise waters make it one of Brazil's top spots for diving. Nearby Búzios, with its many beaches, year-round sunshine and vibrant nightlife, is a popular weekend holiday destination for wealthy *cariocas* as well as foreign visitors to Rio.

North of Rio de Janeiro. Northeast of Rio de Janeiro lies Petrópolis, whose opulent imperial palace was once the emperor's summer home. A twisting road through the mountains takes you to Teresópolis, named for Empress Teresa Christina. Nestled between these two towns is Parque Nacional da Serra dos Órgãos, famous for its curious rock formations.

TOP REASONS TO GO

Glamorous Búzios: Hang out with the young and beautiful on the beach at Búzios in the morning, then enjoy the sunset on Orla Bardot.

Water Sports: Sail a schooner to a deserted island for some scuba diving, then watch the dolphins play in your wake on the way home.

Mountain Excursions: Get lost in time at the Imperial Museum in mountainous Petrópolis.

Glorious Ilha Grande: Take an early-morning hike through the Atlantic rain forests of Ilha Grande.

Historic Paraty: Stroll the cobbled streets of this colonial town, before boarding a sailboat for an island-hopping afternoon.

Fresh Beach Food: Tuck into freshly caught sardines at beach kiosks in Búzios and Arraial do Cabo, washing them down with coconut water sipped straight from the shell.

The Green Coast. West of Rio de Janeiro, the Costa Verde sees wild jungle tumbling down rocky mountains to a seemingly endless string of beaches. Angra dos Reis is the jumping-off point for 365 islands that pepper a picturesque bay. The largest, Ilha Grande, is a short boat ride from Angra dos Reis or nearby Conceição de Jacareí. Paraty, a UNESCO World Heritage Site, is a perfectly preserved colonial town farther down the coast whose proximity to secluded beaches makes it one of the region's highlights.

PLANNING

WHEN TO GO
The towns along the Costa do Sol and Costa Verde are packed solid between Christmas and Carnival, so reservations should be made well in advance. The populations of Paraty and Búzios can more than double as young people arrive from nearby Rio de Janeiro and São Paulo on the weekend. Paraty books up well ahead of its annual literary festival (July) and cachaça festival (August).

The weather along the coast is fairly predictable: summers are hot. During low season, from March to June and September to November, the weather is milder and there is plenty of elbow room on the beach. To top it off, prices can be half of what they are in high season. In the interior, Petrópolis and Teresópolis provide a refreshing change from the oppressive heat of the coast.

PLANNING YOUR TIME
The many attractions of Rio de Janeiro fan out in all directions from the city itself, so it makes sense to focus your time on one region, whether it be the mountainous inland, the Sun Coast, or the Green Coast. Whichever direction you head, trips along the coast invariably merit a few days. Anyone heading down the Costa Verde should allow for at least a couple of nights' stay on lovely Ilha Grande, and once back on the mainland, it's a couple of hours' scenic drive to Paraty. While the

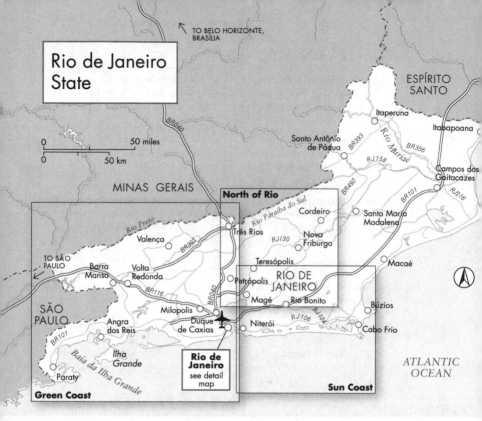

highlights of this historic town can be seen in one day and night, those who can spare the time may well want to head to the tranquil beach village of Trindade nearby.

The highlights of Rio's sister city, Niterói, can be seen in a morning or afternoon, and sun lovers will want to set aside at least a couple of nights to visit the beach resorts that lie farther up the coast. The aptly named Costa do Sol is home to some of the best beaches in the state. Make your base in Búzios, where chic accommodation options abound, and take a day trip to the beaches of Cabo Frio and Arraial do Cabo as well as setting aside at least one full day to take a boat trip to some of Búzios's best beaches. Partiers should allow time in their schedules for late nights and lazy mornings.

The mountainous north is often visited as a day trip from Rio, taking in the imperial town of Petrópolis, but hikers and climbers may want to spend a couple of days scaling the peaks that surround nearby Teresópolis.

GETTING HERE AND AROUND
While most resort towns boast an airport of some kind, the area is small enough that few people fly to destinations within the state. The roads along the coasts and to the towns in the mountains tend to be well maintained, so most Brazilians travel by car or bus. Check weather

conditions before heading to the mountains, however, as heavy rains can cause serious landslips.

Along the Green Coast, collective transfer services such as Easy Transfer provide door-to-door services, complete with boat connections that are a convenient and cost-effective way to travel in the region. At the beach resorts of Búzios, driving from beach to beach in a buggy is great fun, and the cost of renting works out to be a reasonable value.

Driving within the city of Rio can be a daunting experience, but outside the city it's fairly easy to get around. The roads, especially to the major tourist destinations, are well signposted. Buses are cheap, comfortable, and efficient, but the vast terminal in Rio can be uncomfortably hot and the surrounding area is a little edgy. It's best to leave plenty of time to buy tickets and locate your boarding point. Don't rely on using the ATMs here as they are frequently out of service. Note that non-Brazilians may have problems buying advance tickets online, as a CPF (Brazilian social security number) is usually required. At popular times, it may be preferable to arrange a group or private transfer, or to book through a travel agent.

■ TIP➜ Avoid leaving the city on Friday afternoons when residents flee the city en masse and the traffic is horrific. For the same reason, try to avoid returning on a Monday.

BUS TRAVEL

As a rule, private buses in Rio such as Autoviacao 1001 and Costa Verde tend to be clean, punctual, air-conditioned, and comfortable. Buses leave from the Rodoviária Novo Rio, and most destinations are within three hours of the city. Expect to catch a taxi from the bus station to your hotel.

Outside the city, local bus service within towns, or districts, tends to be regular and cheap, but buses rarely have air-conditioning and are not well maintained. There are few routes, and the bus driver will either nod or shake his head if you tell him where you want to go. You can buy your ticket on the bus, but don't use large notes. Bus terminals and stands are easy to spot. Beware of pickpockets if the stand or bus is particularly crowded.

Bus Contacts Autoviacao 1001. ✉ *Estrada Velha Da Usina 444, Centro, Búzios* ☎ *022/2623-2050* ⊕ *www.autoviacao1001.com.br.* **Costa Verde.** ✉ *Rio de Janeiro* ☎ *021/3622-3123* ⊕ *www.costaverdetransportes.com.br.* **Easy Transfer.** ✉ *Rio de Janeiro* ☎ *21/ 99386-3919* ⊕ *www.easytransferbrazil.com.* **Rodoviária Novo Rio.** ✉ *Av. Francisco Bicalho 1, Santo Cristo, Rio de Janeiro* ☎ *021/3213-1800* ⊕ *www.novorio.com.br* Ⓜ *No metro.*

CAR TRAVEL

The roads in Rio de Janeiro State are generally in good condition and well marked, especially in the areas frequented by holidaymakers. If you plan to travel around and spend a few nights in different towns, it makes sense to rent a car in Rio, although it can be a bit tricky finding your way out of the city. Remember that if you travel to Ilha Grande, you will have to leave your car on the mainland, so be sure to remove all valuables.

■ **TIP➜** Car-rental prices in resort towns can be exorbitant, so if you plan to rent a car, do it in Rio. In Cabo Frio and Búzios, it is a better value and more fun to rent a beach buggy—numerous agencies offer this service.

RESTAURANTS

The food here is nothing if not eclectic. Expect to find sushi bars, Italian restaurants, and German *biergartens* sitting alongside restaurants selling typical Brazilian cuisine. Coastal towns serve a large selection of fresh seafood, and most have a local specialty that's worth trying. Beachfront restaurants, especially the ubiquitous *baracas* (kiosks), can be a pleasant surprise and most will bring food and drink right up to your chosen spot on the sands.

Paraty and Búzios have excellent restaurants serving international cuisine. During high season they fill up beginning at 10 pm and may not close until after sunrise. Restaurants in Petrópolis and Teresópolis serve European cuisine and *comida mineira*, the hearty, meaty fare from Minas Gerais. Generally, dinner starts at seven and restaurants close around midnight.

■ **TIP➜** To be on the safe side, don't buy seafood from venders strolling along the beach. Be especially careful about the oysters in Búzios and Cabo Frio, which may not be as fresh as the vendor claims.

HOTELS

There are hotels for all budgets and all tastes, from beachfront *pousadas* offering simple rooms with barely more than a bed and a ceiling fan to boutique hotels with luxurious amenities and on-site spas. Paraty and Petrópolis have gorgeous 18th-century inns, some of which can be a bit drafty in winter. *Hotel reviews have been shortened. For full information, visit Fodors.com.*

WHAT IT COSTS IN REALS			
$	**$$**	**$$$**	**$$$$**
Restaurants	under R$31	R$31–R$45	R$46–R$60	over R$60
Hotels	under R$251	R$251–R$375	R$376–R$500	over R$500

Restaurant prices are the average cost of a main course at dinner or, if dinner is not served, at lunch. Hotel prices are the lowest cost of a standard double room in high season, excluding tax.

TOURS

Fodor's Choice **Cruz the Coast Brazil.** A fun way for time-pressed travelers to see as
★   much of Rio's coastline as possible is to take a bus tour with Cruz the Coast Brazil. This hassle-free hop-on, hop-off service makes a four-day loop from Rio to Paraty and Ilha Grande, or from Rio to Cabo Frio and Búzios, with all travel and accommodations prearranged and excursions such as boating trips, surfing lessons and even Portuguese classes included. ✉ *Rio de Janeiro* ☎ *021/97827–3256* ⊕ *www. cruzthecoastbrazil.com* ✍ *From R$400 for Rio State Loops.*

Rio Xtreme. Rio Xtreme offers group and private adventure tours and activities in Rio de Janeiro State. The friendly, English-speaking guides and instructors can take you scuba diving in Cabo Frio, zip-lining in

A Bit of History

The history of Rio de Janeiro State is as colorful as it is bloody. The first Portuguese trading post was established in 1502 in Cabo Frio to facilitate the export of *Pau-Brasil* (brazilwood). This led to confrontations with Tamoios Indians and their French allies.

The discovery of gold in the state of Minas Gerais in 1696 and the construction of the "Caminho de Ouro" (Path of Gold) from the mines to Paraty brought prosperity. In its wake came pirates and corsairs who used the islands and bays of Angra dos Reis as cover while they plundered the ships bound for Rio de Janeiro.

The mines gave out in the late 1700s, but the relatively new crop called coffee, introduced to the state around 1770, brought another boom. In the mid-19th century the state produced more than 70% of Brazil's coffee. Sadly, vast tracts of Atlantic rain forest were destroyed to make room for the crop across the interior of the state.

In 1808, threatened by Napoléon, King Dom Joáo VI of Portugal moved his court to Rio. He returned to Portugal in 1821 and left his son, Dom Pedro I, behind as prince regent. The following year Dom Pedro I was called back to Portugal, but he refused to leave. Instead, he declared Brazil an independent state and himself its emperor. In 1847, his son, Dom Pedro II, inaugurated Petrópolis as the summer capital of Brazil.

Rio, or hiking through thick jungle on Ilha Grande. Climbing tours in and around Teresópolis and Petrópolis can be arranged on demand. ☏ *021/98516–1146* ⊕ *www.rioxtreme.com* ✉ *From R$200.*

THE SUN COAST

This stretch of coastline is where you'll find the resort towns of Cabo Frio, Arraial do Cabo, and Búzios. The most popular of the three is Búzios, reminiscent of the French Riviera gone tropical. On its 8-km (5-mile) peninsula are 23 beaches. Cabo Frio is a family town famous for its bikini shops and blue water. Arraial do Cabo, jutting into the Atlantic Ocean, still retains the rustic charms of a fishing village. The wind blows year-round, and sports such as windsurfing, kitesurfing, and sailing are popular.

NITERÓI

14 km (9 miles) east of Rio.

Cariocas joke that the best thing about Niterói is the view—on a clear day you can see Rio de Janeiro with the Corcovado and Sugarloaf across the bay. But Niterói has the last laugh, as the city is ranked as having the highest quality of life in the state.

Catch a ferry from Rio's Praça 15 de Novembro and cross the bay in 20 minutes. From the Praça Araribóia or at the Terminal Hidroviário de

Charitas, walk along the esplanade to the Forte de Gragoatá and then walk to Museu de Arte Contemporânea, whose Oscar Niemeyer–designed building and views of Rio are more impressive than the art exhibitions, which rarely thrill. Icaraí beach attracts local beach lovers, and offers spectacular panoramic views of Rio. If you have time, enjoy a beer on the beach and watch the sunset over Sugarloaf and the Corcovado. Don't plan to spend more than one afternoon in Niterói. Instead head up the Costa do Sol to Búzios or Cabo Frio. The tourist office is located next to the ferry terminal.

> **POUSADA DEFINED**
>
> Wherever you travel in Rio de Janeiro State, you're likely to stay in a *pousada*. The name translates as "rest stop," and a pousada may be anything from a simple guesthouse to a luxury boutique lodging with pool and spa. The one thing all pousadas have in common is that they are independently run and managed. Generally smaller than hotels, they tend to offer more personalized service. For detailed listings of quality pousadas throughout Brazil, visit the website of Hidden Pousadas Brazil ⊕ *www.hiddenpousadasbrazil.com*.

GETTING HERE AND AROUND

The best way to get to Niterói is by passenger ferry from the Praça 15 de Novembro in Rio de Janeiro. The trip takes about 20 minutes with CCR Barcas boats (R$4.80). Don't travel here by car unless you have somebody driving for you. The roads in Niterói are even more confusing than in Rio. Viação Mauá's Bus 100 (R$4.35) departs for Niterói from Praça 15 de Novembro (in front of the ferry terminal). The trip takes 15 minutes, not counting traffic delays, which can be severe during rush hour.

ESSENTIALS

Boat Contact CCR Barcas. ⊠ *Praça Araribóia 6–8, Niterói* ☎ *0800/721-1012 toll-free information line* ⊕ *www.grupoccr.com.br/barcas.*

Bus Contact Viação Mauá. ☎ *021/2607-0485* ⊕ *www.vmaua.com.br.*

Taxi Contact Rádio Táxi Niterói. ⊠ *Niterói* ☎ *021/2610-0609.*

Visitor Information Niterói Tourism Office. ⊠ *Estrada Leopoldo Fróes 773, Niterói* ☎ *021/2710-2727* ⊕ *www.neltur.com.br.*

EXPLORING

Fortaleza de Santa Cruz. Built in 1555, the impressive Fortaleza de Santa Cruz was the first fort on Guanabara Bay. The cannons are distributed over two levels, but more impressive are the 17th-century sun clock and Santa Barbara Chapel. The views over Rio de Janeiro span out in all directions, so keep your camera on hand. It takes 15 minutes by taxi to reach the fort from downtown Niterói, and costs about R$35. The on-site restaurant serves good coffee and light meals. ⊠ *Estrada General Eurico Gaspar Dutra, Jurujuba, Niterói* ☎ *021/2710-2354* ⊠ *R$6* ⊙ *Tues.–Sun. 9–4.*

Fodor's Choice
★

Museu de Arte Contemporânea. Designed by the late, great modernist architect Oscar Niemeyer, the cliff-top Museum of Contemporary Art looks like a spaceship that has touched down to admire the views. The

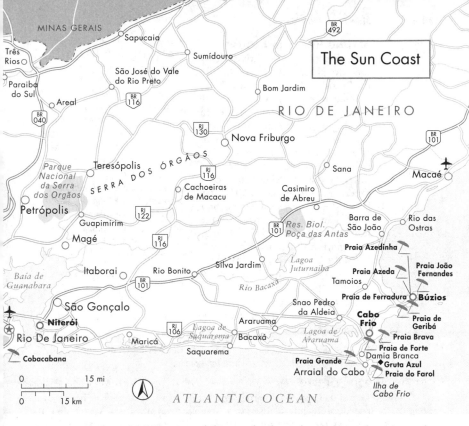

museum's visiting art exhibits tend to be underwhelming, but it's worth a trip here just to see the building. The museum is a five-minute cab ride from Praça Araribóia, by the ferry terminal in downtown Niterói, or take the 47B bus. The on-site bistro is a good spot for lunch. ✉ *Mirante de Boa Viagem s/n, Niterói* ☎ *021/2620–2400* ✇ *www.macniteroi.com. br* 🖃 *R$10, free Wed.* ☉ *Tues.–Sun. 10–6.*

CABO FRIO

155 km (101 miles) east of Rio.

One of the oldest settlements in Brazil, Cabo Frio was established in the early 1500s as a port from which wood was shipped to Portugal. Today it's best known for its beaches with clear blue waters, its party scene, and its water sports. However, it has recently been dogged by crime problems, and the town itself is less than beautiful. Of far greater appeal is the smaller and more tranquil Arraial do Cabo, with its crystal clear waters—making it a top spot for diving—and icing-sugar beaches.

Hotels in Cabo Frio are both less appealing and more expensive than those in nearby Búzios. If you are looking for chic lodgings, you're better off staying in Búzios and taking a day trip to Cabo Frio.

GETTING HERE AND AROUND

From Rio de Janeiro, drive across the Rio–Niterói Bridge (officially the President Costa e Silva Bridge) and bear left, following the BR 101. At Rio Bonito take the exit to the Region dos Lagos and follow the signs to Cabo Frio. The trip takes approximately two-and-a-half hours—expect to be held up in traffic outside Niterói for some time. Cabo Frio–bound 1001 buses leave the Rodoviária every half hour. The trip takes around three hours and costs R$57. Tourist information desks at Cabo Frio's bus station can provide maps. Shuttle transfers from Rio hotels and airports can be arranged for around R$100—speak to hotel staff.

> ## BATHING BEAUTIES
>
> No visit to Cabo Frio is complete without a walk past the bikini shops along Rua das Biquínis. Local lore has it that everything began with a woman selling her homemade bathing suits on the street here. Today more than 70 stores—the largest collection of bikini stores in Latin America, according to the Guinness World Records—sell all manner of beach fashions. In summer, many shops stay open past midnight.

ESSENTIALS

Bus Contact Terminal Rodoviário Cabo Frio. ☒ *Av. Julia Kubitschek s/n, Parque Riviera, Cabo Frio.*

Taxi Contact Associação dos Taxistas de Cabo Frio. ☒ *Cabo Frio* ☎ *022/2645–5463* ⊕ *www.cabofriotaxi.com.br.*

EXPLORING

FAMILY
Fodor's Choice
★

Arraial do Cabo. Nicknamed the "Caribbean of Brazil" in honor of its translucent white sands and crystal clear warm waters, Arraial do Cabo is a favorite destination for divers and sunseekers alike and lies just 10 km (6 miles) south of Cabo Frio. The village is surrounded by gorgeous beaches and craggy rock formations—don't miss the Gruta Azul—a 15-meter-tall cave over the blue sea. PADI-accredited dive schools can be found in abundance here, and skippers wait at the harbor to whisk visitors to the best beaches and vantage points, often stopping for lunch at a floating restaurant. The sunsets over the small beach Prainha Pontal do Atalaia are often quite stunning. There's a handful of pousadas here, but there are cheaper and better options in nearby Búzios, which is a quick bus or cab ride away. ☒ *Arraial do Cabo, Cabo Frio.*

BEACHES

FAMILY
Praia do Forte. The longest and most famous of Cabo Frio's beaches, Praia do Forte is very popular with families for its soft sands and gentle waves. On summer weekends it's jammed with colorful beach umbrellas, swimmers, sun lovers, and food kiosks that extend their services to tables on the sand. Praia do Forte is also very popular with partiers and after dark, during the summer, live music (and dancing) take over the beach. **Amenities:** food and drink. **Best for:** swimming; partiers. ☒ *Avenida do Contôrno, Cabo Frio.*

Praia do Foguete. This beach is famous for its almost transparent soft white sand and the equally clear waters that shelter sea creatures such as turtles, dolphins, and even penguins. The 6-km (4-mile) strand is almost deserted in low season, and while even in summer the water is chilly, the constant strong breeze here creates waves that are perfect for surfing and bodyboarding. During summer, a few vendors operate kiosks with food and drink, but if you visit between March and November you should bring your own refreshments. **Amenities:** food and drink (in summer). **Best for:** solitude; surfing. ✉ *Foguete, Cabo Frio.*

WHERE TO STAY

$$ HOTEL FAMILY 🏨 **Malibu Palace Hotel.** Cabo Frio's most convenient option for partiers and beachgoers sits across the avenue from Praia do Forte and mere blocks from the shops and restaurants of the town center. **Pros:** rooms have great views; hotel provides umbrellas on the beach; delicious breakfast. **Cons:** can be noisy at night; somewhat rowdy area; property showing signs of wear and tear. [$] *Rooms from: R$300* ✉ *Av. do Contorno 900, Praia do Forte, Cabo Frio* ☎ *022/2647–8000* 🌐 *www.malibupalace.com.br* 🛏 *102 rooms, 6 suites* 🍴 *Breakfast.*

SPORTS AND THE OUTDOORS

TOUR OPERATORS

Over Sea Dive Center. This PADI-accredited diving school and trip operator offers highly professional service, with modern boats, well-maintained equipment, and enthusiastic English-speaking staff. Over Sea Dive Center runs dive trips to the best spots around Cabo Frio and farther afield. ✉ *Rua Jose Augusto Saraiva 2, Ilha da Draga, Cabo Frio* ☎ *22/2647–5375* 🌐 *www.overseadivecenter.com.br* 🎟 *Dives from R$200.*

BÚZIOS

24 km (15 miles) northeast of Cabo Frio; 176 km (126 miles) northeast of Rio.

Fodor's Choice ★ Around two hours from Rio de Janeiro, Búzios is a string of beautiful beaches on an 8-km-long (5-mile-long) peninsula. It was the quintessential sleepy fishing village until the 1960s, when the French actress Brigitte Bardot holidayed here to escape the paparazzi and the place almost instantly transformed into a vacation sensation. Búzios has something for everyone. Some hotels cater specifically to families and provide plenty of activities and around-the-clock child care. Many have spa facilities, and some specialize in weeklong retreats. For outdoor enthusiasts, Búzios offers surfing, windsurfing, kitesurfing, diving, hiking, and mountain biking, as well as leisurely rounds of golf.

GETTING HERE AND AROUND

From Rio de Janeiro, drive across the Rio–Niterói Bridge and bear left, following the BR 101. At Rio Bonito take the exit to the Region dos Lagos. At São Pedro de Aldeia, turn left at the sign for Búzios. The trip takes about three hours, of which at least an hour may be spent caught in traffic around Niterói.

Búzios-bound 1001 buses leave from Rio's Novo Rio bus station every half hour. The trip takes around 3½ hours and costs R$48. Transfers from Rio hotels can be arranged for around R$150. Speak to hotel staff who should be happy to set this service up for you. Shuttle transfers from Rio's airports are also available for about the same price. Malizia Tour is a reliable shuttle operator and provides currency exchange services as well.

ESSENTIALS

Taxi Information Búzios Radio Taxi.
☎ *22/2623–2509.*

Visitor and Tour Information

Búzios Tourism Office. ✉ *Praça Santos Dumont s/n, Centro, Búzios* ☎ *022/2623–2099* ⊕ *www.buziosonline.com.br.*

TOURS

Malizia Tour. This prominent tourist agency provides collective and private shuttle transfers to Rio de Janeiro, stopping at airports and Zona Sul hotels, as well as sightseeing trips in and around Búzios. ✉ *Shopping Praia do Canto, Estrada José Bento Ribeiro Dantas, Loja 16, Centro, Búzios* ☎ *22/2623–1226* ⊕ *www.maliziatour.com.br.*

BRIGITTE & BÚZIOS

A walk along the Orla Bardot will bring you to the bronze statue of a seated woman looking out over the cobalt-blue waters. This is the statue of the actress Brigitte Bardot, who put Búzios on the map when she came here on holiday. Bardot, world-famous at the time for her role in director Roger Vadim's provocative *And God Created Woman* and other films, declared the city the one place where she was able to relax. She stayed in Búzios until photographer Denis Albanèse's candid shots allowed the international press to discover her and, in turn, Búzios.

SAFETY AND PRECAUTIONS

A few simple rules: don't eat fresh oysters sold anywhere but in a restaurant, and make sure you only take boat trips with accredited groups or individuals. Crime here is rare, but don't walk along dark and deserted streets after dark, and don't leave your belongings unattended on the beach.

BEACHES

Búzios boasts 23 beautiful beaches, which can be reached by schooner boat trips or speedier taxi boats. There is a taxi boat "terminal" on Orla Bardot, with skippers ready to whisk passengers off to any of the beaches on the island. Prices are per person and start at R$7 to get to the closest beaches, rising to around R$30 for farther-flung sands. There's a minimum two-person fare but solo travelers can wait for others to come along and bump up the numbers. Schooners depart from the end of a small pier nearby and take groups on beach-hopping trips that might last from a couple of hours to a full day. Prices start at around R$40 per person for a two-hour trip, rising to around R$150 for a full-day trip with stops for swimming and snorkeling.

Praia Azeda. Two beaches, Praia Azeda and its smaller neighbor, Praia Azedinha, have clear, calm waters and are accessible via a trail from Praia dos Ossos, or by taxi boat (R$10). The view as you descend to the beach on foot is breathtaking. Vendors at kiosks on the beach sell coconut water and frozen caipirinhas, and you can rent beach chairs and umbrellas. Azedinha is one of the few beaches here where women can sunbathe topless. During summer, arrive early to secure a good spot—the beaches start to get crowded by 11 am. **Amenities:** food and drink; toilets. **Best for:** swimming. ⊠ *João Fernandes, Búzios.*

FAMILY **Praia da Ferradura.** On a cove that protects it from the winds that often blow elsewhere on the peninsula, Praia da Ferradura has calm waters that make it a perfect choice for families with children. The beach adjoins one of Búzios' most exclusive areas—some mansions back right onto it—but maintains a relaxed ambience. Sun loungers and umbrellas are provided as a courtesy for clients of the many beach *barracas* (simple makeshift kiosks selling food and drink). Arrive early for a good spot on summer weekends. **Amenities:** food and drink; toilets; water sports. **Best for:** swimming. ⊠ *Ferradura, Búzios.*

Fodor'sChoice **Praia de Geribá.** This long half-moon of white sand is fashionable with
★ a young crowd, and its breaks and swells make it popular with surfers and windsurfers. The walk from one end to the other takes 30 minutes, so there's plenty of elbow room here even in high season. The relaxed bars and beach kiosks make it easy to while away whole days here. The surrounding Geribá neighborhood makes a great base for beach lovers, with plenty of good pousadas near the sands. **Amenities:** food and drink; water sports. **Best for:** walking; surfing. ⊠ *Geribá, Búzios.*

FAMILY **Praia João Fernandes.** Praia João Fernandes and the smaller adjoining beach, Praia João Fernandinho, are a short taxi-boat ride (R$10) from the center of town; both are beloved for their crystal waters and soft sands. The sounds of live samba music at nearby restaurants and bars can be heard on the beach, and you can bring cocktails out to your chosen spot on the sand if you're not ready to abandon your sun lounger. This beach can get a little busy, but the sunset here is spectacular. **Amenities:** food and drink; toilets; water sports. **Best for:** sunset; swimming. ⊠ *João Fernandes, Búzios.*

WHERE TO EAT

$$ ✕ **Buzin.** Behind fashionable Rua das Pedras is a buffet restaurant fea-
BRAZILIAN turing many varieties of seafood, steaks, salads, and pizzas. The rea-
FAMILY sonable prices, ample choices, and casual atmosphere make it a great post-beach stop. Try the shrimp fried in oil and garlic or the *picanha* beef, a very tender cut found in every churrascaria. The house opens at noon and closes when the last person leaves in the evening. Ⓢ *Average main: R$45* ⊠ *Rua Manoel Turíbio de Farias 273, Centro, Búzios* ☎ *022/2633–7051* ⊕ *www.buzinbuzios.com.*

$$$ ✕ **Capricciosa.** The Búzios branch of this pizzeria serves the same high-
PIZZA quality pies as the main location in Rio. The Margarita Gourmet is a classic, with a thin crust topped with tomatoes and buffalo mozzarella. Imported Italian cheeses and pizza flour make Capricciosa a hit with foodies in Búzios. Ⓢ *Average main: R$50* ⊠ *Orla Brigitte Bardot 500, Centro, Búzios* ☎ *022/2623–2691* ⊕ *www.capricciosa.com.br* ☽ *No lunch.*

$ ✕ **Chez Michou.** A pancake house might seem an unlikely meeting point
BELGIAN for partiers, but this Belgian-owned *crêperie* is indeed the hangout of
FAMILY choice for many hip young things in Búzios. Locals and tourists alike flock to the street-side tables after dark to soak up the scene and listen to live DJ sets while tucking into their choice of over 50 savory and

3

sweet fillings. By day it's a quieter affair and popular with families. [$] *Average main: R$25* ✉ *Av. José Bento Ribeiro Dantas 90, Centro, Búzios* ☎ *022/2623–2169* 🌐 *www.chezmichou.com.br.*

$$$ FRENCH Fodor's Choice ★ 🍴 **Cigalon.** Often cited as the best restaurant in Búzios, Cigalon is an elegant establishment with a veranda overlooking the beach. Though the waiters are bow-tied and the tables covered with crisp linens and lighted by flickering candles, the place still has an unpretentious feel. The food is French-inspired and includes thyme-infused lamb steak, braised duck breast, and prawns in a lemongrass sauce with almonds. Set menus start at R$60 including a starter, a main, and a dessert, and are a terrific value. [$] *Average main: R$55* ✉ *Rua das Pedras 199, Centro, Búzios* ☎ *022/2623–6284* 🌐 *www.cigalon.com.br.*

$$ ARGENTINE FAMILY 🍴 **Estancia Don Juan.** Take a walk through the center of Búzios and you could be forgiven for thinking you've suddenly landed in Argentina. The country's cuisine has arrived in the city in a big way, and you'll hear restaurant staff speaking Spanish almost as much as Portuguese. Argentina's beef is legendary and is traditionally served grilled at a *parrilla*. Of the several parrillas in town, Estancia Don Juan is the most established. Its perfectly grilled cuts of prime beef can be washed down with a glass of Malbec from the well-stocked cellar as you take in a live tango show. [$] *Average main: R$45* ✉ *Rua das Pedras 178, Centro, Búzios* ☎ *22/2623–2169* ⏲ *No lunch* 💳 *No credit cards.*

$$$$ MEDITERRANEAN Fodor's Choice ★ 🍴 **Mistico.** With dazzling views over the bay and out across the mountains, the intimate restaurant at boutique hotel Abracadabara offers impeccable service and exquisitely presented dishes. Enjoy the sunset while sipping a signature cocktail of sugarcane rum with ginger, mango, and orange, and choose from light, fresh dishes such as quinoa salad with avocado, cherry tomato, and basil, or potato croquettes with cod and salmon. The seafood taster plate of tuna ceviche, octopus carpaccio with citrus sauce, and grilled calamari is a wonderful dish for two to share. The creative amuse-bouches surprise the palate with offerings such as tiny cups of tangy chilled kiwi soup. [$] *Average main: R$80* ✉ *Pousada Abracadabara, Alto do Humaitá 13, Centro, Búzios* ☎ *22/2623–1217* 🌐 *www.abracadabrapousada.com.br* ✍ *Reservations essential.*

$$$$ SEAFOOD 🍴 **Rocka Beach Lounge & Restaurant.** Overlooking beautiful Praia Brava, relaxed but sophisticated Rocka is one of Búzios's gastronomic highlights. Superbly fresh locally sourced seafood is combined with seasonal fruit, vegetables, and herbs to wonderful effect. Order a frozen cocktail, or splurge on a bottle of Veuve Clicquot, and soak up the ambience as you wait for your food. The fish and shrimp ceviche is terrific, while the chocolate fondant with hazelnut makes for an appropriately decadent closer. If you're here for lunch (all that's served during low season), you can enjoy your meal from the comfort of a sun bed—literally, a bed, not a plastic lounger—on a grassy slope with perfect beach views. Aim to be here at sunset for a romantic end to the day. [$] *Average main: R$85* ✉ *Praia Brava 13, Brava, Búzios* ☎ *022/2623–6159* ⏲ *No dinner Mar.–Nov.* ✍ *Reservations essential.*

$$$$ SEAFOOD 🍴 **Satyricon.** The Italian fish restaurant famous in Rio has a branch here as well, and the beachfront location adds an extra dash of romance to the

proceedings. The dishes are expensive, but seafood lovers will find them worth the splurge. Go all out and try the grilled mixed-seafood plate with cream-of-lemon risotto. On weekends, reservations are normally required for parties of four or more. $ *Average main: R$110* ⊠ *Av. José Bento Ribeiro Dantas (Orla Bardot) 500, Centro, Búzios* ☎ *022/2623–2691* ⊕ *www.satyricon.com.br* ☽ *No lunch* ⌔ *Reservations essential.*

WHERE TO STAY

Be sure to book well in advance if you plan to visit Búzios on a weekend between Christmas and Carnival. You'll find good accommodation options in the center of town—handy for nightlife, shopping, and organized tours—but there's no real beach there. For beachfront lodgings, you'll have to head a little out of town.

$$$$
HOTEL
Fodor'sChoice
★

▦**Abracadabra.** Rooms at this gorgeous, centrally located boutique hotel are simply but stylishly appointed and have soft white linens and fresh flowers, but the crowning glory is an infinity pool that has stunning views over the bay and out to sea. **Pros:** stunning views; wonderful breakfasts; excellent service. **Cons:** the best beaches are a taxi boat ride away. $ *Rooms from: R$550* ⊠ *Alto do Humaitá 13, Centro, Búzios* ☎ *022/2623–1217* ⊕ *www.abracadabrapousada.com.br* ⇄ *16 rooms* ⵁ *Breakfast.*

$$$
B&B/INN

▦**Aquabarra Boutique Hotel and Spa.** A Zen-like calm pervades the rooms and living spaces at this casual-chic spot just a few-minutes' walk from Geribá Beach. **Pros:** gorgeous space; excellent spas; most rooms have lovely views; close to beach. **Cons:** need to cab or bus to get to Centro. $ *Rooms from: R$456* ⊠ *Rua de Corina 16, Centro, Búzios* ☎ *022/2623–6186* ⊕ *www.aquabarra.com* ⇄ *15 rooms* ⵁ *Breakfast.*

$$$$
HOTEL
Fodor'sChoice
★

▦**Casas Brancas.** Each of the 32 rooms at this timelessly chic hotel is unique, and many have deep baths, beach views, and private balconies. **Pros:** unique accommodations; friendly service; multilingual staff; pool with stunning views; beautiful setting; excellent spa and restaurants; relaxed ambience. **Cons:** a taxi ride to the best beaches. $ *Rooms from: R$900* ⊠ *Alto do Humaitá 10, Centro, Búzios* ☎ *022/2623–1458* ⊕ *www.casasbrancas.com.br* ⇄ *32 rooms, 3 suites* ⵁ *Breakfast.*

$$$$
HOTEL

▦**Hotel le Relais de la Borie.** This historic villa sits right on the edge of Gériba Beach and has a pool area with sweeping views out to sea. **Pros:** on the beach; great restaurant; friendly staff. **Cons:** it's a bus or cab ride from the center. $ *Rooms from: R$900* ⊠ *Rua dos Gravatás 1374, Geribá, Búzios* ☎ *022/2620–8504* ⊕ *www.laborie.com.br* ⇄ *38 rooms, 1 suite* ⵁ *Breakfast.*

$
B&B/INN
FAMILY

▦**Maresia de Búzios.** Small but stylish, this guesthouse close to Geribá Beach provides clean, budget-friendly accommodations. **Pros:** friendly staff; contemporary decor; fine buffet breakfast; pleasant communal spaces; children welcome. **Cons:** small rooms; no TVs in rooms; need to take a taxi to get to town. $ *Rooms from: R$160* ⊠ *Rua das Pitangueiras 12, Bosque de Geribá, Geribá, Búzios* ☎ *022/8822–2384* ✉ *contato@maresiadebuzios.com* ▭ *No credit cards* ⇄ *5 rooms, 1 dorm* ⵁ *Breakfast.*

$
B&B/INN
FAMILY

▦**Pousada Barcarola.** With a large pool and sun terrace, bright and spacious rooms, generous breakfasts, and free parking and Wi-Fi, this family-friendly guesthouse offers excellent value for its price range.

Pros: spacious rooms; helpful staff; lovely pool and gardens. **Cons:** 10 minutes' walk to the beach or town center. [$] *Rooms from: R$150* ✉ *Rua G-5 Lote 14, Ferradura, Búzios* ☎ *22/ 2623–7254* 🌐 *www.pousadabarcarola.com* 🛏 *16 rooms* 🍴 *Breakfast.*

$$$ HOTEL FAMILY 🏨 **Rio Búzios Beach Hotel.** This hotel has a great location a few steps from João Fernandes Beach, and a glass-walled elevator provides sweeping views over the sands. **Pros:** good games room; fantastic breakfast; helpful, friendly staff. **Cons:** 20-minute walk to the center. [$] *Rooms from: R$420* ✉ *Praia de João Fernandes s/n, João Fernandes, Búzios* ☎ *022/2633–6400* 🌐 *www.riobuzios.com.br* 🛏 *63 rooms* 🍴 *Breakfast.*

NIGHTLIFE

BARS

Anexo. A slightly lower-key alternative to the city's more frenetic clubs, Anexo plays ambient house and has a veranda where you can kick back and enjoy one of the many specialty cocktails alongside the *gente bonita* of Búzios. ✉ *Av. José Bento Ribeiro Dantas 392, Centro, Búzios* ☎ *022/2623–6837* 🌐 *www.anexobarbuzios.com.br.*

Terraço no Morro. Head here in the early evening for relaxed drinks and *petiscos* (light snacks) on the wooden patio and enjoy a perfect view as the pumpkin sun dips over the harbour. A place where you won't feel out of place in beachwear and Havaianas, this casual bar holds regular Sunday afternoon *feijoada*s, a hit with locals and visitors looking to soothe their hangovers with Brazil's hearty national dish and a caipirinha. ✉ *Av. José Bento Ribeiro Dantas 575, Centro, Búzios* ☎ *022/2623–0859.*

DANCE CLUBS

Pacha. If you want to sip potent cocktails with beautiful people in scanty clothing, this slick beachfront nightclub is the place to do it. The party set dances here until dawn to contemporary tunes spun by visiting DJs from Europe and the United States, as well as some of the biggest names on the Brazilian dance-music circuit. With room for 1,000 party people, the vast, colorfully lit space can feel a little empty in the low season, but it's packed to the rafters during the summer high season. Tickets for New Year's celebrations sell out well in advance. ✉ *Rua das Pedras 151, Centro, Búzios* ☎ *022/2633–0592* 🌐 *www.pachabuzios.com* 🎟 *From R$50* ⏲ *Closed Sun.–Wed.*

Privilège. A vast space with room for more than 1,000 people, Privilège is one of the top places to party in Búzios. There are six separate areas, including a lounge, two dance floors, four bars, a sushi restaurant, and a pizzeria. Resident DJs play techno on Thursdays and Sundays, while top DJs from around the world fly in to spin tunes on Fridays and Saturdays. This is also a late-night hangout for the rich and famous, who head to the two exclusive VIP areas. ✉ *Av. José Bento Ribeiro Dantas 550, Orla Bardot, Manguinhos, Búzios* ☎ *022/2620–8585* 🌐 *www.privilegebrasil.com/casa/buzios* 🎟 *From R$70* ⏲ *Closed Mon.–Wed. except for Carnival and other major holidays.*

WELCOME TO THE RIO OLYMPICS

In August 2016 athletes from more than 200 nations will head to Rio de Janeiro, one of the world's most stunning cities, to compete in South America's first Olympic Games. Hosting the games is a major coup for Brazil, allowing the nation to bask in the world's attention as it flaunts its spectacular natural beauty and vibrant cultures.

Brazil has a strong performance history at the Olympics: since the 1920s, Brazilian athletes have brought home 108 medals. Surprisingly, Brazil has never won a gold medal in soccer; and the national team will be keen to correct that on its hallowed home turf.

No matter the number of medals earned by the hosts in 2016, visitors can expect to find Rio in full party mode during the 17-day festivities.

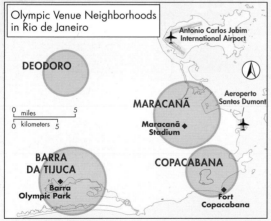

Olympic Venue Neighborhoods in Rio de Janeiro

Antonio Carlos Jobim International Airport

DEODORO

MARACANÃ

Aeroperto Santos Dumont

Maracanã Stadium

0 miles 5

0 kilometers 5

BARRA DA TIJUCA

COPACABANA

Barra Olympic Park

Fort Copacabana

Although Barra has towering condos, wide avenues, and large shopping malls that make the area feel less "Brazilian" than most of Rio (indeed, it is often referred to by locals as "the United States of Barra"), its soft sand beach is the biggest in the city, stretching for more than 13 km (8 miles). The bars, restaurants, and nightclubs attract a hip crowd.

The **Olympic Village** and press camp will be located in Barra, and the largest concentration of games, including many of the big-ticket events such as diving, swimming, and gymnastics, will be held at a total of 14 competition venues making up the **Olympic Park**. Golf will also return to

BARRA DA TIJUCA
With vastly more available land than Rio's built-up urban heart, Barra da Tijuca was an obvious choice as the hub of the 2016 Olympics. Known locally as Barra

(pronounced "Baha"), this affluent beach suburb feels like a city apart from the rest of Rio, even though it's only 25 miles west of the city center.

the Summer Olympics after an absence of more than a century, the new **Olympic Golf Course** will be in Barra da Tijuca.

Occupying a peninsula jutting out into the ocean, the Olympic Park will have venues connected by curved pathways that are designed to resemble Brazil's twisty Amazon River. Those without tickets can watch the games live on giant screens at a green waterfront space within the park.

Barra has traditionally suffered from poor transpor-

tation links to Rio's South Zone and downtown, but it is fast becoming better connected. The first of several rapid bus corridors is already in place, and the metro is scheduled to reach Barra by late 2015.

DEODORO

This nondescript area of Rio holds little tourist appeal outside of its Olympic events, but it will be the setting for the second-largest concentration of venues during the Games. Nine venues will be located here. The zone is best accessed by rail, with trains leaving for Deodoro rail station from Central do Brasil in downtown Rio.

(top left) The sprawling beach in Barra da Tijuca. (top right) Gabby Douglas of the U.S. national team.

FAST FACTS

Dates: August 5–21, 2016

Total Sports: 42

Total Medal Events: 306

Total Venues: 33

Opening and Closing Ceremonies: Maracanã Stadium

Ticket Prices: $25–$350

Where to Purchase Tickets: www.rio2016.org/tickets

The official Rio 2016 website: www.rio2016. org/en

The official Olympics website: www.olympic.org/ rio-2016-summer-olympics

Brazil Tourism Board website: www.visitbrasil. com

Deodoro will host a mix of traditional and more modern events at venues such as the Olympic Shooting Stadium and Equestrian Arena. The modern X-Park includes an Olympic BMX Centre and will leave a legacy for future extreme sporting events. In addition, Deodoro will host rugby, which returns to the Olympics after a 92-year absence.

With little visual appeal and limited tourist infrastructure in the immediate vicinity of the venues, the area is not a good base for visitors.

(top left) The Maracanã Stadium. (top right) Rio's famed Copacabana beach.

MARACANÃ

This area north of the city center will host events in three locations: the iconic **Maracanã Stadium;** the nearby **Sambódromo,** where Rio's famous Carnival parades take place; and the **Engenhão Stadium** in the residential neighborhood of Engenho de Dentro.

The Maracanã Stadium was given a multimillion-dollar overhaul ahead of the 2014 FIFA World Cup. It is here that Rio's spectacular opening and closing ceremonies will be held. Appropriately, the men's and women's soccer finals will take place in the Maracanã Stadium as well.

One of the Olympics' most popular sports, volleyball, will take place in the **Mara-canãzinho Gymnasium,** next to the Maracanã Stadium.

The marathon will begin and end in Rio's Sambódromo, which was recently renovated and can now hold up to 72,000 spectators.

The J. Havelange Olympic Stadium, or "Engenhão," was built for the 2007 Pan-American Games and will host high-profile track-and-field events during the Olympics.

The area is not Rio's most beautiful, but good metro links mean that visitors making their base in Centro or the South Zone will be able to reach the stadiums without much trouble.

COPACABANA

For many people, Copacabana *is* Rio. The long, curved ribbon of sand here is one of the world's most famous beaches, anchored by a perfect view of Sugar Loaf and frequented by bronzed beauties in skimpy swimsuits. It's fitting that Copacabana is the location for the Olympic beach volleyball events in **Copacabana Stadium,** which was purpose-built for the games.

Marathon swimming will take place at the western end of Copacabana beach, and the scenic surrounding area will host some of the Olympics' most exciting events, including cycling at **Flamengo Park** and the triathlon at **Fort Copacabana.**

Copacabana is one of Rio's liveliest neighborhoods, and the beach here is sure to teem with sports fans eager to touch up their tans in between games. Free-flowing caipirinhas, impromptu music performances, and cooling breezes will create a party atmosphere on the beach throughout the games.

Even though hotels are plentiful here, visitors should expect to pay a premium for beachfront lodgings, and loud parties are likely to continue late into the night. Those looking for quieter accommodations will find good options in nearby Ipanema, while budget visitors will find a lively scene in nearby Botafogo.

WHERE TO SEE SELECT EVENTS

Basketball: Barra da Tijuca and Deodoro

Beach Volleyball: Copacabana

Boxing: Barra da Tijuca

Diving: Barra da Tijuca

Equestrian Events: Deodoro

Fencing: Barra da Tijuca

Field Hockey: Deodoro

Golf: Barra da Tijuca

Gymnastics: Barra da Tijuca

Road Cycling: Barra da Tijuca and Copacabana

Rowing: Copacabana

Rugby: Deodoro

Sailing: Copacabana

Soccer: Maracanã

Swimming: Barra da Tijuca

Tennis: Barra da Tijuca

Track and Field: Maracanã

Triathlon: Copacabana

Volleyball: Maracanã

Water Polo: Barra da Tijuca and Maracanã

Weight Lifting: Barra da Tijuca

Wrestling: Barra da Tijuca

Four additional cities will host soccer games during the Olympics: São Paulo, Belo Horizonte, Brasília, and Salvador.

Hurdlers compete for the gold.

For sports fans visiting Rio during the 2016 Olympics, finding lodging and getting around will be the most pressing issues. The games will take place in four neighborhoods spread across this sprawling city.

LODGING

Most sporting events, along with the newly constructed Olympic Village, will be in Barra da Tijuca, an upscale beach community 25 miles west of the city center. Many new hotels are being built here ahead of the games to accommodate the throngs of visitors seeking a convenient base near the main venues.

Those looking for more independence or affordable lodgings will have plenty of options. As happened during the 2014 FIFA World Cup in Brazil, numerous locals will rent out apartments or spare rooms, while residents in some of Rio's favelas have proven themselves excellent hosts for those priced out of lodgings in the city's touristic heartland.

Visitors can use online agencies such as *Booking.com* to get the best prices for Olympic stays. *Airbnb.com* is widely used by Rio locals renting everything from spare sofa beds to penthouse apartments. The go-to source for chic guesthouse accommodation across Brazil is Hidden Pousadas Brazil *(www.hiddenpousadasbrazil.com)*. Those curious to try a favela stay should look to agencies such as Favela Experience *(www.favelaexperience.com)*, which was a reliable and socially responsible operator during the 2014 FIFA World Cup.

TRAVEL

Flights to Rio de Janeiro are available via major carriers from most global destinations, and the city's international airport is getting much-needed renovations as it prepares to receive a mass influx of international visitors. It is wise to book airline tickets as far in advance as possible to avoid ramped-up last-minute prices.

A major overhaul of Rio de Janeiro's public transportation system has been initiated ahead of the games, with plans to extend the metro system to the Olympic Village in Barra da Tijuca. A new light railway system and fast bus corridors will improve transportation connections between the city's airports, inter-city bus terminal, tourist hot spots, and the Olympic Village.

There will be four Bus Rapid Transit (BRT) fast bus corridors. The first connects the international airport with Barra da Tijuca, the main competition zone for the games. The other three will be completed by the time the games begin, and will transport athletes and spectators between the city and the Olympic pavilions. The bus lanes will be open to the general public, with tickets bought on board at the time of travel.

However you get around the city, leave plenty of travel time in your schedule and don't try to cram too many events in multiple venues into one day. Attempts to fit in games in different neighborhoods on the same day may not be realistic unless the schedule allows for several hours of travel. While taxis are widely available and affordable, the metro and fast bus corridors will provide speedier links between venues.

TICKETS TO THE EVENTS

Tickets will be available on the official site: *www.rio2016.org*. Of the 7.5 million tickets available, roughly half will cost US$30 or less. The Olympics Organizing Committee has announced that it will use multiple official vendors and round-the-clock sales in order to ensure that venues are filled to capacity.

Carnival parades at Rio's Sambódromo.

TIPS FOR ATTENDING AN EVENT

■ Arrive an hour or so early to soak up the atmosphere and sample traditional snacks from the street sellers. Be on the lookout for white-clad Bahian women selling Northeastern specialties such as tapioca pancakes and spicy acaraje bean meal patties.

■ Save queuing time with a pre-pay metro card. With machines (cash only) available at all metro stations, these cards can be preloaded with amounts from R$5–R$50.

■ Allow plenty of extra time when heading to a game for any transportation disruptions.

■ Don't plan on walking around the areas surrounding stadiums in Deodoro or Maracanã, especially after dark.

■ Bring a lightweight jacket and an umbrella; it can be chilly after dark in Rio.

■ If you plan to take a taxi and don't speak Portuguese, write down the name of the destination to show the driver.

■ Don't bring outside food or drinks into the stadium.

Visitors marvel at the Escadaria Selarón in Lapa, one of the best neighborhoods for nightlife in Rio.

TEAM SPIRIT

If you don't have tickets to the events, you can still find ways to root for your country. Most bars and restaurants will have their televisions permanently tuned to the sports channels. It is also common during sporting events to see someone's living room television hooked up on the street—a scene that is often accompanied by locals selling cold beers and soft drinks from a cooler.

There will be three live sites scattered through Rio where crowds will be able to follow Olympic events on massive screens. For a peek at the local sporting scene, simply stroll along Rio's many beachfronts to watch cariocas engage in beach volleyball, water sports, and, in particular, soccer, the national sport.

To show your team spirit, paint your country's colors on your nails. At Rio's legendary beauty salons, skilled technicians are renowned for their devotion to perfectly painted nails. Nearly every street in the city has a salon where you can receive an affordable mani-pedi that would cost a fortune elsewhere.

HIT THE TOWN

Rio's downtown Port Zone is currently being transformed into a cultural hot spot through the **Porto Maravilha** project. The **Museum of Tomorrow,** a modern science museum designed by renowned architect Santiago Calatrava, is scheduled to open here before the Games, along with a wealth of upscale restaurants and shops. As of this writing, work is under way to construct a new 28-km (17-mile) light-rail network that will connect the port with Rio's metro system and domestic airport.

For nightlife, Barra da Tijuca draws a sophisticated crowd at its chic wine bars and nightclubs, while Copacabana has a livelier, more casual vibe with beachfront kiosks enticing tourists with bargain caipirinhas. But if you really want to party with the locals, head to the downtown district of **Lapa.** This formerly rundown neighborhood is now Rio's party hub, filled with live music venues where you can dance samba or just watch while fleet-footed locals show how it's done. It's the perfect place to barhop or just wander through street stalls selling potent cocktails.

SPORTS AND THE OUTDOORS

BOATING

FAMILY **Babylon Búzios.** Babylon Búzios runs a number of water-based trips and activities, the most popular of which whisks passengers to the peninsula's best beaches during a 2½-hour excursion, with stops for swimming and snorkeling (masks provided). A great option for families, the schooner *Babylon Búzios* is equipped with a splash pool and a waterslide that flows right into the ocean. It departs three times a day from the main pier in Búzios. ✉ *Rua das Pedras 232, Centro, Búzios* ☎ *022/2623–2350* ⊕ *www.babylonbuzios.com.br* ✆ *R$50 per person* ⊙ *Daily departures 11:45, 2:45, 5:45.*

DIVING

The clear waters of Búzios teem with colorful marine life, making the peninsula a thrilling place to dive.

Mares del Sur Brasil. This professional dive outfit has 5-Star PADI accreditation and operates daily dive trips in Búzios as well as nearby Arraial do Cabo, and offers a full range of instruction from diving "baptisms" to advanced courses. Instructors speak English as well as Spanish and Portuguese. Look out for special promotions such as two diving for the price of one. ✉ *Rua Lagosta 114 , Ferradurinha, Ferradura, Búzios* ☎ *22/99233–7035* ✉ *buceomares@gmail.com.*

GOLF

Búzios Golf Club and Resort. Designed by the acclaimed American golf-course architects Pete and Perry Dye, this well-maintained 18-hole course is challenging thanks to the winds that blow here, but the scenic backdrop of hills, natural pools, and tropical vegetation makes a round here worth the effort. The course is about 10 km (6 miles) from the town center, but it's easily accessed by car or taxi. ✉ *Av. José Bento Ribeiro Dantas 9, Búzios* ☎ *022/2629–1240* ⊕ *www.buziosgolf.com. br* ✆ *R$190* ⚑ *18 holes, 6652 yards, par 72.*

KITE SURFING

Búzios Kitesurf School. The certified instructors here are an upbeat team dedicated to helping you get the most out of your lessons. ✉ *José Bento Ribeiro Dantas 9, Praia Raza, Búzios* ☎ *022/9956–0668* ⊕ *www. kitenews.com.br* ✆ *R$500.*

SURFING

Surf schools set up tents along Geribá Beach, and also rent out boards. Expect to pay around R$70 an hour for a private lesson, including board rental, and R$300 to rent a board for an hour.

Shark's Surf School. With a kiosk at the western end of Geribá Beach, this outfit rents equipment and offers personalized classes for children and adults of all experience levels. The energetic, enthusiastic instructor, Marcio, has years of experience, and the school has International Surfing Association accreditation. ✉ *Praia de Geribá, Geribá, Búzios* ⚓ *At the right hand corner of the beach as you face the sea* ☎ *022/2623–1134.*

TOUR OPERATORS

FAMILY **Tour Shop Búzios.** The largest tour operator in Búzios conducts white-water rafting and boat trips, 4x4 adventures in the dunes, and a popular trolley tour that takes in 12 of the peninsula's best beaches and some spectacular view points. Alongside a wealth of adventure activities, there are family-friendly pursuits such as horseback riding. ⊠ *Orla Bardot 550, Centro, Búzios* ☎ *022/2623–4733, 022/2623–0292* ⊕ *www.tourshop.com.br* ⊠ *From R$50.*

SHOPPING

Adriana Fernandez Bikinis. There are branches of chic bikini stores Bum-Bum Ipanema and Lenny on Rua das Pedras, but for something with a little more local flavor check out the sexy-but-stylish swimwear at Adriana Fernandez Bikinis, where curve-enhancing bikinis are sold alongside one-pieces whose striking prints, deep-scooped backs, and cut-out side panels keep frumpiness firmly at bay. ⊠ *Rua das Pedras 199, Centro, Búzios* ☎ *22/2623–6121* ⊕ *www.adrianafernandezbikinis.com.*

Gatos de Rua. This store sells gorgeous beaded bags, artsy home furnishings, and even bikinis, all made using recycled materials by young people working as part of a community arts project aimed at helping adolescents at risk. The project is admirable, but the pieces stand out as works of art in their own right. The cute beaded cats make great souvenirs or gifts for folks back home. ⊠ *Travessa dos Pescadores 306, Passeio das Palmeiras, Loja 3, Búzios* ✛ *Next to the pier* ☎ *22/2623–4602* ⊕ *www.gatosderua.com.br.*

NORTH OF RIO

Petrópolis is a charming historical village that was once the summer home of the imperial family. If you enjoy hiking, visit the Parque National da Serra dos Órgãos between Teresópolis and Petrópolis. Temperatures in the mountains are low by Brazilian standards—an average of 55°F (13°C) in winter—providing a welcome change from the stifling heat of the city.

PETRÓPOLIS

68 km (42 miles) northeast of Rio.

The highway northeast of Rio de Janeiro rumbles past forests and waterfalls en route to a mountain town so refreshing and picturesque that Dom Pedro II, Brazil's second emperor, moved there with his summer court. From 1889 to 1899 it was the country's year-round seat of government. Horse-drawn carriages clip-clop between the sights, passing flowering gardens, shady parks, and imposing pink mansions. Be sure to visit the Crystal Palace and the Gothic cathedral, São Pedro de Alcântara. The city is also home to the Encantada—literally "Enchanted"— the peculiar house created by Santos Dumont, an inventor and early aviator. Fashion-conscious bargain hunters from across Rio de Janeiro State generally make a beeline for Rua Teresa, a hilly street just outside the historic center that's lined with discount clothing stores.

GETTING HERE AND AROUND

From Rio by car head north along BR 040 to Petrópolis. The picturesque drive (once you leave the city) takes about an hour if traffic isn't heavy. Única buses leave every 40 minutes—less often on weekends—from

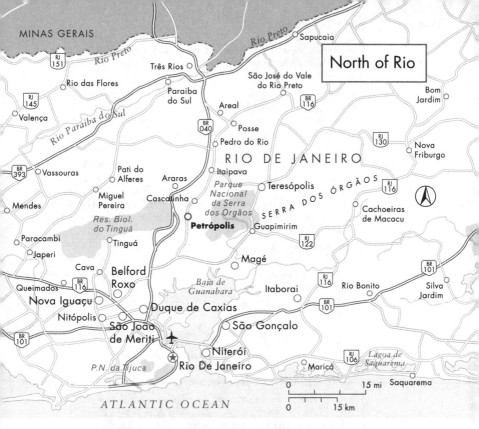

Rio's Rodoviária Novo Rio. The 90-minute journey costs R$22. Upon arrival at Rodoviária Petrópolis, the bus station, you'll be several miles from downtown, so you'll need to take a taxi (R$15–30, depending on traffic), especially if you're laden with luggage.

The easiest and safest way to get to Petrópolis from Rio, though, is to arrange a shuttle at your hotel or to take a tour either privately or as part of a group.

ESSENTIALS

Bus Contacts Rodoviária Petrópolis. ✉ *BR 40–Rodovia Washington Luiz, Km 82.9–Fazenda Inglesa, Petrópolis* ☎ *024/2249–9858.* **Única.** ☎ *024/2244–1600* ⊕ *www.unica-facil.com.br.*

Taxi Contact Ponto de Taxi Elite. ✉ *Petrópolis* ☎ *024/2242–4090.*

Visitor Information Petrópolis Tourism Office. ✉ *Centro de Cultura Raul de Leoni, Praça Visconde de Mauá 305, Petrópolis* ☎ *024/2233–1200* ⊕ *www. petropolis.rj.gov.br.*

TOURS

FAMILY

Fodor'sChoice

★

Rio Cultural Secrets. The private tours to Petrópolis run by Rio Cultural Secrets are led by knowledgeable English-speaking guides and include door-to-door transport in comfortable air-conditioned cars. Ask for Fabio, who runs the tours with great enthusiasm and knowledge of

Petrópolis's history. Trips take around six hours, including a stop for lunch. ✉ *Rio de Janeiro* ☎ *021/ 98031–2692* ⊕ *www.rioculturalsecrets. com.br* 🖳 *From R$220, excluding entrance fees.*

Rio Turismo Radical. This well-established Rio company leads hiking trips up to Teresópolis, Petrópolis, and the surrounding mountains. Treks last from a few hours up to two days, and hikers can expect cascading waterfalls, mammoth granite walls, and astonishing views over dense jungle. ☎ *021/9224–6963* ⊕ *www.rioturismoradical.com.br/petropolis.htm.*

Terra Vertical. Adventurous types can enjoy white-knuckle activities including rappelling, cascading, and hiking in the mountains with this experienced and professional group. There's a strong emphasis on safety, and the team, led by the highly experienced Anderson, has enormous enthusiasm for their high-altitude adventures. ⊕ *www. terravertical.com.br* 🖳 *From R$100.*

EXPLORING
TOP ATTRACTIONS

Fodor'sChoice
★
Catedral São Pedro de Alcântara. The imposing Cathedral of Saint Peter of Alcantara, a fine example of Gothic architecture and the city's most recognizable landmark, sits at the base of a jungle-clad hill. Inside the building, whose construction began in 1884, lie the tombs of Dom Pedro II, his wife, Dona Teresa Cristina, and their daughter, Princesa Isabel. Elegant sculptures and ornate stained-glass windows add to the interior's visual appeal. Drift further back in time by arriving via a horse-drawn carriage, easily hailed in the historic center of town. ✉ *Rua São Pedro de Alcântara 60, Petrópolis* ☎ *024/2242–4300* ☉ *Daily 8–6.*

FAMILY
Museu Imperial. The magnificent 44-room palace that was the summer home of Dom Pedro II, emperor of Brazil, and his family in the 19th century is now the Imperial Museum. The colossal structure is filled with polished wooden floors, artworks, and grand chandeliers. You can also see the diamond-encrusted gold crown and scepter of Brazil's last emperor, as well as other royal jewels. Visitors are handed soft slippers on arrival and asked to slip them over their own shoes to avoid damaging the antique floors. (Children will love sliding around on the polished floors in their slippered feet.) ✉ *Rua da Imperatriz 220, Petrópolis* ☎ *024/2245–5550* ⊕ *www.museuimperial.gov.br* 🖳 *R$8* ☉ *Tues.–Sun. 11–6.*

Palácio de Cristal. The Crystal Palace, a stained-glass and iron building made in France and assembled in Brazil, is rather less grand than its name suggests, resembling a large and very ornate greenhouse, but is worth a visit nonetheless. The palace was a wedding present to Princesa Isabel from her consort, the French Count d'Eu. Their marriage was arranged by their parents—Isabel, then 18, learned of Dom Pedro II's choice only a few weeks before her wedding. The count wrote to his sister that his bride to be was "ugly," but after a few weeks of marriage decided he rather liked her. During the imperial years the palace was used as a ballroom: the princess held a celebration dance here after she abolished slavery in Brazil in 1888. Surrounded by pleasant gardens, the Crystal Palace is now open to the public and often hosts live classical music performances. ✉ *Praça da Confluência, Rua Alfredo Pachá*

s/n, Petrópolis ☎ 024/2247–3721
⊙ Tues.–Sun. 9–6.

WORTH NOTING

FAMILY **Casa de Santos Dumont.** Known as "Encantado" or "enchanted," this diminutive cottage wouldn't look out of place in a fairy-tale wood. Santos Dumont, one of the world's first aviators, built the house in 1918 to a scale in keeping with his own tiny size. The eccentric genius's inventions fill the house, including a heated shower he developed before most homes even had running water. The home doesn't have a kitchen because Dumont ordered his food from a nearby hotel—the first documented restaurant delivery service in Brazil. ✉ Rua do Encantado 22, Petrópolis ☎ 024/2247–3158 💷 R$5 ⊙ Tues.–Sun. 9:30–5.

WHERE TO EAT

$$$ ✕ **Churrascaria Majórica.** A classic steak house in the heart of Petrópolis's
BRAZILIAN historic center, Majórica has been a huge hit with meat lovers since
FAMILY it opened in 1962. Every cut is cooked to perfection and served with flair by attentive waitstaff, and there are excellent fish dishes and sides, too. There's a decent wine list, although it may be even more tempting to opt for one of the very well-made caipirinhas. $ Average main: R$50 ✉ Rua de Emperador 754, Petrópolis ☎ 024/ 2242–2498 ⊕ www.majorica.com.br.

$$ ✕ **Trutas do Rocio.** It's off the beaten track—ask a local for directions—
SEAFOOD and only open on weekends, but this rustic, riverside restaurant is really something special. "Trutas" means trout and that's what you'll find on the menu—trout, trout, and more trout served fresh from the river in many imaginative ways: as appetizers mashed into a pâté or baked in cassava-dough pastry, and as entrées grilled or cooked with a choice of almond, mustard, or orange sauce. The restaurant seats only 22, so reservations are a must. On sunny afternoons, the food is served alfresco. $ Average main: R$40 ✉ Estrada da Vargem Grande 6333, Rocio, Petrópolis ☎ 024/2291–5623 ⊕ www.trutas.com.br ▭ No credit cards ⊙ No dinner. Closed Mon.–Thurs. ⚑ Reservations essential.

WHERE TO STAY

$$$$ ▦ **Locanda della Mimosa.** Sitting in a valley with walking trails winding
B&B/INN through colorful bougainvillea trees, this cozy pousada has six well-appointed suites decorated in a classical style with imperial influences. **Pros:** spacious rooms; great restaurant; massages and afternoon tea service are included in the rates. **Cons:** need to book well in advance; some suites have traffic noise; minimum two-night stay. $ Rooms from: R$700 ✉ BR 040, Km 71.5, Alameda das Mimosas 30, Vale

WALKING IN THE CLOUDS

The Parque Nacional da Serra dos Órgãos, created in 1939 to protect the region's natural wonders, covers more than 101 square km (39 square miles) of mountainous terrain between Petrópolis and Teresópolis. The Petrópolis to Teresópolis trail—a tough three-day hike with spectacular views—is a must for hard-core hikers. Inexperienced hikers should go with a guide, but everyone should check weather forecasts in advance as heavy rainfall in the region has caused mudslides in recent years.

3

Florido, Petrópolis ☎ *024/2233–5405* 🌐 *www.locanda.com.br* 🛏 *6 suites* 🍴 *Breakfast.*

$$$ B&B/INN FAMILY 🏨 **Pousada de Alcobaça.** Just north of Petrópolis, this 1914 mansion is owned by descendents of the family that built it, and great pride is taken in managing the building and its beautiful flower-filled gardens. **Pros:** tasty food; great views; breakfast can be taken at any hour. **Cons:** need to book far in advance; 15-minute drive from the city. [$] *Rooms from: R$385* ✉ *Agostinho Goulão 298, Correias, Petrópolis* ☎ *024/2221–1240* 🌐 *www.pousadadaalcobaca.com.br* 🛏 *11 rooms* 🍴 *Breakfast.*

$ B&B/INN 🏨 **Pousada Monte Imperial.** A 10-minute walk from downtown, this Bavarian-style inn has a lobby with a fireplace, a comfortable restaurant and bar area, and rustic rooms that are cozy, if a bit spartan. **Pros:** close to downtown; friendly, attentive staff; great sunset views. **Cons:** spartan rooms; chilly in winter; uphill walk from the city. [$] *Rooms from: R$245* ✉ *Rua José de Alencar 27, Centro, Petrópolis* ☎ *024/2237–1664* 🌐 *www.pousadamonteimperial.com.br* 🛏 *15 rooms* 🍴 *Breakfast.*

$$$ HOTEL FAMILY Fodor's Choice ★ 🏨 **Solar do Imperio.** Occupying a tastefully restored 1875 neoclassical building and smaller outlying houses amid Petrópolis's historic center, this elegant hotel provides stylish, comfortable accommodations. **Pros:** excellent location; good in-house restaurant; great service; modern spa facilities. **Cons:** insects from the gardens occasionally find their way into the rooms. [$] *Rooms from: R$500* ✉ *Av. Koeler 376, Petrópolis* ☎ *024/2242–0034* 🌐 *www.solardoimperio.com.br* 🛏 *24 rooms* 🍴 *Breakfast.*

THE GREEN COAST

Italy has the charming Costa Azurra, but Brazil has the Costa Verde. The emerald waters in the bay at Angra dos Reis have fabulous diving spots, with abundant marine life and near year-round visibility. If you're not a diver, though, don't fret. There are plenty of boat tours to places like Ilha Grande. With its unspoiled beaches and rough-hewn nature trails, the bay's biggest island attracts sunseekers and adventure tourists alike.

During Carnival, pristine nature takes a backseat when the normally quiet Paraty celebrates its roots with Bloco da Lama, a parade for which participants get down and dirty—literally—and smear mud from local Praia do Jabaquara on one another. The ritual reenacts one the region's prehistoric tribes practiced to drive away evil spirits.

ANGRA DOS REIS

168 km (91 miles) west of Rio.

Angra dos Reis (Bay of Kings) has it all: colonial architecture, beautiful beaches, and clear green waters. Schooners, yachts, and fishing skiffs drift among the bay's 365 islands, one for each day of the year. Indeed, Angra dos Reis's popularity lies in its strategic location near the islands. Some are deserted stretches of sand, others patches of Atlantic rain forest surrounded by emerald waters perfect for swimming or snorkeling.

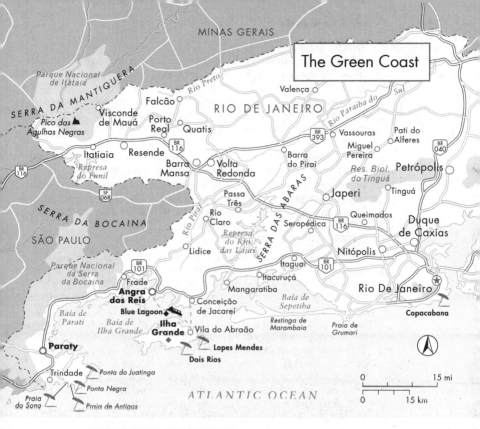

GETTING HERE AND AROUND

Angra dos Reis-bound Costa Verde buses leave Rio every hour. The 2½-hour trip costs R$48. Ferries leave the terminal at Angra dos Reis for Ilha Grande every day at 3:30 pm. The 90-minute trip costs R$14.

From Rio by car, get onto the Rio-Santos highway (BR 101) and follow it south for 190 km (118 miles) until you get to Angra dos Reis. Expect the trip to take between two and three hours, depending on traffic.

ESSENTIALS

Bus Contact Rodoviária Angra dos Reis. ⊠ Av. Almirante Jair Toscano de Brito 110, Balneário, Angra dos Reis ☎ 024/3365–2041 ⊕ www.socicam.com.br/terminais/terminais_rodoviarios.php?ID=15.

Ferry Contact CCR Barcas. ⊠ Cais da Lapa, 15-113 Avenida Júlio Maria, Angra dos Reis ☎ 0800/ 721–1012 toll free ⊕ www.grupoccr.com.br.

Taxi Contact Ponto de Táxi. ⊠ Rua do Comércio 201, Centro, Angra dos Reis ☎ 024/3365–2792.

Visitor Information Angra dos Reis Tourism Office. ⊠ Av. Ayrton Senna da Silva 580, Praia do Anil, Angra dos Reis ☎ 024/3367–7826, 024/3367–7789 ⊕ www.turisangra.com.br.

TOURS

Associação dos Barqueiros. This group runs boat tours to the islands around Angra dos Reis, and rents out boats, plus skipper, for up to 10 people. One great tour is to Ilha da Gipóia and its beautiful beaches, such as the famous Jurubaíba, which is perfect for snorkeling or diving. Some boats have a reputation for playing loud music. Check before you book if you prefer a tranquil environment. ✉ *Rua Júlio Maria 92, Centro, Angra dos Reis* ☎ *024/3365–3165* 🎟 *From R$50.*

FAMILY **Mar de Angra.** This reliable outfit sails its schooners, catamarans, and other boats on day trips to the islands around Angra dos Reis with stops for swimming, snorkeling, and sunbathing. Fresh fruit and soft drinks are provided on board. The boats are also available for private group hire, with skipper. ✉ *Av. Júlio Maria 16, Angra dos Reis* ☎ *024/3365–1097* 🌐 *www.mardeangra.com.br* 🎟 *From R$50.*

WHERE TO STAY

$$$$ HOTEL 🏨 **Hotel do Bosque.** Inside Parque Perequê, this resort hotel has boat service to its private beach across the river and lays on breakfast, dinner, and activities such as boat trips, kayaking, water skiing, fishing, and rafting. **Pros:** plenty of activities; private beach; spacious rooms. **Cons:** out-of-the-way location. [$] *Rooms from: R$2,150* ✉ *BR 101, Km 533, Mambucaba, Angra dos Reis* ☎ *024/3362–3130* 🌐 *www.hoteldobosque.com.br* 🛏 *98 rooms, 4 suites* 🍴 *Some meals.*

$ HOTEL FAMILY 🏨 **Pousada dos Corsarios.** Its location right on the beach at scenic Praia do Bonfim makes this simple hotel a great option for its price range. **Pros:** beachfront location; abundant breakfast; friendly service. **Cons:** few frills; a half-hour walk or 10-minute taxi ride to town center. [$] *Rooms from: R$216* ✉ *Praia do Bonfim 5, Bonfim, Angra dos Reis* ☎ *024/3365–4445* 🌐 *www.corsarios.com.br* 🛏 *10 rooms* 🍴 *Breakfast.*

ILHA GRANDE

21 km (13 miles) south of Angra dos Reis or Mangaratiba via 90-minute ferry ride.

Ilha Grande, 90 minutes via ferry from Angra dos Reis, is one of the most popular island destinations in Brazil. It boasts 86 idyllic beaches, some of which are sandy ribbons with backdrops of tropical foliage, while others are densely wooded coves with waterfalls tumbling down from the forest.

Ferries, catamarans, and schooners arrive at Vila do Abraão. As there are no cars, it's wise to take only what you can carry. Men waiting at the pier make a living helping tourists carry luggage for about R$10 per bag. Take cash out in Angra. There aren't any ATMs on the island, and credit cards aren't always accepted.

GETTING HERE AND AROUND

By far the simplest and most cost-effective way to get to the island is by a bus and boat transfer service. Easy Transfer's comfortable, air-conditioned vans pick travelers up from their lodgings in Rio (the service covers the South Zone, Centro, and Santa Teresa) and make the two-hour journey to Conceição de Jacareí, where the company's own double-decker schooner boat waits to ship passengers over to Abraão, Ilha Grande's only real town. Traveling with a transfer service works out cheaper (R$85 with Easy Transfer) and is far easier than arranging taxis to the bus station, buses down the coast, and then a boat trip out to the island. Easy Transfer and its competitors offer the same service back to Rio, as well as transfers between Ilha Grande and Paraty.

For those that choose to make the trip independently, the quickest route is to go via Conceição de Jacareí. Comfortable coaches leave from Rio's Novo Rio bus station approximately once an hour, a journey of around one-and-a-half hours. Several operators run schooners (40 minutes) and speedier flexboats (15 minutes) to Ilha Grande roughly every hour, with the first crossing at 7:30 am and the last at 9 pm. The fare starts at R$20 per person.

Most boats used to sail to Ilha Grande from Angra dos Reis, and it's still possible to take this route, although most travelers coming from Rio make the quicker trip via Conceição de Jacareí. Buses from Rio's Novo Rio bus station take 2 hours and 15 minutes to reach Angra dos Reis's bus station, from where it's a 10-minute cab ride or hot 20-minute walk to the town center and the boat terminal. Catamarans (R$25) leave at 10:30 am and take 40 to 50 minutes, while the ferry (R$14) takes about 1 hour 40 minutes, leaving at 3:30 pm on weekdays, 1:30 pm on weekends and holidays. A daily ferry also sails from Mangaratiba, but it's slow and inconveniently scheduled at 8 am daily, except on Fridays when it leaves at 10 pm.

SAFETY AND PRECAUTIONS
Avoid taking unlicensed boats. Verify the condition of any boat you plan to board, and check that it has a life preserver for every person aboard.

ESSENTIALS
Boat Contacts Saveiro Andréa. ⊠ *Cais de Conceição de Jacareí* ⊹ *A couple of minutes' downhill walk from the bus stop* ☎ *024/9744–0732.*

Visitor Information Tourist Information Center. ⊠ *Estacao Abraao, Abraão, Ilha Grande* ⊹ *At the entrance to the pier* ☎ *024/3365–5186* ⊕ *www.angra. rj.gov.br/turisangra/atendimento.asp.*

TOURS
FAMILY **Pinguim Tours.** Book a full-day or half-day boat trip around Ilha Grande
Fodor's Choice taking in highlights such as the Blue Lagoon and Lopes Mendes. The
★ excursions are family-friendly with a strong emphasis on water safety. There are stops for swimming and lunch, but it's a good idea to bring along a cool box with fruit, drinks and sandwiches as food at the beach restaurants tends to be heavy on both stomach and wallet. ⊠ *Rua da Praia s/n, Abraão, Ilha Grande* ⊹ *Facing the pier* ☎ *024/9814–4307* ᗌ *From R$40.*

EXPLORING
Visitors to Ilha Grande can follow well-marked nature trails that lead to isolated beaches and waterfalls and past the ruins of the former prison. Walks may last from 20 minutes to six hours, and there are maps at strategic points. Bring along water and insect repellent, and

wear lightweight walking shoes. For a less taxing experience, take a schooner or taxi boat out to the unspoiled beaches. Schooners make regular trips out to the most popular beaches and lagoons, with stops for swimming and snorkeling, while the taxi boats whisk passengers to any point on the island.

FAMILY **Blue Lagoon.** This natural pool forms at low tide and is home to thousands of brightly colored fish that will literally eat out of your hands. Many tour operators include a stop here as part of their boat trips around the island, and most provide floats for children. Be sure to bring a mask and snorkel. ✉ *Lagoa Azul, Ilha Grande.*

BEACHES

Dois Rios. With its pristine white sands and turquoise waters, this beautiful, unspoiled beach sits in stark contrast to the dark prison ruins that sit behind it. Visitors have the place practically to themselves, as few people make the arduous 5-km (3-mile) trek through hot jungle to get here. Those who do are rewarded with one of the island's most gorgeous beaches, and the sense of achievement that comes with really getting off the beaten track. The prison ruins are worth exploring, but be sure to head back several hours before sundown. **Amenities:** none. **Best for:** solitude. ✉ *Dois Rios, Ilha Grande.*

Fodor's Choice ★ **Lopes Mendes.** Locals and visitors alike regard Lopes Mendes, a 3-km (2-mile) stretch of dazzling-white sand lapped by emerald waters, as the most beautiful beach on Ilha Grande. It's often cited as one of the most beautiful in all Brazil. Strict environmental protection orders have kept the jungle-fringed beach from being spoiled by development: expect makeshift beach kiosks, not upscale bars. Take a taxi boat from Vila do Abraão (R$15), if you don't feel up to the two-hour hike through the forest, or hike here and take the boat back—the rough jungle trail and sticky heat can tax even the most hearty of ramblers. While here, use plenty of sunblock, as the rays rebounding off the white sand are particularly strong. **Amenities:** food and drink. **Best for:** swimming; walking. ✉ *Lopez Mendes, Ilha Grande.*

WHERE TO EAT

$$ SEAFOOD 🍴 **Lua e Mar.** Expect fresh, well-prepared seafood at this longtime favorite. It's a casual establishment, so you can stroll in from the beach still wearing your Havaianas. Try Dona Cidinha's specialty, fish with half-ripe bananas, or the famous *moqueca* (seafood stew), which many islanders claim is the best in Rio de Janeiro State. [$] *Average main: R$45* ✉ *Praia do Canto, Abraão, Ilha Grande* ☎ *024/3361–5113* 🌐 *www.ilhagrande.org/luaemar* 🕒 *Closed Wed.*

$$ SEAFOOD 🍴 **O Pescador.** Inside the pousada of the same name, this restaurant serves local seafood prepared using Italian cooking techniques. The specialty is grilled fish (the types vary according to the season) bought from local fishermen. After dark, you can dine alfresco on the beach by candlelight, or just pop in for a cocktail and nibbles from the bar. [$] *Average main: R$45* ✉ *Rua da Praia 647, Abraão, Ilha Grande* ☎ *024/3361–5114* 🌐 *www.opescador.org.*

$$$ BRAZILIAN 🍴 **Pé Na Areia.** For the ultimate I'm-on-vacation feeling, take a seat at a straw-roofed table right on the sands at this relaxed beachfront

restaurant. Quirky illuminated parasols hang from the trees overhead, musicians strum acoustic guitars, and waiters bring delicious *moquecas* (seafood stew with palm oil and coconut milk) to diners as they sit sipping caipirinha cocktails. The candlelit tables and gentle music—a change from the reggae that's played everywhere else on the island—make Pé Na Areia an ideal option for a romantic dinner. [$] *Average main: R$55* ✉ *Rua da Praia s/n, Abraão, Ilha Grande* ✥ *About five minutes' walk along the beach from the pier* ☎ *024/ 3361–9572* ⏲ *No lunch. Closed Mon.* 💳 *No credit cards.*

ILHA GRANDE'S SWEET SPOT

They appear late in the afternoon to tempt you with their sweet aromas and delicate flavors. We're talking about Vila do Abraão's sweet carts, of course. They first appeared in 1998, when a resident of the island started producing baked goods at his home. His success inspired other dessert makers to sell their sweets on the streets of Abraão. The carts stay out late at night, tempting even the most resolute of travelers.

$$ PIZZA FAMILY 🍴 **Pizza na Praça.** On the flagstones of Ilha Grande's main square, this simple restaurant serves up more than four-dozen types of pies, from simple margheritas to exotic seafood combinations. There are low-cal versions made with fresh vegetables and soft ricotta cheese on a wholegrain base, but also indulgent options such as the sweet pizzas with chocolate, or *doce de leite* (thick sweet milk), or both. The pizza menu is available from 6 pm until the early hours, while at lunchtime the restaurant serves vast, tasty salads and good-value set meals. This is a great spot for evening meals on Friday and Saturday nights, when live bands play in the square. [$] *Average main: R$40* ✉ *Praça São Sebastião, Abraão, Ilha Grande* ☎ *024/3361–9566* 💳 *No credit cards.*

WHERE TO STAY

$$ B&B/INN Fodor's Choice ★ 🏨 **Aratinga Inn.** Cooled by gentle hill breezes and shaded by trees and coconut palms, Aratinga Inn is rated by Hidden Pousadas Brazil—experts in chic lodgings across the country—as one of the best in the region. **Pros:** lovely gardens; complimentary afternoon teas; knowledgeable and helpful owner. **Cons:** an uphill walk from the pier. [$] *Rooms from: R$330* ✉ *Rua das Flores 232, Abraão, Ilha Grande* ☎ *024/3361–9559* 🌐 *aratingailhagrande.com.br* 🛏 *7 chalets* 🍽 *Breakfast.*

$ HOTEL FAMILY 🏨 **Farol dos Borbas.** Practical rather than luxurious, Farol do Borbas has simple but comfortable and well-equipped rooms, a vast buffet breakfast, and attentive staff who are happy to arrange trips around the island on guests' behalf. **Pros:** walking distance from the pier; close to everything; attentive staff; private schooner. **Cons:** can be noisy at night. [$] *Rooms from: R$250* ✉ *Rua da Praia 881, Abraão, Ilha Grande* ☎ *024/3361–5832* 🌐 *www.ilhagrandetour.com.br* 🛏 *14 rooms* 🍽 *Breakfast.*

$$ B&B/INN FAMILY 🏨 **Pousada do Canto.** In a colonial-style house, this family-friendly pousada with a tropical atmosphere faces lovely Praia do Canto. **Pros:** on the beach; pretty pool. **Cons:** rooms can get chilly in winter; small bathrooms; a bit of a walk to the boat pier, shops, and restaurants. [$] *Rooms from: R$265* ✉ *Rua da Praia 121, Vila do Abraão, Ilha*

Grande ☎ *021/3717–3262* 🌐 *www.canto-ilhagrande.com* 🛏 *11 rooms* 🍴 *Breakfast.*

$ B&B/INN 🏨 **Pousada Naturalia.** A beachfront location, excellent service, and sumptuous breakfasts all contribute to the appeal of Pousada Naturalia. **Pros:** excellent service; sumptuous breakfasts; sea views; lush tropical gardens. **Cons:** 10-minute walk to the ferry terminal means that you may need to pay a carrier at the harbor around R$20 to transport your luggage. [$] *Rooms from: R$230* ✉ *Rua da Praia 149, Abraão, Ilha Grande* ☎ *024/3361–9583* 🌐 *www.pousadanaturalia.net* 🛏 *14 rooms* 🍴 *Breakfast.*

A POTENT BREW

One telling has it that cachaça was invented around 1540 by slaves working on the sugarcane plantations. A liquid called *cagaço* was removed from the sugarcane to make it easier to transport. The slaves noticed that after a few days this liquid would ferment into a potent brew.

SPORTS AND THE OUTDOORS

Elite Dive Center. This PADI-accredited dive school offers diving classes from beginner to Dive Master level, rents out equipment, and runs daytime and nocturnal diving excursions to numerous places around the island. ✉ *Travessa Bouganville, Loja 1, Vila do Abraão, Ilha Grande* ☎ *024/99936–4181* 🌐 *www.elitedivecenter.com.br.*

PARATY

99 km (60 miles) southwest of Angra dos Reis; 261 km (140 miles) southwest of Rio.

Fodor's Choice ★ This stunning colonial city—also spelled Parati—is one of South America's gems. Giant iron chains hang from posts at the beginning of the mazelike grid of cobblestone streets that make up the historic center, closing them to all but pedestrians, horses, and bicycles. Until the 18th century this was an important transit point for gold plucked from the Minas Gerais—a safe harbor protected by a fort. (The cobblestones are the rock ballast brought from Lisbon, then unloaded to make room in the ships for their gold cargoes.) In 1720, however, the colonial powers cut a new trail from the gold mines straight to Rio de Janeiro, bypassing the town and leaving it isolated. It remained that way until contemporary times, when artists, writers, and others "discovered" the community and UNESCO placed it on its list of World Heritage Sites.

Paraty isn't a city peppered with lavish mansions and opulent palaces; rather, it has a simple beauty. By the time the sun breaks over glorious Paraty Bay each morning—illuminating the whitewashed, colorfully trimmed buildings—the fishermen have begun spreading out their catch at the outdoor market. The best way to explore is simply to begin walking winding streets banked with centuries-old buildings that hide quaint inns, tiny restaurants, shops, and art galleries.

Paraty holds Brazil's largest literary festival, FLIP (Festival Literaria de Paraty) each July, followed in quick succession by the more raucous Festival da Pinga (Cachaça Festival), at which cachaça producers from around the country unveil their latest brews. The Carnival celebrations here are also a spectacle to behold, with costumed revelers covering themselves in mud to parade through the streets at the Bloco da Lama. Book well in advance if you plan to visit during the festivals.

GETTING HERE AND AROUND
From Rio de Janeiro, it's a four-hour drive along the BR 101 to Paraty. Costa Verde buses leave Rio daily every two hours, more frequently before noon. The journey costs R$63, and buses arrive at the *rodoviária* in the new town, about 20 minutes' walk from the pedestrianized historic center. It pays to travel light as taxis may not be able to take you to your hotel door.

ESSENTIALS
Bus Contact Rodoviária Paraty. ⊠ *Rua Jango Pádua, Centro, Paraty* ☎ *024/3371–1238.*

Taxi Contact Tuim Taxi Service. ⊠ *Centro, Paraty* ☎ *024/9918–7834* ⊕ *www. eco-paraty.com/taxi.*

Visitor Information Paraty Tourism Office. ⊠ *Rua Dr. Samuel Costa 29, Centro Histórico, Paraty* ☎ *024/3371–1897* ⊕ *www.paraty.com.br.*

TOURS
Paraty Tours. This outfit conducts six-hour Jeep tours that head into Serra da Bocaina National Park, crossing rivers and visiting fantastic waterfalls, with stops for swimming in natural pools, hiking through rain forest, and even visiting sugarcane-rum distilleries (complete with tastings). Paraty Tours also runs boat trips, adventure sports excursions, and transfers to Rio and São Paulo. ⊠ *Av. Roberto Silveira 11, Centro, Paraty* ☎ *024/3371–2651* ⊕ *www.paratytours.com.br* ⊠ *From R$100.*

EXPLORING
TOP ATTRACTIONS
Forte Defensor Perpétuo. Paraty's only fort was built in the early 1700s, and rebuilt in 1822, as a defense against pirates. It's a pleasant short climb through jungle to get here and the views from the fort itself are terrific. Visitors can also see heavy British-made cannons, still in their original positions. ⊠ *Morro da Vila Velha, Paraty* ☎ *024/3371–2289* ⊠ *R$4* ⊘ *Wed.–Sun. 9–12 and 1–5.*

Igreja de Nossa Senhora dos Remédios. Also known as Igreja Matriz, the neoclassical Church of Our Lady of Remedies was built in 1787 and is one of Paraty's most iconic buildings, with its gray-and-white facade shaded by a towering imperial palm tree. The small art gallery within, Pinacoteca Antônio Marino Gouveia, has paintings by modern artists such as Djanira, Di Cavalcanti, and Anita Malfatti. ⊠ *Rua da Matriz, Centro Histórico, Paraty* ☎ *024/ 3371–1467* ⊕ *www.igrejaparati.com. br* ⊠ *R$4* ⊘ *Tues.–Sun. 8–noon and 1–4.*

Igreja de Santa Rita. The oldest church in Paraty, the simple whitewashed Church of Saint Rita sits on a grassy square with a mountain backdrop and makes for a terrific photo opportunity. The church was built in 1722 by and for freed slaves and has a typical Jesuit layout with a bell tower and domed front. Inside, the carved angels and ornate wood and iron work catch the eye, and there are many valuable religious artifacts

3

on display in the church's small religious art museum. ✉ *Largo de Santa Rita, Rua Santa Rita s/n, Centro Histórico, Paraty* ☎ *024/3371–1206* 🌐 *www.igrejaparati.com.br* 🎟 *R$4* 🕒 *Wed.–Sun. 9–noon and 2–5.*

FAMILY **Trindade.** About 30 km (20 miles) from Paraty, Trindade was once a hippie hangout. Today Trindade's several gorgeous beaches attract everybody from backpackers to Cariocas on vacation, and the natural pools are perfect for children. Regular buses run from the bus station in Paraty. If you're looking to stay overnight, you'll find simple lodgings and campsites near the beaches. ✉ *Trindade, Paraty.*

WORTH NOTING

Casa da Cultura. The largest cultural center in Paraty, Casa da Cultura is dedicated to telling the story of the city and its people. Permanent and visiting exhibitions illustrate the area's rich history and its abundant native flora and fauna. There's a pleasant coffee shop and patio, and the gift shop downstairs, one of the best in town, sells crafts made by local artisans. ✉ *Rua Dona Geralda 177, at Rua Dr. Samuel Costa, Centro Histórico, Paraty* ☎ *024/3371–2325* 🌐 *www.cultura.rj.gov.br/espaco/casa-da-cultura-de-paraty* 🎟 *R$8* 🕒 *Wed.–Mon. 10–6:30.*

BEACHES

Praia de Antigos. An environmental protection order keeps beautiful Antigos Beach wonderfully unspoiled—you can swim amid rugged nature here. The thick jungle reaches right down to the sands, and the beach is famous for the large rocks that jut into the transparent water, separating Antigos from the adjoining smaller beach, Antiginhos, whose calmer waters are better for swimming. The beach can be reached via a 20-minute walking trail from equally scenic Sono Beach, which in turn can be reached by boat from Paraty. **Amenities:** none. **Best for:** solitude; snorkeling; sunbathing. ✉ *Take trail from Sono Beach, Trindade, Paraty.*

Praia do Sono. Secluded Sono Beach is one of the Paraty area's most beautiful strands, with thick jungle framing the crescent of light, soft sand bordering crystal clear waters teeming with colorful fish. Campers base themselves here during the summer, when there's a relaxed, bohemian air. In the off-season, the beach is virtually deserted—sunbathers bask in what feels like a private tropical paradise. Although Sono is a bit off the beaten track, the gorgeous setting makes it worth the effort to reach it. The best way to access the beach is by boat from Paraty (about R$35); otherwise you must take a one-hour bus ride and then hike for about 40 minutes. **Amenities:** food and drink (in high season). **Best for:** solitude; swimming; walking. ✉ *Trindade, Paraty.*

WHERE TO EAT

$$$ BRAZILIAN 🍴 **Banana da Terra.** Seafood is always excellent at this long-standing favorite on Paraty's dining scene, and it's a great place to try giant shrimp when they are in season. The restaurant is in a colonial house decorated with cachaça labels (the caipirinhas here are another strong suit) and 19th-century pictures of the city. The name of the place comes from another of its specialties: *banana da terra* (plantain), which is incorporated into many dishes, among them grilled fish with garlic butter, herbs, plantains, and rice. [$] *Average main: R$55* ✉ *Rua Doutor*

Samuel Costa 198, Centro Histórico, Paraty ☎ *024/3371–1725* 🕒 *No lunch Wed. and Thurs. Closed Tues.*

$$$ ITALIAN Fodor's Choice ★ 🍴 **Punto Divino.** A covered outdoor space means that diners at Punto Divino can enjoy meals alfresco even when the famously torrential Paraty rains start to pour. Tuscan and Sicilian dishes are at the fore, and are prepared with care. Evening live-music performances lend a touch of festivity to the proceedings, and the crisp, generously topped pizzas here are the best in town. The salads are fresh and tasty, and dishes such as the risotto with squid, squid ink, and chili peppers will tempt adventurous eaters. The restaurant's convenient location, at the heart of the historic center opposite the main square, only adds to its popularity. [$] *Average main: R$55* ✉ *Rua Marechal Deodoro 129, Centro Histórico, Paraty* 🕒 *No lunch.*

$$$ SEAFOOD 🍴 **Refúgio.** Near the water in a quiet part of town, this seafood restaurant is a great place for a romantic dinner, with candle-lit tables and a good wine list. It serves excellent cod, sea bass, and shellfish dishes as well as colorful, fresh salads. On chilly days, heat lamps warm the café tables out front. Note that there is an extra "artistic cover" charged when live music is performed. [$] *Average main: R$60* ✉ *Praça do Porto 1, Centro, Paraty* ☎ *024/3371–2447* 🌐 *www.restauranterefugio.com.*

$$$ BRAZILIAN 🍴 **Restaurante do Hiltinho.** The specialty at this elegant restaurants is *camarão casadinho,* fried colossal shrimp stuffed with hot *farofa* (cassava flour). Even if you're familiar with jumbo shrimp, you might be astonished at the size of these beauties. Seafood outnumbers other dishes two to one, but the filet mignon is very good. Glass doors that open onto the street are both welcoming and lend a meal here a touch of grandeur, as does the gracious, professional service. [$] *Average main: R$60* ✉ *Praça da Matriz, Rua Marechal Deodoro 233, Centro, Paraty* ☎ *024/3371–1432* 🌐 *www.hiltinho.com.br.*

WHERE TO STAY

$$ B&B/INN Fodor's Choice ★ 🏨 **Pousada do Príncipe.** Owned by the great-grandson of Emperor Pedro II, this inn at the edge of the Centro Histórico has rooms decorated in colonial style that face either the interior garden or the swimming pool, which is set in a pleasant courtyard. **Pros:** historic building; good location a short walk from the bus station; nice pool and courtyard; welcoming, attentive staff. **Cons:** small rooms; some rooms need repainting. [$] *Rooms from: R$268* ✉ *Av. Roberto Silveira 289, Centro, Paraty* ☎ *024/3371–2266* 🌐 *www.pousadadoprincipe.com.br* 🛏 *34 rooms, 3 suites* 🍽 *Breakfast.*

$$$ B&B/INN 🏨 **Pousada do Sandi.** This welcoming, centrally located pousada offers terrific service and a great location close to the main square in Paraty's historic center. **Pros:** close to all the main sights; large rooms; welcoming lobby and pool area; noteworthy restaurant; great breakfasts. **Cons:** street noise and creaky building; hard to maneuver for people with some disabilities; two-night minimum stay. [$] *Rooms from: R$490* ✉ *Largo do Rosário 1, Centro, Paraty* ☎ *024/3371–2100* 🌐 *www.pousadadosandi.com.br* 🛏 *25 rooms, 1 suite* 🍽 *Breakfast.*

$$$$ HOTEL Fodor's Choice ★ 🏨 **Pousada Literária de Paraty.** A totally renovated colonial mansion is the setting for this timelessly chic luxury guesthouse that celebrates the literary spirit of Paraty. **Pros:** elegant decor; great heated pool; superb Old Town location. **Cons:** books up well ahead of July literary

festival; streets nearby can flood during rainy season. [$] *Rooms from: R$860* ✉ *Rua Ten Francisco Antônio 36, Centro Histórico, Paraty* ☎ *024/3371–1568* 🌐 *www.pousadaliteraria.com.br/pousada-literaria* 🛏 *20 rooms, 3 suites* 🍴 *Breakfast.*

$$$ B&B/INN 🏨 **Pousada Pardieiro.** This is one of the oldest guesthouses in Paraty, and the residences that make up this property are decorated in 19th-century colonial style. **Pros:** close to the historic center; great pool and garden. **Cons:** no TVs in rooms; cold floors in winter. [$] *Rooms from: R$440* ✉ *Rua Tenente Francisco Antônio 74, Centro Histórico, Paraty* ☎ *024/3371–1370* 🌐 *www.pousadapardieiro.com.br* 🛏 *27 rooms, 2 suites* 🍴 *Breakfast.*

SHOPPING

Paraty is known countrywide for its fine cachaça, including brands like Coqueiro, Corisco, Vamos Nessa, Itatinga, Murycana, Paratiana, and Maré Alta.

Empório da Cachaça. This shop stocks more than 300 brands—both local and national—of sugarcane liquor as well as bottled chili peppers and locally produced preserves. It stays open well into the evening. ✉ *Rua Doutor Samuel Costa 22, Centro Histórico, Paraty* ☎ *024/3371–6329.*

Porto da Pinga. If you're looking for cachaça, Porto da Pinga is a worthy stop. It stocks many brands of the liquor, along with fiery bottled chilis, *doce de leite* (thick, sweet milk), and other local specialties. ✉ *Rua da Matriz 12, Centro Histórico, Paraty* ☎ *024/3371–1563.*

SÃO PAULO

Updated By
Claire Rigby

A sprawling, high-rise megacity, São Paulo might not have Rio's beaches and sultry good looks, but for urban explorers, it's a thoroughly rewarding destination. Blessed with its own unique charisma and a kind, courteous population, charmingly unused to tourists, it's brimming with culture and boasts some of the most varied options for eating out on the continent. The incessant urban landscape in this 20-million-strong metropolis won't be to everyone's taste, but for most visitors, one taste of São Paulo will leave them wanting more.

São Paulo is Brazil's main financial hub and its most cosmopolitan city, with top-rate nightlife and restaurants and impressive cultural and arts scenes. Most of the wealthiest people in Brazil live here—and the rest of them drop by at least once a year to shop for clothes, shoes, accessories, luxury items, and anything else money can buy. *Paulistanos* (São Paulo inhabitants) work hard and spend a lot, and there's no escaping the many shopping and eating temptations.

Despite—or because of—these qualities, many tourists, Brazilian and foreigners alike, avoid visiting the city. Too noisy, too polluted, too crowded, they say, and they have a point. São Paulo is hardly a beautiful city with nothing as scenic as Rio's hills and beaches. But for travelers who love big cities and prefer nights on the town to days on the sand, São Paulo is the right place to go. It's fast-paced and there's a lot to do. So even as the sea of high-rise buildings obstructs your view of the horizon, you'll see there's much to explore here.

ORIENTATION AND PLANNING

GETTING ORIENTED

Situated 70 km (43 miles) inland from the Atlantic Ocean with an average elevation of around 800 meters (2,625 feet), São Paulo has a flat and featureless metropolitan area, apart from a few elevated areas, including those around Avenida Paulista and Centro. A major expressway called the "Marginal" runs along the city's northern edge, accompanying the polluted River Tietê, and down the western side along the equally fetid River Pinheiros, with most business and tourist activity occurring in the southeastern, western, and central neighborhoods. No matter where you are, though, it's difficult to gain a visual perspective of your relative location, thanks to the legions of buildings in every direction. A good map or app is a necessity.

TOP REASONS TO GO

Shop Till You Drop: Shop along with Brazil's rich and famous in the Jardins or Itaim areas, or at one of the city's many fashion malls.

Food, Glorious Food: Adventurous eating is a sport in São Paulo. The 12,500 restaurants here serve dozens of different cuisines, from across Brazil and beyond.

Art Attack: Some of the finest galleries on the continent make up São Paulo's buzzing art scene.

Hopping Nightlife: Bars of all shapes, styles, and sizes beckon the thirsty traveler—quench your thirst with a cold beer or strong caipirinha.

The Beautiful Game: *Futebol*, or soccer, is truly "the beautiful game" in Brazil. São Paulo, with no fewer than three major teams, is a great place to feel the passion.

4

Centro. This downtown area has the city's most interesting historic architecture and some of its most famous sights; however, many parts are also quite daunting and dirty, so be prepared. Area highlights include Praça da Sé, geographical center of the São Paulo municipal district, and attractions around the revitalized Vale do Anhangabaú. Some of São Paulo's prime guilty pleasures can be snacked on at Mercado Municipal. Parque da Luz is just to the north and next to a number of important buildings, including the Estação da Luz railway station, part of which now houses the Museum of the Portuguese Language.

Liberdade. Southeast of Centro, Liberdade (meaning "freedom" or "liberty" in Portuguese) is the center of São Paulo's Japanese, Korean, and Chinese communities, and features a range of Asian-style streetscapes and shopfronts. It's a popular area with travelers, thanks to the many culturally motivated markets and restaurants.

Barra Funda. Once a desert of abandoned warehouses, this region has experienced a renaissance in recent years. The construction of various high-rise apartment buildings and trendy nightlife venues has returned life to a neighborhood boasting many of São Paulo's samba schools, architecture by Oscar Niemeyer, and the Allianz Parque stadium, home to Palmeiras soccer club.

Avenida Paulista. The imposing Avenida Paulista is home to some of the city's best-located hotels, biggest financial companies, and most important businesses. Many of São Paulo's cultural institutions center around this impressive, eight-lane-wide thoroughfare. Just 2.8 km (1.7 miles) long, the avenue begins west of Centro and spans several of the city's chicest neighborhoods as it shoots southeast toward the Atlantic.

Bixiga. Officially called Bela Vista, this is São Paulo's Little Italy. Here are plenty of restaurants, theaters, and nightlife hot spots. Southwest of Centro and right next to Avenida Paulista, Bixiga is an old, working-class neighborhood—the kind of place where everybody knows everybody else's business.

Jardins. On the southern side of Avenida Paulista sits Jardins, an upscale neighborhood that's ideal for shopping and eating out. The gently sloping, tree-filled area is one of the nicer parts of São Paulo for walking around; it's also one of the city's safest neighborhoods.

Itaim Bibi. Moving farther south, Itaim (locals always drop the Bibi part) is similar to Jardins because it's also filled with fashionable bars, restaurants, and shops. Another of the city's most impressive roads transects the suburb, Avenida Brigadeiro Faria Lima, which, along with its many cross-streets, has a ton of expensive and exclusive nightlife options. At its western border, Itaim stretches down to the Marginal.

Pinheiros. Just north of Itaim and west of Jardins sits Pinheiros (pine trees), another nightlife hot spot chock-full of bars, clubs, and late-night restaurants. The area, with some of the city's most expensive low-rise housing, is also traversed by the popular Avenida Brigadeiro Faria Lima and has the Marginal as its western boundary.

Vila Madalena. One of the hillier parts of São Paulo with impressive views across the city from the uppermost buildings, Vila Madalena is a relatively small enclave just to the north of Pinheiros. It's yet another nightlife mecca with bohemian-style haunts that stay open until dawn. Bars are stacked one on top of the other, making it a great place for a pub crawl, particularly because it's also one of the city's safest after-dark spots. Scores of boutiques, bookstores, cafés, galleries, and street-art displays also contribute to the neighborhood's pull on the free-spirited.

PLANNING

WHEN TO GO

Cultural events—film and music festivals, and fashion and art exhibits—usually take place between April and December. In South American summer (from January through March) the weather is rainy, and floods can disrupt traffic. Be sure to make reservations for beach resorts as far in advance as possible, particularly for weekend stays. In winter (June and July), follow the same rule for visits to Campos do Jordão. Summers are hot—35°C (95°F). In winter temperatures rarely dip below 10°C (50°F). ■TIP→ The air pollution might irritate your eyes, especially in July and August (dirty air is held in the city by thermal inversions), so pack eye drops.

PLANNING YOUR TIME

A walk along Avenida Paulista is a good way to ease gently in to São Paulo while still soaking up the big-city atmosphere. A long, prominent ridge topped with huge TV and radio antennae, Paulista is a handy geographical reference: you can stroll down into chic, leafy Jardins from here, or grab a cab and head the other way into revitalizing Centro. On Paulista itself, the boxlike MASP art museum has to be seen to be believed, while the little park just opposite, Trianon, is a beautiful scrap of native forest. Centro is where much of the city's remaining historic architecture can be found—don't miss a trip to the foodie-heaven market, the Mercado Municipal, and close to Praça da República, the view from the top of towering Edifício Itália is truly spectacular.

Parque do Ibirapuera is a great favorite with paulistanos, especially on weekends, when a stroll in the park is a chance to see locals of all stripes taking their leisure; while a day spent sauntering around Vila Madalena is a pleasant, undemanding way to see another side to the city. The neighborhood is packed with boutiques, cafés, restaurants and bars—but beware the steep hills. Don't miss Beco do Batman, a copiously graffitied pair of alleyways. Finish up at one of the many lovely restaurants here, or in neighboring Pinheiros.

GETTING HERE AND AROUND

Navigating São Paulo is not easy, and staying either in the central areas or at least near an inner-city subway station is advisable, especially if you don't plan on renting a car or taking cabs. The subway is quick, easy, inexpensive, and covers much of the city, with stops near the most interesting sites for travelers. Buses can be hard to navigate if you don't speak Portuguese. Driving in São Paulo, particularly in peak hours, can be slow and difficult. For longer stays, obtain a provisional driver's license and a good map or GPS—with a little care and a lot of confidence, you can get by. Parking can be perplexing, so it's probably best to use a parking lot (*estacionamento*), which are numerous and relatively cheap, depending on the neighborhood. Cabs are reasonably priced, safe, and abundant in the popular neighborhoods.

AIR TRAVEL

Nearly all international flights stop in São Paulo, so it's easy to get from São Paulo to everywhere else in Brazil. There are flights every half hour covering the short (around one hour) trip between São Paulo and Rio (starting from around R$100 one-way). There are also multiple departures per day to other major cities such as Brasília and Belo Horizonte.

AIRPORTS São Paulo's international airport, Aeroporto Internacional de São Paulo/ Guarulhos (GRU) or "Cumbica," is in the suburb of Guarulhos, 30 km (19 miles) and a 45-minute drive (longer during rush hour or on rainy days) northeast of Centro. Much closer to the Zona Sul region is Aeroporto de Congonhas (CGH), 14 km (9 miles) south of Centro (a 15- to 45-minute drive, depending on traffic), which serves regional airlines, including the Rio–São Paulo shuttle.

Airports Aeroporto Internacional de Congonhas (*CGH*). ⊠ *Avenida Washington Luís s/n, Campo Belo* ☎ *011/5090–9000* ⊕ *www.infraero.gov.br.* **Aeroporto Internacional de São Paulo/Guarulhos** (*GRU*). ⊠ *Rod. Hélio Smidt s/n, Guarulhos* ☎ *011/2445–2945* ⊕ *www.infraero.gov.br.*

AIRPORT TRANSFERS: BUSES AND TAXIS State government–operated EMTU's Airport Bus Service buses (air-conditioned blue-and-white vehicles) shuttle between Guarulhos and Congonhas airports every 30 to 40 minutes from 5:30 am to midnight and every 60 to 90 minutes from midnight to 5:30 am (R$36.50). Look for the EMTU stand near the private bus and cab stalls outside the arrivals terminal. You may also be able to arrange a free transfer with your airline as part of your ticket.

The EMTU buses travel between Guarulhos and the Tietê bus terminal (which is also on the main subway line) from 5 am to midnight, every 30 to 60 minutes; the downtown Praça da República (5:40 am to midnight, every 60 to 90 minutes); and Avenida Paulista (5:50 am to 11:10 pm,

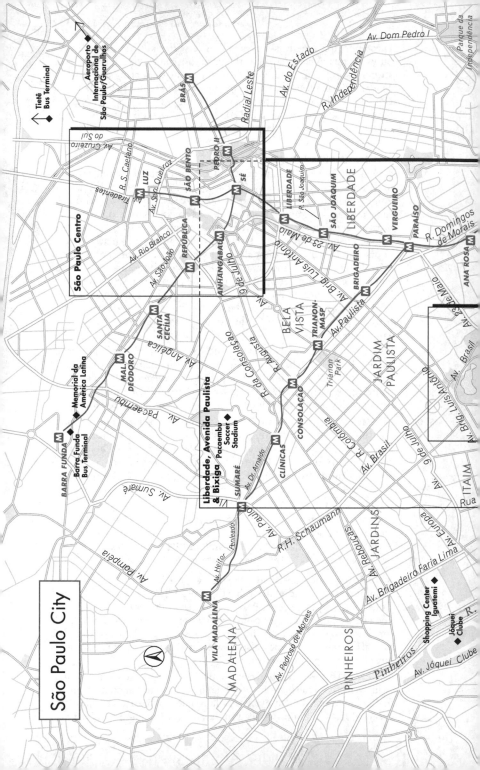

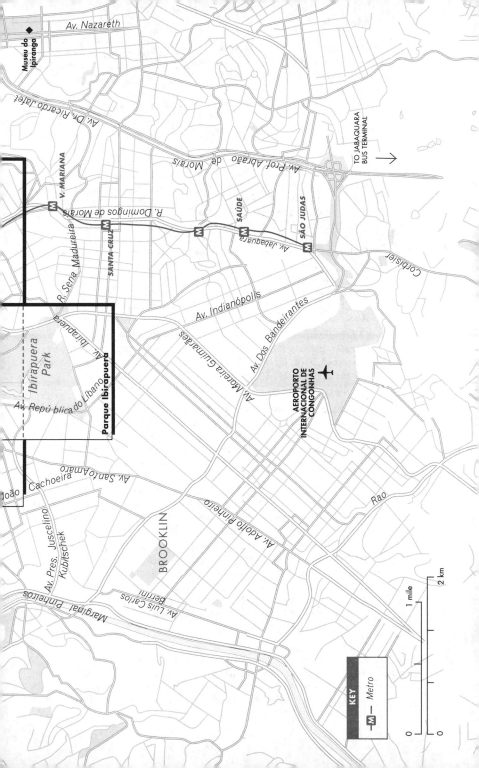

every 60 to 70 minutes), stopping at most major hotels around Avenida Paulista. Lines also connect Guarulhos to the Barra Funda bus terminal, Brooklin, and Itaquera. The cost is R$36.50. Alternatively, there is also a local, non-air-conditioned line that connects to metro Tatuapé for R$4.45.

The blue-and-white, air-conditioned Guarucoop radio taxis are the official taxis at Guarulhos Airport and can take you to Centro for around R$105 and Paulista for around R$125. It can cost up to R$170 to more distant destinations such as Morumbi. The price is set before the trip based on your drop-off address or suburb and can take from 45 minutes to two hours in peak traffic. The line for the cabs forms just outside the arrivals terminal and moves quickly. Congonhas is much closer to downtown and the Zona Sul, so it usually costs no more than R$50 with the airport's offical radio taxi company, Vermelho e Branco. Prices are not set before the trip, so fares can vary.

> **A VIEW OF THE PAST**
>
> Although modern-day São Paulo is a tough place to navigate thanks to the jungle of tall buildings, this wasn't always the case. During the city's first few hundred years, before skyscrapers appeared, there were impressive views from Avenida Paulista, which runs along a natural ridgeline extending all the way to Vila Madelena and beyond.

Transfer Contacts EMTU. ☏ *0800/770–2287* ⊕ *www.airportbusservice.com.br.* **Guarucoop.** ☏ *011/2440–7070* ⊕ *www.guarucoop.com.br.* **Rádio Taxi Vermelho e Branco.** ☏ *011/3146-4000* ⊕ *www.radiotaxivermelhoebranco.com.br.*

BUS TRAVEL

The three key bus terminals in the city of São Paulo are connected to metro (subway) stations and serve more than 1,100 destinations combined. The huge main station—serving all major Brazilian cities (with trips to Rio every 10 minutes during the day and every half hour at night, until 2 am) as well as Argentina, Uruguay, Chile, and Paraguay—is the Terminal Tietê in the north, on the Marginal Tietê Beltway. Terminal Jabaquara, near Congonhas Airport, serves coastal towns. Terminal Barra Funda, in the west, near the Memorial da América Latina, has buses to and from western Brazil. Socicam, a private company, runs all the bus terminals in the city of São Paulo.

Bus Contacts EMTU. ☏ *0800/7702287* ⊕ *www.airportbusservice.com.br.* **Socicam.** ☏ *011/3866–1100* ⊕ *www.socicam.com.br.* **Terminal Barra Funda.** ✉ *Rua Auro Soares de Moura Andrade, 664, Barra Funda* ☏ *011/3866–1100* ⊕ *www.socicam.com.br* Ⓜ *Barra Funda.* **Terminal Jabaquara.** ✉ *Rua dos Jequitibás, s/n, Jabaquara* ☏ *011/3866–1100* ⊕ *www.socicam.com.br* Ⓜ *Jabaquara.* **Terminal Tietê.** ✉ *Av. Cruzeiro do Sul, 1800, Santana* ☏ *011/3866–1100* ⊕ *www.socicam.com.br* Ⓜ *Tietê.*

TRAVEL WITHIN SÃO PAULO Municipal bus service is frequent and covers the entire city, but regular buses are overcrowded at rush hour and when it rains. If you don't speak Portuguese, it can be hard to figure out the system and the stops. The stops are clearly marked, but routes are spelled out only on the buses themselves. Buses don't stop at every bus stop, so if you're waiting, you'll have to flag one down.

Bus fare is R$3.50. You enter at the front of the bus, pay the *cobrador* (fare collector) in the middle, and exit from the rear of the bus. To pay, you can use either money or a rechargeable electronic card *bilhete único*. The card allows you to take four buses in three hours for the price of one fare. Cards can be bought and reloaded at special booths at major bus terminals or at lottery shops.

For bus numbers and names, routes, and schedules, go to the (Portuguese-language) website of Transporte Público de São Paulo (SPTrans), the city's public transport agency, or use Google Maps, which is linked to the SPTrans system and shows all bus routes. The *Guia São Paulo Ruas,* published by Quatro Rodas and sold at newsstands and bookstores for about R$15, is another option.

Contact Transporte Público de São Paulo. ☎ *156* ∰ *www.sptrans.com.br.*

CAR TRAVEL
The principal highways leading into São Paulo are: the Dutra, from the northeast (and Rio); Anhangüera and Bandeirantes, from the north; Washington Luis, from the northwest; Raposo Tavares, from the west; Régis Bittencourt, from the south; and Anchieta-Imigrantes, from Santos in the southeast. Driving in the city isn't recommended, however, because of the heavy traffic (nothing moves at rush hour, especially when it rains), daredevil drivers, and inadequate parking. You'll also need to obtain a temporary driver's license from *Detran,* the State Transit Department, which can be a time-consuming endeavor.

MAJOR HIGHWAYS AND ROADS The high-speed beltways along the Rio Pinheiros and Rio Tietê rivers—called Marginal Tietê and Marginal Pinheiros—sandwich the main part of São Paulo. Avenida 23 de Maio runs south from Centro and beneath the Parque do Ibirapuera via the Ayrton Senna Tunnel. Avenida Paulista splits Bela Vista and Jardins with Higienópolis and Vila Mariana as bookends.

You can cut through Itaim en route to Brooklin and Santo Amaro by taking avenidas Brasil and Faria Lima southwest to Avenida Santo Amaro. Avenida João Dias and Viaduto José Bonifácio C. Nogueira cut across the Pinheiros River to Morumbi. The Elevado Costa e Silva, also called Minhocão, is an elevated road that connects Centro with Avenida Francisco Matarazzo in the west.

PARKING In most commercial neighborhoods you must buy hourly tickets (called Cartão Zona Azul) to park on the street during business hours. Buy them at newsstands, not from people on the street, who may overcharge or sell counterfeited copies. Booklets of 10 one-hour tickets cost R$45. Fill out each ticket, one for every hour you plan to park, with the car's license plate and the time you initially parked. Leave the tickets in the car's window so they're visible to officials from outside. After business hours or at any time near major sights, people may offer to watch your car. If you don't pay these "caretakers," there's a chance they'll damage your car (R$2 is enough to keep your car's paint job intact). But to truly ensure your car's safety, park in a guarded lot, where rates are R$5–R$7 for the first hour and R$1–R$2 each hour thereafter.

Invest in the *Guia São Paulo Ruas,* published by Quatro Rodas, which shows every street in the city. It's sold at newsstands and bookstores for about R$30.

SUBWAY TRAVEL

Five color-coded lines compose the São Paulo Metrô, known simply as the metro by locals, which interconnects with six train lines administered by the Companhia Paulista de Trens Metropolitanos (CPTM) to blanket most of São Paulo in rail. The most glaring gaps exist around the Ibirapuera, Moema, and Morumbi neighborhoods, as well as near the airports. You can print maps of the entire network from the metro's English-language website, where you'll also find ticket prices and schedules. The first four lines are the most useful to tourists. Most notably they cover the center, Avenida Paulista, and Vila Madalena.

Kiosks at all metro and train stations sell tickets; vendors prefer small bills for payment. You insert the ticket into the turnstile at the platform entrance, and it's returned to you only if there's unused fare on it. Seniors (65 or older) ride without charge by showing photo IDs at the turnstiles. Transfers within the metro system are free. A single ticket costs R$3.50. You can also buy a rechargeable *bilhete único* (good for combination tickets for the bus and the metro, R$5.45) at metro stations.

Subway Information Metrô. ☎ *0800/770–7722* ⊕ *www.metro.sp.gov.br.*

TAXI TRAVEL

Taxis in São Paulo are white. Owner-driven taxis are generally well maintained and reliable, as are radio taxis. Fares start at R$4.10 and run from R$2.70 for each kilometer (½ mile) or R$0.55 for every minute sitting in traffic. After 8 pm and on weekends, fares rise up to 50%. You'll pay a tax if the cab leaves the city, as is the case with trips to Cumbica Airport. Good radio-taxi companies, among them Coopertax, Ligue-Taxi, and Radio Taxi Vermelho e Branco, usually accept credit cards, but you must call ahead and request the service. Smartphone apps like Easy Taxi and 99Taxis are popular, reliable, and highly recommended.

Taxi Contacts Coopertaxi. ☎ *011/2095–6000, 011/3511–1919* ⊕ *www. coopertax.com.br.* **Ligue-Taxi.** ☎ *011/2101–3030, 011/3873–3030* ⊕ *www. ligue-taxi.com.br.* **Radio Taxi Vermelho e Branco.** ☎ *011/3146–4000* ⊕ *www. radiotaxivermelhoebranco.com.br.*

SAFETY

Stay alert and guard your belongings at all times. Avoid wearing expensive sneakers or watches and flashy jewelry, and be careful with cameras, smartphones, and tablets—all of which attract attention. Muggers love to target the airports, tourist-frequented neighborhoods, and ATMs, so be vigilant while in these spaces.

If driving, stay alert during traffic jams and at stop signs, especially at night, and don't deviate from the main streets and beltways. Watch out for motorcycles with pillion passengers, as this is a popular mode of transport for thieves. It's best to keep your windows up and doors locked.

VISITOR INFORMATION

The most helpful contact is the São Paulo Convention and Visitors Bureau, open weekdays from 9 to 6. Branches of the city-operated São Paulo Turismo are open daily from 9 to 6. The Secretaria de Turismo do Estado de São Paulo, open weekdays from 9 to 6, is less helpful, but has maps and information about the city and state of São Paulo. The Secretaria also has a booth at the arrivals terminal in Guarulhos airport; it's open daily from 9 am to 10 pm.

Visitor Information **São Paulo Convention and Visitors Bureau.** ✉ *Alameda Ribeirão Preto 130, conjuntos 121, Jardins* ☎ *011/3736–0600, 011/3289–7588* ⊕ *www.spcvb.com.br.* **São Paulo Turismo S/A.** ✉ *Anhembi Convention Center, Av. Olavo Fontoura 1209, Santana* ☎ *011/2226–0400* ⊕ *www.spturis.com.* **São Paulo Turismo S/A.** ✉ *Praça da República, Rua 7 de Abril, Centro* ⊕ *www.spturis. com* Ⓜ *República.* **São Paulo Turismo S/A.** ✉ *Av. Paulista 1853, Cerqueira César* ⊕ *www.spturis.com* Ⓜ *Trianon-Masp.* **São Paulo Turismo S/A.** ✉ *Bus station, Av. Cruzeiro do Sul 1800, Tietê* ⊕ *www.spturis.com* Ⓜ *Tietê.* **São Paulo Turismo S/A.** ✉ *Guarulhos Airport Terminals 1 and 2, Aeroporto de Guarulhos* ⊕ *www.spturis. com.* **Secretaria de Turismo do Estado de São Paulo.** ✉ *Praça Antônio Prado 9, Centro* ☎ *011/3241–5822* ⊕ *www.turismo.sp.gov.br.*

TOURS

You can hire a bilingual guide through a travel agency or a hotel concierge (about R$15 an hour with a four-hour minimum), or you can design your own itineraries. The São Paulo tourist board's Cidade São Paulo website offers various themed walking itineraries and English-language audio guides, and it outlines tours facilitated by subway through the TurisMetrô program. SPTuris conducts three half-day bus tours on Sunday, one covering the parks, one centered on the museums, and one focused on the historical downtown area. Officially, the board's guides don't speak English, but it's sometimes possible to arrange for an English speaker.

Check Point. Check Point's daily tours specialize in general sightseeing. They don't have a physical location, so reservations are online-only. ☎ *011/2791–1316 business hours, 011/99187–1393 after-hours* ⊕ *www.checkpointtours.com.br* ✆ *From R$450 for three people.*

Easygoing Brazil. Brazilian cooking lessons, kart rides at the Interlagos Formula One racetrack, and fly-and-dine tours that include a helicopter trip are part of Easygoing's personalized services. You can book tours in English if you reserve by phone. ✉ *Perdizes* ☎ *011/3801–9540* ⊕ *www. easygoing.com.br* ✆ *From R$373.*

Gol Tour Viagens e Turismo. This company offers half-day city tours, and they also do custom and out-of-town tours for small groups to cities such as Campos do Jordão. ✉ *Centro* ☎ *011/3256–2388* ⊕ *www. goltour.com.br* ✆ *From R$155.*

Sampa Bikers. Specializing in city bicycle tours and excursions outside town, Sampa Bikers has a two-hour tour every Wednesday. ✉ ☎ *011/5517–7733* ⊕ *www.sampabikers.com.br* ✆ *From R$50.*

SP Free Walking Tours. To explore the city's historic center or the gleaming towers and old mansions around Avenida Paulista, join one of the free, English-language group tours run by this outfitter. Tours are around three hours long and leave from Praça República and Avenida Paulista. ⊕ *www.saopaulofreewalkingtour.com.*

Terra Nobre. This company's four-hour car tours include a driver and an English-speaking guide, for one or two people. ⊠ *Rua Tagipuru 235, Conjuntos 44, Perdizes* ☎ *011/3662–1505* ⊕ *www.terranobre.com.br* ✒ *From US$310.*

EXPLORING SÃO PAULO

CENTRO

The downtown district is one of the few places in São Paulo where a significant amount of pre-20th-century history remains visible. You can explore the areas where the city began and view examples of architecture, some of it beautifully restored, from the 19th century. Petty criminals operate in this area, so keep your wits about you while you tour. The best way to get here is by metro.

> **STAY ALERT**
>
> Pickpocketing can be a problem in Centro, so keep a low profile, don't wear expensive jewelry or watches, and bring only what money you absolutely need. Touring with a guide usually provides some extra security.

For an easy glimpse of Centro, start at the Anhangabaú metro station and head northwest along the valley (Vale do Anhangabaú). Pass under the historic Viaduto do Chá viaduct and take in the sight of the magnificent, baroque Theatro Municipal to your left. A bit farther along near the São Bento metro station, find your way to the monastery of the same name, uphill to the right. Then continue on over the hill, and make your way downhill, zigzagging through the crowded shopping streets towards Mercado Municipal.

TOP ATTRACTIONS

Catedral da Sé. The imposing, 14-tower neo-Gothic Catedral da Sé occupies the official center of São Paulo—the 0 Km point, as it's called here. Tours of the church wind through the crypt, which contains the remains of Tibiriçá, a native Brazilian who helped the Portuguese back in 1554. ⊠ *Praça da Sé s/n, Centro* ☎ *011/3106–2709, 011/3107–6832 for tour information* ⊕ *www.catedraldase.org.br/site* ✒ *Tour R$5* ☉ *Church weekdays 8–7, Sat. 8–5, Sun. 8–1 and 2–6; tours weekdays 1–4:30, weekends 9–3* Ⓜ *Sé.*

Edifício Itália. One way to catch the astounding view from atop the Itália Building is to drop in for lunch or dinner at the Terraço Itália restaurant, starting on the 41st floor. The main dining room features central columns, candlelit tables, and a terrace. A live band and dance floor jazz up the panoramic parlor upstairs Monday to Saturday. The restaurant is expensive, making a drink at the piano bar, with its upholstered seating and wood lining, a more affordable strategy. Thriftier still is a visit to the outside terrace, which is free weekdays 3–4 pm. ⊠ *Av. Ipiranga 344, Centro* ☎ *011/2189–2929 restaurant* ⊕ *www.*

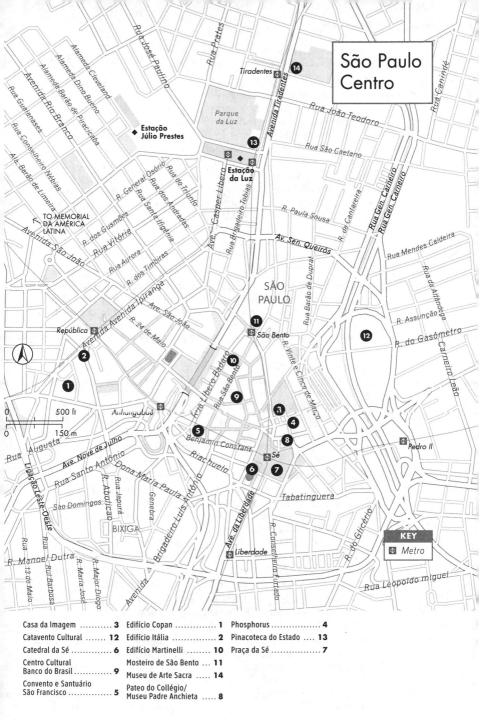

São Paulo
Centro

Tiradentes **14**

Parque
da Luz

Estação
Júlio Prestes

13

Estação
da Luz

TO MEMORIAL
DA AMÉRICA
LATINA

Rua João Teodoro

Rua São Caetano

R. Paula Sousa

SÃO
PAULO

República

11

São Bento

12

2

1

10

9

Anhangabaú

5

Benjamin Constant

Riachuelo

1

4

8

Sé

6

7

Pedro II

Tabatinguera

São Domingos

BIXIGA

Liberdade

Rua Leopoldo miguel

KEY

🚇 Metro

terracoitalia.com.br ✉ *Piano bar R$30 entrance fee* ☉ *Daily noon–midnight* Ⓜ *República.*

Fodor's Choice ★ **Edifício Martinelli.** Amid São Paulo's modern 1950s-era skyscrapers, the Gothic Martinelli Building is a welcome anomaly. Built in 1929 by Italian immigrant–turned-count Giuseppe Martinelli, it was the city's first skyscraper. The whimsical penthouse is worth checking out, and the rooftop has a great view. ⊠ *Av. São João 35, Centro* ☎ *011/3104–2477* ⊕ *www.predio martinelli.com.br/visitas.php* ✉ *Free* ☉ *Weekdays 9:30–11:20 and 2–4, weekends 9–1* Ⓜ *São Bento.*

Mosteiro de São Bento. The German architect Richard Berndl designed this Norman–Byzantine church that was completed in 1922. Ecclesiastical imagery abounds, and soaring archways extend skyward. The church's enormous organ has some 6,000 pipes, and its Russian image of the Kasperovo Virgin is covered with 6,000 pearls from the Black Sea. On the last Sunday of each month, paulistanos compete for space at the church's popular brunch (noon–3:30, R$178 per person), which also includes a tour and varying performances, from dance to choir. To join the party, call *011/2440–7837* early to reserve your seat. The don't-miss religious event at Mosterio de São Bento is Sunday Mass at 10 am, when the sound of monks' Gregorian chants echoes through the chamber. ⊠ *Largo de São Bento, Centro* ☎ *011/3328–8799* ⊕ *www. mosteiro.org.br* ✉ *Free* ☉ *Weekdays 6–6, weekends 6–noon and 4–6* Ⓜ *São Bento.*

Museu de Arte Sacra (*Museum of Sacred Art*). If you can't get to Bahia or Minas Gerais during your stay in Brazil, you can get a taste of the fabulous baroque and rococo art found there at the Museum of Sacred Art. On display are 4,000 wooden and terra-cotta masks, jewelry, and liturgical objects from all over the country (but primarily Minas Gerais and Bahia), dating from the 17th century to the present. The on-site convent was founded in 1774. ⊠ *Av. Tiradentes 676, Centro* ☎ *011/5627–5393* ⊕ *www.museuartesacra.org.br* ✉ *R$6, free Sat.* ☉ *Tues.–Fri. 9–5, weekends 10–6* Ⓜ *Tiradentes or Luz.*

Pinacoteca do Estado. The highlights of the State Art Gallery's permanent collection include paintings by the renowned Brazilian artists Tarsila do Amaral and Cândido Portinari. Amaral, who died in São Paulo in 1973, applied avant-garde techniques, some of which she acquired while hanging out with the cubists in 1920s Paris, with Brazilian themes and content. Portinari, born in São Paulo State and known for his neo-realistic style, also dealt with social and historical themes. The museum occupies a 1905 structure that was renovated in the late 1990s. The exterior recalls a 1950s brick firehouse, while the view through the

A Bit of History

São Paulo wasn't big and important right from the start. Jesuit priests founded it in 1554 and began converting native Indians to Catholicism. The town was built strategically on a plateau, protected from attack and served by many rivers. It remained unimportant to the Portuguese crown until the 1600s, when it became the departure point for the *bandeira* (literally, "flag") expeditions, whose members set out to look for gemstones and gold, to enslave Indians, and, later, to capture escaped African slaves. In the process, these adventurers established roads into vast portions of previously unexplored territory. São Paulo also saw Emperor Dom Pedro I declare independence from Portugal in 1822, by the Rio Ipiranga (Ipiranga River), near the city.

It was only in the late 19th century that São Paulo became a driving force in the country. As the state established itself as one of Brazil's main coffee producers, the city attracted laborers and investors from many countries. Italians, Portuguese, Spanish, Germans, and Japanese put their talents and energies to work. By 1895, 70,000 of the 130,000 residents were immigrants. Their efforts transformed the place from a sleepy mission post into a dynamic financial and cultural hub, with people of all colors and religions living and working together peacefully.

Avenida Paulista was once the site of many a coffee baron's mansion. Money flowed from these private domains into civic and cultural institutions. The arts began to flourish, and by the 1920s São Paulo was promoting such great artists as Mário and Oswald de Andrade, who introduced modern elements into Brazilian art.

In the 1950s the auto industry began to develop and contributed greatly to São Paulo's contemporary wealth—and problems. Over the next 30 years, people from throughout Brazil, especially the Northeast, came seeking jobs, which transformed the city's landscape by increasing slums and poverty. Between the 1950s and today, the city's main revenue has moved from industry to banking and commerce.

Today, like many major European or American hubs, São Paulo struggles to meet its citizens' transportation and housing needs, and goods and services are expensive. Like most of its counterparts elsewhere in the world, it hasn't yet found an answer to these problems.

---

central courtyard's interior windows evokes the cliffs of Cuenca, Spain. Admission is valid for same-day admission to the Estação Pinacoteca, the Pinacoteca's second branch, which is a short walk away at Largo General Osório 66. The area is sketchy so stay alert as you go, especially at night. ⊠ *Praça da Luz 2, Centro* ☎ *011/3324–1000* ⊕ *www. pinacoteca.org.br* ⊠ *R$6, free Thurs. 5–10 and Sat.* ⊙ *Mon.–Wed. and weekends 10–8, Thurs. 10–10* Ⓜ *Luz.*

Praça da Sé. Two major metro lines cross under the busy Praça da Sé, the large plaza that marks the city's geographical center and holds its main cathedral. Migrants from Brazil's poor Northeast often gather here to enjoy their music and to purchase and sell regional items such as medicinal herbs, while street children hang out and try to avoid the periodic police sweeps to remove them. ✉ *Praça da Sé s/n, Centro* Ⓜ *Sé.*

WORTH NOTING

Casa da Imagem. This museum dedicated to São Paulo–themed photography opened in 2012 on the site of Casa No. 1, named for its original address in 1689. The 84,000-image collection, which traces the city's expansion and increasing complexity, includes flashbacks to the days when nearby park Vale do Anhangabaú hosted ceremonies for the rich and regal. Casa da Imagem speaks to São Paulo's earliest foundations, but also captures its contemporary composition. ✉ *Rua Roberto Simonsen 136-B, Centro* ☎ *011/3106–5122* ⊕ *www.museudacidade.sp.gov. br/casadaimagem.php* 💳 *Free* ◷ *Tues.–Sun. 9–5* Ⓜ *Sé.*

> **GAROA**
>
> One of São Paulo's most famous nicknames is *terra da garoa,* which basically means land of drizzling rain. A dearth of sufficient rain in recent years has put an end to that nickname, but especially in the summertime, when afternoon rains wash over the city most days, a lightweight umbrella is a sensible item to carry.

FAMILY **Catavento Cultural.** Traveling families will find education and entertainment for their children at this interactive science museum in the former city hall building. For architecture fans, the early-20th-century structure, with its interior courtyard, alone justifies a visit. Stepping into human-size soap bubbles or touching actual meteorites, meanwhile, are the big attractions for kids. The museum's exhibits are organized along four thematic lines: the universe, life, ingenuity, and society. ✉ *Parque Dom Pedro II, Palácio das Indústrias s/n, Brás* ☎ *011/3315–0051* ⊕ *www.cataventocultural.org.br* 💳 *R$6* ◷ *Tues.–Sun. 9–5, last admission 4* Ⓜ *Pedro II.*

Centro Cultural Banco do Brasil. The greenhouse-size skylight of this cultural center's 1901 neoclassical home makes the modern and contemporary art exhibits here seem almost to sprout organically. Past ones include "The Magic World of Escher." Plays and small film festivals, the latter celebrating filmmakers from Quentin Tarantino to Louis Malle, further broaden the venue's appeal. The center's facilities include a theater, an auditorium, a movie theater, a video room, and three floors of exhibition rooms. ✉ *Rua Álvares Penteado 112, Centro* ☎ *011/3113–3651, 011/3113–3652* 💳 *Free; performances R$10; movies R$4* ◷ *Wed.–Mon. 9–9* Ⓜ *Sé.*

Convento e Santuário São Francisco. One of the city's best-preserved Portuguese colonial buildings, this baroque structure—two churches, one run by Catholic clergy and the other by lay brothers—was built between 1647 and 1790. The image inside of Saint Francis was rescued from a fire in 1870. ✉ *Largo São Francisco 133, Centro* ☎ *011/3291–2400* ⊕ *www.franciscanos.org.br* 💳 *Free* ◷ *Mon.–Sat. 7:30–5:50* Ⓜ *Sé or Anhangabaú.*

Edifício Copan. The architect of this serpentine apartment and office block, Oscar Niemeyer, went on to design much of Brasília, the nation's capital. The building has the clean, white, undulating curves characteristic of Niemeyer's work. The Copan was constructed in 1950, and its 1,160 apartments house about 5,000 people. Pivô (*www.pivo. org.br*), a stunning new art gallery inside the Copan, has exhibitions, workshops, residencies, and educational activities; admission is free. ✉ *Av. Ipiranga 200, Centro* ☎ *011/3257–6169* ⊕ *www.copansp.com. br* Ⓜ *República.*

Café Floresta. Drop in at this standing-room-only coffee bar for a cup of java and to soak up the atmosphere inside the Copan building, which includes shops, restaurants, and cafés on the ground floor. ✉ *Av. Ipiranga 200, Loja 21, Centro* ☎ *011/3259–8416* ⊕ *www.cafefloresta.com.br* Ⓜ *República.*

Pateo do Collegio / Museu Padre Anchieta. São Paulo was founded by the Jesuits José de Anchieta and Manoel da Nóbrega in the College Courtyard in 1554. The church was constructed in 1896 in the same style as the chapel built by the Jesuits. In the small museum you can see a fascinating relief map of Centro in colonial times and an exhibition of early sacred art and relics. ✉ *Praça Pateo do Collegio 2, Centro* ☎ *011/3105–6899* ⊕ *www.pateocollegio.com.br* 💲 *Museum R$6* ☉ *Museum Tues.–Sun. 9–4:30; church Mon.–Sat. 8:15–7, Sun. Mass at 10* Ⓜ *Sé.*

Phosphorus. This wonderful contemporary art gallery, which also encompasses a second gallery, Sé, on the top floor, occupies one of the oldest buildings in the area, which it shares with a vintage clothing company, Casa Juisi. ✉ *Rua Roberto Simonsen 108, Centro* ☎ *011/3107–7074* ⊕ *www.phosphorus.art.br/about* 💲 *Free* ☉ *Thurs.–Fri. noon–7, Sat. noon–5* Ⓜ *Sé.*

Café do Páteo. A great place to rest your feet while touring Centro, this café on a large balcony overlooking the east side of town serves cold and hot drinks along with typical snacks, such as *pão de queijo* (cheese bread). ✉ *Praça Pateo do Collegio 2, Centro* ☎ *011/3105–6899* ⊕ *www. pateodocollegio.com.br* ☉ *Tue.–Sun. 9–4:30* Ⓜ *São Bento.*

LIBERDADE

The red-porticoed entryway to Liberdade (which means "Freedom") is south of Praça da Sé, behind the cathedral. The neighborhood is home to many first-, second-, and third-generation Nippo-Brazilians, as well as to more recent Chinese and Korean immigrants. Clustered around Avenida Liberdade are shops with everything from imported bubble gum to miniature robots and Kabuki face paint.

The best time to visit Liberdade is on Sunday during the street fair at Praça Liberdade, where Asian food, crafts, and souvenirs are sold. The fair will very likely be crowded, so keep your wits about you and do not wander around at night.

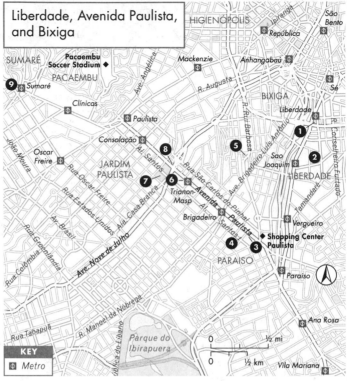

TOP ATTRACTIONS

Museu Histórico da Imigração Japonesa no Brasil. The three-floor Museum of Japanese Immigration has exhibits about Nippo-Brazilian culture and farm life, and about Japanese contributions to Brazilian horticulture. There are also World War II memorials. Relics and life-size re-creations of scenes from the Japanese diaspora line the walls, and paintings hang from the ceiling like wind chimes. Most of the museum's labels are in Portuguese. ⊠ *Rua São Joaquim 381, Liberdade* ☎ *011/3209–5465* ⊕ *www.museubunkyo.org.br* ☒ *R$7* ⊙ *Tues.–Sun. 1:30–5:30* Ⓜ *São Joaquim.*

WORTH NOTING

Praça Liberdade. To experience the eclectic cultural mix that keeps São Paulo pulsing, visit Praça Liberdade on a weekend, when the square hosts a sprawling Asian food and crafts fair. You might see Afro-Brazilians dressed in colorful kimonos hawking grilled shrimp on a stick, or perhaps a religious celebration such as April's Hanamatsuri, commemorating the birth of the Buddha. Many Japanese shops and restaurants worth a stop can be found near the square. ⊠ *Av. da Liberdade and Rua dos Estudantes, Liberdade* ⊙ *Fair weekends 10–7* Ⓜ *Liberdade.*

AVENIDA PAULISTA AND BIXIGA

Money once poured into and out of the coffee barons' mansions that lined Avenida Paulista, making it, in a sense, the financial hub. And so it is today, though the money is now centered in the major banks. Like the barons before them, many of these financial institutions generously support the arts. Numerous places have changing exhibitions—often free—in the Paulista neighborhood. Nearby Bixiga, São Paulo's Little Italy, is full of restaurants—Italian, of course.

TOP ATTRACTIONS

Casa das Rosas. Peek into the Paulista's past at one of the avenue's few remaining early-20th-century buildings, the House of the Roses. A 1935 French-style mansion with gardens inspired by those at Versailles, it seems out of place next to the surrounding skyscrapers. The famous paulistano architect Ramos de Azevedo designed the home for one of his daughters, and the same family occupied it until 1986, when it was made an official municipal landmark. The site, now a cultural center, hosts classes and literary events. Coffee drinks and pastries are served at the café on the terrace. ⊠ *Av. Paulista 37, Paraíso* ☎ *011/3285–6986, 011/3288–9447* ⊕ *www.casadasrosas.org.br* ⊠ *Free* ⊙ *Tues.–Sat. 10–10, Sun. 10–6; café noon–5* Ⓜ *Brigadeiro.*

NEED A BREAK?

Ponto Chic. Stop here for a delicious *bauru*—a sandwich with roast beef, tomato, cucumber, and a mix of melted cheeses. This branch of the Paissandu restaurant that invented the bauru is a block east of the Instituto Itaú Cultural, across Avenida Paulista. ⊠ *Praça Osvaldo Cruz 26, Paraíso* ☎ *011/3289-1480* ⊕ *www.pontochic.com.br* ⊙ *Daily 11 am–2 am.*

Fodor's Choice ★ **Museu de Arte de São Paulo (MASP).** A striking low-rise building elevated on two massive concrete pillars holds one of the city's premier fine-arts collections. The highlights include works by Van Gogh, Renoir, Delacroix, Cézanne, Monet, Rembrandt, Picasso, and Degas. The baroque sculptor Aleijadinho, the expressionist painter Lasar Segall, and the expressionist/surrealist painter Cândido Portinari are three of the many Brazilian artists represented. The huge open area beneath the museum is often used for cultural events and protests, and is the site of a charming Sunday antiques fair. ⊠ *Av. Paulista 1578, Bela Vista* ☎ *011/3251–5644* ⊕ *www.masp.art.br* ⊠ *R$15; free Tues.* ⊙ *Tues.–Wed. and Fri.–Sun. 10–6, Thurs. 10–8* Ⓜ *Trianon-MASP.*

Parque Trianon. Created in 1892 as a showcase for local vegetation, the park was renovated in 1968 by Roberto Burle Marx, the Brazilian landscaper famed for Rio's mosaic-tile beachfront sidewalks. You can escape the noise of the street and admire the flora and the 300-year-old trees while seated on one of the benches sculpted to look like chairs. ⊠ *Rua Peixoto Gomide 949, Jardim Paulista* ☎ *011/3289–2160, 011/3253–4973* ⊠ *Free* ⊙ *Daily 6–6* Ⓜ *Trianon-MASP.*

WORTH NOTING

Centro Cultural FIESP–Ruth Cardoso. Adorned with LED lights, the cultural center's pyramid-shaped facade serves as an open-air digital-art gallery. Past exhibits at this facility of São Paulo State's Federation of

TAKE A WALK

The imposing and almost dead-straight Avenida Paulista is a great place to explore on foot. Running from Paraíso (paradise) to Consolação (consolation), two bookending metro stations, the avenue also serves as paulistanos' tongue-in-cheek comparison to marriage, but many couples of all ages will be found strolling here hand-in-hand. The Museu de Arte de São Paulo (MASP) has one of Brazil's best collections of fine art. Right across the street is shady Parque Trianon, where locals hang out and eat lunch. Leaving the park, veer right and head for the Centro Cultural FIESP. Here you may be able to catch one of its art shows or performances. A few blocks away is the Instituto Itaú Cultural, a great place to see contemporary Brazilian art. Finally, rest your weary feet in Casa das Rosas, a cultural center and café, with a pretty rose garden attached.

Industry have broadcast towering games of Pac-Man and Space Invaders to pedestrians and nearby residents. The center has a theater, a library of art and photography, galleries that host temporary exhibitions, and areas for lectures, films, and other events. ⊠ *Av. Paulista 1313, Jardim Paulista* ☎ *011/3146–7405* ⊕ *www.fiesp.com.br/centro-cultural-fiesp-ruth-cardoso* ⊠ *Free* ◷ *Mon. 11–8, Tues.–Sat. 10–8, Sun. 10–7* Ⓜ *Trianon-MASP.*

Centro da Cultura Judaica. A short cab or metro trip northwest of Avenida Paulista, this Torah-shape concrete building is one of the newest architectural hot spots in town. Inaugurated in 2003 to display Jewish history and culture in Brazil, it houses a theater and an art gallery and promotes exhibits, lectures, and book fairs. The center's café was inspired by New York delis and serves local Jewish cuisine. ⊠ *Rua Oscar Freire 2500, Pinheiros* ☎ *011/3065–4333* ⊕ *www.culturajudaica. org.br* ⊠ *Free* ◷ *Tues.–Sun. noon–7* Ⓜ *Sumaré.*

Feira do Bixiga. Strolling through this flea market is a favorite Sunday activity for paulistanos. Crafts, antiques, and furniture are among the wares. Walk up the São José staircase to see **Rua dos Ingleses,** a typical and well-preserved fin-de-siècle Bixiga street. ⊠ *Praça Dom Orione s/n, Bixiga* ⊠ *Free* ◷ *Sun. 8–5.*

Itaú Cultural. Maintained by Itaú, one of Brazil's largest private banks, this cultural institute has art shows as well as lectures, workshops, and films. It also maintains an archive with a photographic history of São Paulo, a library that specializes in works on Brazilian art and culture, and a new permanent exhibition tracing the formation of Brazil. ⊠ *Av. Paulista 149, Paraíso* ☎ *011/2168–1777* ⊕ *www.itaucultural.org.br* ⊠ *Free* ◷ *Tues.–Fri. 9–8, weekends 11–8* Ⓜ *Brigadeiro.*

PARQUE IBIRAPUERA

Ibirapuera is São Paulo's Central Park, though it's slightly less than half the size and is often more crowded on sunny weekends than its New York City counterpart. In the 1950s the land, which originally contained the municipal nurseries, was chosen as the site of a public park to commemorate the city's 400th anniversary. Architect Oscar Niemeyer and landscape architect Roberto Burle Marx joined the team of professionals assigned to the project. The park was inaugurated in 1954, and some pavilions used for the opening festivities still sit amid its 160 hectares (395 acres). It has jogging and biking paths, a lake, and rolling lawns. You can rent bicycles near some of the park entrances for about R$5 an hour.

TOP ATTRACTIONS

Museu Afro Brasil. Among Parque Ibirapuera's various attractions, natural and architectural, this museum might easily pass unnoticed. But in terms of its content—a thorough if sometimes patchily organized survey of Brazil's profoundly important but underreported black history—it's highly recommended. English available only to download as audio, so bring your headphones. ⊠ *Av. Pedro Álvares Cabral, Gate 10, Parque Ibirapuera* 🕾 *011/3320–8900* ⊕ *www.museuafrobrasil.org.br* ⊠ *R$6, free Thurs. and Sat.* ☉ *Tues.–Sun. 10–5* Ⓜ *Brigadeiro.*

Museu de Arte Contemporânea (MAC). The Museum of Contemporary Art expanded its Ibirapuera presence in 2012 by renovating and moving into the eight-floor former Department of Transportation building. Now shorn of its bureaucratic coldness, the space ranks among Parque Ibirapuera's architectural highlights (even though it is just over the road, rather than inside the park). The museum houses the MAC's entire 10,000-piece collection, including works by Picasso, Modigliani, and Chagall. ⊠ *Av. Pedro Álvares Cabral 1301, Parque Ibirapuera* 🕾 *011/5573–9932 direct line, 011/3091–3039* ⊕ *www.macvirtual.usp. br* ⊠ *Free* ☉ *Tues. 10–9, Wed–Sun. 10–6.*

Museu de Arte Moderna (*MAM*). More than 4,500 paintings, installations, sculptures, and other works from modern and contemporary artists such as Alfredo Volpi and Ligia Clark are part of the Museum of Modern Art's permanent collection. Temporary exhibits often feature works by new local artists. The giant wall of glass, designed by Brazilian architect Lina Bo Bardi, serves as a window beckoning you to glimpse inside; an exterior mural painted in 2010 by Os Gêmeos, São Paulo twin brothers famous for their graffiti art, shows a little of MAM's inner appeal to the outside world. ⊠ *Av. Pedro Álvares Cabral, Gate 3, Parque Ibirapuera* 🕾 *011/5085–1300* ⊕ *www.mam.org.br* ⊠ *R$6, free Sun.* ☉ *Tues.–Sun. 10–6.*

NEED A BREAK?

Prêt no MAM. The café inside the Museum of Modern Art serves dishes from many lands, Brazil, France, and Italy among them. Except for hot-dog stands, this is one of the few places in Parque Ibirapuera to buy food. It's open for lunch only (buffet R$49.90). ⊠ *Av. Pedro Álvares Cabral, Gate 3, Parque Ibirapuera* 🕾 *011/5085–1306* ⊕ *www.mam.org.br* ☉ *Tues.–Sun. noon–4.*

Parque Ibirapuera

Pavilhão da Bienal. In even-numbered years this pavilion hosts the *Bienal* (Biennial), an exhibition that presents the works of artists from more than 60 countries. The first such event was held in 1951 in Parque Trianon and drew artists from 21 countries. After Ibirapuera Park's inauguration in 1954, the Bienal was moved to this Oscar Niemeyer–designed building that's noteworthy for its large open spaces and floors connected by circular slopes. ⊠ *Av. Pedro Álvares Cabral, Gate 3, Pavilhão Ciccillo Matarazzo, Parque Ibirapuera* ☎ *011/5576–7600, 011/5576–7641* ⊕ *www.bienal.org.br.*

WORTH NOTING

Auditório do Ibirapuera. The final building in Oscar Niemeyer's design for the park, the Auditório opened in 2005. It has since become one of São Paulo's trademark sights, with what looks like a giant red lightning bolt striking a massive white daredevil ramp. Seating up to 800, the concert hall regularly welcomes leading Brazilian and international musical acts. Its back wall can be retracted to reveal the stage to thousands more on the lawn outside. ⊠ *Gate 3, Av. Pedro Álvares Cabral, Parque Ibirapuera* ☎ *011/3629–1075* ⊕ *www.auditorioibirapuera.com.br.*

Oca. A spacecraft-like building that's pure Oscar Niemeyer, the Oca often hosts popular temporary art exhibitions. The building isn't usually open to the public when there is no show on. ⊠ *Av. Pedro Álvares*

Cabral, Gate 3, Parque Ibirapuera
☎ *011/3105–6118,   011/5082–*
1777 ⊕ *www.parqueibirapuera.org*
🖭 *Price varies depending on show.*

Pavilhão Japonês. An exact replica
of the Katsura Imperial Palace in
Kyoto, Japan, the Japanese Pavilion is one of the structures built
for the Parque Ibirapuera's inauguration. Designed by professor
Sutemi Horiguti of the University
of Tokyo, it was built in Japan and
reassembled here beside the man-
made lake in the Japanese-style
garden. The main building displays

> **PEOPLE'S PARK**
>
> One of the city's all-too-few parks,
> Parque Ibirapuera is a great place
> to find a bit of peace and quiet
> during the week, and for people-
> watching on weekends, when
> the packed park plays host to
> paulistanos of every background.
> Weekdays, it can be hard to find
> snacks as you wander the park, so
> consider bringing an energy bar
> or an apple along for the ride.

samurai clothing, pottery, and sculpture from several dynasties; rooms
upstairs are used for traditional tea ceremonies. ⌷ *Av. Pedro Álvares
Cabral, Gate 10, Parque Ibirapuera* ☎ *011/5081–7296* ⊕ *www.bunkyo.
org.br* 🖭 *R$6* ⊙ *Wed. and weekends 10–noon and 1–5.*

GREATER SÃO PAULO

Several far-flung sights are worth a taxi ride to see. West of Centro is the
Universidade de São Paulo (USP), which has two interesting museums: a
branch of the Museu de Arte Contemporânea and the Instituto Butantã,
with its collection of creatures that slither and crawl. Close by, Parque
Villa-Lobos is a smaller but still significant alternative to Ibirapuera for
sporty locals. Head southwest of Centro to the Fundação Maria Luisa e
Oscar Americano, a museum with a forest and garden in the residential
neighborhood of Morumbi. In the Parque do Estado, southeast of Centro, are the Jardim Botânico and the Parque Zoológico de São Paulo.

TOP ATTRACTIONS

Fundação Maria Luisa e Oscar Americano. A beautiful, quiet private
wooded estate is the setting for the Maria Luisa and Oscar Americano
Foundation. Paintings, furniture, sacred art, silver, porcelain, engrav-
ings, tapestries, sculptures, and personal possessions of the Brazilian
royal family are among the 1,500 objects from the Portuguese colonial
and imperial periods on display here, and there are some modern pieces
as well. Having afternoon high tea here is an event, albeit an expensive
one, and Sunday concerts take place in the auditorium. ⌷ *Av. Morumbi
4077, Morumbi* ☎ *011/3742–0077* ⊕ *www.fundacaooscaramericano.
org.br* 🖭 *R$10* ⊙ *Tues.–Sun. 10–5:30.*

Memorial da América Latina. The memorial's massive concrete hand sculpture, its fingers reaching toward the São Paulo sky, is one of the city's
signature images. Part of a 20-acre park filled with Oscar Niemeyer–
designed structures, the Memorial da América Latina was inaugurated in 1989 in homage to regional unity and its greatest champions,
among them Simón Bolívar and José Martí. Aside from the monument, the grounds' highlights include works by Cândido Portinari
and an auditorium dedicated to musical and theatrical performances.

Free two-hour guided visits for individuals or groups of up to 40 people can be scheduled in advance for Tuesday and Sunday at 10 am or 3 pm. ⊠ *Av. Auro Soares de Moura Andrade 664, Barra Funda* ☎ *011/3823–4600, 011/3823-4655 For guided visit reservations only, Tues.–Fri. 2–6* ⊕ *www.memorial. org.br* ✉ *Free* ☉ *Tues.–Sun. 9–6* Ⓜ *Barra Funda.*

FAMILY **Parque Zoológico de São Paulo.** The 200-acre São Paulo Zoo has more than 3,200 animals, and many of its 410 species—such as the *micoleão-dourado* (golden lion tamarin monkey)—are endangered. If you visit the zoo, don't miss the monkey houses, built on small islands in the park's lake, and the Casa do Sangue Frio (Cold-Blooded House), with reptilian and amphibious creatures. ⊠ *Av. Miguel Stéfano 4241, Água Funda, Parque do Estado* ☎ *011/5073–0811* ⊕ *www.zoologico.com.br* ✉ *R$18* ☉ *Tues.–Sun. 9–5* Ⓜ *Jabaquara.*

> **STARCHITECT**
>
> World-famous paulistano landscape architect Roberto Burle Marx (1909–94) is responsible for the design of many of São Paulo's top sites, including a host of contemplative gardens and parks. Also an artist, ecologist, and naturalist, Burle Marx has been honored by the naming of a beautiful park in the Morumbi region southwest of the city: Parque Burle Marx features a number of weaving tracks among thick Atlantic Forest as well some fine examples of his design work.

WORTH NOTING

FAMILY **Instituto Butantan.** In 1888 a Brazilian scientist, with the aid of the state government, turned a farmhouse into a center for the production of snake serum. Today the Instituto Butantan has more than 70,000 snakes, spiders, scorpions, and lizards in its five museums. It still extracts venom and processes it into serum that's made available to victims of poisonous bites throughout Latin America. ⊠ *Av. Vital Brasil 1500, Butantã* ☎ *011/3726–7222* ⊕ *www.butantan.gov.br* ✉ *R$6* ☉ *Tues.–Sun. 9–4:30* Ⓜ *Butantã.*

Instituto Tomie Ohtake. The futuristic green, pink, and purple exterior of this contemporary art museum designed by Ruy Ohtake makes it one of the city's most recognizable buildings. The institute, named for Ohtake's mother, a renowned painter who emigrated from Japan to Brazil, mounts interesting photography and design-related exhibitions. It also houses the independently operated Brazilian restaurant Santinho, which has a popular Sunday brunch. ⊠ *Av. Brigadeiro Faria Lima 201, Pinheiros* ☎ *011/2245–1900* ⊕ *www.institutotomieohtake. org.br* ✉ *Free* ☉ *Tues.–Sun. 11–8* Ⓜ *Faria Lima.*

FAMILY **Jardim Botânico.** A great spot for a midday picnic, the Botanical Gardens contain about 3,000 plants belonging to more than 340 native species. Orchids, aquatic plants, and Atlantic rain-forest species thrive in the gardens' greenhouses. The hundred-plus bird species that have been observed at Jardim Botânico make it a favorite stopover for São Paulo birders. ⊠ *Av. Miguel Stéfano 3031, Água Funda, Parque do Estado* ☎ *011/5073–6300* ⊕ *www.ibot.sp.gov.br* ✉ *R$5* ☉ *Tues.–Sun. 9–5.*

WHERE TO EAT

São Paulo's dynamic social scene centers on dining out, and among the 12,500-plus restaurants, most of the world's cuisines are covered. The most popular options include Portuguese, Japanese, Italian, French, and Lebanese; contemporary fusions are popular and plentiful. The city also offers a massive selection of pizza and hamburger joints with some world-class offerings. Most places don't require jacket and tie, but paulistanos tend to dress to European standards, so if you're going to pricey establishments, looking elegant is key.

On the domestic front the Brazilian *churrascarias* are a carnivore's dream, with their all-you-can-eat skewers of barbecued meats and impressive salad buffets. For in-between times, just about every bar will offer a selection of grilled meats, sandwiches, and deep-fried favorites for casual grazing. On Wednesday and Saturday, head to a Brazilian restaurant for *feijoada*—the national dish of black beans and pork. Ask about the other traditional and regional Brazilian dishes as well.

WHAT IT COSTS IN REAIS				
	$	$$	$$$	$$$$
AT DINNER	under R$31	R$31–R$45	R$46–R$60	over R$60

Restaurant prices are the average cost of a main course at dinner or, if dinner is not served, at lunch.

BIXIGA

$$$
ITALIAN

✕ **Cantina Roperto.** Wine casks and bottles adorn the walls at this typical Bixiga cantina, located on a street so charmingly human-scaled you'll hardly believe you're still in São Paulo. You won't be alone if you order the ever-popular fusilli—either *ao sugo* (with tomato sauce) or *ao frutos do mar* (with seafood)—or the traditional baby goat's leg with potatoes and tomatoes. $ *Average main: R$60* ✉ *Rua 13 de Maio 634, Bixiga* ☎ *011/3288–2573* ⊕ *www.cantinaroperto.com.br* ☾ *Closed Sun.* Ⓜ *Brigadeiro* ✛ *2:C5.*

$$
ITALIAN

✕ **Lazzarella.** Generous portions at reasonable prices and live music—that's the Lazzerella way. The cantina, a classic Italian joint founded in 1970, is hardly extravagant, but the rich flavors of a meal here and the Neapolitan stylings of the crooners circling among the red-and-white checkered tabletops linger in memory. The signature house lasagna dish, made old-style with ground beef and mozzarella in a Bolognese sauce, is meal enough for two. All the pastas here are worth a try. $ *Average main: R$40* ✉ *Rua Treze de Maio 589, Bixiga* ☎ *011/3289–3000* ⊕ *www.lazzarella.com.br* ✛ *2:C5.*

$$$$
ITALIAN PIZZA

✕ **Speranza.** One of the most traditional pizzerias in São Paulo, this restaurant is famous for its margherita pie. In 2010, Speranza became the first pizzeria in Latin America to win recognition from the Italian pizza quality-control board Associazione Verace Pizza Napoletana. The crunchy *pão de linguiça* (sausage bread) appetizers have a fine reputation as well. Pastas and chicken and beef dishes are also

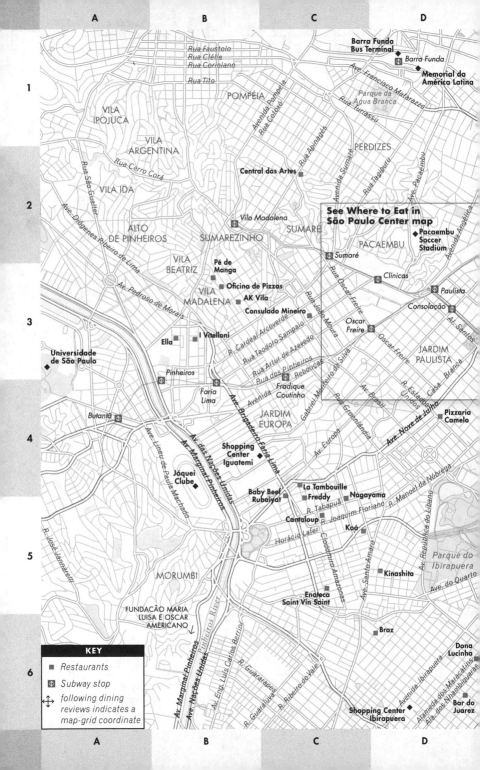

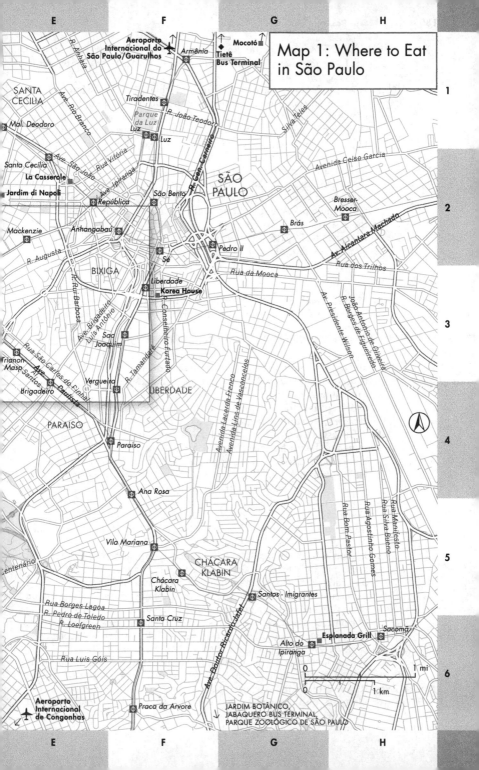

served. $ *Average main: R$80* ⊠ *Rua 13 de Maio 1004, Bela Vista* 🖀 *011/3288–8502* ⊕ *www.pizzaria.com.br* ☉ *No lunch* ⚠ *Reservations not accepted* ✢ *2:C5.*

$$$$ ╳ **Templo da Carne Marcos Bassi.** The brainchild of the late Marcos Bassi,
BRAZILIAN a former butcher turned restaurateur and radio host, Templo da Carne (Temple of Meat) makes no bones about its specialty. *Contrafilé* (sirloin) and famed Brazilian *picanha* (rump cap) are among the highlights. Unlike at all-you-can-eat churrascarias, dining here is an à la carte experience. The decor departs from the nostalgic interiors found in Bixiga's surrounding Italian cantinas without entirely abandoning the neighborhood's traditional coziness. The wait for a table regularly exceeds an hour, so try to arrive before your hunger peaks. You can fill the time perusing the emporium for wines and other items used in the restaurant. $ *Average main: R$150* ⊠ *Rua Treze de Maio 668, Bixiga* 🖀 *011/3288–7045* ⊕ *www.marcosbassi.com.br* ☉ *No dinner Sun.* ⚠ *Reservations essential* ✢ *2:C5.*

CENTRO

$ ╳ **Café Girondino.** Photos of old São Paulo, a winding wooden bannis-
CAFÉ ter, and antique light fixtures transport Café Girondino's patrons back to the trolley-car era. On the ground floor is a coffee shop known for its espresso drinks and the wildly flavorful Miguel Couto (ice cream, espresso, bourbon, whipped cream, and cinnamon). Typical café fare and mouthwatering desserts are also served—the *arroz doce* (rice pudding) is among the city's best. (A saloon occupies the second floor, and a full restaurant is on the third.) $ *Average main: R$30* ⊠ *Rua Boa Vista 365, Centro* 🖀 *011/3229–1287, 011/3229–4574* ⊕ *www.cafegirondino. com.br* ☉ *No dinner weekends* Ⓜ *São Bento* ✢ *2:A6.*

$$$ ╳ **La Casserole.** Facing a little Centro flower market, this romantic Pari-
FRENCH sian-style bistro has been around for five decades and has witnessed more than its share of wedding proposals. Surrounded by wood-paneled walls decorated with art that nods at famous French artists, you can dine on such delights as *gigot d'agneau aux soissons* (roast leg of lamb in its own juices, served with white beans), *canard à l'orange* (roast duck in an orange sauce), and cherry strudel. $ *Average main: R$50* ⊠ *Largo do Arouche 346, Centro* 🖀 *011/3331–6283* ⊕ *www.lacasserole.com.br* ☉ *Closed Mon. No dinner Sun.* Ⓜ *República* ✢ *1:E2.*

$ ╳ **Estadão Bar & Lanches.** Quests for quick, cheap, and good food should
DELI start near São Paulo's origins at this greasy spoon that's open 24 hours a day. Estadão's recipe for staying in business for more than four decades is its succulent *pernil* (roast pork) sandwich, a staple of the local street-food scene. Depending on the hour, the clientele ranges from partygoers and bohemians to politicians and bus drivers. $ *Average main: R$25* ⊠ *Av. Nove de Julho 193, Centro* 🖀 *011/3257–7121* ⊕ *www.estadolanches. com.br* ⚠ *Reservations not accepted* Ⓜ *Anhangabaú* ✢ *2:A6.*

$$$$ ╳ **Famiglia Mancini.** This busy little cantina is well loved for both its
ITALIAN cuisine and location. It's on an unforgettable restaurant-lined strip of
Fodors Choice Rua Avandhandava, where you may find yourself admiring the cob-
★ blestones on the street as you wait for a table. An incredible buffet with cheeses, olives, sausages, and much more makes finding a tasty

appetizer a cinch. The menu has many terrific pasta options, such as the cannelloni with palm hearts and a four-cheese sauce. All dishes serve two people. [$] *Average main: R$120* ✉ *Rua Avanhandava 81, Centro* ☎ *011/3256–4320* 🌐 *www.famigliamancini.com.br* ✍ *Reservations not accepted* [M] *Anhangabaú* ✥ *2:A5.*

$$$$ ITALIAN 🍴 **Gigetto.** When the menu of this São Paulo classic was slimmed down a few years back, dedicated locals successfully lobbied to have its more than 150 delicious options restored. Try the cappelletti *à romanesca* (pasta with chopped ham, peas, mushrooms, and white cream sauce), osso buco with polenta, or the popular *cabrito com batata e brócolis* (baby goat with potatoes and broccoli). Main courses serve two people. [$] *Average main: R$90* ✉ *Rua Avanhandava 63, Centro* ☎ *011/3256–9804* 🌐 *www.gigetto.com.br* [M] *Anhangabaú* ✥ *2:A5.*

4

CERQUEIRA CÉSAR

$ PIZZA 🍴 **Pedaço da Pizza.** At one of São Paulo's few pizzerias where you can order by the slice (R$6), the options for toppings range from pepperoni and other traditional favorites to shimeji mushrooms, kale, and other innovative ingredients. Open until 4 am on Friday and Saturday night, this is a good place to stop after clubbing. [$] *Average main: R$30* ✉ *Rua Augusta 1463, Cerqueira César* ☎ *011/3061–0004* 🌐 *www.opedacodapizza.com.br* ⏲ *No lunch Sun.* [M] *Consolação* ✥ *2:D2.*

$$$$ ECLECTIC 🍴 **Spot.** A few blocks west of MASP, this quaint yet futuristic glass-encased diner occupies a lonely single-story building tucked between government skyscrapers. Entrées—Argentine beef is a favorite—don't come with sides, so you'll have to order a dish such as rice with broccoli to fill the plate. Come early if you want to eat—as the night wears on, the extensive drink menu becomes the focus of partying patrons. [$] *Average main: R$70* ✉ *Alameda Rocha Azevedo 72, Cerqueira César* ☎ *011/3284–6131* 🌐 *www.restaurantespot.com.br* [M] *Consolação or Trianon-Masp* ✥ *2:C4.*

$$$$ BRAZILIAN 🍴 **Tordesilhas.** Typically Brazilian from its decor to its daily specials, rustic-elegant Tordesilhas prides itself on spotlighting recipes from across the republic. Feijoada takes center stage on Wednesdays and Saturdays, while a Brazilian tasting menu is served from Tuesday through Saturday. Among the daily staples you'll find *tacacá* (shrimp soup), from Brazil's northern region, and *moqueca* (fish and shrimp stew), from Espírito Santo State. [$] *Average main: R$80* ✉ *Alameda Tietê 489, Cerqueira César* ☎ *011/3107–7444* 🌐 *www.tordesilhas.com* ⏲ *Closed Mon. No lunch weekdays. No dinner Sun.* [M] *Paulista* ✥ *2:C3.*

CONSOLAÇÃO

$$$$ ECLECTIC 🍴 **Mestiço.** Even the fabulous people have to hang at the bar before being shown to a table in this large, sleek dining room; but especially for vegetarians, dishes such as the tofu and vegetable curry make the wait worthwhile. The restaurant makes a point of using free-range chicken and other ecologically responsible ingredients. The decidedly eclectic menu includes Italian, Brazilian, Bahian, and even Thai cuisine. [$] *Average main: R$80* ✉ *Rua Fernando de Albuquerque 277, Consolação*

☎ *011/3256–3165* 🌐 *www.mestico.com.br* ✍ *Reservations essential* [M] *Consolação* ✥ *2:B3.*

MEAL TIME

Eating out in São Paulo can be an all-night affair, so most restaurants open late and close even later. The majority will officially throw their doors open around 8 pm but will only get busy after 9 pm, regardless of what day it is. Try a bar that has a good happy hour if you want to eat earlier.

$$$ BRAZILIAN 🍴 **Sujinho–Bisteca d'Ouro.** Occupying corners on both sides of the street, the modest Sujinho honors its roots as an informal bar by serving churrasco without any frills: this is the perfect place for diners craving a gorgeous piece of meat to down with a cold bottle of beer. The portions are so Jurassic in size that one dish can usually feed two. Sujinho stays open until 5 am, making it a leading stop on the post-bar circuit. [$] *Average main: R$50* ✉ *Rua da Consolação 2078, Cerqueira César* ☎ *011/3231–1299* 🌐 *www.sujinho.com.br* 💳 *No credit cards* [M] *Consolação or Paulista* ✥ *2:B3.*

$$$$ FRENCH 🍴 **La Tartine.** An ideal place for an intimate dinner, this small bistro has a good wine selection and an upstairs bar furnished with mismatched sofas and armchairs. The menu changes daily; a favorite is the classic coq au vin, but you can also fill up on entrées such as beef tenderloin, pasta, soups, and quiches. The frogs' legs come off like a Tangier-style chicken wing. If Moroccan couscous is being served, don't pass it up. The trendy set loves La Tartine; on weekends you might have to wait a bit to get a table. [$] *Average main: R$65* ✉ *Rua Fernando de Albuquerque 267, Consolação* ☎ *011/3259–2090* ⏲ *Closed Sun. No lunch* [M] *Consolação* ✥ *2:B3.*

HIGIENÓPOLIS

$$$$ CONTEMPORARY 🍴 **Carlota.** TV host, author, and chef Carla Pernambuco introduces Brazilian elements to a multicultural array of recipes at her popular restaurant. The four-cheese polenta and the red-rice risotto with lobster are among the many well-calibrated dishes served here. All-white brick walls outside and inside lend Carlota a soothing, stylish feel. The clientele, befitting the neighborhood's demographics, tends to be older than elsewhere in town. Save room for the signature dessert, a guava jam soufflé with melted-cheese sauce. [$] *Average main: R$95* ✉ *Rua Sergipe 753, Higienópolis* ☎ *011/3661–8670* 🌐 *carlota.com.br* ⏲ *No dinner weekends. Closed Mon.* ✥ *2:A3.*

$$$$ ITALIAN 🍴 **Jardim di Napoli.** The classic neon sign that adorns this restaurant's exterior cues diners about what to expect inside: traditional Italian cuisine. No surprises here, but dishes such as the unchanging and unmatchable *polpettone alla parmigiana*, a huge meatball with mozzarella and tomato sauce, inspire devotion among the local clientele. Many other meat dishes can be found on the menu, along with pastas and pizzas. [$] *Average main: R$70* ✉ *Rua Doutor Martinico Prado 463, Higienópolis* ☎ *011/3666–3022* 🌐 *www.jardimdenapoli.com.br* ✥ *1:E2.*

$$$$ PIZZA Fodor's Choice ★ 🍴 **Veridiana.** Owner Roberto Loscalzo transformed a 1903 mansion into a remarkable dining space; expansive yet intimate, grandiose yet welcoming. At one end of the room chefs pull Napoli-style pizzas from the three mouths of a two-story brick oven that looms over diners like a

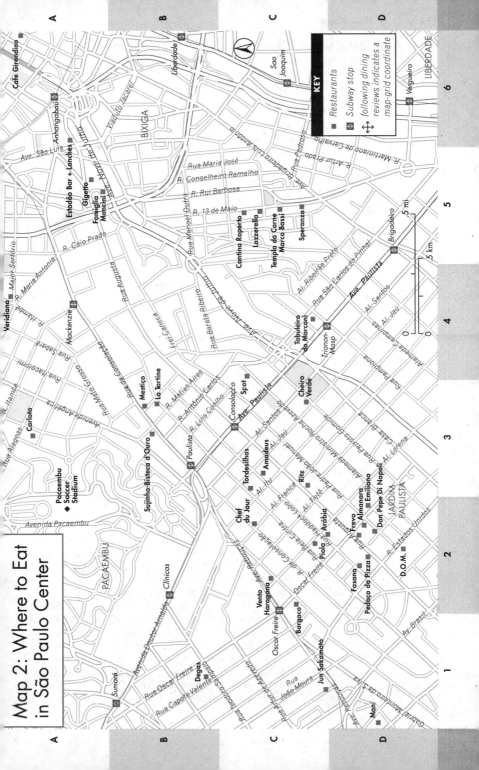

Map 2: Where to Eat in São Paulo Center

KEY

- ■ Restaurants
- Ⓜ Subway stop
- ✛ following dining reviews indicates a map-grid coordinate

A

Café Girondino
Estádão Bar + Lanches
Gigetto
Famiglia Mancini
Veridiana
Carlola
Pacaembu Soccer Stadium
Sujinho-Bisteca d'Ouro
Mestiço
La Tartine
Chef du Jour
Vento Haragano
Bargaço
Degas
Jun Sakamoto
Mani

B

Liberdade
BIXIGA
PACAEMBU
Ave. São Luís
R. Caio Prado
R. Maria Antonia
Mackenzie
Frei Caneca
Rua Augusta
Rua Barata Ribeiro
Paulista
Clínicas
Avenida Pacaembu
Avenida Doutor Arnaldo
Sumaré
Rua Oscar Freire
Rua Capote Valente

C

São Joaquim
Rua Maria José
R. Conselheiro Ramalho
R. Rui Barbosa
R. 13 de Maio
Cantina Roperto
Lazzerella
Templo do Carne Marco Bassi
Speranza
Consolação
Spot
Ave. Paulista
Cheiro Verde
Tordesilhas
Amadeus
Al. Itu
Al. Franca
Ritz
Piola
Arábia
Fasano
Pedaço da Pizza
Oscar Freire
Rua João Moura

D

LIBERDADE
Vergueiro
R. Artur Prado
R. Martiniano de Carvalho
Ave. Brigadeiro Luís Antônio
Al. Ribeirão Preto
Rua São Carlos do Pinhal
Ave. Paulista
Brigadeiro
Trianon-Masp
Tabuleira do Marconi
Al. Santos
Al. Jaú
Alameda Campinas
Rua Pamplona
Almanara
Frevo
Emiliano
Don Pepe Di Napoli
JARDIM PAULISTA
R. Estados Unidos
D.O.M.
Av. Brasil

0 —— 5 mi
0 —— 5 km

6 5 4 3 2 1

cathedral organ. Different place-names lead to different taste combinations: Napoli in Beruit blends goat cheese and *za'atar*, a spice mixture that includes herbs and sesame seeds, while Napoli in Brasili contains sun-dried meat and Catupiry, the creamy Brazilian cheese invented in Minas Gerais a century ago. If you don't feel like globe-trotting, go for the Do Nonno, topped with juicy grilled tomatoes. A sister branch of Veridiana operates in the Jardins neighborhood. The Higienópolis location is not well marked. The restaurant is directly across from the Iate Clube (Yacht Club) de Santos. $ *Average main: R$70* ⊠ *Rua Dona Veridiana 661, Higienópolis* 🕾 *011/3120–5050* ⊕ *www.veridiana.com. br* ⊘ *Closed Sun. No lunch* Ⓜ *Santa Cecilia* ✛ *2:A4.*

ITAIM BIBI

$$$$
BRAZILIAN

✕ **Baby Beef Rubaiyat.** The family that owns and runs this restaurant serves meat from its ranch in Mato Grosso do Sul State. Charcoal-grilled fare—baby boar (request at least two hours in advance of your visit), steak, chicken, salmon, and more—is served at the buffet, and options abound at the salad bar. Wednesday and Saturday are feijoada nights, and on Friday the emphasis is on seafood. $ *Average main: R$150* ⊠ *Av. Brigadeiro Faria Lima 2954, Itaim Bibi* 🕾 *011/3165–8888* ⊕ *www.rubaiyat.com.br* ⊘ *No dinner Sun.* Ⓜ *Faria Lima* ✛ *1:C5.*

$$
BRAZILIAN

✕ **Bar do Juarez.** With the look of an old-style saloon, Bar do Juarez has won awards for its draft beers and buffet of *petiscos* (small tapas-like dishes), but *picanha* (rump cap of beef) is this gastropub's calling card. Served raw on a mini-grill, the platter is perfect for small groups and gives individuals direct control over how their meat is done. Bow-tied waiters with A-plus attentiveness add to Juarez's appeal. The Itaim location is the best of four in the city, with the Moema, Pinheiros, and Brooklin houses coming close. $ *Average main: R$40* ⊠ *Av. Pres. Juscelino Kubitschek 1164, Itaim Bibi* 🕾 *011/3078–3458* ⊕ *www. bardojuarez.com.br* ⊘ *No lunch weekdays* ✛ *1:D6.*

$$$$
EUROPEAN

✕ **Cantaloup.** That paulistanos take food seriously has not been lost on the folks at Cantaloup. The converted warehouse has two dining areas: oversize photos decorate the walls of the slightly formal room, while a fountain and plants make the second area feel more casual. Try the veal cutlet with blinis of yucca or the stuffed shrimp with clams. Save room for macerated strawberries in port wine sauce or a particularly velvety crème brûlée with ice cream. $ *Average main: R$130* ⊠ *Rua Manoel Guedes 474, Itaim Bibi* 🕾 *011/3078–9884, 011/3078–3445* ⊕ *www. cantaloup.com.br* ⊘ *No dinner Sun.* ✛ *1:C5.*

$$$$
FRENCH

✕ **Freddy.** A pioneer in bringing French cuisine to São Paulo, Freddy opened originally in 1935. Despite moving from its original location, Freddy has managed to retain the feel of an upscale Parisian bistro, thanks to a number of small touches as well as some larger ones, like the grand chandeliers hanging from its ceiling. Try the duck with Madeira sauce and apple purée, coq au vin, or the hearty cassoulet with white beans, lamb, duck, and garlic sausage. $ *Average main: R$100* ⊠ *Rua Pedroso Alvarenga 1170, Itaim Bibi* 🕾 *011/3167–0977* ⊕ *www. restaurantefreddy.com.br* ⊘ *No dinner Sun. No lunch Sat.* ✛ *1:C5.*

$$$$ JAPANESE 🍴 **Nagayama.** Low-key, dependable, and well loved, Nagayama consistently serves excellent sushi and sashimi. The chefs like to experiment: the California *uramaki* Philadelphia has rice, cream cheese, grilled salmon, roe, cucumber, and spring onions rolled together. [$] *Average main: R$110* ✉ *Rua Bandeira Paulista 369, Itaim Bibi* ☎ *011/3079–7553* 🌐 *www.nagayama.com.br* 🕒 *Closed Sun.* ✣ *1:C5.*

$$$$ ECLECTIC 🍴 **La Tambouille.** This Italo-French restaurant with a partially enclosed garden isn't just a place for businesspeople and impresarios to see and be seen; it also has some of the best food in town. Among chef Giancarlo Bolla's recommended dishes are the linguine with fresh mussels and prawn sauce, the eggplant Parmesan, and the filet mignon *rosini* (served with foie gras and saffron risotto). [$] *Average main: R$100* ✉ *Av. Nove de Julho 5925, Itaim Bibi* ☎ *011/3079–6277, 011/3079–6276* 🌐 *www.tambouille.com.br* ✣ *1:C4.*

A TASTE OF LEBANON

While in São Paulo, be sure to try a *beirute*, a Lebanese sandwich served hot on toasted Syrian bread and filled with roast beef, cheese, lettuce, and tomato. Another quick bite from Lebanon that has established itself in the city is *esfiha*, an open-faced pastry topped with cheese or spiced meat. Fast-food restaurants serving these snacks are scattered around the city.

4

JARDINS

$$$ LEBANESE 🍴 **Almanara.** Part of a chain of Lebanese semifast-food outlets, Almanara is perfect for a quick lunch of hummus, tabbouleh, grilled chicken, and rice. A full-blown restaurant also on the premises offers up Lebanese specialties *rodízio* style, meaning you're served continuously until you can ingest no more. [$] *Average main: R$60* ✉ *Rua Oscar Freire 523, Jardins* ☎ *011/3085–6916* 🌐 *www.almanara.com.br* ✣ *2:D2.*

$$$$ SEAFOOD 🍴 **Amadeus.** Because São Paulo isn't on the ocean, most restaurants here don't base their reputations on seafood, but Amadeus is an exception. Appetizers such as fresh oysters and salmon and endive with mustard, and entrées like shrimp in cognac sauce make it a challenge to find better fruits of the sea elsewhere in town. The restaurant is popular with the business-lunch crowd. [$] *Average main: R$100* ✉ *Rua Haddock Lobo 807, Jardins* ☎ *011/3061–2859* 🌐 *restauranteamadeus.com.br* 🕒 *No dinner Sun.* [M] *Consolação* ✣ *2:C3.*

$$$$ LEBANESE 🍴 **Arábia.** For almost 20 years Arábia has served traditional Lebanese cuisine at this beautiful high-ceilinged restaurant. Simple dishes such as hummus and stuffed grape leaves are executed with aplomb, and the lamb melts in your mouth. Meat-stuffed artichokes are great for sharing, and the reasonably priced "executive" lunch menu includes one appetizer, one cold dish, one meat dish, a drink, dessert, and coffee. Don't miss the crepe-like *ataife*, filled with pistachio nuts or cream, for dessert. [$] *Average main: R$70* ✉ *Rua Haddock Lobo 1397, Jardins* ☎ *011/3061–2203* 🌐 *www.arabia.com.br* ✣ *2:D2.*

$$$ ECLECTIC 🍴 **Chef du Jour.** Despite the name, there's indeed a permanent chef installed here: Renato Frias, who hails from the state of Pernambuco, though his cuisine straddles France and Italy. Take your pick from a

vast buffet with more than 30 different salads, along with sushi, risottos and pastas, and fish and meat dishes. Colorful tiles decorate the spacious dining room. Ⓢ *Average main: R$60* ⊠ *Rua da Consolação 3101, Jardins* ☎ *011/3845–6843* ☽ *No dinner. Closed Sun.* ✛ *2:C2.*

$
VEGETARIAN

✕**Cheiro Verde.** A São Paulo pioneer in meat-free dining, Cheiro Verde has attracted a devoted following over the past three decades for its simple but tasty vegetarian fare. (One couple fancied the restaurant so much they ended up buying it.) Whole-wheat mushroom pasta and delicious empanadas are among the many good bets here. Ⓢ *Average main: R$30* ⊠ *Rua Peixoto Gomide 1078, Jardim Paulista* ☎ *011/3289–6853* ⊕ *www.cheiroverderestaurante.com.br* ☽ *No dinner. Closed Sun.* Ⓜ *Trianon-MASP* ✛ *2:C3.*

$$$$
CONTEMPORARY

✕**D.O.M.** Regularly named among the best restaurants in South America and the world, D.O.M. is synonymous with exclusivity in São Paulo's gastronomic circles—its popularity is limited only by a self-imposed cap on the number of customers served. This is some of the finest food to be had on the continent, with prices as dizzying as celebrity chef Alex Atala's inspired cooking. The focus is on Brazilian fare with added flair, such as *filhote* (Amazonian catfish) with tapioca in *tucupi* (manioc root) sauce and sweet potato in a Béarnaise made from maté, a South American tea. Try the tapas-esque tasting menu for the full, unforgettable experience, at R$380 for four courses, or R$527 for eight. Make your reservations at least a week in advance. Ⓢ *Average main: R$250* ⊠ *Rua Barão de Capanema 549, Jardins* ☎ *011/3088–0761* ⊕ *www. domrestaurante.com.br* ☽ *Closed Sun. No lunch Sat.* ⚐ *Reservations essential* ✛ *2:D2.*

$$$$
ITALIAN

✕**Don Pepe Di Napoli.** Good and simple Italian food is what you'll find at this traditional spot. Choose from a great variety of pastas, salads, and meat dishes. A good option is *talharina a Don Pepe,* pasta with meat, broccoli, and garlic. Ⓢ *Average main: R$70* ⊠ *Rua Padre Joao Manoel 1104, Jardins* ☎ *011/3081–4080* ⊕ *www.donpepedinapoli.com. br* ✛ *2:D2.*

$$$$
ITALIAN

✕**Fasano.** A family-owned Northern Italian classic tucked away behind the elegantly modern lobby of the hotel of the same name, this restaurant is as famous for its superior cuisine as for its exorbitant prices. The luxe decor oozes class—marble, mahogany, and mirrors, all crowned by a breathtaking skylight—and suggests that proof of one's captainship of industry or other such mastery of the universe must be shown at the door for entrance. In the kitchen, a 20-strong brigade of chefs, butchers, and bakers commanded by Luca Gozzani sends out exquisite, sinfully rich dishes like agnollottis of Angola chicken on heart-of-mozzarella cream. Ⓢ *Average main: R$120* ⊠ *Rua Vittorio Fasano 88, Jardins* ☎ *011/3062–4000* ⊕ *www.fasano.com.br* ☽ *Closed Sun. No lunch* ⚐ *Reservations essential* ✛ *2:D2.*

$
BRAZILIAN

✕**Frevo.** Paulistanos of all types and ages flock to this luncheonette on the stylish Rua Oscar Freire for its *beirute* sandwiches, filled with ham and cheese, tuna, or chicken, and for its draft beer and fruit juices in flavors such as *acerola* (Antilles cherry), passion fruit, and papaya. Ⓢ *Average main: R$30* ⊠ *Rua Oscar Freire 603, Jardins* ☎ *011/3082–3434, 011/4003–2665 delivery* ⊕ *www.frevinho.com.br* ✛ *2:D2.*

$$$ CONTEMPORARY Fodor's Choice ★ 🍴 **Maní.** With world-class chef-proprietor Helena Rizzo at the helm, Maní has made its way to the top of the restaurant charts in São Paulo. A sophisticated take on Brazilian country cuisine meshed with modern cooking techniques, dishes like chicken and rice with okra might not sound like much, but one bite will be enough to explain why local and visiting foodies beat a path to Maní's door. Go for the tasting menu (R$195) or for the great-value lunch platters (around R$40). [$] *Average main: R$50* ✉ *Rua Joaquim Antunes 210, Jardins* ☎ *011/3085-4148* 🌐 *www.manimanioca.com.br* ⏲ *Closed Mon. No dinner Sun.* [M] *Faria Lima* ✥ *2:D1.*

PURPLE POWER

Açai, an antioxidant-rich super fruit, has recently made its way to juice bars around the world. Don't miss your chance to get it close to the source, where it's cheaper and purer than the versions you'll find back home. Always frozen, scoops of it are blended together with syrup of the energy-filled guaraná berry. The most popular way to get it is *na tigela,* in a glass bowl with bananas and granola, though juice stands dedicated to the fruit should serve up a pure milk-shake-thick *suco* (juice) as well.

4

$$$ PIZZA FAMILY 🍴 **Piola.** Part of a chain started in Italy, this restaurant serves pizzas loaded with toppings like Gorgonzola, Brie, ham, salami, mushrooms, and anchovies. It also has good pasta dishes, like the penne with smoked salmon in a creamy tomato sauce. The young, hip crowd matches the trendy contemporary decor, and there's also a recreational area for kids to play while the grown-ups finish their meals. [$] *Average main: R$55* ✉ *Alameda Lorena 1765, Jardins* ☎ *011/3064–6570, 011/3061–2221 delivery* 🌐 *www.piola.com.br* ⏲ *No lunch* ✥ *2:C2.*

$$ PIZZA 🍴 **Pizzaria Camelo.** Though it's neither fancy nor beautiful, Pizzaria Camelo has kept paulistanos enthralled for ages with its many thin-crust pies. The *chopp* (draft beer) is great, too. Avoid Sunday night unless you're willing to wait an hour for a table. [$] *Average main: R$45* ✉ *Rua Pamplona 1873, Jardins* ☎ *011/3887–8764* 🌐 *www.pizzariacamelo.com.br* ⏲ *No lunch* ✥ *1:D4.*

$$ ECLECTIC 🍴 **Ritz.** An animated, gay-friendly crowd chatters at this restaurant with Italian, Brazilian, French, and mixed cuisine, as contemporary pop music plays in the background. Although Ritz serves some of the best hamburgers in the city, another popular dish is *bife à milanesa* (breaded beef cutlet) with creamed spinach and french fries. [$] *Average main: R$40* ✉ *Alameda Franca 1088, Jardins* ☎ *011/3088–6808 delivery, 011/3062–5830* 🌐 *www.restauranteritz.com.br* ⏲ *No dinner Mon.–Wed.* [M] *Consolação* ✥ *2:C3.*

LIBERDADE

$$$ KOREAN 🍴 **Korea House.** Camper cooking meets Korean at this Liberdade mainstay. For the *bul go gui* (Korean barbecue), diners blend raw meat, spices, sauces, and veggies and cook them over small, do-it-yourself gas stoves. One order feeds two. You can prepare other Korean dishes, and there are Chinese options, including several involving tofu. Everything is reasonably priced. The design is unimpressive but the atmosphere is lively, with hipsters and gringos sprinkled among neighborhood

residents. $ *Average main: R$60* ✉ *Rua Galvão Bueno 43, 1° andar, Liberdade* ☎ *011/3208–3052* ⊘ *Closed Wed.* Ⓜ *Liberdade* ✛ *1:F3.*

MOEMA

$$$
PIZZA
Fodor'sChoice
★

✕ **Bráz.** This restaurant's name comes from one of the most traditional Italian neighborhoods in São Paulo, and no one argues that Bráz doesn't have the right. The pies are of a medium thickness with high, bubbly crusts. And each of the nearly 20 varieties is delicious, from the traditional margherita to the house specialty, pizza *Bráz*, with tomato sauce, zucchini, and mozzarella and Parmesan cheeses. The *chopp* (draft beer) is also very good. Reservations aren't accepted on weekends. $ *Average main: R$60* ✉ *Rua Graúna 125, Moema* ☎ *011/5561–1736* ⊕ *www. brazpizzaria.com.br* ⊘ *No lunch* ✛ *1:D6.*

$$$
BRAZILIAN

✕ **Dona Lucinha.** Mineiro dishes are the specialties at this modest eatery with plain wooden tables. The classic cuisine is served as a buffet only: more than 50 stone pots hold dishes like *feijão tropeiro* (beans with manioc flour) and *frango com quiabo* (chicken with okra). Save room for a dessert of ambrosia. The menu is in English, French, and Spanish. $ *Average main: R$60* ✉ *Av. Chibarás 399, Moema* ☎ *011/5051–2050* ⊕ *www.donalucinha.com.br* ⊘ *Closed Mon. No dinner Sun.* ✛ *1:D6.*

$$$
JAPANESE
Fodor'sChoice
★

✕ **Kinoshita.** Contemporary Japanese plates with international influences are the draw at Kinoshita, where foie gras might accompany a Kobe beef hamburger or truffles might enliven salmon roe and shellfish. The freshness of the ingredients available on any given day determines the fare of chef Tsuyoshi Murakami, one of São Paulo's culinary superstars. Geishas serve guests in the Krug Room (available only for groups of 6 to 12), where slippers replace shoes and diners sit on floor mats. For a real, if pricey, treat opt for one of the *omakase* (tasting) menus—seven or nine courses, plus dessert—and let chef Murakami decide what you eat. $ *Average main: R$50* ✉ *Rua Jacques Félix 405, Moema* ☎ *011/3849–6940, 011/5318–9014* ⊕ *restaurantekinoshita.com.br* ⊘ *Closed Sun.* ⩔ *Reservations essential* ✛ *1:D5.*

MORUMBI

$$$
BRAZILIAN

✕ **Esplanada Grill.** The beautiful people hang out in the bar of this highly regarded churrascaria. The thinly sliced *picanha* (similar to rump steak) is excellent; it goes well with a house salad (hearts of palm and shredded, fried potatoes), onion rings, and creamed spinach. The version of the traditional *pão de queijo* (cheese bread) served here is widely viewed as among the city's best. $ *Average main: R$50* ✉ *Morumbi Shopping Center, Av. Roque Petroni Jr. 1089, Morumbi* ☎ *011/5181–8156* ✛ *1:G6.*

PINHEIROS

$$$$
BRAZILIAN
Fodor'sChoice
★

✕ **Consulado Mineiro.** During and after the Saturday crafts and antiques fair in Praça Benedito Calixto, it may take an hour to get a table at this homey restaurant. Among the shareable, traditional *mineiro* (from Minas Gerais State) dishes are the *mandioca com carne de sol* (cassava with salted meat) appetizer and the *tutu* (pork loin with beans, pasta, cabbage, and rice) entrée. The cachaça menu is extensive, with rare, premium, and homemade brands of the sugarcane-based spirits, and several types of *batidas* (fruit-and-alcohol mixtures) and caipirinhas are served. [$] *Average main: R$70* ✉ *Rua Praça Benedito Calixto 74, Pinheiros* ☎ *011/3064–3882* 🌐 *www.consuladomineiro.com.br* ⏲ *Closed Mon.* ✣ *1:C3.*

WOK THIS WAY

In a street-food scene dominated by hamburgers and hot dogs, Yakisoba stands out—keep an eye peeled for the spectacle of stir-fried noodles tossed over an open flame in the middle of the crowded sidewalk. Another delicious option is homemade *espetinhos* or *churrascos*, wooden kebabs of beef, chicken, or pork whose juices send towers of fragrant smoke into the air. A calmer alternative is the corn cart. Rather than on the cob, try *pamonha*, steam-cooked sweetened cornmeal wrapped in a husk, or *curau*, sweet creamed corn.

4

$$ ITALIAN FAMILY

🍴 **Degas.** Humble-looking Degas owes its more than 50 years in existence to word-of-mouth among the residents of São Paulo's western neighborhoods. Its famed filet mignon Parmigiana has gained near-legendary status, attracting foodies from across the city. The dish, along with almost anything else on the menu, easily feeds two, if not a family of four. Even the salads seem to be small vegetable gardens on a platter. Lunchtime usually brings a business crowd. Dinner, when the restaurant fires up its pizza ovens, is more of a family affair. [$] *Average main: R$35* ✉ *Rua Teodoro Sampaio 568, Pinheiros* ☎ *011/3062–1276, 011/3085–3545* 🌐 *www.degasrestaurante.com.br* [M] *Clinicas* ✣ *2:B1.*

$$ ITALIAN Fodor's Choice ★

🍴 **Ella.** A diminutive restaurant tucked away on a nondescript Pinheiros street, Ella is all about the simple pleasure of fresh homemade pasta, risotto, and the like, with a fantastic-value executive lunch menu, at R$37 for three courses. Try the ruby-red beetroot tortelloni with sage and ricotta. [$] *Average main: R$45* ✉ *Rua Costa Carvalho 138, Pinheiros* ☎ *011/3034–1267* ⏲ *Closed Mon. No dinner Sun.* [M] *Pinheiros* ✣ *1:B3.*

$$$ PIZZA

🍴 **I Vitelloni.** At perhaps the most creative pizza restaurant in town, owner Hamilton Mello Júnior combines disparate ingredients for his specialty pies, while serving up tasty classics as well. In the Pinheiros neighborhood, lively at night, the restaurant sits on a quiet residential street, away from the sidewalk bars an avenue away, so it's prized by locals and well worth searching out. We recommend the authentic arugula pie. There's a stand-up bar outside that's a nice place to finish your drinks before you head off. [$] *Average main: R$50* ✉ *Rua Conde Sílvio Álvares Penteado 31, Pinheiros* ☎ *011/3819–0735* 🌐 *www.ivitelloni.com.br* ⏲ *No lunch. Closed Mon.* ✣ *1:B3.*

$$$ JAPANESE Fodor's Choice ★

🍴 **Jun Sakamoto.** Arguably the best Japanese restaurant in a town famous for them, Jun Sakamoto stands out for serving fish of the highest quality and for employing the most skillful of sushi chefs to slice them. This is haute gastronomy at its haughtiest. You're best served if you let the waiters wearing futuristic earpieces guide you through the menu based on what's freshest the day you visit. [$] *Average main: R$60* ✉ *Rua Lisboa 55, Pinheiros* ☎ *011/3088–6019* 🕒 *No lunch. Closed Sun.* ✥ *2:C1.*

$$$$ BARBECUE Fodor's Choice ★ 🍴 **Vento Haragano.** São Paulo has a certain fame for its all-you-can-eat steak houses. Vento Haragano, just a few blocks from Avenida Paulista, has the best location in town, attentive staff in slightly kitsch historic-reenactment-style garb, and a truly magnificent salad bar. And, naturally, a never-ending parade of succulent meat, served table-side until you cry uncle. [$] *Average main: R$116* ✉ *Av. Rebouças 1001, Pinheiros* ☎ *011/3083-4265* 🌐 *www.ventoharagano.com.br* [M] *Consolação* ✥ *2:C2.*

POMPÉIA

$ ECLECTIC 🍴 **Central das Artes.** Come for the view, stay for the crepes. Or vice versa. A back wall made of windows faces out to a verdant valley and, beyond that, Avenida Paulista. The panorama makes Central das Artes a popular place to grab drinks as well. Crepes are named for famous artists. The Cocteau, with salmon, shiitake, and cream, is as smooth on the taste buds as its namesake was with the written word. [$] *Average main: R$25* ✉ *Rua Apinajés 1081, Pompéia* ☎ *011/3865–0116* 🌐 *www.centraldasartes.com.br* ✥ *1:C2.*

VILA MADALENA

$$$ CONTEMPORARY 🍴 **AK Vila.** Putting a premium on freshness, chef Andrea Kaufmann shifts her menu weekly to keep pace with seasonal ingredients. Her restaurant's multicultural, contemporary cuisine ranges from salads and sandwiches to ceviche and octopus couscous. The chef made her name cooking Jewish favorites, and she often makes room on her menu for bagels or salads with smoked salmon. A touch of the burlesque softens AK Vila's industrial-sleek design. On nice nights, sit outside and soak in the Vila Madalena scene. [$] *Average main: R$50* ✉ *Rua Fradique Coutinho 1240, Vila Madalena* ☎ *011/3231–4496, 011/3231–4497* 🌐 *www.akvila.com.br* 🕒 *No dinner Sun.–Mon.* ✥ *1:B3.*

$$$ PIZZA 🍴 **Oficina de Pizzas.** This restaurant looks like something designed by the Spanish architect Gaudí had he spent his later years in the tropics, but the pizzas couldn't be more Italian and straightforward. Try a pie with mozzarella and toasted garlic. [$] *Average main: R$50* ✉ *Rua Purpurina 517, Vila Madalena* ☎ *011/3816–3749* 🌐 *www.oficinadepizzas.com.br* 🕒 *No lunch* ✥ *1:B3.*

$$ BRAZILIAN 🍴 **Pé de Manga.** The restaurant's name and charm come from a massive mango tree. Tables surrounding the trunk spread across a shaded patio, which is usually packed with professionals in their 30s and 40s. A two-story covered seating area lends the whole affair a Robinson Crusoe touch. High-end, Brazilian-style pub grub pads stomachs for Pé de Manga's beers and caipirinhas. The feijoada buffet is a top option on Saturdays. [$] *Average main: R$35* ✉ *Rua Arapiraca 152, Vila Madalena* ☎ *011/3032–6068* 🌐 *www.pedemanga.com.br* ✥ *1:B3.*

VILA OLÍMPIA

$$$$ WINE BAR **🍴 Enoteca Saint Vin Saint.** A snug bistro on as secluded a street as you're apt to find in São Paulo's hip southern neighborhoods, Enoteca triples as a wineshop, restaurant, and live-music venue. Marble-top tables fill two rooms brimming with bottle racks, bookshelves, and bullfighting posters. Friends and thirtysomething couples toast each other with an international array of wines, many from France, Spain, Italy, and Chile. The kitchen's specialty is a risotto with wine-braised beef whose taste more than compensates for its plain appearance. There's a $R15 cover for live tango, jazz, and flamenco music from Wednesday through Saturday night, but it's well worth it. [$] *Average main: R$100* ✉ *Rua Professor Atílio Innocenti 811, Vila Olímpia* ☎ *011/3846–0384* 🌐 *www.saintvinsaint.com.br* 🕒 *Closed Sun. No lunch Sat.* ✥ *1:C5.*

> **JAPANESE FRUIT**
>
> Along with the famous Japanese cuisine, which can be found just about everywhere in São Paulo, Brazil's Japanese immigrants are credited with introducing persimmons, azaleas, tangerines, and kiwis to Brazil.

$$$ CONTEMPORARY Fodor's Choice ★ **🍴 Kaá.** Contemporary cuisine, attentive service, and a luxurious, secret-garden charm help Kaá maintain its status as one of São Paulo's leading fine-dining establishments. The gorgeously designed restaurant, complete with fountains, a sunken bar, and a rain forest–like wall, attracts a mostly mature and well-to-do clientele. The crayfish au gratin in endive cream is a top choice among the appetizers; appealing entrées include rack of lamb ribs and beer-cooked duck. Though the wine list is extensive, many diners opt for the signature orchid martini. [$] *Average main: R$60* ✉ *Av. Presidente Juscelino Kubitschek 279, Vila Olímpia* ☎ *011/3045–0043* 🌐 *kaarestaurante.com.br* 🕒 *No dinner Sun.* ✥ *1:C5.*

$$ BRAZILIAN Fodor's Choice ★ **🍴 Mocotó.** This far-flung restaurant is an exceptional take on the classic boteco, run by the young, charismatic chef Rodrigo Olveira. Try his Northeastern Brazilian classics like *escondidinho*, a rich little meat-and-manioc pie, and don't miss the homemade *torresmo*, crunchy morsels of pork rind. [$] *Average main: R$40* ✉ *Av. Nossa Senhora do Loreto 1100* ☎ *011/2951-3056* 🌐 *www.mocoto.com.br* 🕒 *No dinner Sun.* ✥ *1:G1.*

$$ BRAZILIAN **🍴 Tabuleiro do Marconi.** Owner Marconi Silva started his little slice of Bahia by selling *acarajé* (deep-fried bean balls usually stuffed with paste made from shrimp and other ingredients) on the sidewalk in front of where his restaurant now stands. Since moving indoors, he's expanded his menu to include favorites such as *escondidinho* (a lasagna-like dish with cheese, meat, and manioc) and shrimp risotto in a coconut shell. Kitsch is this tiny eatery's other calling card: keepsakes and curios line the walls. [$] *Average main: R$45* ✉ *Rua Ribeirão Claro 319, Vila Olímpia* ☎ *011/3846–9593* 🌐 *www.tabuleirodomarconi.com.br* 🕒 *Closed Mon.* ✥ *2:C4.*

WHERE TO STAY

São Paulo puts an emphasis on business, and for the most part so do its hotels. Most of them are near Avenida Paulista, along Marginal Pinheiros, or in the charming Jardins neighborhood, where international businesses are located. But catering to business doesn't mean they've forgotten about pleasure. On the contrary, if you're willing to pay for it, the city can match London or New York for unfettered elegance.

Because of the business influence, rates often drop on weekends. Breakfast is a sumptuous affair and is oftentimes included in the room rate. International conventions and the annual Brazilian Grand Prix in November can book hotels completely, so it's wise to make reservations in advance. *Hotel reviews have been shortened. For full information, visit Fodors.com.*

WHAT IT COSTS IN REAIS				
	$	$$	$$$	$$$$
FOR 2 PEOPLE	under R$251	R$251–R$375	R$376–R$500	over R$500

Hotel prices are the lowest cost of a standard double room in high season, excluding tax.

BELA VISTA

$ HOTEL [H] **Ibis São Paulo Paulista.** One of the best bargains on Avenida Paulista, all rooms at this large hotel feature queen-size beds and contemporary decor, with the focus on function, not beauty. **Pros:** a nonaffiliated airport shuttle bus has a stop next door; close to major thoroughfares. **Cons:** heavy traffic all day long. [$] *Rooms from: R$229* ✉ *Av. Paulista 2355, Bela Vista* ☎ *011/3523–3000* 🌐 *www.ibishotel.com* 🛏 *236 rooms* 🍴 *No meals* [M] *Consolação or Paulista* ✣ *D3.*

$ HOTEL [H] **San Gabriel.** Expect no frills at this budget hotel in a lively neighborhood close to Avenida Paulista—rooms are small (though there are some larger suites), but have all the basics and are clean, and the rates are unbeatable for this part of town. **Pros:** close to malls, bars, and restaurants; in-house convenience store. **Cons:** surrounding area isn't well lighted; room rate doesn't include breakfast; no Internet. [$] *Rooms from: R$172* ✉ *Rua Frei Caneca 1006, Bela Vista* ☎ *011/3253–2279* 🌐 *www.sangabriel.com.br* 🛏 *134 rooms* 🍴 *No meals* [M] *Consolação* ✣ *E3.*

BROOKLIN

$$ HOTEL [H] **Hilton São Paulo Morumbi.** The brightest star in Brooklin and the hot spot of the São Paulo business world, this venue is one of three skyscrapers that form an office park loaded with Fortune 500 companies. **Pros:** attached by tunnel to D&D Shopping mall; art exhibits at Canvas Bar; spa uses treatments from the Amazon. **Cons:** far from anything cultural or historical; charge for Internet access. [$] *Rooms from: R$320* ✉ *Av. das Nações Unidas 12901, Torre Leste, Brooklin* ☎ *011/2845–0000* 🌐 *www.hiltonmorumbi.com.br* 🛏 *503 rooms, 13 suites* 🍴 *Breakfast* ✣ *B6.*

CENTRO

$$ HOTEL [H] **Bourbon.** Rich woodwork runs at waist level throughout the halls of this small, classy hotel near Praça da República, just one block away from Largo do Arouche, a bar-lined square that sees a largely gay

crowd at night. **Pros:** great location for exploring Centro; next door to metro. **Cons:** small workstations; Praça da República can be dodgy at night. [$] *Rooms from: R$290* ✉ *Av. Vieira de Carvalho 99, Centro* ☎ *011/3337–2000, 011/3331–8187, 011/3337–1414* 🌐 *www.bourbon.com.br* 🛏 *127 rooms* 🍴 *Breakfast* [M] *República* ✣ *E2.*

$ HOTEL 🏨 **Novotel São Paulo Jaraguá Conventions.** Built in 1951 to be the headquarters of one of the main newspapers in the city, the building that now houses this hotel is a landmark in downtown São Paulo and has hosted Queen Elizabeth II, Fidel Castro, and Errol Flynn. **Pros:** pleasant rooms at good prices; close to many restaurants and sights; 10-minute taxi ride to Paulista. **Cons:** no pool; weak water pressure; area can be spooky at night. [$] *Rooms from: R$250* ✉ *Rua Martins Fontes 71, Centro* ☎ *011/2802–7000* 🌐 *www.novotel.com.br* 🛏 *415 rooms, 99 suites* 🍴 *No meals* [M] *Anhangabaú* ✣ *E2.*

4

CERQUEIRA CÉSAR

$$$$ HOTEL Fodor's Choice ★ 🏨 **Tivoli São Paulo–Mofarrej.** The five-star Tivoli Mofarrej reopened a few years ago after renovations that raised the standard of lavishness for São Paulo hotels. **Pros:** chance of meeting a prince or princess (literally); Thai spa's Rainmist Steam Bath; steps from Avenida Paulista. **Cons:** Wi-Fi access not included in price; extremely expensive. [$] *Rooms from: R$720* ✉ *Alameda Santos 1437, Cerqueira César* ☎ *011/3146–5900* 🌐 *www.tivolihotels.com* 🛏 *220 rooms, 35 suites* 🍴 *No meals* [M] *Tirianon-MASP* ✣ *D3.*

CONSOLAÇÃO

$ HOTEL 🏨 **Ibis Budget.** With hotels at both ends of Paulista and other properties in Jardins, Morumbi, and the city center, the Ibis Budget (formerly the Formule 1) is a great choice if you value location and price over luxury. **Pros:** close to metro and convenience stores; perfect for travelers who plan to be out and about. **Cons:** unspectacular breakfast; often fully booked; no pool. [$] *Rooms from: R$175* ✉ *Rua da Consolação 2303, Consolação* ☎ *011/3123–7755* 🌐 *www.ibisbudget.com* 🛏 *399 rooms* 🍴 *No meals* [M] *Paulista* ✣ *D3.*

HIGIENÓPOLIS

$$ HOTEL 🏨 **Hotel Ville.** In the lively Higienópolis neighborhood of apartment buildings, bars, and bookstores abutting Mackenzie University, this hotel has plain, clean rooms with little decoration. **Pros:** walking distance to shopping mall; supermarket next door is open until midnight; university campus is pretty. **Cons:** only one person at desk on weekends; heavy evening-rush-hour traffic. [$] *Rooms from: R$290* ✉ *Rua Dona Veridiana 643, Higienópolis* ☎ *011/3257–5288* 🌐 *www.hotelville.com.br* 🛏 *56 rooms* 🍴 *Breakfast* [M] *Santa Cecilia* ✣ *E2.*

$$$ HOTEL 🏨 **Tryp Higienópolis.** Tucked imperceptibly among stately apartment buildings in one of the city's oldest and most attractive residential neighborhoods, this hotel built in 2000 has bright and spacious rooms with contemporary light-wood furnishings. **Pros:** cool half-indoor,

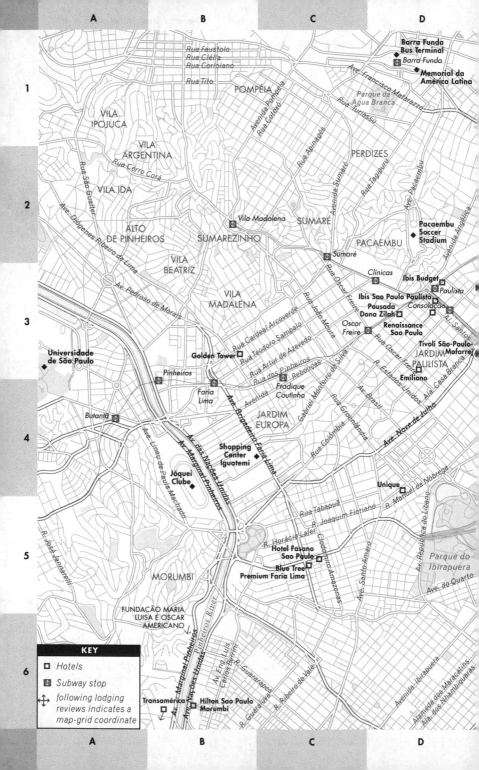

half-outdoor pool; breakfast menu in Braille; 10-minute taxi ride from Centro. **Cons:** small bathrooms; boring furniture. $ *Rooms from: R$500* ✉ *Rua Maranhão 371, Higienópolis* ☎ *011/3665–8200, 0800/892–1356* 🌐 *www.melia.com* 🛏 *207 rooms* 🍴 *No meals* [M] *Paulista* ✥ *E2.*

ITAIM BIBI

$$ HOTEL 🏨 **Blue Tree Premium Faria Lima.** Techno beats enliven the lobby of this chic business hotel halfway between Paulista and Brooklin whose rooms have clean lines and dark-wood furnishings that contrast with the bright-white walls and fabrics. **Pros:** courteous staff; on major thoroughfare close to many multinationals; close to restaurants. **Cons:** taxi needed to visit sights; heavy rush hour. $ *Rooms from: R$310* ✉ *Av. Brigadeiro Faria Lima 3989, Itaim Bibi* ☎ *011/3896–7544, 011/3896–7545* 🌐 *www.bluetree.com.br* 🛏 *338 rooms* 🍴 *Breakfast* [M] *Faria Lima* ✥ *C5.*

JARDINS

$$$$ HOTEL 🏨 **Emiliano.** For pure luxury, the Emiliano would match any modern hotel in Europe's best cities: rooms are large, with blonde-wood floors and furnishings—including Eames lounge chairs—and creamy leather sofas and banquettes. **Pros:** on São Paulo's chicest avenue; pillow menus; complimentary wine bottles. **Cons:** stratospheric prices. $ *Rooms from: R$1,780* ✉ *Rua Oscar Freire 384, Jardins* ☎ *011/3069–4369* 🌐 *www.emiliano.com.br* 🛏 *56 rooms, 19 suites* 🍴 *No meals* [M] *Trianon-Masp* ✥ *D3.*

$$$$ HOTEL Fodor's Choice ★ 🏨 **Hotel Fasano São Paulo.** With a decor that hints at 1940s modern but is undeniably 21st-century chic, the Hotel Fasano caters to those for whom money is a mere detail. **Pros:** attentive, knowledgeable staff; top-floor pool with stunning view. **Cons:** paying for it all. $ *Rooms from: R$1,240* ✉ *Rua Vittorio Fasano 88, Jardins* ☎ *011/3896–4000* 🌐 *www.fasano.com.br* 🛏 *60 rooms, 10 suites* 🍴 *No meals* [M] *Consolação* ✥ *C5.*

$$$$ HOTEL 🏨 **L'Hotel Porto Bay São Paulo.** Compared to the top-of-the line chain hotels on Paulista, L'Hotel stands out as a truly special experience. **Pros:** small number of rooms makes for personalized service; L'Occitane bath products. **Cons:** expensive. $ *Rooms from: R$700* ✉ *Alameda Campinas 266, Jardins* ☎ *011/2183–0500, 011/2183–0505* 🌐 *www.lhotel.com.br* 🛏 *83 rooms, 8 suites* 🍴 *Breakfast* [M] *Trianon-MASP* ✥ *E3.*

$$$$ HOTEL 🏨 **InterContinental São Paulo.** One of the city's most attractive top-tier establishments, the InterContinental consistently receives rave reviews because of the attention paid to every detail, including the pillows (guests choose among six different types). **Pros:** Japanese breakfast; PlayStation in rooms; gym with personal trainers. **Cons:** suites aren't much bigger than regular rooms. $ *Rooms from: R$941* ✉ *Alameda Santos 1123, Jardins* ☎ *011/3179–2600, 0800/770–0858, 011/3179–2666* 🌐 *www.intercontinental.com* 🛏 *195 rooms, 38 suites* 🍴 *No meals* [M] *Trianon-MASP* ✥ *E3.*

$$$ HOTEL 🏨 **Maksoud Plaza.** Once the top choice for luxury accommodations in São Paulo, Maksoud must now share the bill with a bevy of high-end hotels; still, its facilities, comfort, and good location make it one of the best choices in the city. **Pros:** four full-service restaurants and five bars;

huge atrium. **Cons:** dingy exterior; rush-hour traffic. Ⓢ *Rooms from: R$400* ✉ *Alameda Campinas 1250, Jardins* ☎ *011/3145–8000, 888/551–1333 toll-free in U.S.* ⊕ *www.maksoud.com.br* ⇆ *416 rooms* ❍*Breakfast* Ⓜ *Trianon-MASP* ✛ *E3.*

$$
B&B/INN

🛏 **Pousada Dona Zilah.** Marvelously located in the retail-heavy part of the Jardins district and easily navigable both to and from, this homey pousada, while not exactly cheap, might be a more affordable alternative if you're seeking to momentarily escape the skyscraper experience. **Pros:** close to Oscar Freire shopping; excellent breakfast. **Cons:** can be noisy. Ⓢ *Rooms from: R$275* ✉ *Alameda Franca 1621, Jardins* ☎ *011/3062–1444* ⊕ *www.zilah.com* ⇆ *14 rooms* ❍*Breakfast* Ⓜ *Paulista* ✛ *D3.*

MOTELS AND POUSADAS

If you check into a reasonably priced motel with the hope of humble-but-cheap lodging alternative, you may be surprised to find a heart-shape bed and strategically placed mirrors. Yes, motels in Brazil are specifically set aside for romantic rendezvous. The market is large because most unmarried people live with their parents until well into their 20s or 30s, not to mention the soap-opera lives that many Brazilians lead. If you're looking for a bed that doesn't vibrate, the name of what you seek is *pousada*.

$$$
HOTEL

🛏 **Renaissance São Paulo.** In case the rooftop helipad doesn't say it all, the striking lines of the red-and-black granite lobby announce one serious business hotel. **Pros:** you never have to leave hotel; professional staff. **Cons:** Internet and breakfast aren't included; uninspired decor. Ⓢ *Rooms from: R$400* ✉ *Alameda Santos 2233, Jardins* ☎ *011/3069–2233, 888/236–2427 in U.S.* ⊕ *www.renaissancehotels.com* ⇆ *444 rooms, 56 suites, 45 club rooms* ❍*No meals* Ⓜ *Consolação* ✛ *D3.*

$$$$
HOTEL
Fodor's Choice
★

🛏 **Unique.** It's hard not see a familiar shape (some say watermelon, some say boat, but neither hits the mark) in the wild but harmonious design of this boutique hotel. **Pros:** steps from Ibirapuera Park and a taxi ride to many top restaurants; attractive, modern design. **Cons:** nonstop techno music in public spaces; very expensive. Ⓢ *Rooms from: R$1,000* ✉ *Av. Brigadeiro Luís Antônio 4700, Jardins* ☎ *011/3055–4700, 011/3889–8100* ⊕ *www.unique.com.br* ⇆ *95 rooms* ❍*No meals* ✛ *D4.*

PINHEIROS

$$$
HOTEL

🛏 **Golden Tower.** Its ideal location close to important hubs and to Vila Madalena and spacious rooms make this a good choice. **Pros:** close to Marginal Pinheiros; quiet neighborhood. **Cons:** far from Centro. Ⓢ *Rooms from: R$400* ✉ *Rua Deputado Lacerda Franco 148, Pinheiros* ☎ *011/3094–2200* ⊕ *www.goldentowerhotel.com.br* ⇆ *96 rooms, 8 suites* ❍*Breakfast* Ⓜ *Faria Lima* ✛ *B3.*

SANTO AMARO

$$$$
HOTEL

🛏 **Transamérica.** Directly across the Pinheiros River from the Centro Empresarial office complex, the home of many U.S. companies, this hotel is a convenient choice for those working in the area. **Pros:** great location for business travelers; free Wi-Fi; tennis courts; 3-hole chip-and-putt golf course. **Cons:** Pinheiros River smells terrible; traffic paralyzes the area at rush hour. [$] *Rooms from: R$835* ✉ *Av. das Nações Unidas 18591, Santo Amaro* ☎ *011/5693–4050, 0800/012–6060* 🌐 *www.transamerica.com.br* 🛏 *400 rooms, 11 suites* 🍴 *Breakfast* [M] *Santo Amaro* ✛ *B6.*

VILA MARIANA

$$$$ HOTEL 🏨 **Hotel Pullman São Paulo Ibirapuera.** Renovated in 2013 and looking fresh, the Pullman brings contemporary design and reasonable prices to the Ibirapuera area. **Pros:** near Ibirapuera Park, Avenida Paulista, and museums; affordable. **Cons:** considerable ride from main business and nightlife districts; small pool. [$] *Rooms from: R$900* ✉ *Rua Joinville 515, Vila Mariana* ☎ *011/5088–4000* 🌐 *www.pullmanhotels.com* 🛏 *350 rooms* 🍴 *No meals* [M] *Paraíso* ✛ *E4.*

$$$$ HOTEL 🏨 **Grand Mercure São Paulo Ibirapuera.** Near the Congonhas Airport and Ibirapuera Park, this modern, luxury hotel is noted for its French style, and its restaurant serves French cuisine. **Pros:** many amenities; convenient helipad for millionaires; park views. **Cons:** afternoon traffic; far from business centers. [$] *Rooms from: R$505* ✉ *Rua Sena Madureira 1355, Bloco 1, Vila Mariana* ☎ *011/3201–0800, 011/5575–4544* 🌐 *www.accorhotels.com.br* 🛏 *215 rooms* 🍴 *No meals* ✛ *E5.*

NIGHTLIFE AND PERFORMING ARTS

NIGHTLIFE

São Paulo's nightlife options are seemingly endless, so knowing where to go is key. The chic and wealthy head for establishments, most of which serve food, in the Vila Olímpia, Jardins, and Itaim neighborhoods. The Pinheiros and Vila Madalena neighborhoods have a large concentration of youthful clubs and bars, and many trendy clubs have opened in Barra Funda. Jardins and Centro have many gay and lesbian spots, with the area around Rua Augusta catering to hipsters.

Most clubs open at 9 pm, but people tend to arrive late (around midnight) and dance until 5 or 6 am. Still, you should arrive early to be at the front of the lines. Don't worry if the dance floor appears empty at 11 pm; things will start to sizzle an hour or so later.

Clubbing can get expensive. Most clubs charge at least R$20 at the door (sometimes women are allowed in for free), and the most popular and upscale places as much as R$300 just for entry. At the hottest clubs, expect to wait in line for a bit, especially if you head out late. Expect to wait in line on the way out again, too—the system is usually that you charge your drinks on an electronic tab, presenting the card and paying upon leaving. It can mean long queues: smart clubbers think ahead and pay up in good time.

A word about happy hour: Unlike in some countries, where the term refers to those few early-evening hours when drinks are cheaper, happy hour (pronounced and written in English) in Brazil simply means the time just after the work day ends, around 6 pm, when you might head to a bar for a drink with friends or colleagues. Despite the lack of discounted cocktails, paulistanos love to use the term, and many bars are judged purely on their suitability as a happy hour venue.

> **GETTING AROUND AFTER DARK**
>
> For safety reasons, we strongly suggest taking cabs at night—it's convenient and relatively cheap. Ask your concierge about transportation if finding a cab proves difficult.

BARRA FUNDA, ÁGUA BRANCA, AND LAPA

DANCE CLUBS

D.Edge. Electronic music is the main attraction at this popular club with a Death Star–meets–Studio 54 appeal. As many as nine DJs, often including internationally renowned turntablists, spin music on Thursday, Friday, and Saturday nights; on Sunday the party starts at 6 am and runs into the afternoon, and Monday is rock night. The terrace here has views of a park of Oscar Niemeyer design. Cover charges dip as low as R$20 but sometimes exceed R$100. ⊠ *Av. Auro Soares de Moura Andrade 141, Barra Funda* ☎ *011/3665–9500, 011/3667–8799* ⊕ *www.d-edge.com.br* ✉ *Average entry R$20* Ⓜ *Barra Funda.*

Villa Country. This is *the* place to dance to American country music and *sertanejo*, Brazilian country music. The huge club has a restaurant, bars, shops, game rooms, and a big dance floor. The decor is strictly Old West. ⊠ *Av. Francisco Matarazzo 774, Água Branca* ☎ *011/3868–5858* ⊕ *www.villacountry.com.br* ✉ *Average entry R$40 women, R$60 men* Ⓜ *Barra Funda.*

GAY AND LESBIAN BARS AND CLUBS

Blue Space. In a huge colonial blue house in an old industrial neighborhood, Blue Space is one of the largest gay nightclubs in São Paulo. Every Saturday and Sunday, two dance floors and four bars, along with lounge and private rooms, fill with a large crowd, mostly 40 and over, interested in the house DJs and go-go-boy and drag shows. ⊠ *Rua Brigadeiro Galvão 723, Barra Funda* ☎ *011/3666–1616, 011/3665–7157* ⊕ *www.bluespace.com.br* ✉ *Average entry R$30* Ⓜ *Marechal Deodoro.*

The Week. Occupying a nearly 6,000-square-meter (64,500-square-foot) space, this club popular with gay men has two dance floors, three lounge rooms, a deck with a swimming pool, six bars, and a massage bed. Several DJs playing house, electro, and techno animate an often shirtless crowd on Friday and Saturday night. ⊠ *Rua Guaicurus 324, Lapa* ☎ *011/3868–9944* ✉ *Average entry R$100.*

BELA VISTA

MUSIC CLUBS

Café Piu Piu. The café is best-known for its live-rock nights—Thursday, Friday, and Saturday. On other nights, it hosts groups that play rock jazz, blues, bossa nova, and sometimes tango. Potato latkes are among the menu highlights. ⊠ *Rua 13 de Maio 134, Bela Vista* ☎ *011/3258–8066* ⊕ *www.cafepiupiu.com.br* ✉ *Average entry R$20.*

CENTRO

BARS

Bar Brahma. First opened in 1948, Bar Brahma used to be the meeting place of artists, intellectuals, and politicians. The decor is a time warp to the mid-20th century, with furniture, lamps, and a piano true to the period. This is one of the best places in São Paulo for live music, with traditional samba and Brazilian pop groups scheduled every week. Caetano Veloso immortalized the intersection of Ipiranga and São João Avenues, where the bar is located, in his 1978 song "Sampa."⊠ *Av. São João 677, Centro* ☎ *011/3224–1250 reservations, 011/3367–3601* ⊕ *www.barbrahmacentro.com* ☒ *Average entry R$35* Ⓜ *República.*

DANCE CLUBS

Alberta #3. A linchpin of the nightlife revival pulling hipsters back to Centro, this club across from the Novotel Jaraguá caters to crowds from happy hour to the bewitching hours. Head upstairs to the lounge for cocktails and imported beers or downstairs to shake it out on the dance floor to indie and classic rock. ⊠ *Av. São Luís 272, Centro* ☎ *011/3151–5299* ⊕ *www.alberta3.com.br* ☒ *Average entry R$30* Ⓜ *República.*

Cine Joia. One of the city's newer live-music venues, Cine Joia may also be its loveliest. It takes the form of a resurrected vintage cinema, minus the seating but with the added attraction of a top-notch video-mapping system. See the site for live dates, or check out regular club nights like Talco Bells, spinning soul classics for a faithful party crowd. ⊠ *Praça Carlos Gomes 82, Centro* ☎ *011/3101–1385* ⊕ *www.cinejoia.tv* ☒ *Average entry R$40* Ⓜ *Liberdade.*

CONSOLAÇÃO

BARS

Drosophyla. Your creepy aunt's house filled with bizarre keepsakes meets quaint garden bar at Drosophyla. Young professionals and midlife free spirits assemble here for exotic caipirinhas, shots of vodka with cranberry syrup, and other zesty cocktails. If here for a meal, try the *huahine*, a French-Polynesian dish with marinated raw tuna, carrot, peppers, cherry tomatoes, and coconut milk. ⊠ *Rua Pedro Taques 80, Consolação* ☎ *011/3120–5535* ⊕ *www.drosophyla.com.br* Ⓜ *Consolação or Paulista.*

Riviera Bar. A firm nighttime favorite, Riviera reinvented a much-loved corner bar dating from 1949 as a chic, modern nightspot owned by star chef Alex Atala and nightclub entrepreneur Facundo Guerra. Drop in for a drink at the curvaceous bar, head upstairs and find a table for an evening of dinner and jazz, or stop by for the good buffet lunch. ⊠ *Av. Paulista 2584, Consolação* ☎ *011/3258–1268* ⊕ *www.rivierabar.com.br* ☒ *Average entry R$30* Ⓜ *Paulista.*

GAY AND LESBIAN BARS AND CLUBS

A Lôca. A mixed gay, lesbian, and straight crowd often dances until dawn at A Lôca to everything from pop and rock to disco and techno. ⊠ *Rua Frei Caneca 916, Consolação* ☎ *011/3159–8889* ⊕ *www.aloca.com.br* ☒ *Average entry R$40* Ⓜ *Consolação.*

FREGUESIA DO Ó
BARS

Frangó. A stop at off-the-beaten-path Frangó, northwest of Centro, makes you feel as if you've been transported to a small town. The bar has more than 300 varieties of beer, including the Brazilian craft beer Colorado. The Indica brew, an IPA made with sugarcane, nicely complements the bar's unforgettable *coxinhas de frango com queijo* (fried balls of chicken with cheese). ✉ *Largo da Matriz de Nossa Senhora do Ó 168, Freguesia do Ó* ☎ *011/3932–4818* ⊕ *www.frangobar. com.br.*

GAY PRIDE PARADE
São Paulo hosts one of the world's biggest and most famous gay parades each year on the Sunday of the Corpus Christi holiday, which generally falls at the end of May or in early June. The Gay Pride Parade, which was first held in 1997, runs along Avenida Paulista and attracts more than 2 million people.

ITAIM BIBI
BARS

Na Mata Café. Close to the northern border of Itaim, Na Mata ranks among the city's best live-music venues. It's a great place to catch some upmarket Brazilian entertainment. ✉ *Rua da Mata 70, Itaim* ☎ *011/3079–0300* ⊕ *www.namata.com.br* 💳 *Average entry R$45 women, R$55 men.*

GAY AND LESBIAN BARS AND CLUBS

Vermont Itaim. A major lesbian hangout in Itaim, this venue offers dining, live music, and dancing. Ten acts divvy up the showtimes from Wednesday to Saturday; on Sunday a nine-piece all-girl samba band takes the stage. When the bands stop playing, DJs spin music late into the night. ✉ *Rua Pedroso Alvarenga 1192, Itaim Bibi* ☎ *011/3071–1320, 011/3707–7721* ⊕ *www.vermontitaim.com.br* 💳 *Average entry R$20.*

MUSIC CLUBS

Kia Ora Pub. Rock and pop cover bands perform at this Down Under-themed pub. Seven international draft beers and happy hour specials make Kia Ora popular after businesses close. ✉ *Rua Dr. Eduardo de Souza Aranha 377, Itaim* ☎ *011/3846–8300* ⊕ *www.kiaora.com.br* 💳 *Average entry R$30 women, R$70 men.*

JARDIM PAULISTA
BARS

Balcão. Balcão means "bar" in Portuguese, and this artsy place has a long, curving one. If you'd like a little food to accompany your drinks and conversation, try one of the famous sandwiches on ciabatta bread. ✉ *Rua Doutor Melo Alves 150, Jardim Paulista* ☎ *011/3063–6091* Ⓜ *Consolação.*

DANCE CLUBS

8 Bar. The DJs at this intimate space play electronic, disco, and hip-hop, often interacting with the crowd on the dance floor and accepting requests. The bar closes occasionally for private events, so call ahead to be sure it's open. ✉ *Rua José Maria Lisboa 82, Jardim Paulista*

4

☎ *011/3889–9927, 011/97085–5718* ⊕ *www.8bar.com.br* ⌨ *Average entry R$10.*

JARDINS
BARS
O'Malley's. A self-proclaimed "gringo" hangout, this is a good place to catch international sporting events, perhaps that major one back home it's killing you to miss. O'Malley's has three bars, a game room, and more than a dozen TVs spread across two floors. Seven beers are on tap, along with more than four dozen by the bottle. Bands play nightly, so there's always a cover after happy hour ends. ⊠ *Alameda Itú 1529, Jardins* ☎ *011/3086–0780* ⊕ *www.omalleysbar.net* ⌨ *Average entry R$10* Ⓜ *Consolação.*

MOEMA
MUSIC CLUBS
Bourbon Street. With a name right out of New Orleans, it's no wonder that Bourbon Street is where the best jazz and blues bands, Brazilian and international, play. Performances start at 9:30 pm. On Sunday, you can merengue and mambo at the Caribbean dance party. ⊠ *Rua dos Chanés 127, Moema* ☎ *011/5095–6100* ⊕ *www.bourbonstreet.com.br* ⌨ *Average entry R$30.*

PARAÍSO
BARS
Barnaldo Lucrécia. Live MPB and pub fare such as the *carne seca com mandioca frita* (sun-dried beef with fried manioc) draws an intense but jovial crowd to this bohemian spot. ⊠ *Rua Abílio Soares 207, Paraíso* ☎ *011/3885–3425* ⊕ *www.barnaldolucrecia.com.br* ⌨ *Average entry R$35* Ⓜ *Paraíso.*

Fodor's Choice
★ **Veloso.** Tables here are as disputed as a parking spot in front of a downtown apartment. An intimate corner bar on a quiet cobblestone plaza, Veloso dispenses some of São Paulo's best caipirinhas, including exotic versions such as tangerine with red pepper, and *coxinhas* (fried balls of chicken with cheese). ⊠ *Rua Conceição Veloso 56, Paraíso* ☎ *011/5572–0254* ⊕ *www.velosobar.com.br* Ⓜ *Ana Rosa.*

PINHEIROS
DANCE CLUBS
Bar Secreto. Madonna and band members from U2 are former patrons of this once esoteric and invitation-only dance club. Though entrance is no longer just for Bruce Wayne, to make sure you can mingle with the moneyed partygoers, you should still try to put your name on the list—through the website or by email invitation. List or not, you'll still have to pay a cover charge that might wade into the triple digits. Bar Secreto opens at 11 pm from Wednesday to Saturday, and at 7 on Sunday. Or does it? ⊠ *Rua Álvaro Anes 97, Pinheiros* ⊕ *barsecreto.com.br* ⌨ *Average entry R$40* Ⓜ *Faria Lima.*

Casa 92. Giving new meaning to the concept house party, Casa 92 was fashioned out of a converted domicile. The living room has been fitted with disco lighting; the patio and terrace each have bars. An upstairs dance floor resides where a bedroom otherwise would. The music is eclectic with an emphasis on (what else?) house. ✉ *Rua Cristovão Gonçalves 92, Pinheiros* ☎ *011/3032–0371* ⊕ *www.casa92.com.br* ☷ *Average entry R$50* Ⓜ *Faria Lima.*

GAY AND LESBIAN BARS AND CLUBS

Bubu Lounge Disco. Disco balls dangle over the dance floor at gay Bubu, where shirtless is the new fully clothed. Drag performers strut their stuff at Sunday matinees, and the last Thursday of the month is girls-only night. ✉ *Rua Dos Pinheiros 791, Pinheiros* ☎ *011/3081–9546, 011/3081–9659* ⊕ *www.bubulounge.com.br* ☷ *Average entry R$30* Ⓜ *Faria Lima.*

MUSIC CLUBS

Canto da Ema. At what's widely considered the best place in town to dance *forró* (music/dance from Brazil's Northeast), you'll find people of different ages and styles coming together on the dance floor. *Xiboquinha* is the official forró drink, made with *cachaça* (a Brazilian sugarcane-based alcohol), lemon, honey, cinnamon, and ginger. The doors open at 10:30 pm from Wednesday through Saturday; the hours on Sunday are from 7 pm to midnight. ✉ *Av. Brigadeiro Faria Lima 364, Pinheiros* ☎ *011/3813–4708* ⊕ *www.cantodaema.com.br* ☷ *Average entry R$25.*

Carioca Club. A *carioca* is a person from Rio de Janeiro, and Carioca Club has the decor of old-style Rio clubs. Its large dance floor attracts an eclectic mix of up to 1,200 college students, couples, and professional dancers who move to samba, *gafieira,* and *pagode* from Thursday through Saturday starting at varying times. ✉ *Rua Cardeal Arcoverde 2899, Pinheiros* ☎ *011/3813–8598, 011/3813–4524* ⊕ *www.carioca club.com.br* ☷ *Average entry R$25* Ⓜ *Faria Lima.*

VILA MADALENA

BARS

Astor. The 1960s and 1970s bohemian-chic decor here sends you back in time. The quality draft beer and tasty snacks and meals mean that Astor is always hopping—the menu is full of specialties from classic bars in Brazil. Don't miss the *picadinho:* beef stew with rice and black beans, poached eggs, banana, farofa, and beef *pastel* (a type of dumpling). To finish up, head downstairs, where SubAstor, a speakeasy-style sister bar, serves the kind of cocktails that inspire you to attempt knockoffs at your next house party. ✉ *Rua Delfina 163, Vila Madalena* ☎ *011/3815–1364* ⊕ *www.barastor.com.br.*

Filial. When it comes to ending the night, Filial is considered by many to be the best bar in town. Many musicians stop by for an after-hours taste of its draft beer, along with the flavorful snacks (such as *bolinho de arroz,* or rice fritters) and meals (try *galinha afogada,* a stew with incredibly moist chicken and rice). ✉ *Rua Fidalga 254, Vila Madalena* ☎ *011/3813–9226* ⊕ *www.barfilial.com.br.*

Gràcia. A flirtatious clientele frequents this hot spot. Named for a Barcelona neighborhood, Gràcia is clothed in Catalan imagery and serves tapas and Sangria from the region. Sidewalk seating is available when the weather cooperates. ✉ *Rua Coropes 87, Vila Madalena* ☎ *011/3034–1481* ⊕ *graciabar.com.br* Ⓜ *Faria Lima.*

Posto 6. One of four comparable and fashionable bars at the corner of Mourato Coelho and Aspicuelta streets, Posto 6 pays homage to Rio de Janeiro and its Botafogo soccer club. The bar gets gold stars for its chopp and *escondidinho de camarão* (a lasagna-type dish with shrimp). ⊠ *Rua Aspicuelta 646, Vila Madalena* ☎ *011/3812–4342.*

DANCE CLUBS

Fodor's Choice
★ **Ó do Borogodó.** With live samba and MPB music every night of the week, this packed little club is a firm local favorite and provides a reliably good time, every time. ⊠ *Rua Horácio Lane 21, Vila Madalena* ☎ *011/3814–4087* ⊟ *Average entry R$20.*

UP Club. DJs spin hip-hop and rap, and dancers pack the floor on Friday night at the UP Club. If things get too steamy, you can take a breather in the backyard garden. ⊠ *Rua Harmonia 21, Vila Madalena* ☎ *011/2309–7159* ⊕ *www.upclubsp.com.br* ⊟ *Average entry R$20.*

MUSIC CLUBS

Grazie a Dio. The fashionable patrons at this club may vary in age, but they all appreciate good music. The best time to go is at happy hour for daily live performances. Samba, soul, and jazz figure prominently, with Brazilian pop represented as well. The natural decorations, including trees and constellations, complement the Mediterranean food served in the back. ⊠ *Rua Girassol 67, Vila Madalena* ☎ *011/3031–6568* ⊕ *www.grazieadio.com.br* ⊟ *Average entry R$10.*

Fodor's Choice
★ **Madeleine.** The riffs heard at Madeleine place it in an exclusive stratum of São Paulo music clubs, but it's the mix of music, food, drinks, and atmosphere that lends the bar its comprehensive appeal. Jazz ensembles play in the exposed-brick lounge, which has clear sightlines from the mezzanine. Better for chatting are the candlelit tables in the well-stocked wine cellar, and the seats on the veranda, with its panoramic views of Vila Madalena. Wherever you sit, the gourmet pizzas go great with the craft beers poured here. ⊠ *Rua Aspicuelta 201, Vila Madalena* ☎ *011/2936–0616* ⊕ *www.madeleine.com.br.*

VILA OLÍMPIA

BARS

Bar Do Arnesto. More than 500 types of the rumlike liquor cachaça—the main ingredient in caipirinhas, Brazil's national cocktail—line a huge wall at this traditional Brazilian *botequim.* These casual bars generally specialize in cold bottled beer, snack foods, and caipirinhas. ⊠ *Rua Ministro Jesuíno Cardoso 207, Vila Olímpia* ☎ *011/3848–9432, 011/3848-6041 after 6 pm* ⊕ *www.bardoarnesto.com.br* ⊟ *Average entry R$20.*

DANCE CLUBS

Disco. Big names in electronic music command the turntables at Disco, where you might end up sharing the dance floor with members of the national glitterati—or just some very–São Paulo playboys. ⊠ *Rua Professor Atílio Innocenti 160, Brooklin* ☎ *011/3078–0404* ⊕ *www.clubdisco.com.br* ⊟ *Average entry men R$150, women free.*

Rey Castro. Salsa, merengue, zouk, and Latin pop predominate at Rey Castro; and during the breaks between live performances, you can take dance classes. The Caribbean-influenced drinks and snacks include mojitos and ham croquettes. ⊠ *Rua Ministro Jesuíno Cardoso 181, Vila Olímpia* ☎ *011/3842–5279* ⊕ *www.reycastro.com.br* ⊟ *Average entry R$40.*

MUSIC CLUBS
All of Jazz. People come here to listen quietly to good jazz and bossa nova in an intimate environment—there's even a CD store upstairs with more than 3,000 discs. Local musicians jam from 10 pm on except on Sunday. The club gets crowded on weekends, when it's best to reserve a table. ✉ *Rua João Cachoeira 1366, Vila Olímpia* ☏ *011/3849–1345* ⊕ *www.allofjazz.com.br* 🍽 *Average entry R$30.*

PERFORMING ARTS

The world's top orchestras, opera and dance companies, and other troupes always include São Paulo in their South American tours. Many free concerts—with performances by either Brazilian or international artists—are presented on Sunday in Parque Ibirapuera. City-sponsored events are frequently held in Centro's Vale do Anhangabaú area or in Avenida Paulista.

The Centro Cultural São Paulo near Paraíso metro and an ample network of Serviço Social do Comércio (SESC) cultural centers feature inexpensive dance, theater, and musical performances daily. Listings of events appear in the "Veja São Paulo" insert of the newsweekly *Veja*. The arts sections of the dailies *Folha de São Paulo* and *O Estado de São Paulo* also have listings and reviews. Both papers publish a weekly guide on Friday. The Portuguese-language website Catraca Livre (⊕ *catracalivre.com.br/brasil*)is the authority on free entertainment options.

Tickets for many events are available through the Ingresso Rápido, Ingresso, and Tickets for Fun websites. Many of these venues and sites offer ticket delivery to your hotel for a surcharge.

Ticket Information Ingresso Rápido. ☏ *011/4003–1212* ⊕ *www.ingressorapido.com.br.* **Ingresso.com.** ☏ *011/4003–2330* ⊕ *www.ingresso.com.br.* **Show Tickets.** ✉ *Iguatemi São Paulo, Av. Brigadeiro Faria Lima 1191, 3rd fl., Jardim Paulistano* ☏ *011/3031–2098* ⊕ *www.showtickets.com.br.* **Tickets for Fun.** ☏ *011/4003–5588* ⊕ *premier.ticketsforfun.com.br.*

CLASSICAL MUSIC AND OPERA
Fodor'sChoice ★ **Sala São Paulo.** Despite being housed in a magnificent old train station, Sala São Paulo is one of the most modern concert halls for classical music in Latin America. It's home to the **São Paulo Symphony** (OSESP). ✉ *Praça Júlio Prestes 16, Centro* ☏ *011/3367–9500* ⊕ *www.salasaopaulo.art.br* Ⓜ *Luz.*

Theatro São Pedro. Built in the neoclassical style in 1917, São Paulo's second-oldest theater is one of its best venues for chamber concerts and operas. Free morning events take place on Sunday and Wednesday. ✉ *Rua Albuquerque Lins 207, Barra Funda* ☏ *011/3667–0499 ticket booth* ⊕ *www.theatrosaopedro.org.br* Ⓜ *Marechal Deodoro.*

CONCERT HALLS
Credicard Hall. One of the biggest theaters in São Paulo, Credicard Hall can accommodate up to 7,000 people. The venue frequently hosts concerts by famous Brazilian and international artists. Tickets can be bought by phone or online through Tickets for Fun. ✉ *Av. das Nações Unidas 17995, Santo Amaro* ☏ *011/4003–5588* ⊕ *www.credicardhall.com.br.*

SESC Pompéia. Part of a chain of cultural centers throughout the city, SESC Pompéia incorporates a former factory into its design. There are multiple performance spaces, but the *choperia* (beer hall) and theater host the most prominent Brazilian and international musical acts— from jazz and soul to rock and hip-hop. ⊠ *Rua Clélia 93, Vila Olímpia* ☎ *011/3871–7700* ⊕ *www.sescsp.org.br.*

Teatro Alfa. International musicals and ballet, as well as occasional musical performances, are held at Teatro Alfa, which seats more than a thousand people. The sound and lighting technology are top of the line. Tickets can be bought by phone and through Ingresso Rápido, then picked up a half hour before the performance. ⊠ *Rua Bento Branco de Andrade Filho 722, Santo Amaro* ☎ *011/5693–4000, 0300/789–3377* ⊕ *www.teatroalfa.com.br.*

Theatro Municipal. Inspired by the Paris Opéra, the Municipal Theater was built between 1903 and 1911 with art nouveau elements. *Hamlet* was the first play presented, and the house went on to host such luminaries as Isadora Duncan in 1916 and Anna Pavlova in 1919. Plays and operas are still staged here; local newspapers, as well as the theater's website, have schedules and information on how to get tickets. The auditorium, resplendent with gold leaf, moss-green velvet, marble, and mirrors, has 1,500 seats and is usually open only to those attending cultural events, although prearranged visits are also available. A museum dedicated to the theater's history is located close by at Praça das Artes. Call the theater to arrange a free guided tour in English. ⊠ *Praça Ramos de Azevedo, Centro* ☎ *011/3397–0300, 011/3397–0327* ⊕ *www.prefeitura.sp.gov.br/cidade/secretarias/cultura/ theatromunicipal* Ⓜ *Anhangabaú.*

DANCE

Balé da Cidade. The City Ballet, São Paulo's official dance company, has performed for many years at the magnificent Theatro Municipal. ⊠ *Rua João Passaláqua 66, Bela Vista* ☎ *011/3241–3883, 011/3241–1740* Ⓜ *Anhangabaú.*

Ballet Stagium. The ballet performs contemporary works incorporating Brazilian pop and bossa nova music. Founded in 1971 during Brazil's period of dictatorship, the company made its name performing dances with political and social-justice themes. ⊠ *Rua Augusta 2985, 2nd fl., Cerqueira César* ☎ *011/3085–0151.*

FILM

Centro Cultural São Paulo. The cultural center has temporary alternative film screenings, particularly of Brazilian titles, but also presents plays, concerts, and art exhibits. Major renovations finished in 2013 added new projection and sound equipment and saw improvements in the lighting and acoustics. Admission is free or low-price for some events. ⊠ *Rua Vergueiro 1000, Paraíso* ☎ *011/3397–4002* ⊕ *www. centrocultural.sp.gov.br* Ⓜ *Vergueiro.*

Cidade Jardim Cinemark. The prices are elite but so are the amenities, such as gourmet food service. Cidade Jardim Cinemark set the bar much higher for blockbuster-screening, luxury theaters in São Paulo. ⊠ *Av.*

Magalhães de Castro 12000, Morumbi ☎ *011/3552–1800* ⊕ *www. shoppingcidadejardim.com/cinema.*

CineSESC. Titles already out of other theaters and independent openings show for discounted prices at CineSESC. The screen is visible from the snack bar. ✉ *Rua Augusta 2075, Cerqueira César* ☎ *011/3087–0500* ⊕ *www.sescsp.org.br* Ⓜ *Consolação.*

Espaço Itaú de Cinema, Augusta. Brazilian, European, and other non-block-buster films are shown at the Espaço Itaú. ✉ *Rua Augusta 1475, Consolação* ☎ *011/3288–6780* ⊕ *www.itaucinemas.com.br* Ⓜ *Consolação.*

Reserva Cultural. The complex contains four movie theaters, a small library, and a deck-style restaurant from which you can see—and be seen by—pedestrians on Paulista Avenue. ✉ *Av. Paulista 900, Jardim Paulista* ☎ *011/3287–3529* ⊕ *www.reservacultural.com.br* Ⓜ *Trianon-MASP or Brigadeiro.*

SAMBA SHOWS
Escolas de samba or samba schools are the heart and soul of many communities. Most people only associate them with the dancing groups that perform during Carnival, but they keep busy all year round. In addition to samba lessons, they organize a range of community services, especially education and health outreach programs. Check them out anytime, but from November to February they're gearing up for Carnival, and often open their rehearsals to the public.

Mocidade Alegre. Up to 3,000 people at a time attend rehearsals at Mocidade Alegre just before Carnival. ✉ *Av. Casa Verde 3498, Limão* ☎ *011/3857–7525* ⊕ *www.mocidadealegre.com.br.*

Rosas de Ouro. One of the most popular rehearsals takes place at Rosas de Ouro. ✉ *Rua Coronel Euclides Machado 1066, Freguesia do Ó* ☎ *011/3931–4555* ⊕ *www.sociedaderosasdeouro.com.br.*

SPORTS AND THE OUTDOORS

Maybe it's the environment or maybe the culture, but participating in organized sports isn't usually a huge part of a paulistano's regime. An exception is soccer, or *futebol*, which you will see being played in most parks, either on full fields, half-size arenas, or even sandy courts, every weekend and on weeknights. Basketball and volleyball also have loyal, if smaller, followings at parks and SESC centers around the city.

AUTO RACING

Brazilian Grand Prix. Racing fans from all over the world come to São Paulo in November for the Brazilian Grand Prix, a Formula 1 race that attracts massive national attention, especially when a Brazilian driver is in the mix. The race is held at Autódromo da Interlagos, which at other times hosts auto races on weekends. ✉ *Autódromo da Interlagos, Av. Senador Teotônio Vilela 261* ☎ *021/2221–4895 tickets* ⊕ *www. gpbrasil.com.*

CYCLING AND JOGGING

Parque Ibirapuera. Going for a ride or a run in one of São Paulo's parks is a good choice if you want a little exercise. For cyclists there are usually plenty of rental options (from R$5 per hour) available and special lanes just for riders. Parque Ibirapuera gets busy on the weekends, but it's still worth coming here. ⊠ *Av. Pedro Álvares Cabral, Parque Ibirapuera* ☎ *011/5574–5045* ⊕ *www.parqueibirapuera.org.*

Parque Villa-Lobos. It may have fewer trees and less of a history than Parque Ibirapuera, but Parque Villa-Lobos is big and has plenty of winding pathways wide enough to accommodate cyclists and runners. There are bike-rental stands inside the park (from R$7 per hour), as well as a few soccer pitches and a big, concrete square with basketball halfcourts. There are some food-and-drink options, too. ⊠ *Av. Professor Fonseca Rodrigues 2001, Alto de Pinheiros* ☎ *011/3021–6285* ⊕ *www. ambiente.sp.gov.br/parquevillalobos* ☉ *Daily 6–6.*

SOCCER

São Paulo State has several well-funded teams with some of the country's best players. The four main teams—Corinthians, São Paulo, Palmeiras, and Santos—attract fans from other states. Corinthians and Palmeiras opened new stadiums in 2014. São Paulo's Morumbi and the municipally run Pacaembu, meanwhile, continue to host matchups featuring Brazilian clubs. Covered seats offer the best protection, not only from the elements but also from rowdy spectators.

Buy tickets at the stadiums or online at ⊕ *www.ingressofacil.com.br.* Futebol Tour (⊕ *www.futeboltour.com.br*) also sells packages starting at R$60 for select games that include transportation to and from the stadiums, admission, and information folders. Regular games usually don't sell out, but finals and classicos between the big four—for which you can buy tickets up to five days in advance—generally do. For a history lesson on the "beautiful game," check out the interactive Soccer Museum at the Pacaembu stadium.

Allianz Parque (*Nova Arena*). This new arena opened in 2014 and is configured to seat about 46,000 people for soccer and other events. The home team, Palmeiras, plays here. ⊠ *Rua Turiassu 1840, Barra Funda* ☎ *011/3874–6500* ⊕ *www.allianzparque.com.br* Ⓜ *Barra Funda.*

Arena Corinthians. The home of Corinthians soccer club hosted the opening of the 2014 World Cup. It holds 48,000 spectators. ⊠ *Av. Miguel Inácio Curi 111, Vila Carmosina* ☎ *011/2095–3000, 011/2095–3175* ⊕ *www.corinthians.com.br/arena* Ⓜ *Corinthians-Itaquera.*

Canindé. The home team, Portuguesa, is the main attraction here, though the *bolinhos de bacalhau* (salt-cod fritters), popular among the Portuguese immigrants filling the stadium's 21,000 seats, run a close second. ⊠ *Rua Comendador Nestor Pereira 33, Canindé* ☎ *011/2125–9400* ⊕ *www.portuguesa.com.br.*

Estádio da Javari (*Estádio Conde Rodolfo Crespi*). The 4,000-seat Estádio da Javari, also known as Estádio Conde Rodolfo Crespi, is where third-division Juventus plays. It's an ideal place to soak up some

Italian atmosphere—Moóca is an Italian neighborhood—and eat a cannoli while cheering for the home team. ✉ *Rua Javari 117, Moóca* ☎ *011/2693–4688, 011/2292–4833* ⊕ *www.juventus.com.br* Ⓜ *Moóca.*

Morumbi. The home stadium of São Paulo Futebol Clube seats 67,000 people. When soccer isn't being played here, other events take place, including concerts by stars such as Lady Gaga. ✉ *Praça Roberto Gomes Pedroza 1, Morumbi* ☎ *011/3742–3377, 011/3749–8000* ⊕ *www.saopaulofc.net.*

Pacaembu (*Estádio Municipal Paulo Machado de Carvalho*). The first games of the 1950 World Cup were played at this stadium. The plaza it inhabits is named for the Englishman who introduced Brazil to soccer. While it isn't used by any team in particular, it does host games occasionally and still houses the Museu de Futebol (soccer museum). ✉ *Praça Charles Miller s/n, Pacaembú* ☎ *011/3664–4650, 011/3663–6888* Ⓜ *Clínicas.*

SHOPPING

Fashionistas from all over the continent flock to São Paulo for the clothes, shoes, and accessories. In fact, shopping is a tourist attraction in its own right. You can get a sampling of what's on offer six days a week: stores are usually open on weekdays from 9 to 6:30 and Saturdays from 9 to 1; many are closed on Sunday. Mall hours are generally weekdays and Saturday from 10 am to 10 pm; some malls only open on Sunday around 2 pm.

Well-heeled paulistanos famously love shopping malls, and there are plenty of those in the city. Perhaps of more interest for visitors, almost every neighborhood has a weekly outdoor food market, complete with loudmouthed hawkers, exotic scents, and mountains of colorful produce. Nine hundred of them happen every week in São Paulo, so you'll be able to hit at least one; ask around to find out when and where the closest one happens.

Antiques and secondhand furniture are the big draws at the Sunday flea market at the Praça Dom Orione in **Bela Vista**. You'll also find clothing, CDs, and other (mostly) reasonably priced items here. In **Centro**, Rua do Arouche is noted for leather goods. Rua Barão de Paranapiacaba is lined with jewelry shops and is nicknamed the "street of gold." The area around Rua João Cachoeira in **Itaim** has evolved from a neighborhood of small clothing factories into a wholesale- and retail-clothing sales district. Several shops on Rua Tabapuã sell small antiques. Also, Rua Dr. Mário Ferraz is stuffed with elegant clothing, gift, and home-decoration stores.

In **Jardins,** centering on Rua Oscar Freire, double-parked Mercedes-Benzes and BMWs point the way to the city's fanciest stores, which sell leather items, jewelry, gifts, antiques, and art. Shops that specialize in high-price European antiques are on or around Rua da Consolação. Lower-price antiques stores and thrift shops line Rua Cardeal Arcoverde in **Pinheiros.** Flea markets with secondhand furniture, clothes, and CDs take place on Saturday at the popular Praça Benedito Calixto in Pinheiros, where you can also eat at food stands and listen to music all day long. Arcades along Praça Benedito Calixto and many streets in neighboring **Vila Madalena**, like Ruas Aspicuelta and Harmonia, house boutique clothing stores.

BOM RETIRO

BEACHWEAR

Beira Mar Beachwear. This Brazilian brand, founded in 1948, is known for innovative and high-quality products. Beira Mar has its own factory and produces many types of bikinis and swimming suits. ⊠ *Rua Silva Pinto 254, 3rd fl., Bom Retiro* ☎ *011/3222–7999* ⊕ *www. maiosbeiramar.com.br* Ⓜ *Tiradentes.*

CENTRO

BEAUTY

O Boticário. The Brazilian brand O Boticário was founded by dermatologists and pharmacists from Curitiba in the 1970s. The company creates products for men, women, and children, and through its foundation funds ecological projects throughout Brazil. The shops can be found in most neighborhoods and malls in the city. ⊠ *Av. Brig. Luis Antonio 282, Centro* ☎ *011/3115–0712* ⊕ *www.oboticario.com.br.*

LEATHER GOODS AND LUGGAGE

Inovathi. A shop you'll find in many malls all over town, Inovathi has leather accessories at good prices. ⊠ *Av. Ipiranga 336, Centro* ☎ *011/2179–2050* ⊕ *www.inovathi.com.br* Ⓜ *República.*

MARKETS

Fodor'sChoice **Mercado Municipal.** The city's first grocery market, this huge 1928 neo-
★ baroque-style building is the quintessential hot spot for gourmets and food lovers. The building, nicknamed Mercadão (Big Market) by locals, houses about 300 stands that sell just about everything edible, including meat, vegetables, cheese, spices, and fish from all over Brazil. It also has restaurants and traditional snack places. The Hocca Bar is justly famous for its *pastel de bacalhau* (salt-cod pastry) and heaping mortadella sandwich. ⊠ *Rua da Cantareira 306, Sé, Centro* ☎ *011/3313–3365, 011/3313–7456* ⊕ *www.oportaldomercadao.com.br* ☒ *Free* ☺ *Mon.– Sat. 6–6, Sun. 6–4* Ⓜ *São Bento.*

Praça da República arts and crafts fair. Vendors sell jewelry, embroidery, leather goods, toys, clothing, paintings, and musical instruments at the Sunday-morning arts-and-crafts fair in Praça da República. If you look carefully, you can find reasonably priced, out-of-the-ordinary souvenirs. ⊠ *Praça da República, Centro* Ⓜ *República.*

MUSIC

Baratos Afins. Heaven for music collectors, Baratos Afins opened inside the popular Galeria do Rock in 1978 and is also a record label. The company was the brainchild of Arnaldo Baptista, guitar player in the influential 1960s Brazilian rock band Os Mutantes. The store sells all kinds of music, but it specializes in Brazilian popular music. If you're looking for rare records, ask for the owner, Luiz Calanca. ⊠ *Galeria do Rock, Av. São João 439, 2nd fl., Centro* ☎ *011/3223–3629* ⊕ *www. baratosafins.com.br* Ⓜ *República.*

Ventania. Browse through more than 100,000 records at this huge store that specializes in Brazilian popular music. You can find old 78s, contemporary CDs, and everything in between. ⊠ *Rua 24 de Maio 188, 1st fl., Centro* ☎ *011/3331–0332* ⊕ *www.ventania.com.br* Ⓜ *República.*

CERQUEIRA CÉSAR

ANTIQUES

Patrimônio. Head to Patrimônio for Brazilian antiques at reasonable prices. The shop also sells Indian artifacts, as well as modern furnishings crafted from iron. ⊠ *Alameda Ministro Rocha Azevedo 1077, 1st fl., Cerqueira César* ☎ *011/99225–7570* ⊕ *www.patrimonioantiguidades. com* ⊙ *Fri. and by appointment other days.*

CONSOLAÇÃO

JEWELRY

Antonio Bernardo. Carioca Antonio Bernardo is one of the most famous jewelry designers in Brazil. He creates custom pieces with gold, silver, and other precious metals and stones. ⊠ *Rua Bela Cintra 2063, Consolação* ☎ *011/3083–5622* ⊕ *www.antoniobernardo.com.br* ⊙ *Closed Sun.*

HIGIENÓPOLIS

BEACHWEAR

Cia. Marítima. The Brazilian beachwear brand known for its bikinis and swimsuits has a presence in this and many other high-class malls. ⊠ *Shopping Pátio Higienópolis, Av. Higienópolis, Higienópolis* ☎ *011/3661–7602* ⊕ *www.ciamaritima.com.br.*

CENTERS AND MALLS

Shopping Pátio Higienópolis. One of the most upscale shopping malls in São Paulo, Shopping Pátio Higienópolis is a mixture of old and new architecture styles. It has plenty of shops and restaurants, as well as six screens in the Cinemark movie theater. ⊠ *Av. Higienópolis 618, Higienópolis* ☎ *011/3823–2300* ⊕ *www.patiohigienopolis.com.br.*

ITAIM BIBI

ANTIQUES

Pedro Corrêa do Lago. The shop's namesake owner, a consultant for Sotheby's auction house, sells and auctions rare and used books, as well as antique maps, prints, and drawings of Brazil. ⊠ *Rua Afonso Braz 473, Conjuntos 31 and 32, Itaim* ☎ *011/3063–5455.*

CENTERS AND MALLS

JK Iguatemi. Natural light illuminates the atrium and walkways of this luxury mall for the elite, where international brands from AW Store to Zara mix it up with national brands like Animale and Carlos Miele.

There are plenty of fancy dining spots. If scheduled beforehand, the mall will supply you with a personal shopper. ⊠ *Av. Presidente Juscelino Kubitschek 2041, Itaim Bibi* ☎ *011/3152–6800, 011/3152–6809 Schedule personal shopper* ⊕ *www.jkiguatemi.com.br.*

JARDIM PAULISTA

HANDICRAFTS

Amoa Konoya Arte Indigena. Inspired by contact with indigenous peoples, Walter Gomes opened this store to promote awareness about and economic opportunities for Brazil's native communities. Artisans of 230 indigenous tribes create the crafts and artworks, from musical instruments to earthenware, sold here. ⊠ *Rua João Moura 1002, Jardim Paulista* ☎ *011/3061–0639* ⊕ *www.amoakonoya.com.br.*

JARDIM PAULISTANO

ANTIQUES

Juliana Benfatti. The antiques shop run by Juliana Benfatti and her two sons has inventory that dates back to the 18th century. The buyers have a discerning eye for what was unique and special in many lands over many generations. ⊠ *Rua Sampaio Vidal 786, Jardim Paulistano* ☎ *011/3083–7858* ⊕ *www.julianabenfatti.com.br* Ⓜ *Faria Lima.*

CENTERS AND MALLS

Iguatemi São Paulo. This may be the city's oldest mall, but it has the latest in fashion and fast food. The Cinemark movie theaters often show films in English with Portuguese subtitles. The Gero Caffé, built in the middle of the main hall, has a fine menu. If you're in São Paulo at Christmastime, the North Pole–theme displays here are well worth a detour. ⊠ *Av. Brigadeiro Faria Lima 2232, Jardim Paulistano* ☎ *011/3816–6116* ⊕ *www.iguatemisaopaulo.com.br.*

JEWELRY

Tiffany & Co. The world-famous store sells exclusive pieces for the very wealthy. Go for the diamonds—you know you want to. ⊠ *Iguatemi São Paulo, Av. Brigadeiro Faria Lima 2232, Jardim Paulista* ☎ *011/3815–7000* ⊕ *www.tiffany.com.*

JARDINS

On Sunday there are antiques fairs near the Museu de Arte de São Paulo (MASP).

ANTIQUES

Legado. At this antiques showroom that holds monthly auctions you'll find plenty of heirlooms looking for new homes—Baccarat bowls and vases, art nouveau and art deco sideboards, and a slew of silver trays and tea sets among them. Past oddities include the helmet of the late race-car legend Ayrton Senna. ⊠ *Alameda Lorena 882, Jardins* ☎ *011/3063–3400* ⊕ *www.legadoantiguidades.com.br.*

Renée Behar Antiques. This shop has that prim and proper look one expects from a reputable, longtime dealer known for classic 18th- and

19th-century silver, ceramics, and other antiques. The craftsmanship in the items for sale here is consistently top-drawer. ✉ *Rua Peixoto Gomide 2088, Jardins* ☎ *011/3085–3622* ⊕ *www.reneebehar.com.br.*

ART GALLERIES

Arte Aplicada. A respected Jardins gallery, Arte Aplicada is known for its high-quality Brazilian paintings, sculptures, and prints. ✉ *Rua Haddock Lobo 1406, Jardins* ☎ *011/3062–5128, 011/3064–4725* ⊕ *www. arteaplicada.com.br.*

Bel Galeria. Paintings and sculptures from Brazilian and international artists go up for auction at Bel Galeria. ✉ *Rua Paraguaçú 334, Perdizes* ☎ *011/3663–3100* ⊕ *www.belgaleriadearte.com.br.*

Dan Galeria. Specializing in 20th-century Brazilian art, this gallery is a must for serious art lovers and monied collectors, and educational for interested amateurs. Look out for works by modernist stars such as Tarsila do Amaral and di Cavalcanti. ✉ *Rua Estados Unidos 1638, Jardins* ☎ *011/3083–4600* ⊕ *www.dangaleria.com.br* ☉ *Closed Sun.*

Galeria Luisa Strina. One of the city's oldest and best established galleries, Luisa Strina is a serious player in the international art world, representing artists of the stature of Cildo Meireles and Anna Maria Maiolino, as well as a stable of young stars such as Renata Lucas, Clarissa Tossin, and Fernanda Gomes. ✉ *Rua Padre João Manuel 755, Jardins* ☎ *011/3088–2471* ⊕ *www.galerialuisastrina.com.br.*

Galeria Renot. At this gallery you'll find oil paintings by such Brazilian artists as Vicente Rego Monteiro, Di Cavalcanti, Cícero Dias, and Anita Malfatti. ✉ *Alameda Ministro Rocha Azevedo 1327, Jardins* ☎ *011/3083–5933.*

Mônica Filgueiras Galeria. Many a trend has been set at this gallery, which sells all types of art but mostly paintings and sculpture. ✉ *Rua Bela Cintra 1533, Jardins* ☎ *011/3082–5292* ⊕ *www.monicafilgueiras.com.br.*

BEAUTY

Granado. As with the other locations of this Brazilian beauty-supplies chain that dates back to 1870, the Jardins shop maintains the old-time appearance of an apothecary. ✉ *Rua Haddock Lobo 1353, Jardins* ☎ *011/3061–0891* ⊕ *www.granado.com.br.*

BEACHWEAR

Track & Field. This brand's shops, which you'll find in nearly every mall in São Paulo, are good places to buy beachwear and sports clothing. The store sells bikinis and swimsuits from Cia. Marítíma, a famous Brazilian beachwear brand. ✉ *Rua Oscar Freire 959, Jardins* ☎ *011/3062–4457* ⊕ *www.tf.com.br.*

BOOKS

Livraria Cultura. São Paulo's best selection of travel literature can be found here, along with many maps. ✉ *Av. Paulista 2073, Jardins* ☎ *011/3170–4033* ⊕ *www.livrariacultura.com.br* Ⓜ *Consolação.*

CLOTHING

Alexandre Herchcovitch. The Brazilian designer Alexandre Herchcovitch sells prêt-à-porter and tailor-made clothes at his store. ⊠ *Rua Melo Alves 561, Jardins* ☎ *011/3063-2888* ⊕ *www.herchcovitch.com.br.*

Animale. With a deft line in cool, sophisticated fashion, Animale has long been a go-to brand for hip young Brazilian women. Known for its striking prints and sultry yet wearable garments, Animale isn't cheap—but these are clothes you'll be slipping into for years. ⊠ *Rua Bela Cintra 2164, Jardins* ☎ *011/3063-2038* ⊕ *www.animale.com.br* Ⓜ *Consolação.*

BO.BÔ. Brazilian models and soap-opera stars wear this brand, which blends bohemian and bourgeois (coincidentally, the type of bank account needed to shop here). ⊠ *Rua Oscar Freire 1039, Jardins* ☎ *011/3062-8145* ⊕ *www.bobo.com.br.*

Fórum. High-class evening attire for young men and women is the specialty of Fórum, which also sells sportswear and shoes. ⊠ *Rua Oscar Freire 916, Jardins* ☎ *011/3085-6269* ⊕ *www.forum.com.br.*

Le Lis Blanc. This chain is Brazil's exclusive purveyor of the French brand Vertigo. Look for party dresses in velvet and sheer fabrics. ⊠ *Rua Oscar Freire 1119, Jardins* ☎ *011/3809-8950* ⊕ *www.lelis.com.br.*

Lita Mortari. The designer Lita Mortari sells her feminine festive wear in four stores in São Paulo, including two in Jardins. ⊠ *Rua Bela Cintra 2195, Jardins* ☎ *011/3064-3021* ⊕ *litamortari.com.br.*

Mulher Elástica. Outfits built around leggings are no stretch for Mulher Elástica. Looks range from sporty to business casual. ⊠ *Rua Dr. Melo Alves 381, Jardins* ☎ *011/3060-8263* ⊕ *mulherelastica.com.br.*

Reinaldo Lourenço. Sophisticated, high-quality women's clothing is Reinaldo Lourenço's calling card. ⊠ *Rua Bela Cintra 2167, Jardins* ☎ *011/3085-8150* ⊕ *www.reinaldolourenco.com.br.*

Richards. The collections at Richards include casualwear for men, women, and kids. ⊠ *JK Iguatemi, Av. Presidente Juscelino Kubitschek 2041, Vila Olímpia* ☎ *011/3073-1332* ⊕ *www.richards.com.br.*

HANDICRAFTS

Galeria de Arte Brasileira. Since 1920 Galeria de Arte Brasileira has specialized in art and handicrafts from all over Brazil. Look for objects made of *pau-brasil* (brazilwood), hammocks, jewelry, T-shirts, *marajoara* pottery (from the Amazon), and lace. ⊠ *Alameda Lorena 2163, Jardins* ☎ *011/3062-9452* ⊕ *www.galeriaartebrasileira.com.br.*

JEWELRY

H.Stern. An internationally known Brazilian brand for jewelry, especially featuring precious Brazilian gems, H.Stern has shops in more than 30 countries. This one has designs made especially for the Brazilian stores. ⊠ *Rua Oscar Freire 652, Jardins* ☎ *011/3068-8082* ⊕ *www.hstern.com.br.*

LEATHER GOODS AND LUGGAGE
Le Postiche. One of the biggest brands for luggage and leather goods in Brazil, Le Postiche has 96 shops around the country. You can find one in almost any mall in São Paulo. ⊠ *Rua Haddock Lobo 1307, Jardins* ☎ *011/3081–9702* ⊕ *www.lepostiche.com.br.*

Schutz. Boots, sandals, wedges, stilettos—if you can't find a pair of shoes you like at Schutz, you're probably not looking properly. This flagship store carries a huge variety of fashion footwear, from statement heels to fun prints on sneakers. ⊠ *Rua Oscar Freire 944, Jardins* ☎ *011/4508-1499* ⊕ *www.schutz.com.br* Ⓜ *Consolacão.*

MOEMA

CLOTHING
Fil du Fil. The women's clothing brand Fil du Fil maintains three locations across Moema and Vila Olímpia. This address is dedicated to plus-size attire. Looks are casual with colorful blouses and dresses featuring prominently. ⊠ *Rua Canário 1253, Moema* ☎ *011/5561-2645* ⊕ *www.fildufil.com.br.*

Vila Romana Factory Store. The prices for suits, jackets, jeans, and some women's clothing (silk blouses, for example) at Vila Romana Factory Store are unbeatable. The store is a 40-minute drive from Centro. In-town mall branches are more convenient, but prices are higher. ⊠ *Via Anhanguera, Km 17.5, Rua Robert Bosch 1765, Osasco* ☎ *011/3604–5293* ⊕ *www.vilaromana.com.br.*

HANDICRAFTS
Casa do Amazonas. As its name suggests, Casa do Amazonas has a wide selection of products from the Amazon. ⊠ *Alameda dos Jurupis 460, Moema* ☎ *011/5051–3098* ⊕ *www.arteindigena.com.br.*

MUSIC
Painel Musical. In shopping malls, look out for Painel Musical, a small record shop that carries CDs and DVDs. It usually has a good selection of instrumental Brazilian music and local rock. ⊠ *Shopping Ibirapuera, Av. Ibirapuera 3103, Moema* ☎ *011/5561–9981.*

MORUMBI

CENTERS AND MALLS
MorumbiShopping. Though it's taken a backseat to newer malls Cidade Jardim and JK Iguatemi, MorumbiShopping is still a slice of São Paulo's upper crust, seasoned with swank boutiques, record stores, bookstores, and restaurants. The atrium hosts art exhibits. ⊠ *Av. Roque Petroni Jr. 1089, Morumbi* ☎ *011/4003–4132* ⊕ *www.morumbishopping.com.br.*

Shopping Cidade Jardim. The feeling here is almost as though archaeologists have uncovered a lost jungle city's ancient temples—only they're to upscale shopping and gourmet dining, not deities and potentates. Trees outside sprout three stories high, and a bevy of plants inside shrouds boutiques with names like Valentino, Omega, and Louis Vuitton. For resting, there's a huge open garden with splendid city views. If you get hungry, head to the Argentine steak house Pobre Juan for a hearty meal or, for lighter fare, drop in at bright and breezy The Gourmet Tea. ✉ *Av. Magalhães de Castro 12000, Morumbi* ☎ *011/3552–1000* ⊕ *www.shoppingcidadejardim.com.*

CLOTHING

FAMILY **Camu Camu.** Founded in 1974, Camu Camu sells stylish clothing for young girls and boys. ✉ *Shopping Marketing Place, Av. Dr. Chucri Zaidan 902, Morumbi* ☎ *011/5181–1567* ⊕ *www.camucamu.com.br.*

PARAÍSO

HANDICRAFTS

Marcenaria Trancoso. The wooden products this shop sells are an elegant mixture of interior design and handicraft. ✉ *Rua Mateus Grou 282, Pinheiros* ☎ *011/3816–1298* ⊕ *www.marcenariatrancoso.com.br.*

LEATHER GOODS AND LUGGAGE

Arezzo. A leader in the leather game, with stores in most São Paulo shopping malls, Arezzo is best known for its footwear. The brand also has an extensive line of bags, wallets, and accessories. ✉ *Shopping Paulista, Rua Treze de Maio 1947, Paraíso* ☎ *011/3171–1183* ⊕ *www.arezzo. com.br* Ⓜ *Brigadeiro.*

VILA MADALENA

ART

Galeria Fortes Vilaça. This fine gallery is one of the city's big hitters and always worth a look. ✉ *Rua Fradique Coutinho 1500, Vila Madalena* ☎ *011/3032–7066* ⊕ *www.fortesvilaca.com.br.*

CLOTHING

Uma. Women of all ages lust after the simple elegance of Uma's swimsuits, dresses, shorts, shirts, and pants—they're not cheap, but they're good. ✉ *Rua Girassol 273, Vila Madalena* ☎ *011/3813–5559* ⊕ *www.uma.com.br.*

HANDICRAFTS

Ôoh de Casa. Souvenirs and presents, from vividly colored hammocks to papier-mâché piggy banks (cows, actually), are for sale here. ✉ *Rua Fradique Coutinho 899, Vila Madalena* ☎ *011/3812–4934, 011/3815–9577* ⊕ *www.oohdecasa.com.br.*

VILA MARIANA

ART

Galeria Jacques Ardies. If you like *art naïf*—as the name suggests, the art is simple, with a primitive and handcrafted look—Galeria Jacques Ardies is a must. ✉ *Rua Morgado de Mateus 579, Vila Mariana* ☎ *011/5539–7500* ⊕ *www.ardies.com* Ⓜ *Paraíso.*

SIDE TRIPS FROM SÃO PAULO

Updated By
Angelica Mari

São Paulo's surroundings are perfect for all types of getaways with the peaks of the Serra da Mantiqueira inland and the area's finest beaches up the North Coast. The state has the best highways in the country, making it easy to travel by car or bus to its many small, beautiful beaches, and beyond to neighboring states (Paraná, Rio de Janeiro, and Minas Gerais). Although the North Coast's sandy stretches require two-hour drives, good side trips from the city can be as close as the 30-minute trip to Santos's long strip of sand, Embu's weekend craft market, or Santana de Parnaíba's historical streets.

For a weekend of relaxation, soak up the healing properties of Águas de São Pedro's spas and springs. If you like mountains, head to Campos do Jordão, where cafés and clothing stores are often crowded with oh-so-chic *paulistanos* (natives of São Paulo city; inhabitants of São Paulo State are called *paulistas*). Serra Negra and its surrounding region offer mineral waters and an immersion in the coffee production history of Brazil, as well as several activities for families and couples looking for a romantic getaway. Favor the coast's North Shore beaches and Ilhabela (the name means "beautiful island") if you prefer sun and sand. The island is part of the Mata Atlântica (Atlantic Forest) and has many waterfalls, trails, and diving spots.

ORIENTATION AND PLANNING

GETTING ORIENTED

Along the Coast. On weekends, paulistanos flock to the easily accessible beaches of Santos just south of São Paulo. Farther up the coast, the North Shore has beautiful stretches of sand for every kind of sun or sports enthusiast. In the 1990s the area experienced a building boom, with condos popping up seemingly overnight. Luckily, the North Shore still managed to maintain its pristine environment.

Inland. Just a stone's throw from São Paulo, Embu das Artes is famous for its big handicraft fair with paintings, toys, and candles, as well as scrumptious pastries and breads. Campos do Jordão, known as the Switzerland of Brazil, attracts hordes of chill-seekers in winter, when temperatures drop below tepid. Serra Negra is the main city of São Paulo's Circuito das Águas (Water Circuit) and offers plenty of events and activities for families as well as a refuge for couples seeking romance.

TOP REASONS TO GO

Beach Paradises: Bask on a range of beautiful beaches, from surfer paradises in Ubatuba to coastal islands and sandy rain-forest coves on Ilhabela.

Rich History: Witness Brazil's colonial and rural history in Embu and Santana de Parnaíba.

Great Nightlife: Dance until dawn with a seaside view at Maresias, São Sebastião.

Gorgeous Landscapes: Luxurious forests in Campos do Jordão combine with impressive wildlife and bodies of water in Águas de São Pedro and Serra Negra.

Scrumptious Food: Sample a variety of local dishes made with the freshest ingredients, including artisanal sausages and locally brewed beer.

PLANNING

WHEN TO GO

The area around São Paulo is lovely year-round. Most places have a steady stream of visitors, so it's always wise to book hotels well in advance. Summers are hot and humid, and it's the rainy season, so it's good to have some indoor plans in the back of your mind. In winter, temperatures drop into the 40s°F (5°C–10°C), so be sure to bring some warm clothing.

PLANNING YOUR TIME

Those who crave a couple of days of sunning themselves on a beach should head up to the resort towns and rain-forest fringed sands of the North Shore about 210 km (130 miles) from São Paulo (two to three hours by car; longer by bus). Alternatively squeeze in an afternoon on the sands by joining the paulistanos heading to the port city of Santos less than an hour away. If you prefer spending time in the mountains and have two or three days to spare, aim for Campos do Jordão, Águas de São Pedro, or Serra Negra. For a quicker day-trip, Embu das Artes or Santana de Parnaíba make great choices, especially for those interested in arts, crafts, and architecture, and they can even be reached by taxi.

GETTING HERE AND AROUND

Bus travel to and from the towns around São Paulo can be a time-consuming affair because of heavy traffic to and from the big city to commuter towns along the coast and inland, particularly on weekends. It is also possible to rent a car or take a taxi, particularly as roads are good and traffic isn't too chaotic once you're out of the city. Reaching many of the destinations around São Paulo is feasible by taxi, but expect to pay upwards of R$200 for one-way trips, even for relatively nearby destinations such as Embu das Artes and Santana de Parnaíba. Your taxi driver might agree to a flat fee over turning on the meter.

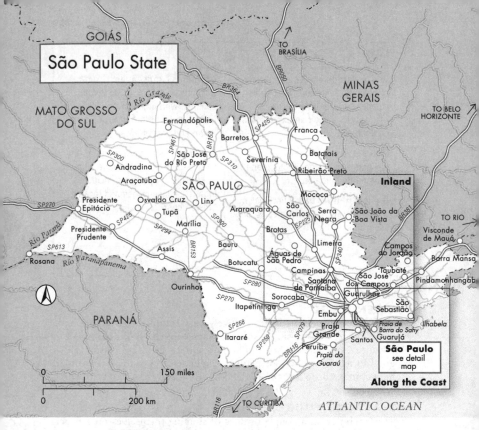

São Paulo State

GOIÁS

TO BRASÍLIA

MINAS GERAIS

TO BELO HORIZONTE

MATO GROSSO DO SUL

Rio Grande

BR364

Fernandópolis

Barretos

Franca

Batatais

São José do Rio Preto

Severínia

Ribeirão Preto

Inland

Andradina

Araçatuba

SÃO PAULO

Mococa

Presidente Epitácio

Osvaldo Cruz

Lins

Araraquara

São Carlos

Serra Negra

São João da Boa Vista

TO RIO

Visconde de Mauá

Tupã

Marília

Brotas

Limeira

Campos do Jordão

Barra Mansa

Presidente Prudente

Assis

Bauru

Águas de São Pedro

Campinas

Taubaté

Pindamonhangaba

Rosana

Rio Paranapanema

Botucatu

Santana de Parnaíba

São José dos Campos

Ourinhos

SP280

Sorocaba

Guarulhos

São Sebastião

PARANÁ

SP270

Itapetininga

Embu

Praia de Barra do Sahy

Ilhabela

SP258

Itararé

Praia Grande

Guarujá

Santos

Peruíbe

São Paulo
see detail map

Praia do Guaraú

Along the Coast

150 miles

200 km

TO CURITIBA

ATLANTIC OCEAN

RESTAURANTS

Restaurants in coastal towns tend to be of the rustic beach-café sort, and predictably serve lots of seafood. For a change of taste, visit Ubatuba and these three neighborhoods in or near São Sebastião—Maresias, Boiçucanga, and Camburi—where you can find good pizzerias and Japanese restaurants. In Campos do Jordão, a popular paulistano mountain retreat, you can find a Brazilian version of Swiss fondue (both the chocolate and the cheese varieties are delicious). In Serra Negra, you'll find typical countryside food, including lots of fresh meat and farm produce, as well as a vast range of local sweets, artisanal beers, and wine.

HOTELS

São Paulo has by far the best lodgings in the state. Elsewhere you can generally find basic *pousadas* (sort of like bed-and-breakfasts), with the occasional gems like Porto Pacuíba on Ilhabela and Shangri-Lá in Serra Negra. Coastal towns are packed in summer (from December to March) and it's almost impossible to get anything without advance reservations. The same holds true for Campos do Jordão and Serra Negra in winter (June and September). *Hotel reviews have been shortened. For full information, visit Fodors.com.*

WHAT IT COSTS IN REAIS				
	$	$$	$$$	$$$$
Restaurants	under R$31	R$31–R$45	R$46–R$60	over R$60
Hotels	under R$251	R$251–R$375	R$376–R$500	over R$500

Restaurant prices are the average cost of a main course at dinner or, if dinner is not served, at lunch. Hotel prices are the lowest cost of a standard double room in high season, excluding tax.

ALONG THE COAST

After visiting the concrete jungle of São Paulo, you'll be pleased to find that there are some lovely beaches in São Paulo State that are within easy reach. The beaches of the South Shore in and around Santos are more urban than those farther up the coast, but pleasant enough for a quick escapade from the big city. The cleanest and best *praias* (beaches) in the region are along what is known as the Litoral Norte (North Shore), where mountains and bits of Atlantic Forest hug numerous small, sandy coves.

Beaches generally have restaurants nearby, or at least vendors in tents selling soft drinks, beer, and *porções* (platters of savory snacks such as shrimp and french fries, perfect for sharing). They often don't have bathrooms or phones right on the sands. Vendors rent beach umbrellas or chairs, especially in summer and on holidays and weekends. It is standard practice on Brazilian beaches to set up a *conta* (tab) with vendors, so you can order food and drinks during your stay and pay it all when you leave. On weekdays when school is in session, the beaches are gloriously deserted.

SANTOS

70 km (43 miles) south of São Paulo.

The biggest city on the São Paulo coast, Santos is the home of the largest container port in South America. At the turn of the 20th century, the local economy was focused on coffee exports, which contributed to the city's wealth and development. Lined with neoclassical buildings, the cobblestone streets of the historic center are compact enough to explore on foot. The main attraction here, though, is the coastline, a full 7 km (4½ miles) long, and adorned with a large beachfront garden. Try visiting on weekdays or Saturday.

GETTING HERE AND AROUND

Buses to Santos leave every 10–15 minutes from São Paulo's Jabaquara terminal, at the south end of the Linha 1 (Blue) of the underground. The journey takes just over an hour and offers views of the spectacular mountain range Serra do Mar. Santos's bus station is located right in the center and is a 10-minute walk to the Museu do Café in the historic center and the Museu Pelé in Valongo. A five-minute cab ride will drop

you off at the Gonzaga and José Menino Beaches, where most of the hotels, bars, and restaurants are located.

ESSENTIALS

Bus Contacts Terminal Rodoviário de Santos. ⊠ *Praça dos Andradas 45, Centro* ☎ *013/3213–2290.*

Visitor Information Tourist Information. ⊠ *Terminal Rodoviário de Santos, Praça dos Andradas 45, Centro* ☎ *0800 /173–887.*

TOURS

FAMILY **Bonde Turístico de Santos.** This delightful tour is on board a restored 1920s tram, which stops at all the main points of interest in the historic center. It's a hop-on, hop-off service, which allows you to jump off, have a look around, and get on the next tram when you're ready to move on. ⊠ *Praça Mauá, Centro* ☎ *013/3201–8000* 💲 *R$6* 🕙 *Tues.–Sun. 11–5.*

SAFETY AND PRECAUTIONS

When walking around at night, prefer the beaches of José Menino and Gonzaga; at these times, avoid walking around the area near the port and the bus station. If you need to get on a bus back to São Paulo at night, get a taxi straight to the station.

A BIT OF HISTORY

In the 19th century, farming, first of sugarcane, and then of coffee, was São Paulo's major industry and brought prosperity to the region.

At the beginning of the 20th century, São Paulo became the center for industry in Brazil, as factories were built at a rapid pace, mostly by an immigrant workforce. By mid-century, São Paulo was one of the largest industrialized centers in Latin America and the state with the highest population in Brazil, thanks in part to mass migration from within Brazil.

Today São Paulo is the richest and most multicultural state in the country. It has about 1 million people of Middle Eastern descent, approximately 6 million people of Italian descent and the largest Japanese community outside of Japan (an estimated 1 million people).

EXPLORING

Museu do Café (*Coffee Museum*). The grand neoclassical Palácio da Bolsa de Café, where the Coffee Museum is located, was home to the coffee exchange up to 1957. Rosewood chairs are set out for traders in the trading hall, whose walls are hung with panels painted by Brazilian Benedicto Calixto. Upstairs are exhibits related to the world of coffee. Visitors can also sample the drink at the museum's cafeteria. ✉ *Rua 15 de Novembro 95* ☎ *013/3213–1750* ⊕ *www.museudocafe.com.br* 🎟 *R$6* ⊙ *Tues.–Sat. 9–5, Sun. 10–5.*

Fodor's Choice **Museu Pelé.** Edson Arantes do Nascimento's, or simply Pelé's, self assess-
★   ment—"I was born for soccer, just as Beethoven was born for music."— may seem a tad self-important, but to many soccer fans, who regard him as one of the world's greatest footballers, it is not far from the truth. Housed in a 19th-century mansion and opened during the 2014 World Cup, Museu Pelé honors Santos's most famous son through displays of his personal items and trophies, plus photos, videos, and documents concerning the footballer. The area surrounding the museum, the Valongo district, is currently being revitalized with restaurants, bars, and cultural centers. ✉ *Largo Marquês de Monte Alegre s/n, Valongo* ☎ *013/3704–6260* ⊕ *museupele.org.br* 🎟 *R$18* ⊙ *Tues.–Sun. 10–6.*

BEACHES

Praia do Santos. The massive, 7-km (4½-mile) strip of sand along Santos's shoreline is made up of a series of lively beaches. The city is crossed by seven channels, which act as borders between districts, and separate each of the beaches from one another. The busiest beaches—José Menino, Gonzaga, and Boqueirão—are between channels 1 and 4, and this is where you'll find the greatest concentration of hotels and restaurants. The sea conditions do not differ greatly from one beach to another, but at José Menino (channels 1 to 2) the waves are a bit stronger and better for surfing. Partiers gather at Gonzaga Beach (channels 2 to 3), where open air concerts often take place. Boqueirão (channels 3 to 4) has Santos's best infrastructure with ATMs, toilets, and showers, as well as a crafts fair on the weekend. Embaré Beach (channels 4 to 5) has many kiosks and bars and is a magnet for the younger set. Aparecida Beach (channels 5 to 6) is the meeting point for families with children, as well as seniors, and the location of the biggest beachfront garden in the world. The calm, almost flat sea at Ponta da Praia (channels 6 to 7) is suitable for water sports such as sailing, windsurfing, and jet skiing. **Amenities:** food and drink; lifeguards; showers; toilets. **Best for:** partiers; walking. ✉ *From Av. Presidente Wilsom 1900 (José Menino beach) to Av. Saldanha da Gama (Ponta da Praia).*

WHERE TO EAT AND STAY

$$$ CONTEMPORARY Fodor's Choice ★ 🍴 **Guaiaó.** A hidden gem and a favorite among well-informed locals, Guaiaó serves up a (successfully) adventurous menu of world dishes with a Brazilian twist created by chef André Ahn, including watermelon carpaccio and smoked *vieira*, a local fish specialty. The coffee pudding is highly recommended, as is the fresh seasonal fruit salad with lemon mousse. [$] *Average main: R$60* ✉ *Rua Dom Lara 65, Boqueirão* ☎ *013/3877–5379* ⏲ *No lunch. Closed Sun.* ✍ *Reservations essential* 💳 *No credit cards.*

$$ HOTEL 🏨 **Mercure Santos Hotel.** Hotel chain Mercure offers a practical base for a short visit to Santos, located near the beach and the historical center, as well as the main bars and restaurants. **Pros:** beach location; rooftop terrace. **Cons:** room service is rather slow. [$] *Rooms from: R$300* ✉ *Av. Washington Luiz 565, Boqueirão, Santos* ☎ *013/3036–1013* 🌐 *mercure.com* 🛏 *107 rooms* 🍽 *Breakfast.*

SÃO SEBASTIÃO

204 km (127 miles) southeast of São Paulo.

São Sebastião stretches along 100 km (62 miles) of the North Shore. Its bays, islands, and beaches attract everyone from the youngsters who flock to Maresias and Camburi to the families who favor Barra do Sahy and Camburizinho. Boating enthusiasts, hikers, and wildlife-seekers also come here, especially on weekends, when hotels are often crowded. Nightlife is good here—the main spots are in Maresias and Boiçucanga. The "beautiful island" of Ilhabela *(below)* is a 15-minute ferry ride away from downtown São Sebastião.

GETTING HERE AND AROUND

Litorânea buses travel four times daily to São Sebastião (to the ferry dock) from São Paulo's Tietê terminal, close to the international airport of Guarulhos, and take about four hours.

The drive from São Paulo to São Sebastião is about three hours if it is not raining. Some of the North Shore's most beautiful houses line the Rio-Santos Highway (SP 055) on the approach to Maresias. However, extra care is required when driving along the 055, as the road conditions and lighting are precarious, particularly past Maresias. To reach the 055, take the Ayrton Senna (SP 070) highway, followed by Mogi-Bertioga (SP 098). Alternatively if you want to get straight to the center of São Sebastião where the Ilhabela ferry docks, take Rodovia Ayrton Senna–Carvalho Pinto (SP 070), followed by Rodovia Tamoios (SP 099) to Caraguatatuba, and then follow the signs.

ESSENTIALS

Bus Contacts **Litorânea.** ☎ *011/3775–3850, 0800/285–3047* 🌐 *www.litoranea.com.br.* **Terminal Rodoviário.** ✉ *Praça Vereador Venino Fernandes Moreira 10, São Sebastião.*

Visitor Information **Sectur.** ✉ *Avenida Altino Arantes 174, São Sebastião* ☎ *012/3892–2620.*

BEACHES

FAMILY **Barra do Sahy.** Families with young children favor small, quiet Barra do Sahy. Its narrow strip of sand (with a bay and a river on one side and rocks on the other) is steep but smooth, and the water is clean and calm. Kayakers paddle about, and divers are drawn to the nearby Ilha das Couves. Area restaurants serve mostly basic fish dishes with rice and salad, as well as sharing platters of snacks, seafood, and fries. Note that Barra do Sahy's entrance is atop a slope and appears suddenly—be on the lookout around marker Km 174. **Amenities:** food and drink; lifeguards; parking (no fee). **Best for:** snorkeling; sunrise. ✉ *Rio-Santos Hwy., SP 055, São Sebastião* ✣ *157 km (97 miles) southeast of São Paulo.*

5

Camburizinho and Camburi. Wealthy paulistanos flock to Camburizinho and Camburi, to sunbathe, surf, and party. While the first beach is more secluded and also where the families head to, the latter, on the other side of the river Camburi, is where the action is, with night owls heading here to play guitar by the moonlight. At the center of the beaches is a cluster of cafés, ice-cream shops, bars, and restaurants. The two beaches are located just north of Barra do Sahy. If you're coming from the south, take the second entrance, which is usually in better shape than the first entrance, at Km 166. **Amenities:** food and drink; lifeguards; parking (fee). **Best for:** partiers; sunset; surfing. ✉ *Rio-Santos Hwy., SP 055, São Sebastião* ✣ *162 km (100 miles) southeast of São Paulo.*

Maresias. Maresias is a 4-km (2-mile) stretch of white sand with clean, green waters that are good for swimming and surfing. Maresias is popular with a young crowd and compared with the others along the North Coast, its beach village is large and has a good infrastructure, with banks, supermarkets, and a wide choice of nightlife entertainment. **Amenities:** food and drink; lifeguards; parking (fee); toilets. **Best for:** partiers; surfing; windsurfing. ✉ *Rio-Santos Hwy, Km 151, SP 055, São Sebastião* ✣ *177 km (109 miles) southeast of São Paulo.*

WHERE TO EAT

$ PIZZA 🍴 **Candeeiro.** On the main street of Camburi, Candeeiro serves delicious Neapolitan-style pizza, as well as crepes. The little gallery where it is located has a very good ice-cream shop, Gelateria Parmalat, tucked at the back, so save room for dessert. [$] *Average main: R$30* ✉ *Estrada do Camburi 87, Camburi, São Sebastião* ☎ *012/3865–3626* 🕓 *No lunch* 💳 *No credit cards.*

$$$$ ITALIAN FAMILY 🍴 **Ristorante Mergellina Maresias.** A traditional restaurant run by a Neopolitan chef, Mergellina serves good, fuss-free Italian fare with generous portions and great desserts. The prices are a little higher than the local average, but this place is absolutely worthwhile. Try the Gorgonzola paste with freshly baked Italian bread to start, followed by risotto Brasil, with heart of palm, zucchini, and mushrooms, and the chocolate

and nut tart to finish. The well-rounded wine list has about 40 local and international varieties. Ask to sit outside, under a giant parasol. [$] *Average main: R$100* ✉ *Rua Dos Navegantes 139, Maresias, São Sebastião* ☎ *012/3865–7272* ⏲ *No lunch Mon. and Tues. Closed Wed.*

WHERE TO STAY

$$$$ HOTEL 🏨 **Amora Boutique Hotel.** Right on São Sebastião's beachfront, with easy access to the town center, this hotel has cozy rooms and a heated outdoor pool, hot tub, and sauna, perfect for days when agitated seas make the beach less appealing. **Pros:** beach service; comfortable rooms. **Cons:** limited and expensive food options. [$] *Rooms from: R$600* ✉ *Av. Dr. Francisco Loup 1285, São Sebastião* ☎ *012/3865–7377* 🌐 *www.amorahotel.com.br* 🌐 🛏 *23 suites* 🍴 *Breakfast.*

$$$$ HOTEL Fodor's Choice ★ 🏨 **Nau Royal.** Tucked away from the main cluster of Camburi's bars and all the noise of weekend partiers, this very special boutique hotel is the perfect choice for couples looking for peace and quiet. **Pros:** unparalled service; good restaurant; beach service. **Cons:** suites near reception area can be noisy. [$] *Rooms from: R$1,000* ✉ *Alameda Patriarca Antônio José Marques 1533, Camburi, São Sebastião* ☎ *012/3865–4486* 🌐 *www.nauroyal.com.br* 🛏 *15 suites* 🍴 *Breakfast.*

$$$ B&B/INN FAMILY 🏨 **Pousada Porto Mare.** On the main street just a stone's throw from the town's clubs and bars, Pousada Port Mare is a great choice for those who like to be close to the action, with plenty of amenities thrown in—a nice pool and sauna facilities, and beach service, too. **Pros:** excellent breakfast; good outdoor facilities. **Cons:** rooms near the breakfast area can be noisy; poor Wi-Fi. [$] *Rooms from: R$400* ✉ *Rua Sebastião Romão César 400, Maresias, São Sebastião* ☎ *012/3865–5272* 🌐 *www.pousadaportomare.com.br* 🛏 *28 rooms* 🍴 *Some meals.*

$$ B&B/INN 🏨 **Villa Bebek.** The owners of this chic hotel sought inspiration from Bali to create the beautiful gardens inlaid with pebbles, sculptures, and tropical plants surrounding the pool and sauna areas. **Pros:** beautiful decor; good service; perfect for relaxing poolside. **Cons:** fewer options at breakfast during low season. [$] *Rooms from: R$300* ✉ *Rua Zezito 251, Camburi, São Sebastião* ☎ *012/3865–3320* 🌐 *www.villabebek.com.br* 🛏 *15 rooms* 🍴 *Breakfast.*

NIGHTLIFE

Morocco. Combining dining with a club environment, Morocco hosts a wide range of live bands. When Sirena (*below*) doesn't appeal, partiers head here to dance. ✉ *Rua Silvina Auta Salles 375, São Sebastião* ☎ *012/3077–0020.*

Santo Gole. Santo Gole is an informal beach-style bar run by three friends that attracts a younger crowd and stays open until dawn. Come here for live rock music, draft beer, and light snacks. ✉ *Av. Rua Sebastião Romão César 477, São Sebastião* ☎ *012/3865–5044.*

Sirena. Wealthy, sun-kissed paulistanos head to Sirena to see and be seen, sip cocktails, and dance the night away, watching the sun rise from the external dance floor. ✉ *Rua Sebastião Romão César 418, Maresias, São Paulo* ☎ *011/3865–6681* 🌐 *www.sirena.com.br.*

ILHABELA

Fodor's Choice
★

7 km (5 miles)/15-minute boat ride from São Sebastião.

Ilhabela is favored by those who like the beach and water sports; indeed, many sailing competitions are held here as well as scuba diving. This is the biggest sea island in the country, with 22 calm beaches along its western shore, which faces the mainland. The hotels are mostly at the north end, though the best sandy stretches are the 13 to the south, which face the open sea. Eighty percent of the island is in a state park area, with some parts accessible by car and others by boat only.

There are two small towns on the island: one is where the locals live; the other is where most visitors stay because of its hotels, restaurants, and stores. During the winter months most businesses that cater to tourists, including restaurants, are open only on weekends.

Scuba divers have several 19th- and early-20th-century wrecks to explore—this region has the most wrecks of any area off Brazil's coast—and hikers can set off on the numerous inland trails, many of which lead to a waterfall (the island has more than 300). ■TIP➜ Mosquitoes are a problem; bring plenty of insect repellent.

GETTING HERE AND AROUND

Balsas (ferries) from São Sebastião to Ilhabela run every 30 minutes from 6 am to midnight and hourly during the night. The São Sebastião Balsa transports vehicles as well as passengers. Fares range from R$15 (weekdays) to R$22.50 (weekends), including a car. To get to the ferry dock in São Sebastião, take Avenida São Sebastião from town to the coast. Make advance ferry reservations, particularly December through February. On rainy days, it is worth checking whether ferries are operating at all.

The best way to get around Ilhabela is by car. There are no rental agencies on the island (or connecting bridges) so be sure to make arrangements beforehand. Public buses also cross the island from north to south daily.

ESSENTIALS

Ferry Information São Sebastião Balsa (Ferry). ⊠ *São Sebastião* ☎ *012/3892-1576.*

Visitor and Tour Information Ilhabela Secretaria do Turismo. ⊠ *Praça Vereador José Leite dos Passos 14, Ilhabela* ☎ *012/3895-7492* ⊕ *www.ilhabela. sp.gov.br.*

TOURS

Maremar Turismo. Maremar Turismo offers a range of scuba diving, Jeep, horseback riding, and hiking tours around Ilhabela's most popular areas, as well as some off-the-beaten track tours. ⊠ *Av. Princesa Isabel 90, Ilhabela* ☎ *012/3896-1418* ⊕ *www.maremar.tur.br* 🛥 *From R$50.*

BEACHES

Praia da Armação. The long strip of white sand and calm sea attract sailing, windsurfing, and kitesurfing aficionados. Busy during most of the year, Praia da Armação has an excellent infrastructure, with bars, restaurants, and kiosks serving food and drinks and renting parasols and beach chairs. Bathrooms, baby changing facilities, and parking bays are available. There is a church on-site, which is said to be one of the oldest buildings on the island. The beach was also once the site of a factory for processing blubber and other resources from whales caught in the waters around Ilhabela. **Amenities:** food and drink; lifeguards; parking (fee); toilets; water sports. **Best for:** snorkeling; sunset; walking; windsurfing. ✉ *14 km (9 miles) north of ferry dock, Ilhabela.*

Praia do Curral. Curral is one of the most famous beaches on Ilhabela, and is popular with tourists as well as young people. It has clear and slightly rough waters and also a large green area, which serves as a refuge for those needing a break from sunbathing. The local vendors provide tables and chairs, fresh showers with clean water, bathrooms, and parking. At night people gather at the many restaurants and bars—some with live music—and there are places to camp. The wreck of the ship *Aymoré* (1921) can be found off the coast of this beach, near Ponta do Ribeirão, where you can also look for a waterfall trail. **Amenities:** food and drink; lifeguards; showers; toilets. **Best for:** partiers; sunset. ✉ *6 km (4 miles) south of Praia Grande, Ilhabela.*

Praia Grande. It's busy, but some of the best infrastructure in Ilhabela can be found here: the kiosks have tables in the shade; you can rent a chair from most vendors along the long sandy strip; showers are available free of charge; and there's even a chapel. The beach is popular for windsurfing, diving, and surfing. The sandy strip is rather inclined, with a tumble in the central part. The sands are thick and yellowish. On the far left there is a small river that ends in the sea. **Amenities:** food and drink; lifeguards; showers; toilets. **Best for:** partiers; surfing; walking; windsurfing. ✉ *13 km (8 miles) south of ferry dock, Ilhabela.*

WHERE TO EAT

$$$$ SEAFOOD 🍴 **Ilha Sul.** The best option on the menu at Ilha Sul is the grilled shrimp with vegetables. Fish and other seafood are also available. [$] *Average main: R$90* ✉ *Av. Riachuelo 287, Ilhabela* ☎ *012/3894–9426* ⏲ *Closed Mon.–Thurs. in the months of Apr.–June and Aug.–Nov.*

$$$$ SEAFOOD FAMILY 🍴 **Viana.** *Camarão* (shrimp) is prepared in various ways at this traditional, petite restaurant with just a few tables. It's popular among locals, who come here to eat and enjoy the gorgeous view and sunsets. Grilled fish is also on the menu. It's open for breakfast Tuesday and on weekends. [$] *Average main: R$65* ✉ *Av. Leonardo Reale 2301, Ilhabela* ☎ *012/3896–1089* 💳 *No credit cards* ⏲ *No lunch Mon. and Thurs. Closed Wed.* ✍ *Reservations essential.*

WHERE TO STAY

$$$$ HOTEL Fodor's Choice ★ 🏨 **DPNY Beach Hotel & Spa.** This luxury hotel is geared up for couples looking for romance and relaxation, with modern, comfortable rooms and direct access to Praia do Curral, one of Ilhabela's most famous beaches. **Pros:** luxuriously comfortable rooms; excellent food; perfect for poolside relaxation. **Cons:** service can be slow at busy times. [$] *Rooms from: R$738* ✉ *Praia do Curral, Av. Jose Pacheco do Nascimento 7668, Ilhabela* ☎ *012/3894–3000* 🛏 *79 suites* 🍽 *Breakfast* 💳 *No credit cards.*

$$$$ HOTEL 🏨 **Maison Joly.** Past guests of this exclusive hotel at the top of the Cantagalo Hill range from kings of Sweden to the Rolling Stones. **Pros:** beautiful surroundings; excellent restaurant. **Cons:** service a little erratic

in busy seasons. [$] *Rooms from: R$575* ✉ *Rua Antônio Lisboa Alves 278, Ilhabela* ☎ *012/3896–1201, 012/3896–2364* 🌐 *www.maisonjoly.com.br* 🛏 *9 rooms* 🍴 *Breakfast.*

$$$ HOTEL FAMILY 🏨 **Porto Pacuíba.** Peaceful and family-friendly, Porto Pacuíba is close to a beach and has easy access to good hikes nearby. **Pros:** excellent service; good restaurant; well-decorated rooms. **Cons:** far from the town center and ferry dock. [$] *Rooms from: R$400* ✉ *Av. Leonardo Reale 2392, Viana, Ilhabela* ☎ *012/3896–2466* 🛏 *29 suites* 🍴 *Breakfast.*

$ B&B/INN 🏨 **Pousada dos Hibiscos.** North of the ferry dock, this red house has midsize rooms, all at ground level. **Pros:** great service; hearty breakfast. **Cons:** couples looking for poolside relaxation may be disturbed by large groups; rooms may feel a little small. [$] *Rooms from: R$220* ✉ *Av. Pedro de Paula Moraes 720, Ilhabela* ☎ *012/3896–1375* 🌐 *www.pousadadoshibiscos.com.br* 🛏 *13 suites* 🍴 *Breakfast.*

SPORTS AND THE OUTDOORS

BOATING AND SAILING

Ilha Sailing Ocean School. Sailing courses here run 12 hours and cost about R$500. ✉ *Av. Pedro de Paula Moraes 578, Ilhabela* ☎ *012/9766–6619* 🌐 *www.ilhasailing.com.br.*

KITE- AND WINDSURFING

BL3. You can take kitesurfing, windsurfing, and sailing lessons at BL3, the biggest school in Ilhabela. Individual lessons are priced from R$200. ✉ *Av. Perimetral Norte 4260, Ilhabela* ☎ *012/3286–5885* 🌐 *www.bl3.com.br.*

SCUBA DIVING

Diving is a popular activity for those visiting Ilhabela. In the calm, transparent waters, you can explore the marine wildlife as well as discover the mysteries surrounding the island's various shipwrecks. It is said that Ilhabela has more than 100 close to its shore. These vessels have formed huge submerged artificial reefs, and are now home to a wide variety of aquatic species such as turtles, octopuses, and the like. It is still possible to actually see the ships. Beginning divers should aim for the most popular wrecks, such as the *Aymoré* (1914; Curral Beach; 3–7 meters) and the *Darth* (1894; Itaboca Beach; 5–15 meters). There are numerous diving schools along nearly every beach, which also rent equipment if you are happy to go solo.

Colonial Diver. You can rent equipment, take diving classes, and arrange for a dive-boat trip through Colonial Diver. The basic course takes up to three days and costs around R$1,190, which includes equipment for the classes, course material, and an international certificate. ✉ *Av. Brasil 1751, Ilhabela* ☎ *012/3894–9459* 🌐 *www.colonialdiver.com.br.*

Fodor's Choice ★ **Ilha das Cabras.** The main attractions of this little piece of paradise—besides the white sand and clear water—are the tiny bars that serve delicious, fresh seafood and the Ecological Sanctuary of Ilha das Cabras. The park, created in 1992, is a secluded reserve around the island and is also a great diving and fish-watching site. While most "baptisms" of diving beginners take place here, seasoned divers head off to their underwater adventures at the diving/snorkeling sanctuary off the shore of the isle, where a statue of Neptune can be found at the 22-foot depth. ⊠ *2 km (1 mile) south of ferry, Ilhabela.*

Fodor's Choice ★ **Ilha de Búzios.** A nearly two-hour boat trip separates Ilhabela from Ilha de Búzios, but the effort is totally worthwhile. Because it is located far from the coast, the water is very transparent, meaning divers will be able to see plenty of colorful fish and other underwater fauna such as rays and sea turtles. The main stars, however, are the dolphins, which fearlessly approach boats. ⊠ *25 km (15 miles) offshore; take boat from São Sebastião, Ilhabela.*

Itaboca. One of best places for diving is Itaboca, where British ship *Darth* sank in 1884, leaving bottles of wine and porcelain dishes that can still be found. ⊠ *17 km (11 miles) south of ferry dock, Ilhabela.*

UBATUBA

234 km (145 miles) southeast of São Paulo.

Many of the more than 70 beaches around Ubatuba are more than beautiful enough to merit the long drive from São Paulo. Young people, surfers, and couples with and without children hang out in the 90-km (56-mile) area, where waterfalls, boat rides, aquariums, diving, and trekking in the wild are major attractions. Downtown Ubatuba also has an active nightlife, especially in summer.

GETTING HERE AND AROUND

Litorânea buses travel eight times a day to Ubatuba from São Paulo. The journey takes about four hours. By car from São Paulo, take Rodovia Ayrton Senna–Carvalho Pinto (SP 070), followed by Rodovia Tamoios (SP 099) to Caraguatatuba. Turn right and head north on SP 055.

ESSENTIALS

Bus Contacts Litorânea. ☎ *011/3775–3850* ⊕ *www.litoranea.com.br.* **Rodoviária.** ⊠ *Av. Thomas Galhardo 513, Ubatuba* ⊕ *www.rodoviariaubatuba. com.*

BEACHES

Praia Grande. For those seeking a party atmosphere, Praia Grande is a great option. It has bars and restaurants by the sea, with local samba and country music playing all day. Chairs and parasols can be hired from beach vendors. The waters here are clean and green, and the hard sands are ideal for football, volleyball, and racquetball; it's also a great place for hiking. Praia Grande is a major surf spot in Ubatuba, with consistent, perfect waves. **Amenities:** food and drink; lifeguards; parking (fee). **Best for:** partiers; surfing; walking. ⊠ *Off Tamoios (SP 099) and Rio-Santos intersection, Ubatuba.*

Praia do Prumirim. Surrounded by rain forest and lined with summer holiday mansions, Prumirim is a small beach of coarse sands and turquoise calm waters. Despite its exuberant natural beauty, Prumirim is not very busy. There's good surfing, but the waves are generally smaller than those at Praia Grande. About a kilometer out to sea, Prumirim Island also has magnificent scenery and is a great place for diving. To reach the island you can pay one of the local fishermen to ferry you out there or, if you're particularly fit, you could even swim. The access to Praia do Prumirim is near Km 29 of SP 055, past the entrance to a private condominium. A beautiful waterfall with a natural pool can also be accessed nearby off the highway. **Amenities:** food and drink. **Best for:** snorkeling; solitude; sunrise; walking. ⊠ *Near Km 29 of BR 101 (Rio-Santos), Ubatuba.*

WHERE TO EAT AND STAY

$ ✕ **Padaria Integrale.** This popular, centrally located *padaria* (bakery)
BRAZILIAN   offers a range of healthy sandwiches and drinks, as well as an excel-
FAMILY   lent deli selection. Even if the place is packed, service is still agile and
friendly. You can either have your breakfast or light meal here, or take
it away like many locals do. $ *Average main: R$25* ⊠ *Rua Dr. Esteves
da Silva 360, Ubatuba* ☎ *012/3836–1836.*

$$$$ ⊞ **Pousada Picinguaba.** A luxury pousada in the beautiful, unspoiled
HOTEL   fishing village of Picinguaba, this place is ideal for couples looking for
Fodor's Choice   peace and quiet. **Pros:** beautiful surroundings; excellent food; unpar-
★   alleled service. **Cons:** the pousada is up a steep hill. $ *Rooms from:
R$1,120* ⊠ *Rua G 130 , Picinguaba, Ubatuba* ☎ *012/3836–9105*
⊕ *www.picinguaba.com* ↝ *10 suites* ¡○¡ *Some meals.*

$ ⊞ **Pousada Torre del Mar.** A simple but comfortable and very clean
B&B/INN   pousada, Torre del Mar is just a stone's throw from the town's main
FAMILY   attractions, beaches, and restaurants. **Pros:** comfortable beds; excellent
homemade breakfast; central location. **Cons:** rooms facing the street can
be noisy; rooms can be quite small. $ *Rooms from: R$200* ⊠ *Av. Milton
de Holanda Maia 210, Itaguá, Ubatuba* ☎ *012/3832–2751* ↝ *18 suites*
¡○¡ *Breakfast* ▭ *No credit cards.*

INLAND

São Paulo's inland region has beautiful mountains, springs, rivers, and waterfalls perfect for outdoor activities like hiking and rafting. Historic attractions are generally fewer than in other states. Save some time for clothing and crafts shopping, and for the lavish regional cuisine.

Highways that lead to inland towns are some of the best in the state. To get to Águas de São Pedro, take Anhangüera–Bandeirantes (SP 330/ SP 348); to Santana de Parnaíba, take Castelo Branco (SP 280); and to Campos de Jordão, take Ayrton Senna–Carvalho Pinto (SP 70). Embu is the exception—it's a 30-minute drive from the capital on the not-so-well-maintained Régis Bittencourt (BR 116). To go by bus, choose between the daily departures from the Tietê and Barra Funda terminals in São Paulo. Both are next to subway stations, making access fairly easy.

ÁGUAS DE SÃO PEDRO

180 km (112 miles) northwest of São Paulo.

Although Águas de São Pedro is one of the smallest cities in Brazil, at a mere 3.9 square km (1.5 square miles), its sulfurous waters made it famous countrywide in the 1940s and '50s. The healing hot springs were discovered by chance in the 1920s when technicians were drilling for oil.

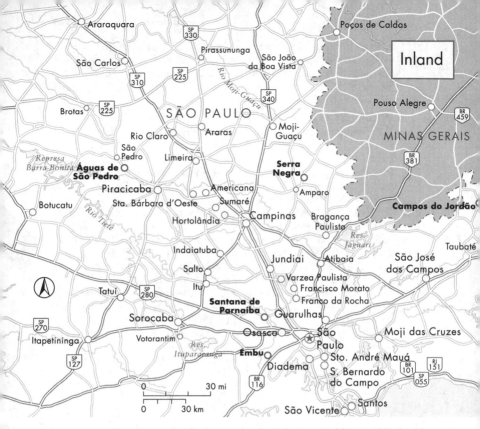

You can access the springs at the Balneário Publico (public bathhouse) or through some hotels. Though a number of illnesses respond to the water, most visitors are just healthy tourists soaking in relaxation. Águas de São Pedro is compact, so it's easy to get around on foot.

GETTING HERE AND AROUND
Águas de São Pedro is about a 2½-hour drive north of São Paulo on Anhangüera-Bandeirantes (SP 330/SP 348) and then SP 304.

ESSENTIALS
Visitor Information Tourist Information. ⊠ *Praça Pref Geraldo Azevedo 153, Águas de São Pedro* ☎ *019/3482–1652* ⊕ *www.aguasdesaopedro.sp.gov.br.*

EXPLORING
Balneário Municipal Dr. Octávio Moura Andrade. Want immersion baths in sulfurous springwater? You can swim in the pool or sweat in the sauna while you wait for your private soak, massage, or beauty treatment. A snack bar and a gift shop round out the spa services. The surrounding forested grounds are perfect for a leisurely stroll or a ride on horseback (R$10 for half an hour). The park is free and open to the public in the morning on weekdays and all day on weekends. ⊠ *Av. Carlos Mauro, Águas de São Pedro* ☎ *019/3482–1333* ⊠ *R$8–R$50* ☺ *Mon.–Thurs. 7:30 am–12:30 pm, Fri. and Sat. 7 am–noon and 3–6 pm, Sun. 7 am–12:30 pm.*

WHERE TO STAY

$$ HOTEL
Avenida Charme Hotel. This hotel, resembling a large ranch house, has an arcaded veranda and well-maintained, but rather dated, rooms. **Pros:** excellent breakfast; friendly service; good pool area. **Cons:** rooms are spacious but plain and sparsely decorated. [$] *Rooms from: R$300* ✉ *Av. Carlos Mauro 246, Águas de São Pedro* ☎ *019/3482–7900,* 🌐 *www.hotelavenida.com.br* 🛏 *53 rooms* 🍴 *All-inclusive.*

$$$$ HOTEL Fodor's Choice ★
Grande Hotel São Pedro. In the middle of a 300,000-square-meter (3.2 million-square-foot) park with more than 1 million trees and local wildlife, this hotel is in a beautiful art deco building that was a casino during the 1940s. **Pros:** beautiful location; excellent service. **Cons:** requires booking months in advance, especially during the winter season. [$] *Rooms from: R$800* ✉ *Parque Dr. Octávio de Moura Andrade, Águas de São Pedro* ☎ *019/3482–7600* 🌐 *www.grandehotelsenac.com.br* 🛏 *96 rooms, 16 suites* 🍴 *No meals.*

$ HOTEL
Hotel Jerubiaçaba. In a 17,000-square-meter (183,000-square-foot) green area with springs and a bathhouse, this hotel features rooms bathed in light colors. **Pros:** excellent location. **Cons:** rather simple furnishings; not very comfortable mattresses. [$] *Rooms from: R$200* ✉ *Av. Carlos Mauro 168, Águas de São Pedro* ☎ *0800/13–1411* 🌐 *www.hoteljerubiacaba.com.br* 🛏 *120 rooms, 8 suites* 🍴 *No meals.*

5

CAMPOS DO JORDÃO

184 km (114 miles) northeast of São Paulo.

In the Serra da Mantiqueira at an altitude of 5,525 feet, Campos do Jordão and its fresh mountain air are paulistanos' favorite winter attractions. In July temperatures drop as low as 32°F (0°C), though it never snows; in warmer months temperatures linger in the 13°C–16°C (55°F–60°F) range.

In the past some people came for their health (the town was once a tuberculosis treatment area), others for inspiration—including such Brazilian artists as writer Monteiro Lobato, dramatist Nelson Rodrigues, and painter Lasar Segall. Nowadays the arts continue to thrive, especially during July's Festival de Inverno (Winter Festival), which draws classical musicians from around the world.

Exploring Campos do Jordão without a car is difficult, as attractions are far-flung. The neighborhood of Vila Capivary is where most restaurants and cafés are located.

GETTING HERE AND AROUND

Six Passaro Marron buses leave São Paulo for Campos do Jordão daily. The journey takes three hours and costs R$43. To reach Campos do Jordão from São Paulo (a 2½-hour drive), take Rodovia Carvalho Pinto (SP 070) and SP 123.

ESSENTIALS

Bus Contacts Passaro Marron. ☎ *0800/2853–047, 011/3775–3890* 🌐 *www.passaromarron.com.br.* **Terminal Rodoviário.** ✉ *Rua Benedito Lourenço 285, Campos do Jordão.*

Visitor Information **Campos do Jordão Tourist Office.** ✉ *At entrance to town, Campos do Jordão* ☎ *012/3664–3525* 🌐 *www.camposdojordao.com.br.*

EXPLORING

TOP ATTRACTIONS

FAMILY **Amantikir Garden.** The Amantikir Garden consists of 17 areas inspired by various ecosystems and famous gardens around the world. On the grounds you can find a cafeteria and a learning center, where there are courses on gardening. Plans are in the works for expanding the area and building a bird-watching center. Reservations are mandatory, as the place receives a limited number of guests per day. An English-speaking guide is available if booked in advance. ✉ *Rodovia Campos do Jordão Eugênio Lefreve 215, Estrada Gavião Gonzaga, Campos do Jordão* ☎ *012/3662–5044* 🌐 *www.parqueamantikir.com.br* 🎫 *R$25* 🕒 *Daily 8–5.*

FAMILY **Estação Ferroviária Emílio Ribas.** A wonderful little train departs from Estação Ferroviária Emílio Ribas for tours of the city and its environs, including the 47-km (29-mile) trip to Reino das Águas Claras, where there's a park with waterfalls and models of Monteiro Lobato's characters (Lobato is a well-loved children's-book author). Be sure to book in advance. ✉ *Av. Dr. Emílio Ribas s/n, Vila Capivari, Campos do Jordão* 🎫 *R$11* 🕒 *Daily departures every hr apart from noon.*

Horto Florestal. Horto Florestal is a natural playground for *macacos-prego* (nail monkeys), squirrels, and parrots, as well as people. The park has a trout-filled river, waterfalls, and trails—all set among trees from around the world and one of the last *araucária* (Brazilian pine) forests in the state. ✉ *Av. Pedro Paulo, Km 13, Campos do Jordão* ☎ *012/3663–3762* 🎫 *R$13* 🕒 *Daily 9–6.*

Morro do Elefante (*Elephant Hill*). Outside town a chairlift ride to the top of Morro do Elefante is a good way to enjoy the view from a 5,850-foot height. ✉ *Av. José Oliveira Damas s/n, Campos do Jordão* ☎ *012/3663–1530* 🎫 *R$7* 🕒 *Tues.–Fri. 1–5, weekends 9–5:30.*

Palácio Boa Vista. Palácio Boa Vista, the official winter residence of the state's governor, has paintings by such famous Brazilian modernists as Di Cavalcanti, Portinari, Volpi, Tarsila do Amaral, and Anita Malfatti. On the same property, the Capela de São Pedro (São Pedro Chapel) has sacred art from the 17th and 18th centuries. ✉ *Av. Dr. Adhemar de Barros 3001, Campos do Jordão* ☎ *012/3662–1122* 🎫 *Free* 🕒 *Wed., Thurs., Sat., and Sun. 10–noon and 2–5.*

WHERE TO EAT AND STAY

$$$ GERMAN Fodor's Choice ★ 🍴 **Baden-Baden.** One of the specialties at this charming German restaurant and *chopperia* in the heart of town is sauerkraut *garni* (sour cabbage with German sausages). The typical dish serves two and is almost as popular as Baden-Baden's cold draft beer from the attached brewery, open 10–5 on weekdays. [$] *Average main: R$60* ✉ *Rua Djalma Forjaz 93, Loja 10, Campos do Jordão* ☎ *012/3663–3610.*

$$$ SWISS 🍴 **Baronesa Von Leithner.** This Switzerland-inspired restaurant on a working berry farm is surrounded by beautiful Brazilian pine trees. Typical fare such as fondue is served and you can buy homemade jellies, fudges, and jams made on-site. [$] *Average main: R$60* ✉ *Av. Fausto Arruda Camargo*

CLOSE UP

Os Bandeirantes

In the 16th and 17th centuries, groups called *bandeiras* (literally meaning "flags" but also an archaic term for an assault force) set out on expeditions from São Paulo. Their objectives were far from noble. Their initial goal was to enslave Native Americans. Later, they were hired to capture escaped African slaves and destroy *quilombos* (communities the slaves created deep in the interior). Still, by heading inland at a time when most colonies were close to the shore, the *bandeirantes* (bandeira members) inadvertently did Brazil a great service.

A fierce breed, bandeirantes often adopted indigenous customs and voyaged for years at a time. Some went as far as the Amazon River; others only to what is today Minas Gerais, where gold and precious gems were found. In their travels they ignored the 1494 Treaty of Tordesilhas, which established a boundary between Spanish and Portuguese

lands. (The boundary was a vague north–south line roughly 1,600 km (1,000 miles) west of the Cape Verde islands.) Other Brazilians followed the bandeirantes, and towns were founded, often in what was technically Spanish territory. These colonists eventually claimed full possession of the lands they settled, and thus Brazil's borders were greatly expanded.

Near Parque Ibirapuera in the city of São Paulo, there's a monument, inaugurated In 1953, to honor the bandeirantes. It's a huge granite sculpture created by Victor Brecheret, a famous Brazilian artist. A major São Paulo highway is named Bandeirantes and several roads across the state are named after these supposedly brave, honorable men. Protests are occasionally staged at the Ibirapuera statue by those who don't believe the bandeirantes deserve any kind of monument whatsoever.

2815, *Alto da Boa Vista, Campos do Jordão* 012/3662–1121 *www. baronesavonleithner.com.br* Closed Mon. No credit cards.

$
CAFÉ
✗ **Chocolates Montanhês.** A well-known chocolate shop and café, and a perfect stop after a meal, where you can stock up on chocolate lollipops and slabs. Don't forget to try the extra-creamy hot chocolate. $ *Average main: R$20* *Praça São Benedito 45, Loja 6, Campos do Jordão* 012/3663–1979 *www.chocolatemontanhes.com.br* No credit cards.

$$$$
RESORT
FAMILY
Fodor'sChoice
★
Grande Hotel Campos do Jordão. A former 1940s casino—just like its sister hotel in Águas de São Pedro—the Grande Hotel is a teaching hotel that boasts extensive grounds with beautiful gardens and plenty of outdoor activities. **Pros:** excellent food; unparalled service; plenty of activities for adults and children. **Cons:** few dining options for vegetarians and others with dietary restrictions. $ *Rooms from: R$800* *Av. Frei Orestes Girardi 3549, Vila Capivary, Campos do Jordão* 012/3668–6000, 0800/770–0790 *for reservations* 95 suites *All meals* No credit cards.

$$
HOTEL
Pousada Villa Capivary. A stay at this cozy guesthouse puts you in the gastronomic and commercial center of Campos. **Pros:** friendly, helpful, and efficient staff; central location. **Cons:** booking well in advance

required, particularly in the winter months. $ Rooms from: R$350 ⊠ Av. Victor Godinho 131, Campos do Jordão ☎ 012/3663-1746 ⊕ www.capivari.com.br ⏎ 15 rooms ⏺⏺ Breakfast.

SHOPPING

Boulevard Genéve. This mall in the busy Vila Capivari district is lined with cafés, bars, and restaurants, making it a nightlife hub. You can also find plenty of clothing stores, and candy shops selling chocolate, the town's specialty. ⊠ Rua Doutor Djalma Forjas 93, Vila Capivari, Campos do Jordão ☎ 012/3663-5060 ⊕ www.boulevardgeneve.com.br.

Maison Genéve. The best handmade embroidered clothing in town is at Maison Genéve, open weekdays 10–7 and weekends 10–10. It also has a café offering a range of cakes, pastries, and drinks. ⊠ Av. Dr. Januário Miráglia 3224, Vila Jaguaribe, Campos do Jordão ☎ 012/3663-3922 ⊕ www.lojageneve.com.br.

SERRA NEGRA

142 km (88.2 miles) northeast of São Paulo.

At 4,265 feet above sea level in the Serra da Mantiqueira, Serra Negra attracts hordes of paulistanos and cruising motorbike fans looking for a bucolic weekend break in the mountains. In addition to various mineral water fountains, there is the Coffee Route, where you can drive through thousands of acres of coffee fields until you reach Cachoeira dos Sonhos (Dreams Waterfall), where it's possible to swim and have a snack. You can also head over to Alto da Serra, the town's highest point, where paragliding aficionados gather on the weekends. To get there, follow the signs from Avenida João Gerosa and drive up Rua 14 de Julho all the way past Hotel São Mateus, until you reach an unpaved road on the left that will lead to the top. The main shopping street in Serra Negra is Rua Coronel Pedro Penteado, where you can find plenty of knitwear, leather bags and clothing, as well as sweets and cheeses of all kinds. The town center is small enough to be explored by foot.

GETTING HERE AND AROUND

Nine Fênix buses leave São Paulo's Tietê bus terminal for Serra Negra daily. The journey takes 3½ hours and costs R$37. To reach Serra Negra from São Paulo (a 2½-hour drive), take Rodovia Fernão Dias (SP 381) to Atibaia, Rodovia Dom Pedro I (SP 065) toward Itatiba, then the SP 360.

ESSENTIALS

Bus Contacts Rápido Fênix. ⊠ Praça Sesquicentenário s/n, Serra Negra ☎ 019/3892-2098 ⊕ www.rapidofenix.com.br.

Visitor Information Serra Negra Tourist Office. ⊠ Praça Sesquicentenário, Serra Negra ✛ Behind the bus station and next to chairlift ☎ 019/3842-2109.

EXPLORING

Monte Alegre do Sul. If you have more than a day to spare and are driving, pay a quick visit to the delightful little town of Monte Alegre do Sul, just 6 km (4 miles) from Serra Negra and known for its September strawberry festival. The buildings of the historic center, including the town's church, Santuario Bom Jesus, date from the 19th century. Check out the shop of local artisan group Associarte, as well as the traditional sweet shop Peschiera nearby. At the old train station, a steam engine used for transporting coffee waits at a decommissioned platform. ✉ *Monte Alegre do Sul, Serra Negra.*

WHERE TO EAT

$$$ FUSION

🍴 **Bar da Fonte.** A delightful restaurant oozing charm, Bar da Fonte serves excellent dishes based on a mix of cuisines. Choices range from risottos to Indian-inspired stews and steaks, as well as feijoada served on Saturdays. A small cachaça distillery is based on-site, and the owner Marcos Kaloy offers tours that include a tasting. Local beers are also available. There's often live music in the evening on weekends. [$] *Average main: R$60* ✉ *Rua Joaquim de Oliveira 116, Monte Alegre do Sul* ☎ *019/3899–1239* 🕑 *Closed Mon.–Wed.* 💳 *No credit cards.*

$$$ BRAZILIAN FAMILY Fodor's Choice ★

🍴 **Café Boteco.** Located by João Zelante Square in what was once a department store, Café Boteco incorporates elements of the traditional Brazilian *boteco* (dive bar) in some of its recipes and decor, but the comparisons end there: smartly dressed, friendly waiters serve excellent *picanha* (rump steak) and *costelinha com polenta* (pork ribs with polenta chips), as well as salad and pasta dishes with a local twist. Draft lager and a range of local beers are available. On weekends, sit outside to hear bands playing in the square. The owners also run a small shop next door selling souvenirs, fine wines, and cold cuts. [$] *Average main: R$60* ✉ *Travessa Tenente Mário Dallari 20 (Praça João Zelante), Serra Negra* ☎ *019/3892–3481* 🌐 *www.cafeboteco.com.br* 🕑 *Closed Mon. and Tues.*

$ CAFÉ FAMILY

🍴 **Gelato Donato.** A small ice-cream parlor at Praça João Zelante, Gelato Donato is a good destination for dessert and a coffee after a meal. The ice cream is made in Serra Negra using locally sourced ingredients, and the typically Brazilian flavors, such as the strange sounding but delicious guava and cheese, change often. [$] *Average main: R$10* ✉ *Travessa Sargento Agostinho de Oliveira 47 (Praça João Zelante), Serra Negra* ☎ *019/3892–7794* 🕑 *Closed Mon.* 💳 *No credit cards.*

$ BRAZILIAN FAMILY

🍴 **Padaria Serrana.** Located at the heart of Serra Negra, Serrana is a bakery that serves breakfast, light snacks, and also meals, as well as sharing platters. The *bolinhos de bacalhau* (cod fritters) are a popular choice, as is Ecobier, the local draft beer. Grab a *pao na chapa* (grilled bread) and coffee for breakfast here on a Sunday morning and sit at one of the tables outside to watch the hordes of motorcycling aficionados—they flock to Serra Negra on weekends from other cities on their amazing touring bikes. [$] *Average main: R$20* ✉ *Rua Padre Joao Batista Lavello 21, Serra Negra* ☎ *019/3892–2289* 💳 *No credit cards.*

WHERE TO STAY

$$ HOTEL FAMILY Fodor's Choice ★

🏨 **Hotel Firenze.** The choice of wealthy paulistanos, the Firenze is the smartest hotel in Serra Negra; its location, a stone's throw from the shopping area and the town's main square, is the primary draw. **Pros:** excellent breakfast; comfortable rooms; unparalled service. **Cons:** the bar and games room close early. [$] *Rooms from: R$350* ✉ *Rua Sete de Setembro 118, Serra Negra* ☎ *019/3942–9999* 🌐 *www.hotelfirenzeserranegra.com.br* 🛏 *76 suites* 🍽 *All-inclusive.*

$$ B&B/INN [icon] **Shangri-Lá.** At the edge of town, 3,600 feet above sea level, this little gem offers a wonderful pool area open 24 hours and gazebos with breathtaking views of the mountains. **Pros:** amazing views; good restaurant; comfortable beds. **Cons:** need to drive to reach the town center. [$] *Rooms from: R$270* ✉ *Estrada das Tabaranas, Km 4 at the end of Av. Juca Preto, Serra Negra* ☎ *019/3892–3765* 🛏 *17 suites* 🍴 *Breakfast* 💳 *No credit cards.*

EMBU

27 km (17 miles) west of São Paulo.

Founded in 1554, Embu, or Embu das Artes, is a tiny Portuguese colonial town of whitewashed houses, old churches, wood-carvers' studios, and antiques shops. It has a downtown handicrafts fair every weekend. On Sunday the streets sometimes get so crowded you can barely walk, so it's worth arriving early. Embu also has many stores that sell handicrafts and wooden furniture; most of these are close to where the street fair takes place.

GETTING HERE AND AROUND

EMTU runs an *executivo* (executive or first-class) bus from São Paulo to Embu–Engenho Velho on Line 179, which departs hourly from Anhangabaú. Regular (intermunicipal) buses travel more often: every 20 minutes, Line 033 leaves from Clínicas to Embu. The ride is less comfortable, though: you might have to stand up.

To make the 30-minute drive from São Paulo to Embu, drive from Avenida Professor Francisco Morato to Rodovia Régis Bittencourt (BR 116) and then follow the signs.

ESSENTIALS

Bus Contacts **EMTU.** ✉ *Embu* ☎ *0800/724-0555* 🌐 *www.emtu.sp.gov.br.*

Visitor Information **Tourist Information.** ✉ *Largo 21 de Abril 139, Embu* ☎ *011/4704-6565* 🌐 *www.embu.sp.gov.br.* **Gol Tour Viagens e Turismo.** ✉ *São Paulo* ☎ *011/3256-2388* 🌐 *www.goltour.com.br.*

EXPLORING

FAMILY **Cidade das Abelhas** (*City of the Bees*). In the Atlantic Rain Forest you can visit the Cidade das Abelhas, a farm with a small museum where you can watch bees at work. You can buy honey and other bee-related natural products while your kids climb the gigantic model of a bee. It's about 10 minutes from downtown; just follow the signs. ✉ *Km 7, Estrada da Ressaca, Embu* ☎ *011/4703-6460* 🎟 *R$20* 🕘 *Tues.–Sun. 8:30–5.*

Igreja Nossa Senhora do Rosário. Igreja Nossa Senhora do Rosário was built in 1690 and it's worth seeking out if you won't have a chance to visit the historic cities of Minas Gerais. The church contains baroque images of saints and is next to a 1730 monastery now turned into a museum of sacred art. ✉ *Largo dos Jesuítas 67, Embu* ☎ *011/4704–2654* 🎟 *R$2* 🕘 *Tues.–Sun. 9–5.*

WHERE TO EAT

$$ BRAZILIAN 🍴 **Casa do Barão.** In this colonial-style spot you find contemporary versions of country plates. Go for the exotic *picadinho jesuítico* (round-steak stew), served with corn, fried bananas, and *farofa* (cassava flour sautéed in butter). Unlike most restaurants in the city, Casa do Barão serves single-person portions. Note that there are no salads or juices on the menu. [$] *Average main: R$40* ✉ *Rua Joaquim Santana 12, Embu* ☎ *011/4704–2053* ⏲ *No lunch Thurs. and Fri. Closed Mon.–Wed.*

$$$ ECLECTIC 🍴 **O Garimpo.** Sit in either the beautiul garden or the dining room with fireplace of Embu's most famous restaurant, and then choose between Brazilian regional dishes such as the house specialty, *moqueca de badejo* (spicy fish-and-coconut-milk stew), and German classics such as *eisbein* (pickled and roasted pork shank). There is live music on weekends, but note that it stops at 10:30 on the dot, regardless of how much patrons might be enjoying themselves. Service is patchy on weekends, when the place is busy. [$] *Average main: R$60* ✉ *Rua da Matriz 136, Embu* ☎ *011/4704–6344* ⏲ *No lunch Mon.–Fri.*

$ ECLECTIC 🍴 **Os Girassóis Restaurante e Choperia.** A great variety of dishes is served at this downtown restaurant next to an art gallery and at the center of the weekend hustle and bustle of the artisan fair. The *picanha brasileira* (barbecued steak) with fries and farofa is recommended. [$] *Average main: R$30* ✉ *Rua Nossa Senhora do Rosário 3, Embu* ☎ *011/4781–6671* ⏲ *Closed Mon.*

SHOPPING

Associação dos Artesãos de Embu das Artes. Maintained by the artisan association of Embu das Artes, this shop has a mix of locally produced craft, with some occasional gems. Many of the artisans help run the shop and so are on hand to answer questions about the work. ✉ *Rua Siqueira Campos 100, Embu* ☎ *011/4781–9387* ⏲ *Wed.–Fri. 9–5, weekends 10–6.*

Cantão Móveis e Galeria. Cantão Móveis e Galeria is a good place to buy ceramics, paintings, sculptures, and antique decorations. ✉ *Largo dos Jesuítas 169, Embu* ☎ *011/4781–6671* ⏲ *Weekends 9–5.*

Fodor's Choice ★ **Oficina da Cor.** Clovis Fau-Nasser runs a collective featuring plenty of interesting paintings and sculptures including some of his own works. Many of the pieces are small enough to easily pack away while traveling. ✉ *Rua Nossa Senhora do Rosário 45, Embu* ☎ *011/3433–1290* ⏲ *Fri.–Sun. 10–5.*

SANTANA DE PARNAÍBA

42 km (26 miles) northwest of São Paulo.

With more than 200 preserved houses from the 18th and 19th centuries, Santana de Parnaíba is considered the "Ouro Preto from São Paulo"—a town rich with history and colonial architecture. Santana was founded in 1580; by 1625 it was the most important point of departure for the bandeirantes.

In 1901 the first hydroelectric power station in South America was built here. Throughout the 20th century, Santana managed to retain

5

its houses and charm while preserving a local tradition: a rural type of samba called "de bumbo," in which the pacing is marked by the *zabumba* (an instrument usually associated with rhythms from the northeastern states of Brazil). The proximity to a couple of São Paulo's finest suburbs explains the region's fine dining. Outdoors lovers feel at home with the canopy-walking and trekking options.

GETTING HERE AND AROUND

EMTU's *executivo* (executive or first-class) bus from Barra Funda in São Paulo to Pirapora do Bom Jesus (Line 385) stops in Santana de Parnaíba daily and takes one hour.

To reach Santana de Parnaíba from São Paulo—a 40-minute drive—take the express lane of Rodovia Castelo Branco (SP 280) and pay attention to the road signs. On weekends parking is scarce in Santana de Parnaíba, and parking lots can be expensive.

ESSENTIALS

Bus Contacts **EMTU.** ✉ *Santana de Parnaíba* ☎ *0800/724–0555.*

Visitor Information **Santana de Parnaíba Secretaria de Cultura e Turismo.** ✉ *Largo da Matriz 19, Santana de Parnaíba* ☎ *011/4154–1874, 011/4154–2377* 🌐 *www.santanadeparnaiba.sp.gov.br.*

EXPLORING

Centro Histórico. The best place to begin your trip to Santana de Parnaíba is in the Centro Histórico, where you'll be able to appreciate numerous examples of 17th- and 18th-century colonial architecture. The more than 200 well-preserved houses are concentrated around three streets: Suzana Dias, André Fernandes, and Bartolomeu Bueno—two of which are named after famous bandeirantes. ✉ *Santana de Parnaíba.*

Igreja Matriz de Sant'Anna. Baroque Igreja Matriz de Sant'Anna was built in 1610 and restored in 1892. It has terra-cotta sculptures and an altar with gold-plated details. ✉ *Largo da Matriz, Santana de Parnaíba* ☎ *011/4154–2401* 🎫 *Free* 🕓 *Daily 8–5.*

Museu Casa do Anhanguera. Museu Casa do Anhanguera provides a sharp picture of the bandeirantes era. In a 1600 house (the second-oldest in the state) where Bartolomeu Bueno—nicknamed Anhanguera, or "old devil," by the Indians—was born, the museum displays objects and furniture from the past four centuries. ✉ *Largo da Matriz 9, Santana de Parnaíba* ☎ *011/4154–5042* 🎫 *R$2* 🕓 *Weekdays 8–4:30, weekends 11–5.*

WHERE TO EAT

$$$ BRAZILIAN FAMILY

🍴 **Bartolomeu.** In a 1905 house, this restaurant serves regional specialties like feijoada and *picadinho* (steak stew served with rice and beans, farofa, fried banana, and fried egg). Salmon and boar ribs are some additional choices. [$] *Average main: R$60* ✉ *Praça 14 de Novembro 101, Santana de Parnaíba* ☎ *011/4154–6566* 🕓 *Closed Mon.*

$$ BRAZILIAN

🍴 **São Paulo Antigo.** In a century-old ranch-style house, a hearty buffet lunch is served with dishes such as *feijão tropeiro* (beans with bacon), *dobradinha com feijão branco* (intestines and white-bean stew), or *galinha atolada* (rural-style hen stew). [$] *Average main: R$40* ✉ *Rua Álvaro Luiz do Valle 66, Santana de Parnaíba* ☎ *011/4154–2726* 🕓 *No dinner.*

UNDERSTANDING RIO DE JANEIRO & SÃO PAULO

Brazilian Portuguese Vocabulary

BRAZILIAN PORTUGUESE VOCABULARY

	ENGLISH	PORTUGUESE	PRONUNCIATION
BASICS			
	Yes/no	Sim/Não	**see** ing/nown
	Please	Por favor	pohr fah- **vohr**
	May I?	Posso?	**poh**-sso
	Thank you (very much)	(Muito) obrigado	(**moo** yn-too) o-bree- **gah**-doh
	You're welcome	De nada	day **nah**-dah
	Excuse me	Com licença	con lee- **ssehn**-ssah
	Pardon me/what did you say?	Desculpe/O que disse?	des- **kool**-peh/o.k. **dih**-say
	Could you tell me?	Poderia me dizer?	po-day- **ree**-ah mee dee- **zehrr**
	I'm sorry	Sinto muito	**seen**-too **moo** yn-too
	Good morning!	Bom dia!	bohn **dee**-ah
	Good afternoon!	Boa tarde!	**boh**-ah tahr-dee
	Good evening!	Boa noite!	**boh**-ah nohee-tee
	Goodbye!	Adeus!/Até logo!	ah- **deh** oos/ah- **teh** **loh**-go
	Mr./Mrs.	Senhor/Senhora	sen- **yor** /sen- **yohr**-ah
	Miss	Senhorita	sen-yo- **ri**-tah
	Pleased to meet you	Muito prazer	**moo** yn-too prah- **zehr**
	How are you?	Como vai?	**koh**-mo **vah**-ee
	Very well, thank you	Muito bem, obrigado	**moo** yn-too **beh**-in, o-bree- **gah**-doh
	And you?	E o(a) Senhor(a)?	eh oh sen- **yor** (**yohr**-ah)
	Hello (on the telephone)	Alô	ah- **low**
NUMBERS			
	1	um/uma	oom/ **oom**-ah
	2	dois	**doh** ees
	3	três	**treh** ys
	4	quatro	**kwa**-troh

ENGLISH	PORTUGUESE	PRONUNCIATION
5	cinco	**seen**-koh
6	seis	**seh** ys
7	sete	**seh**-tee
8	oito	**oh** ee-too
9	nove	**noh**-vee
10	dez	**deh**-ees
11	onze	**ohn**-zee
12	doze	**doh**-zee
13	treze	**treh**-zee
14	quatorze	kwa- **tohr**-zee
15	quinze	**keen**-zee
16	dezesseis	deh-zeh- **seh** ys
17	dezessete	deh-zeh- **seh**-tee
18	dezoito	deh- **zoh** ee-toh
19	dezenove	deh-zeh- **noh**-vee
20	vinte	**veen**-tee
21	vinte e um	**veen**-tee eh **oom**
30	trinta	**treen**-tah
32	trinta e dois	**treen**-ta eh **doh** ees
40	quarenta	kwa- **rehn**-ta
43	quarenta e três	kwa- **rehn**-ta e **treh** ys
50	cinquenta	seen- **kwehn**-tah
54	cinquenta e quatro	seen- **kwehn**-tah e **kwa**-troh
60	sessenta	seh- **sehn**-tah
65	sessenta e cinco	seh- **sehn**-tah e **seen**-ko
70	setenta	seh- **tehn**-tah
76	setenta e seis	seh- **tehn**-ta e **seh** ys
80	oitenta	ohee- **tehn**-ta
87	oitenta e sete	ohee- **tehn**-ta e **seh**-tee
90	noventa	noh- **vehn**-ta

ENGLISH	PORTUGUESE	PRONUNCIATION
98	noventa e oito	noh- **vehn**-ta e **oh** ee-too
100	cem	**seh**-ing
101	cento e um	**sehn**-too e **oom**
200	duzentos	doo- **zehn**-tohss
500	quinhentos	key- **nyehn**-tohss
700	setecentos	seh-teh- **sehn**-tohss
900	novecentos	noh-veh- **sehn**-tohss
1,000	mil	meel
2,000	dois mil	**doh** ees meel
1,000,000	um milhão	oom mee-lee- **ahon**

COLORS

black	preto	**preh**-toh
blue	azul	a- **zool**
brown	marrom	mah- **hohm**
green	verde	**vehr**-deh
pink	rosa	**roh**-zah
purple	roxo	**roh**-choh
orange	laranja	lah- **rahn**-jah
red	vermelho	vehr- **meh**-lyoh
white	branco	**brahn**-coh
yellow	amarelo	ah-mah- **reh**-loh

DAYS OF THE WEEK

Sunday	Domingo	doh- **meehn**-goh
Monday	Segunda-feira	seh- **goon**-dah **fey**-rah
Tuesday	Terça-feira	**tehr**-sah **fey**-rah
Wednesday	Quarta-feira	**kwahr**-tah **fey**-rah
Thursday	Quinta-feira	**keen**-tah fey-rah
Friday	Sexta-feira	**sehss**-tah fey-rah
Saturday	Sábado	**sah**-bah-doh

	ENGLISH	PORTUGUESE	PRONUNCIATION
MONTHS			
	January	Janeiro	jah- **ney**-roh
	February	Fevereiro	feh-veh- **rey**-roh
	March	Março	**mahr**-soh
	April	Abril	ah- **breel**
	May	Maio	**my**-oh
	June	Junho	jy **oo**-nyoh
	July	Julho	jy **oo**-lyoh
	August	Agosto	ah- **ghost**-toh
	September	Setembro	seh- **tehm**-broh
	October	Outubro	owe- **too**-broh
	November	Novembro	noh- **vehm**-broh
	December	Dezembro	deh- **zehm**-broh
USEFUL PHRASES			
	Do you speak English?	O Senhor fala inglês?	oh sen- **yor fah**-lah een- **glehs**
	I don't speak Portuguese.	Não falo português.	nown **fah**-loh pohr-too- **ghehs**
	I don't understand (you)	Não lhe entendo	nown ly **eh** ehn- **tehn**-doh
	I understand	Eu entendo	**eh**-oo ehn- **tehn**-doh
	I don't know	Não sei	nown say
	I am American/ British	Sou americano (americana)/inglês (inglêsa)	sow a-meh-ree- **cah**-noh (a-meh-ree-**cah**-nah)/een- **glehs** (een- **gleh**-sa)
	What's your name?	Como se chama?	**koh**-moh seh **shah**-mah
	My name is . . .	Meu nome é . . .	mehw **noh**-meh eh
	What time is it?	Que horas são?	keh **oh**-rahss **sa**-ohn
	It is one, two, three . . . o'clock	É uma/São duas, três . . . hora/horas	eh **oom**-ah/ **sa**- ohn **doo**-ahss, **treh** ys **oh**-rah/ **oh**-rahs
	Yes, please/No, thank you	Sim por favor/Não obrigado	seing pohr fah- **vohr** / nown o-bree- **gah**-doh

ENGLISH	PORTUGUESE	PRONUNCIATION
How?	Como?	**koh**-moh
When?	Quando?	**kwahn**-doh
This/Next week	Esta/Próxima semana	**ehss**-tah/ **proh**-see-mah seh- **mah**-nah
This/Next month	Este/Próximo mêz	**ehss**-teh/ **proh**-see-moh mehz
This/Next year	Este/Próximo ano	**ehss**-teh/ **proh**-see-moh **ah**-noh
Yesterday/today/ tomorrow	Ontem/hoje/amanhã	**ohn**-tehn/ **oh**-jeh/ ah-mah- **nyan**
This morning/ afternoon	Esta manhã/tarde	**ehss**-tah mah- **nyan** / **tahr**-deh
Tonight	Hoje a noite	**oh**-jeh ah **noh** ee-tee
What?	O que?	oh **keh**
What is it?	O que é isso?	oh **keh** eh **ee**-soh
Why?	Por quê?	pohr- **keh**
Who?	Quem?	**keh**-in
Where is . . . ?	Onde é . . . ?	**ohn**-deh **eh**
the train station?	a estação de trem?	ah es-tah- **sah**-on deh train
the subway station?	a estação de metrô?	ah es-tah- **sah**-on deh meh- **tro**
the bus stop?	a parada do ônibus?	ah pah- **rah**-dah doh **oh**-nee-boos
the post office?	o correio?	oh coh- **hay**-yoh
the bank?	o banco?	oh **bahn**-koh
the hotel?	o hotel . . . ?	oh oh- **tell**
the cashier?	o caixa?	oh **kah** y-shah
the museum?	o museo . . . ?	oh moo- **zeh**-oh
the hospital?	o hospital?	oh ohss-pee- **tal**
the elevator?	o elevador?	oh eh-leh-vah- **dohr**
the bathroom?	o banheiro?	oh bahn-yey-roh
the beach?	a praia de . . . ?	ah prahy-yah deh
Here/there	Aqui/ali	ah- **kee** /ah- **lee**

ENGLISH	PORTUGUESE	PRONUNCIATION
Open/closed	Aberto/fechado	ah- **behr**-toh/ feh- **shah**-doh
Left/right	Esquerda/direita	ehs- **kehr**-dah/ dee- **ray**-tah
Straight ahead	Em frente	ehyn **frehn**-teh
Is it near/far?	É perto/longe?	eh **pehr**-toh/ **lohn**-jeh
I'd like to buy...	Gostaria de comprar...	gohs-tah- **ree**-ah deh cohm- **prahr**
a bathing suit	um maiô	oom mahy- **owe**
a dictionary	um dicionário	oom dee-seeoh- **nah**-reeoh
a hat	um chapéu	oom shah- **peh** oo
a magazine	uma revista	oomah heh- **vees**-tah
a map	um mapa	oom **mah**-pah
a postcard	cartão postal	kahr- **town** pohs- **tahl**
sunglasses	óculos escuros	ah-koo-loss ehs- **koo**-rohs
suntan lotion	um óleo de bronzear	oom **oh**-lyoh deh brohn-zeh- **ahr**
a ticket	um bilhete	oom bee-lyeh-teh
cigarettes	cigarros	see- **gah**-hose
envelopes	envelopes	eyn-veh- **loh**-pehs
matches	fósforos	**fohs**-foh-rohss
paper	papel	pah- **pehl**
sandals	sandália	sahn- **dah**-leeah
soap	sabonete	sah-bow- **neh**-teh
How much is it?	Quanto custa?	**kwahn**-too **koos**-tah
It's expensive/cheap	Está caro/barato	**ehss**-tah **kah**-roh/ bah- **rah**-toh
A little/a lot	Um pouco/muito	oom **pohw**-koh/ **moo** yn-too
More/less	Mais/menos	**mah**-ees / **meh**-nohss
Enough/too much/ too little	Suficiente/demais/ muito pouco	soo-fee-see- **ehn**-teh/ deh- **mah**-ees/ **moo** yn-toh pohw-koh

ENGLISH	PORTUGUESE	PRONUNCIATION
Telephone	Telefone	teh-leh- **foh**-neh
Telegram	Telegrama	teh-leh- **grah**-mah
I am ill.	Estou doente.	**ehss**-tow doh- **ehn**-teh
Please call a doctor.	Por favor chame um médico.	pohr fah- **vohr** shah-meh oom **meh**-dee-koh
Help!	Socorro!	soh- **koh**-ho
Help me!	Me ajude!	mee ah- **jyew**-deh
Fire!	Incêndio!	een- **sehn**-deeoh
Caution!/Look out!/ Be careful!	Cuidado!	kooy- **dah**-doh

ON THE ROAD

Avenue	Avenida	ah-veh- **nee**-dah
Highway	Estrada	ehss- **trah**-dah
Port	Porto	**pohr**-toh
Service station	Posto de gasolina	**pohs**-toh deh gah-zoh- **lee**-nah
Street	Rua	**who**-ah
Toll	Pedagio	peh- **dah**-jyoh
Waterfront promenade	Beiramar/orla	behy-rah- **mahrr** / **ohr**-lah
Wharf	Cais	**kah**-ees

IN TOWN

Block	Quarteirão	kwahr-tehy- **rah**-on
Cathedral	Catedral	kah-teh- **drahl**
Church/temple	Igreja	ee- **greh**-jyah
City hall	Prefeitura	preh-fehy- **too**-rah
Door/gate	Porta/portão	**pohr**-tah/porh- **tah**-on
Entrance/exit	Entrada/saída	ehn- **trah**-dah/ sah- **ee**-dah
Market	Mercado/feira	mehr- **kah**-doh/ **fey**-rah
Neighborhood	Bairro	**buy**-ho
Rustic bar	Lanchonete	lahn-shoh- **neh**-teh

ENGLISH	PORTUGUESE	PRONUNCIATION
Shop	Loja	**loh**-jyah
Square	Praça	**prah**-ssah

DINING OUT

ENGLISH	PORTUGUESE	PRONUNCIATION
A bottle of...	Uma garrafa de...	**oo** mah gah- **hah**-fah deh
A cup of...	Uma xícara de...	**oo** mah **shee**-kah-rah deh
A glass of...	Um copo de...	oom **koh**-poh deh
Ashtray	Um cinzeiro	oom seen- **zeh** y-roh
Bill/check	A conta	ah **kohn**-tah
Bread	Pão	**pah**-on
Breakfast	Café da manhã	kah- **feh** dah mah- **nyan**
Butter	A manteiga	ah mahn-tehy-gah
Cheers!	Saúde!	sah- **oo**-deh
Cocktail	Um aperitivo	oom ah-peh-ree- **tee**-voh
Dinner	O jantar	oh **jyahn**-tahr
Dish	Um prato	oom **prah**-toh
Enjoy!	Bom apetite!	bohm ah-peh- **tee**-teh
Fork	Um garfo	**gahr**-foh
Fruit	Fruta	**froo**-tah
Is the tip included?	A gorjeta esta incluída?	ah gohr- **jyeh**-tah ehss-**tah** een-clue- **ee**-dah
Juice	Um suco	oom **soo**-koh
Knife	Uma faca	**oo** mah **fah**-kah
Lunch	O almoço	oh ahl- **moh**-ssoh
Menu	Menu/cardápio	me- **noo** / kahr-dah-peeoh
Mineral water	Água mineral	**ah**-gooah mee-neh- **rahl**
Napkin	Guardanapo	gooahr-dah- **nah**-poh
No smoking	Não fumante	nown foo- **mahn**-teh

ENGLISH	PORTUGUESE	PRONUNCIATION
Pepper	Pimenta	pee- **mehn**-tah
Please give me	Por favor me dê	pohr fah- **vohr** mee **deh**
Salt	Sal	sahl
Smoking	Fumante	foo- **mahn**-teh
Spoon	Uma colher	**oo** mah koh- **lyehr**
Sugar	Açúcar	ah- **soo**-kahr
Waiter!	Garçon!	gahr- **sohn**
Water	Água	**ah**-gooah
Wine	Vinho	**vee**-nyoh

PRONOUNCING PLACE NAMES

NAME	PRONUNCIATION
Amazônia	ah-mah- **zoh**-knee-ah
Bahia	bah- **ee**-ah
Belém	beh- **lein**
Belo Horizonte	**beh**-loh ho-rih- **zon**-teh
Brasília	brah- **zee**-lee-ah
Fortaleza	for-tah- **leh**-zah
Manaus	mah- **nah**-oos
Minas Gerais	**mee**-nahs jyeh- **rah**-ees
Paraná	pah-rah-nah
Porto Alegre	**pohr**-toh ah- **leh**-greh
Recife	heh- **see**-fee
Rio de Janeiro	**hee**-oh day jah- **ne**-roh
Rio Grande do Sul	**hee**-oh **gran**-deh doh sool
Salvador	sahl-vah- **dohr**
Santa Catarina	sahn- **tah** kah-tah-reeh-nah
São Paulo	saohn **pow**-low

TRAVEL SMART
RIO DE JANEIRO
& SÃO PAULO

GETTING HERE AND AROUND

Road conditions in Brazil vary widely throughout the country, and passenger train travel is almost nonexistent. Private cars and public buses are the main modes of intercity road travel. Buses can range (depending on the route and the price) from luxurious and well maintained to basic and mechanically unsound. Traveling by plane is a good option, especially considering the large distances between cities. It's fast, safe, and you can get good prices on tickets.

TRAVEL TIMES FROM SÃO PAULO TO	BY AIR	BY BUS
Rio de Janeiro	1 hour	6 hours
Salvador	2 hours, 30 minutes	27 hours
Manaus	4 hours	54 hours
Florianópolis	1 hour, 15 minutes	9 hours
Brasília	1 hour, 45 minutes	13 hours

▌ AIR TRAVEL

Within a country as big as Brazil, it's especially important to plan your itinerary with care. Book as far in advance as possible, particularly for weekend travel. Planes tend to fill up on Friday, especially to or from popular destinations like Rio and São Paulo. For more booking tips and to check prices and make online flight reservations, see individual airline sites listed at ⊕ *www.infraero.gov.br.*

The majority of direct flights to Brazil fly to São Paulo's Guarhulhos International Airport, although with the increased demand created by the 2016 Olympics, many more direct flights run from New York to Rio than in the past. It's still the case though that most flights to Rio stop in Miami. Most flights from Los Angeles go through Miami as well, save a few

nonstops to São Paulo, and flight times are about 13 hours, not including layover in Miami. The flying time from New York is 10½ hours to Rio and 10 hours to São Paulo. From Miami it's just under 9 hours to Rio de Janeiro and 8½ hours to São Paulo. Usually the connection time in São Paulo is an hour to 90 minutes.

■ TIP→ Reconfirm flights within Brazil, even if you have a ticket and a reservation, as flights tend to operate at full capacity.

When you leave Brazil, be prepared to pay a hefty departure tax, which runs about R$82 ($30) for international flights. A departure tax also applies to flights within Brazil; amounts run as high as R$22 ($8). Although some airports accept credit cards to pay departure taxes, it's wise to have the appropriate amount in reais.

Airline Security Issues Transportation Security Administration. ⊕ *www.tsa.gov.*

Air Travel Resources in Brazil National Civil Aviation Agency (ANAC). ☎ *61/3905–2645 in Brasília, 0800/725–4445 toll-free within Brazil* ⊕ *www.anac.gov.br.*

TRANSFERS BETWEEN AIRPORTS

In the major hubs, airport transfers are offered between airports: in São Paulo between Guarulhos and Congonhas, and in Rio de Janeiro between Galeão and Santos Dumond. This type of service is not common outside of Rio and São Paulo; most other Brazilian cities have only one commercial airport.

FLIGHTS

TO BRAZIL

Miami, New York, and Toronto are the major North American gateways for flights to Brazil. United Airlines flies nonstop from Houston, Newark, and Chicago; American Airlines has direct service from Dallas, Miami, and New York; and Delta offers nonstop service from Atlanta and New York. Air Canada has nonstop service between Toronto and São Paulo.

LATAM Airlines (still known as TAM within Brazil) flies nonstop from Miami to Rio and São Paulo, and from New York to São Paulo with onward service to Rio and many other cities. GOL Linhas Aéreas Intelligentes covers several American cities, including New York, Miami, Atlanta, Los Angeles, Las Vegas, Detroit, Austin, and Chicago. The Colombian airline Avianca flies from Washington, D.C. to São Paulo, with a brief stopover in Bogotá.

Airline Contacts Air Canada. ☎ 888/247–2262 in North America, 11/3254–6630 in Brazil ⊕ www.aircanada.com. **American Airlines.** ☎ 800/433–7300 in North America, 0300/789–7778 in Brazil ⊕ www.aa.com. **Avianca Airlines.** ☎ 800/284–2622 in North America, 0800/891–8668 in Brazil ⊕ www.avianca.com. **Delta Airlines.** ☎ 800/241–4141 in North America, 0800/881–2121 in Brazil ⊕ www.delta.com. **GOL Linhas Aéreas Intelligentes.** ☎ 855/862–9190 in North America, 0800/704–0465 in Brazil ⊕ www.voegol.com.br. **TAM.** ☎ 888/235–9826 in North America, 21/3212–9400 in Rio, 11/3274–1313 in São Paulo ⊕ www.tam.com.br. **United Airlines.** ☎ 800/864–8331 in North America, 011/3145–4200 in São Paulo, 0800/16–2323 in Rio de Janeiro and other cities within Brazil ⊕ www.united.com.

WITHIN BRAZIL

There's regular jet service within the country between all major and most medium-size cities. Remote areas are also accessible—as long as you don't mind small planes. Domestic airlines include TAM and GOL, a reliable low-cost airline with routes covering most major and medium-size Brazilian cities. Another option is Azul Linhas Aéreas, with service to about 100 domestic destinations. The flight from Rio to São Paulo is 1 hour.

Domestic Airlines Azul Linhas Aéreas. ☎ 11/4003–1118 in São Paulo, 0800/884–4040 toll-free from other cities within Brazil ⊕ www.voeazul.com.br. **GOL Linhas Aéreas Intelligentes.** ☎ 855/862–9190 in North America, 0800/704–0465 in Brazil ⊕ www.voegol.com.br. **TAM.** ☎ 888/235–9826 in North America, 0800/570–5700 in Brazil ⊕ www.tam.com.br.

AIR PASSES

If you reside outside Brazil, you're eligible to purchase air passes from TAM or GOL. If you're planning four or more flights within the country within 30 days, these passes—available online through Miami-based travel agency and tour operator Brol—can save you hundreds of dollars. Prices start around $530 (plus tax), and you must purchase your pass before you enter Brazil. Passes that include flights between Brazil and other South American countries are also available.

Air Pass Information Brol. ☎ 888/527–2745 in North America, 21/3500–6704 in Rio ⊕ www.brol.com.

∎ BUS TRAVEL

The nation's *ônibus* (bus) network is affordable, comprehensive, and efficient—compensating for the lack of trains and the high cost of air travel. Every major city can be reached by bus, as can most small to medium-size communities.

The quality of buses in Brazil is good; in many cases better than in the United States. The number of stops at roadside cafés depends on the length of the journey. Usually buses stop at large outlets with food services, and souvenir and magazine stalls.

Lengthy bus trips can involve travel over some poorly maintained highways, a fact of life in Brazil. When traveling by bus, bring water, toilet paper or tissues, and an additional top layer of clothing (handy if it gets cold or as a pillow). Travel light, dress comfortably, and keep a close watch on your belongings—especially in bus stations. If your bus stops at a roadside café, take your belongings with you.

When buying a ticket, you'll be asked whether you want the *ônibus convencional*, the simplest option; the *ônibus executivo*, which gets you air-conditioning, coffee, water, a sandwich, more space between seats, and a pillow and blanket; or the *ônibus-leito*, where you have all facilities of an executive bus plus a seat that reclines completely. If you're over 5 feet 10 inches, it's prudent to buy the most expensive ticket and try for front-row seats, which usually provide more space.

Most buses used for long trips are modern and comfortable, usually with bathrooms and air-conditioning. Note that regular buses used for shorter hauls may be labeled "ar condicionado" ("air-conditioned") but often are not.

Bus fares are substantially cheaper than in North America or Europe. Between Rio and São Paulo (6½–7 hours), for example, a bus departs every half hour and costs about $28; a night sleeper will run about $60. Sometimes competing companies serve the same routes, so it can pay to shop around.

Tickets are sold at bus-company offices, at city bus terminals, in some travel agencies, and online. Larger cities may have different terminals for buses to different destinations, and some small towns may not have a terminal at all (you're usually picked up and dropped off at the line's office, invariably in a central location). Expect to pay with cash, as credit cards aren't accepted everywhere. Reservations or advance-ticket purchases generally aren't necessary except for trips to resort areas during high season—particularly on weekends—or during major holidays (Christmas, Carnival, etc.) and school-break periods (July and December/January). In general, arrive at bus stations early, particularly for peak-season travel.

Traveling between Argentina and Brazil by bus is also a good idea if time is not an issue. The same can be said for Uruguay, Chile, Peru, and other neighboring countries. It's inexpensive and you can enjoy the landscapes. Expect to pay $200 for the 14-hour trip between São Paulo and Buenos Aires.

■ TIP→ To ensure that your destination is understood, write it down on a piece of paper and present it to bus or taxi drivers, most of whom don't speak English.

Bus Information Expresso Brasileiro.
☎ *0300/700–9000* ⊕ *www.expressobrasileiro. com.* **Itapemirim.** ☎ *0800/723–2121* ⊕ *www. itapemirim.com.br.* **Pluma International.**
☎ *41/3212–2689 long distance from North America, 0800/646–0300 toll-free within Brazil* ⊕ *www.pluma.com.br.*

■ CAR TRAVEL

Traveling by car is recommended if you meet the following criteria: you're not pressed for time, you enjoy driving even in places you do not know well, and you do not want to be limited by airline or bus schedules. Traveling by car is, especially if you avoid driving at night, reasonably safe in most areas and is a wonderful way to see the country and access lesser-known areas.

Driving can be chaotic in cities like São Paulo and Rio. In the countryside the usually rough roads, lack of clearly marked signs, and language difference can make driving a challenge. Further, the cost of renting can be steep. All that said, certain areas are most enjoyable when explored on your own in a car: the beach areas of Búzios and the Costa Verde (near Rio), and the North Shore beaches outside São Paulo, to name a few.

If you are feeling at all unsure, don't forget that hiring a car with a driver gives you almost the same level of flexibility with none of the stress of driving in an unfamiliar country. You could hire a car and driver through your hotel concierge, or make a deal with a taxi driver for extended sightseeing at a long-term rate. Often drivers charge a set hourly rate, regardless of the distance traveled. You'll have to pay cash, but you may actually spend less than you would for a rental car.

ROAD CONDITIONS
Brazil has more than 1.7 million km (1.05 million miles) of highway, about 12% of it paved. While roads in the South are often excellent, the country's highway

department estimates that 40% of the federal highways (those with either the designation *BR* or a state abbreviation such as *RJ* or *SP*), which constitute 70% of Brazil's total road system, are in a dangerous state of disrepair. Evidence of this is everywhere: potholes, lack of signage, inadequate shoulders. Landslides and flooding after heavy rains are frequent and at times shut down entire stretches of key highways. Recent construction has improved the situation, but independent land travel in Brazil definitely has its liabilities.

The Brazilian Federal Government maintains a (Portuguese-language) website with up-to-date information on road conditions throughout the country (⊕ *www. dnit.gov.br*); the site also has downloadable state road maps. A private Brazilian company, Quatro Rodas (⊕ *www. guia4rodas.com.br*), publishes road maps that list local phone numbers for obtaining current road conditions; these cost about R$36 ($14).

FROM	TO	DISTANCE
São Paulo	Rio de Janeiro	430 km (267 miles)
Rio de Janeiro	Búzios	168 km (104 miles)
Rio de Janeiro	Salvador	1,560 km (970 miles)
São Paulo	Belo Horizonte	596 km (370 miles)
São Paulo	Florianópolis	691 km (430 miles)
São Paulo	Foz do Iguaçu	1,037 km (644 miles)

ROADSIDE EMERGENCIES
Apart from toll roads, which generally have their own services, roadside assistance is available only sporadically and informally through local private mechanics. However, the Automóvel Clube do Brasil (Automobile Club of Brazil) provides emergency assistance to foreign motorists who are members of an automobile club in their own nation. If you're

not a member of an automobile club, you can call 193 from anywhere in the country. This is a universal number staffed by local fire departments. The service is in Portuguese only. In case of emergency, the fastest way to summon assistance is to call one of the following services: Fire Brigade (193); Police (190); Federal Highway Patrol (191); Ambulance (192); Civil Defense (199).

RULES OF THE ROAD
Brazilians drive on the right, and in general traffic laws are the same as those in the United States. The use of seat belts is mandatory. The minimum driving age is 18 and children should always sit in the backseat. Do not use your cell phone while driving.

The national speed limit ranges from 50 to 90 kph (31 to 56 mph), although vehicles considered light can often travel at higher speeds on freeways. Pay close attention to signs. Some sections of highway have pedestrian crossings and the speed limit drops as you approach them. In large cities like São Paulo, there are now cameras to detect and fine speeding and aggressive drivers. This has decreased traffic accidents significantly, but you should be careful anyway. Some drivers slow down only when close to these cameras. The worst offenders are bus and truck drivers. In cities be very careful around motorcycles, as their drivers are notorious for flouting traffic rules.

If you get a ticket for some sort of violation, be polite with the police officer and try to solve the issue either by accepting the ticket (if you committed the violation) or by explaining your position (if you did not commit a violation). Even though it's common to see scams in cases like this, the best option is to solve the problem as honestly as possible, especially if you're a foreigner.

TRAFFIC AND PARKING

In major cities, traffic jams are common in rush hours (8 am, 6 pm); the problem is especially bad in São Paulo and Rio de Janeiro. At rush hour you may find the local driving style more aggressive.

Finding a space in Rio or São Paulo is a major task. It's best to head for a garage or a lot and leave your car with the attendant. The cost of parking depends on the city and the neighborhood: downtown garages, close to stores, will certainly be more expensive than those in residential areas. There are no meters; instead you must post a coupon in your car's window, which allows you to park for a certain time period (one or two hours). You can buy them from uniformed street-parking attendants or at newsstands. Should you find a space on the street, you'll probably have to pay a fee for parking services.

■ TIP➔ **No-parking zones are marked by a crossed-out capital letter E (which means estacionamento, Portuguese for "parking").**

TOLL ROADS

Tollbooths, better known as *pedagio* in Portuguese, are common in Brazil. These are located along many highways, especially in the Southeast and around São Paulo. Fees depend on the type of vehicle you're driving. Make sure you carry cash, including some small change.

GASOLINE

In Brazil gasoline costs around R$2.80 per liter, ($1.05 or about $4 per gallon). Unleaded gas, called *especial,* costs about the same. Brazil also has an extensive fleet of ethanol-powered cars, *carro a álcool,* and you might end up with one from a rental agency. Ethanol fuel is sold at all gas stations and is a little cheaper than gasoline. However, these cars get lower mileage, so they offer little advantage over gas-powered cars. Stations are plentiful within cities and on major highways, and many are open 24/7. In smaller towns few stations take credit cards, and their hours are more limited. If you want a receipt, ask for a *recibo.*

DRIVER'S LICENSES

Visitors to Brazil can drive with their home-country driver's license for the first 180 days they are in the country, as long as they also carry a copy of it translated into Portuguese and another piece of ID. You can also drive with an international driver's license. International driving permits (IDPs) are available from the American and Canadian automobile associations. These international permits, valid only in conjunction with your regular driver's license, are universally recognized.

CAR RENTAL

Rates are sometimes—but not always—better if you book in advance or reserve through a rental agency's website. Although international car-rental agencies have better service and maintenance track records than local firms (they also provide better breakdown assistance), your best bet at getting a good rate is to rent on arrival, particularly from local companies. But reserve ahead if you plan to rent during a holiday period or at a particularly popular destination, or need a specific type of car (an SUV or a van). You can contact local agencies through their websites in advance. At many airports, agencies are open 24 hours.

When you reserve a car, ask about cancellation penalties, taxes, drop-off charges (if you're planning to pick up the car in one city and leave it in another), and surcharges (for being under or over a certain age, for additional drivers, or for driving across state or country borders or beyond a specific distance from your point of rental). All these things can add substantially to your costs. Request car seats and extras such as a GPS when you book.

Some common-sense tips: Always give the rental car a once-over to make sure the headlights, jack, and tires (including the spare) are in working condition. Before you set out, establish an itinerary and ask about gas stations. Be sure to plan your daily driving distance conservatively and don't drive after dark.

■TIP→ **Make sure that a confirmed reservation guarantees you a car. Agencies sometimes overbook, particularly for busy weekends and holiday periods.**

CAR-RENTAL INSURANCE

Car insurance is not compulsory when renting a car, but if you have plans to drive in more than one city we strongly recommend buying car insurance, given the bad conditions of Brazilian roads in some states and the risk of accidents. Most car-rental companies offer an optional insurance against robbery and accidents. Minimum age for renting a car is 21, but some companies require foreign clients to be at least 25 or charge extra for those under 26.

If you own a car, your personal auto insurance may cover a rental to some degree, though not all policies protect you abroad; always read your policy's fine print. If you don't have auto insurance, then seriously consider buying the collision- or loss-damage waiver (CDW or LDW) from the car-rental company, which eliminates your liability for damage to the car.

Some credit cards offer CDW coverage, but it's usually supplemental to your own insurance and rarely covers SUVs, minivans, luxury models, and the like. If your coverage is secondary, you may still be liable for loss-of-use costs from the car-rental company. But no credit-card insurance is valid unless you use that card for *all* transactions, from reserving to paying the final bill. All companies exclude car rental in some countries, so be sure to find out about the destination to which you are traveling.

Some rental agencies require you to purchase CDW coverage; many will even include it in quoted rates. All will strongly encourage you to buy CDW—possibly implying that it's required—so be sure to ask about such things before renting. In most cases it's cheaper to add a supplemental CDW plan to your comprehensive travel-insurance policy than to purchase it from a rental company. That said, you don't want to pay for a supplement if you're required to buy insurance from the rental company. Another possibility is to purchase insurance through a third-party provider such as Travel Guard (⊕ *www. travelguide.com*), which can cost significantly less than coverage offered by car-rental companies.

ESSENTIALS

■ ACCOMMODATIONS

All hotels in Rio and São Paulo have bathrooms in their rooms. The simplest type of accommodations usually consists of a bed, TV, table, a little fridge, a telephone, and a bathroom with a shower. In luxury hotels you'll also generally have Internet, cable TV, and a bathroom with a bathtub and shower. Hotels listed with EMBRATUR, Brazil's national tourism board, are rated using stars. Staff training is a big part of the rating, but it's not a perfect system, since stars are awarded based on the number of amenities rather than their quality.

If you ask for a double room, you'll get a room for two people, but you're not guaranteed a double mattress. If you'd like to avoid twin beds, ask for a *cama de casal* ("couple's bed").

■ **TIP→ For top hotels in Rio during Carnival, you must make reservations a year in advance.**

Carnival, the year's principal festival, takes place during the four days preceding Ash Wednesday. Hotel rates rise by at least 30% for Carnival. Not as well known outside Brazil but equally impressive is Rio's New Year's Eve celebration. More than a million people gather along Copacabana Beach for a massive fireworks display and to honor the sea goddess Iemanjá. To ensure a room, book at least six months in advance.

Most hotels and other lodgings require you to give your credit-card details before they will confirm your reservation. However you book, get confirmation in writing and have a copy of it handy when you check in.

Be sure you understand the hotel's cancellation policy. Some places allow you to cancel without any kind of penalty—even if you prepaid to secure a discounted rate—if you cancel at least 24 hours in advance. Others require you to cancel a week in advance or penalize you the cost of one night. Small inns and B&Bs are most likely to require you to cancel far in advance. Most hotels allow children under a certain age to stay in their parents' room at no extra charge, but others charge for them as extra adults; find out the cutoff age for discounts.

BED AND BREAKFASTS

B&Bs in Brazil are comfortable, friendly, and offer a modicum of privacy. They're a nice option if you're looking for something a little more intimate than a hotel.

AirBnB is another option that has become a popular choice in Brazil. You can look up listings of short-term lets and small B&Bs that locals post on the site. Often you will be staying in someone's home while they are away. Usually the rates are a fraction of other accommodations.

Contacts AirBnB. ⊕ *www.airbnb.com.* **Bed & Breakfast.com.** ☎ *844/271–6829, 512/322–2710* ⊕ *www.bedandbreakfast.com.* **BnB Finder.com.** ☎ *888/469–6663* ⊕ *www. bnbfinder.com.*

FAZENDAS

Another accommodations option is to stay on a *fazenda* (farm), or *hotel fazenda,* where you can experience a rural environment. They are ideal for families with kids, as most have adventure sports and programs for children. Some farms in the state of São Paulo date back to colonial times, when they were famous Brazilian coffee farms. Prices range from around $70 to $150 per day for adults, but the actual cost depends a lot on which facilities and activities you choose. The prices we give usually include all meals (but be sure to check this beforehand) and are valid for the months of January, February, July, and December (high season). You can get discounts of up to 30% during the low season.

POUSADAS

If you want the facilities of a hotel plus the family environment of an apartment, but at a lower cost, a *pousada* is a good option. Cheaper than hotels and farms, pousadas are simple inns, often in historic houses. They usually offer breakfast and have swimming pools, parking lots, air-conditioning and/or fans, TVs, refrigerators, and common areas such as bars, laundry, and living rooms. Some have a common kitchen for guests who prefer to cook their own meals. Hidden Pousadas Brazil is a helpful website for locating pousadas.

Contacts Hidden Pousadas Brazil. ☎ *219/8122–2000* ⊕ *www. hiddenpousadasbrazil.com.*

■ ADDRESSES

Finding addresses in Brazil can be frustrating, as streets often have more than one name and numbers are sometimes assigned haphazardly. In some places street numbering doesn't enjoy the wide popularity it has achieved elsewhere; hence, you may find the notation "s/n," meaning *sem número* (without number). In rural areas and small towns, there may only be directions to a place rather than a formal address (i.e., street and number). Often such areas do not have official addresses.

In Portuguese *avenida* (avenue), *rua,* (street) and *travessa* (lane) are abbreviated (as *Av., R.,* and *Trv.* or *Tr.*), while *estrada* (highway) often isn't abbreviated, and *alameda* (alley) is abbreviated (as *Al.*). Street numbers follow street names. Eight-digit postal codes (CEP) are widely used.

In some written addresses you might see other abbreviations. For example, an address might read, "R. Presidente Faria 221-4°, s. 413, 90160-091 Porto Alegre, RS," which translates to 221 Rua Presidente Faria, 4th floor, Room 413 ("s." is short for *sala*), postal code 90160-091, in the city of Porto Alegre, in the state of Rio

Grande do Sul. You might also see *andar* (floor) or *edifício* (building).

The abbreviations for Brazilian states are: Acre (AC); Alagoas (AL); Amapá (AP); Amazonas (AM); Bahia (BA); Ceará (CE); Distrito Federal (Federal District, aka Brasília; DF); Espírito Santo (ES); Goiás (GO); Maranhão (MA); Minas Gerais (MG); Mato Grosso do Sul (MS); Mato Grosso (MT); Pará (PA); Paraíba (PB); Paraná (PR); Pernambuco (PE); Piauí (PI); Rio de Janeiro (RJ); Rio Grande do Norte (RN); Rio Grande do Sul (RS); Rondonia (RO); Roraima (RR); Santa Catarina (SC); São Paulo (SP); Sergipe (SE), Tocantins (TO).

■ COMMUNICATIONS

INTERNET

Internet access is widespread, and Wi-Fi is often available in Rio and São Paulo. Many hotels have in-room access to Wi-Fi, but some charge $5 to $10 per day for the privilege. 3G access in big cities like São Paulo and Rio is common, but check with your local provider to find a plan that mitigates the often-steep roaming charges. Switching your device from cellular data to Wi-Fi whenever it is available should save you money.

Be discreet about carrying laptops, smart phones, and other obvious displays of wealth, which can make you a target of thieves. Conceal your laptop in a generic bag and keep it close to you at all times.

PHONES

The good news is that you can now make a direct-dial telephone call from virtually any point on earth. The bad news? You can't always do so cheaply. Calling from a hotel is almost always the most expensive option; hotels usually add huge surcharges to all calls, particularly international ones. In remote areas you can phone from call centers or sometimes even the post office, but in big cities these call centers don't exist anymore. Calling cards usually keep costs to a minimum, but only if you purchase them locally. And then there are mobile phones, which are sometimes more prevalent—particularly in the developing world—than landlines; as expensive as mobile phone calls can be, they are still usually a much cheaper option than calling from your hotel.

Because of the recent increase in demand for mobile phones in Brazil, an extra digit has been added to mobile phone numbers to make more numbers available. If calling a mobile phone in the states of São Paulo and Rio, make sure to add a 9 in front of the usual eight digits of the number.

The country code for Brazil is 55. When dialing a Brazilian number from abroad, dial the international access code of your home country, the Brazilian country code, the two-digit area code (drop the initial 0 if there is one), and the local number.

Public phones are everywhere and are called *orelhões* (big ears) because of their shape. The phones take phone cards only.

CALLING WITHIN BRAZIL

Local calls can be made most easily from pay phones, which take phone cards only. A bar or restaurant may allow you to use its private phone for a local call if you're a customer.

If you want to call from your hotel, remember long-distance calls within Brazil are expensive, and hotels add a surcharge.

With the privatization of the Brazilian telecommunications network, there's a wide choice of long-distance companies. Hence, to make direct-dial long-distance calls, you must find out which companies serve the area from which you're calling and then get their access codes—the staff at your hotel can help. (Some hotels have already made the choice for you, so you may not need an access code when calling from the hotel itself.) For long-distance calls within Brazil, dial 0 + the access code + the area code and number. To call Rio, for example, dial 0, then 21 (for Embratel, a major long-distance and international

provider), then 21 (Rio's area code), and then the number.

CALLING OUTSIDE BRAZIL

International calls from Brazil are extremely expensive. Hotels also add a surcharge, increasing this cost even more. Calls can be made from public phone booths with a prepaid phone card. You can also try going to a phone office, although with the rise of mobile phones, very few of these still exist. The staff at your hotel may know whether there is one nearby.

For international calls, dial 00 + 23 (for Intelig, a long-distance company) or 21 (for Embratel, another long-distance company) + the country code + the area code and number. For operator-assisted international calls, dial 00–0111. For international information, dial 00–0333. To make a collect long-distance call (which will cost 40% more than a normal call), dial 9 + the area code and the number.

The country code for United States and Canada is 1.

AT&T and Sprint operators are also accessible from Brazil; get the local access codes before you leave home.

Access Codes AT&T Direct. ☎ *0800/703–6335 for individuals* ⊕ *www.att.com/esupport/ traveler.jsp.* **Sprint International Access.** ☎ *866/866–7509* ⊕ *mysprint.sprint.com.*

CALLING CARDS

All pay phones in Brazil take phone cards only. Buy a phone card, a *cartão telefônico*, at a newsstand, drugstore, or post office. Cards come with a varying number of units (each unit is usually worth a couple of minutes), which will determine the price. Buy a couple of cards if you don't think you'll have the chance again soon. These phone cards can be used for international, local, and long-distance calls within Brazil. Be aware that calling internationally using these cards is extremely expensive and your units will expire pretty quickly. It's advisable to buy several cards with the maximum number of units (75 minutes). A 20-minute card costs about $1.25, a 50-minute card about $3.25, and a 75-minute about $5.

In big cities like São Paulo and Rio de Janeiro, you can buy an international phone card, which is around the same price as the 75-minute local card.

MOBILE PHONES

Big cities in Brazil often have 4G Internet available to anyone with a smart phone, although 3G usually works much better and is more readily available. Roaming charges can be extremely high, however, so make sure to check rates with your provider before arriving in Brazil. Your provider may offer international data plans and should be able to provide details on connectivity. It's a good idea to use local Wi-Fi when available and to make international calls with services like Skype, Viber, or WhatsApp.

If you will be making many local calls and will be in the country for a few weeks, consider buying a new SIM card (note that your provider may have to unlock your phone for you), and signing up for a pay-as-you-go plan. You'll then have a local number and can make calls at local rates. Be aware that as a non-Brazilian you must show proof of citizenship (such as a passport) to buy a SIM card, which costs around $10. Note that you'll use up the credit on your SIM card more quickly when calling numbers in a Brazilian state other than the one in which you purchased the card. Many travelers buy a new SIM card in each state they visit. If you plan on visiting rural areas, find out from locals which mobile phone provider works best in the area before buying your SIM card. There are often several available, but one or two providers tend to get better coverage because of tower locations, especially in Amazonas.

▌ EATING OUT

Food in Brazil is delicious, inexpensive (especially compared with North America and Europe), and bountiful. Portions are huge and presentation is tasteful. A lot of restaurants prepare plates for two people; when you order, be sure to ask if one plate will suffice—or even better, glance around to see the size of portions at other tables.

In major cities the variety of eateries is staggering: restaurants of all sizes and categories, snack bars, and fast-food outlets line downtown streets and fight for space in shopping malls. Pricing systems vary from open menus to buffets where you weigh your plate. In São Paulo, for example, Italian eateries—whose risottos rival those of Bologna—sit beside Pan-Asian restaurants, which, like the chicest spots in North America and Europe, serve everything from Thai *satay* to sushi. In addition, there are excellent Portuguese, Chinese, Japanese, Lebanese, and Spanish restaurants.

Outside the cities you find primarily typical, low-cost Brazilian meals that consist simply of *feijão preto* (black beans) and *arroz* (rice) served with beef, chicken, or fish. Manioc, a root vegetable that's used in a variety of ways, and beef are adored everywhere.

Many Brazilian dishes are adaptations of Portuguese specialties. Fish stews called *caldeiradas* and beef stews called *cozidos* (a wide variety of vegetables boiled with different cuts of beef and pork) are popular, as is *bacalhau*, salt cod cooked in sauce or grilled. *Salgados* (literally, "salt-eds") are appetizers or snacks served in sit-down restaurants as well as at stand-up *lanchonetes* (luncheonettes). Brazil's national dish is *feijoada* (a stew of black beans, sausage, pork, and beef), which is often served with rice, shredded kale, orange slices, and manioc flour or meal—called *farofa* if it's coarsely ground, *farinha* if finely ground—that has been fried with onions, oil, and egg.

One of the most avid national passions is the *churrascaria*, where meats are roasted on spits over an open fire, usually *rodízio* style. Rodízio means "going around," and waiters circulate nonstop carrying skewers laden with charbroiled hunks of beef, pork, and chicken, which are sliced onto your plate with ritualistic ardor. For a set price you get all the meat and side dishes you can eat. Starve yourself a little before going to a rodízio place. Then you can sample everything on offer.

At the other end of the spectrum, vegetarians can sometimes find Brazil's meat-centric culture challenging, especially outside of larger cities. Increasingly, though, salads and vegetarian options are offered at nicer restaurants in areas catering to foodies, tourists, and those with more international tastes. You'll also find salads at buffet restaurants, called *quilos,* found throughout Brazil.

Brazilian *doces* (desserts), particularly those of Bahia, are very sweet, and many are descendants of the egg-based custards and puddings of Portugal and France. *Cocada* is shredded coconut caked with sugar; *quindim* is a small tart made from egg yolks and coconut; *doce de banana* (or any other fruit) is banana cooked in sugar; *ambrosia* is a lumpy milk-and-sugar pudding.

Coffee is served black and strong with sugar in demitasse cups and is called *cafezinho.* (Requests for *descafeinado* [decaf] are met with a firm shake of the head "no," a blank stare, or outright amusement.) Coffee is taken with milk—called *café com leite*—only at breakfast. Bottled water (*agua mineral*) is sold carbonated or plain (*com gás* and *sem gás,* respectively).

MEALS AND MEALTIMES

It's hard to find breakfast (*café da manhã*) outside a hotel restaurant, but in bakeries (*padarias*) you can always find something breakfast-like. At lunch (*almoço*) and dinner (*jantar*) portions are large. Often a single dish will easily feed two people; no one will be the least bit surprised if you order one entrée and ask for two plates. In addition some restaurants automatically bring a *couvert* (an appetizer course of such items as bread, cheese, or pâté, olives, quail eggs, and the like). You'll be

charged extra for this, and you're perfectly within your rights to send it back if you don't want it.

Mealtimes vary according to locale. In Rio and São Paulo, lunch and dinner are served later than in the United States. In restaurants lunch usually starts around noon and can last until 3. Dinner is always eaten after 7 and in many cases not until 10.

Unless otherwise noted, the restaurants listed in this guide are open daily for lunch and dinner.

PAYING

Credit cards are widely accepted at restaurants in the major cities. In the countryside all but the smallest establishments generally accept credit cards as well, but check before you order. Smaller, family-run restaurants are sometimes cash-only. Gratuity is 10% of the total sum, and it's usually included in the bill. The tip is always optional; if you weren't happy with the service, you can ask for it to be removed from your bill.

For more tip guidelines, see Tipping.

RESERVATIONS AND DRESS

Appropriate dress for dinner in Brazil can vary dramatically. As a general rule, dress more formally for expensive restaurants. In most restaurants dress is casual.

Regardless of where you are, it's a good idea to make a reservation if you can. We only mention them specifically when reservations are essential (there's no other way you'll ever get a table) or when they're not accepted. For popular restaurants, book as far ahead as you can (often 30 days), and reconfirm as soon as you arrive. (Large parties should always call ahead to check the reservations policy.) We mention dress only when men are required to wear a jacket or a jacket and tie.

WINES, BEER, AND SPIRITS

The national drink is the *caipirinha,* made of crushed lime, sugar, and *pinga* or *cachaça* (sugarcane liquor). When whipped with crushed ice, fruit juices, and condensed milk, the pinga/cachaça becomes a *batida*. A *caipivodka*, or *caipiroska*, is the same cocktail with vodka instead of cachaça. Most bars also make both drinks using a fruit other than lime, such as kiwi and *maracujá* (passion fruit). Brazil has many brands of bottled beer. In general, though, Brazilians prefer tap beer, called *chopp*, which is sold in bars and restaurants. Be sure to try the carbonated soft drink *guaraná*, made using the Amazonian fruit of the same name. It's extremely popular in Brazil.

▌ELECTRICITY

The current in Brazil isn't regulated: in São Paulo and Rio it's 110 or 120 volts (the same as in the United States and Canada). Electricity is AC (alternating current) at 60 Hz, similar to that in Europe. To use electric-powered equipment purchased in the U.S. or Canada, it's wise to bring a converter and adapter, although these days, increasingly, most electronics are designed to convert themselves— if your device specifies a range of 100 to 240 volts, you won't have any problem using it in Brazil. Wall outlets take Continental-type plugs, with two or three round prongs, although you may come across older outlets that take two-pronged flat plugs. Consider buying a universal adapter, which has several types of plugs in one handy unit. Some hotels are equipped to handle various types of plugs and electrical devices.

▌EMERGENCIES

In case of emergency, call one of the services below. Calling the fire brigade is a good option, since they're considered one of the most efficient and trustworthy institutions in Brazil. If you need urgent and immediate support, talk to the people around you. Brazilians are friendly and willing to help. They'll go out of their way to speak your language and find help.

If you've been robbed or assaulted, report it to the police. Unfortunately, you shouldn't expect huge results for your trouble. Call your embassy if your passport has been stolen or if you need help dealing with the police.

General Emergency Contacts
Federal Highway Patrol. ☎ *191.* **Fire Brigade (Bombeiros).** ☎ *193* ⊕ *www. bombeirosemergencia.com.br.* **Police.** ☎ *190.* **Ambulance.** ☎ *192.* **Civil Defence.** ☎ *199.*

▌HEALTH

The most common types of illnesses are caused by contaminated food and water. Especially in developing countries, drink only bottled, boiled, or purified water and drinks; don't drink from public fountains or use ice. It's even prudent to use bottled water to brush your teeth. Make sure food has been thoroughly cooked and is served to you fresh and hot; avoid vegetables and fruits that you haven't washed (in bottled or purified water) or peeled yourself. If you have problems, mild cases of traveler's diarrhea may respond to over-the-counter medications. Be sure to drink plenty of fluids; if you can't keep fluids down, seek medical help immediately.

Infectious diseases can be airborne or passed via mosquitoes and ticks and through direct or indirect physical contact with animals or people. Some, including Norwalk-like viruses that affect your digestive tract, can be passed along through contaminated food. Speak with your physician and/or check the CDC or World Health Organization websites for health alerts, particularly if you're pregnant, traveling with children, or have a chronic illness.

English-speaking medical assistance in Brazil is rare. It's best to contact your consulate or embassy if you need medical help. Seek private clinics or hospitals, since getting an appointment in the government's health-care system is a slow process.

DIVERS' ALERT

Do not fly within 24 hours of scuba diving. Neophyte divers should have a complete physical exam before undertaking a dive. If you have travel insurance that covers evacuations, make sure your policy applies to scuba-related injuries, as not all companies provide this coverage.

FOOD AND DRINK

The major health risk in Brazil is traveler's diarrhea, caused by eating contaminated fruit or vegetables or drinking contaminated water. So watch what you eat—on and off the beaten path. Avoid ice, uncooked food, and unpasteurized milk and milk products, and drink only bottled water or water that has been boiled for at least 20 minutes, even when brushing your teeth. The use of bottled water for brushing your teeth is not necessary in large cities, where water is treated. Don't use ice unless you know it's made from purified water. (Ice in city restaurants is usually safe.) Peel or thoroughly wash fresh fruits and vegetables. Avoid eating food from street vendors.

Choose industrially packaged beverages when you can. Order tropical juices only from places that appear clean and reliable.

HEATSTROKE

Heatstroke and heat prostration are common though easily preventable maladies throughout Brazil. The symptoms for either can vary but always start with headaches, nausea, and dizziness. If ignored, these symptoms can worsen until you require medical attention. In hot weather be sure to rehydrate regularly, wear loose lightweight clothing, and avoid overexerting yourself.

INFECTIOUS DISEASES AND VIRUSES

The Amazon and a few other remote areas are the only places in Brazil where you really need worry about infectious diseases. Most travelers to Brazil return home unscathed. However, you should visit a doctor at least six weeks prior to traveling to discuss recommended vaccinations, some of which require multiple shots over a period of weeks. If you get sick weeks, months, or in rare cases, years after your trip, make sure your doctor administers blood tests for tropical diseases.

Meningococcal meningitis and typhoid fever are common in certain areas of Brazil—and not only in remote areas like the Amazon. Meningitis has been a problem around São Paulo in recent years. Dengue fever and malaria—both caused by mosquito bites—are common in Brazil or in certain areas of Brazil, like Rio de Janeiro. Both are usually only a problem in the Amazon, but dengue can affect urban areas and malaria is sometimes found in urban peripheries. Talk with your doctor about what precautions to take.

OVER-THE-COUNTER REMEDIES

Mild cases of diarrhea may respond to Imodium (known generically as loperamide) or Pepto-Bismol (not as strong), both of which can be purchased over the counter at a *farmácia* (pharmacy). Drink plenty of purified water or *chá* (tea)—*camomila* (chamomile) is a good folk remedy, as is dissolving a tablespoon of cornstarch in a mix of lime juice and water. In severe cases rehydrate yourself with a salt–sugar solution: ½ teaspoon *sal* (salt) and 4 tablespoons *açúcar* (sugar) per quart of *agua* (water).

An effective home remedy for diarrhea is the same as the rehydrating concoction: a teaspoon of sugar plus a quarter teaspoon of salt in a liter of water.

Aspirin is *aspirina*; Tylenol (acetaminophen; paracetamol) is pronounced *tee-luh-nawl*. Advil (ibuprofen) is ah-jee-viu.

SHOTS AND MEDICATIONS

■ TIP→ If you travel a lot internationally—particularly to developing nations—refer to the CDC's Health Information for International Travel (aka Traveler's Health Yellow Book). Info from it is posted on the CDC website (wwwnc.cdc.gov/travel).

The best recommendation to avoid health problems is to see a doctor before and after traveling, just to be on the safe side. Some vaccines must be applied long before traveling so that their protective effect is guaranteed, and some prophylactic medicines must be taken also in advance so that the doctor and the patient are aware of possible side effects.

Vaccinations against hepatitis A and B, meningitis, typhoid, and yellow fever are highly recommended. Consult your doctor about whether to get a rabies vaccination. Check with the CDC's International Travelers' Hotline if you plan to visit remote regions or stay for more than six weeks.

For travel anywhere in Brazil, it's recommended that you have updated vaccines for diphtheria, tetanus, and polio. Children must additionally have current inoculations against measles, mumps, and rubella.

Yellow fever immunization is compulsory to enter Brazil if you're traveling directly from one of the following countries in South America (or from one of several African countries): Bolivia; Colombia; Ecuador; French Guiana; Peru; or Venezuela. You must have an International Certificate of Immunization proving that you've been vaccinated.

Health Warnings National Centers for Disease Control & Prevention (*CDC*). ☎ *800/232–4636* ⊕ *www.cdc.gov.* **World Health Organization** (*WHO*). ⊕ *www.who.int.*

▍ MONEY

Brazil's unit of currency is the *real* (R$; plural: *reais*). One real is 100 *centavos* (cents). There are notes worth 2, 5, 10, 20, 50, and 100 reais, together with coins worth 5, 10, 25, and 50 centavos and 1 real.

ATMS AND BANKS

Your own bank will probably charge a fee for using ATMs abroad; the foreign bank you use may also charge a fee. Nevertheless, you'll usually get a better rate of exchange at an ATM than you will at a currency-exchange office. And extracting

funds as you need them is a safer option than carrying around a large amount of cash.

■ **TIP→** PINs with more than four digits are not recognized at ATMs in many countries. If yours has five or more, remember to change it before you leave.

Nearly all the nation's major banks have ATMs, known in Brazil as *caixas eletrônicos,* for which you must use a card with a credit-card logo. MasterCard/Cirrus holders can withdraw at Banco Itau, Banco do Brasil, HSBC, and Banco24horas ATMs; Visa holders can use Bradesco ATMs and those at Banco do Brasil. American Express cardholders can make withdrawals at most Bradesco ATMs marked "24 horas." To be on the safe side, carry a variety of cards. For your card to function in some ATMs, you may need to hit a screen command (perhaps, *estrangeiro* or *inglês*) if you are a foreign client.

Banks are, with a few exceptions, open weekdays 10 to 4. Avoid using ATM machines alone and at night, and use ATMs in busy, highly visible locations whenever possible.

CREDIT CARDS

It's a good idea to inform your credit-card company before you travel, especially if you're going abroad and don't travel internationally very often. Otherwise, the credit-card company might put a hold on your card owing to unusual activity—not a good thing halfway through your trip. Record all your credit-card numbers—as well as the phone numbers to call if your cards are lost or stolen—in a safe place, so you're prepared should something go wrong. Both MasterCard and Visa have general numbers you can call (collect if you're abroad) if your card is lost, but you're better off calling the number of your issuing bank, since MasterCard and Visa usually just transfer you to your bank; your bank's number is usually printed on your card.

If you plan to use your credit card for cash advances, you'll need to apply for a

PIN at least two weeks before your trip.

Although it's usually cheaper (and safer) to use a credit card abroad for large purchases (so you can cancel payments or be reimbursed if there's a problem), note that some credit-card companies *and* the banks that issue them add substantial percentages to all foreign transactions, whether they're in a foreign currency or not. Check on these fees before leaving home, so there won't be any surprises when you get the bill. Credit card fraud does happen in Brazil, so always conceal PIN numbers and keep your receipts.

■ **TIP → Before you charge something, ask the merchant whether he or she plans to do a dynamic currency conversion (DCC).** In such a transaction the credit-card processor (shop, restaurant, or hotel, not Visa or MasterCard) converts the currency and charges you in dollars. In most cases you'll pay the merchant a 3% fee for this service in addition to any credit-card company and issuing-bank foreign-transaction surcharges.

Dynamic currency conversion programs are becoming increasingly widespread. Merchants who participate in them are supposed to ask whether you want to be charged in dollars or the local currency, but they don't always do so. And even if they do offer you a choice, they may well avoid mentioning the additional surcharges. The good news is that you *do* have a choice. And if this practice really gets your goat, you can avoid it entirely thanks to American Express; with its cards, DCC simply isn't an option.

For costly items use your credit card whenever possible—you'll come out ahead, whether the exchange rate at which your purchase is calculated is the one in effect the day the vendor's bank abroad processes the charge or the one prevailing on the day the charge company's service center processes it at home.

Reporting Lost Cards American Express.
☎ *800/528-4800 in U.S., 336/393-1111 collect from abroad ⊕ www.americanexpress. com.* **Diners Club.** ☎ *800/234-6377 in U.S.,*

514/881-3735 collect from abroad ⊕ www. dinersclub.com. **MasterCard.** ☎ *800/627-8372 in U.S., 636/722-7111 collect from abroad, 0800/891-3294 in Brazil ⊕ www.mastercard. com.* **Visa.** ☎ *800/847-2911 in U.S., 410/581-9994 collect from abroad, 0800/891-3679 in Brazil ⊕ www.visa.com.*

CURRENCY AND EXCHANGE

At this writing, the real is at about 3.12 to the U.S. dollar and 2.52 to the Canadian dollar.

For the most favorable rates, change money through banks. Although ATM transaction fees may be higher abroad than at home, ATM rates are excellent because they're based on wholesale rates offered only by major banks. You won't do as well at *casas de câmbio* (exchange houses), in airports or bus stations, in hotels, in restaurants, or in stores. ATMs also allow you to avoid the often long lines at airport exchange booths.

Outside Rio and São Paulo, changing money in Brazil becomes more of a challenge. When leaving a large city for a smaller town, bring enough cash for your trip.

■ **TIP → Even if a currency-exchange booth has a sign promising no commission, rest assured that there's some kind of huge, hidden fee. And as for rates, you're almost always better off getting foreign currency at an ATM or exchanging money at a bank.**

▌ PACKING

For sightseeing, casual clothing and good walking shoes are appropriate; most restaurants don't require formal attire. For beach vacations, bring lightweight sportswear, a bathing suit, a beach cover-up, a sun hat, and waterproof sunscreen that is at least SPF 30. A sarong or a light cotton blanket makes a handy beach towel, picnic blanket, and cushion for hard seats, among other things.

If you're going to Rio in summer (December, January, and February), dress more informally and feel free to wear flip-flops (thongs) all day—and don't forget your sunglasses. São Paulo, which has lower temperatures, tends to be more formal and more conservative when it comes to clothing (sometimes even Brazilians are shocked by the way people in Rio dress). In both cities it's always a good idea to have some nice outfits for going out at night.

∎ PASSPORTS AND VISAS

At this writing, passports and visas are required for citizens—even infants—of the U.S. and Canada for entry to Brazil. Business travelers may need a special business visa. It has all the same requirements as a tourist visa, but you'll also need a letter on company letterhead addressed to the embassy or consulate and signed by an authorized representative (other than you), stating the nature of your business in Brazil, itinerary, business contacts, dates of arrival and departure, and that the company assumes all financial and moral responsibility while you're in Brazil.

PASSPORTS

When in Brazil, carry your passport or a copy with you at all times. Make two photocopies of the data page (one for someone at home and another for you, carried separately from your passport). If you lose your passport, promptly call the nearest embassy or consulate and the local police.

If your passport is lost or stolen, first call the police—having the police report can make replacement easier—and then call your embassy. You'll get a temporary Emergency Travel Document that will need to be replaced once you return home. Fees vary according to how fast you need the passport; in some cases the fee covers your permanent replacement as well. The new document will not have your entry stamps; ask if your embassy takes care of this, or whether it's your responsibility to get the necessary immigration authorization.

Contacts Brazilian Embassy. ⊠ *3006 Massachusetts Ave. NW,* ☏ *202/238–2700*

⊕ *washington.itamaraty.gov.br/en-us.* **Brazilian Embassy.** ⊠ *450 Wilbrod St.,* ☏ *613/237–1090* ⊕ *ottawa.itamaraty.gov.br/pt-br.*

VISAS

A visa is essentially formal permission to enter a country. Visas allow countries to keep track of you and other visitors—and generate revenue (from application fees).

Go to the website for the Brazilian embassy or consulate nearest you for the most up-to-date visa information. At this writing, tourist visa fees are US$160 for Americans and C$81.25 for Canadians. Additional fees may be levied if you apply by mail. Obtaining a visa can be a slow process, and you must have every bit of paperwork in order when you visit the consulate, so read instructions carefully. (For example, in the United States, the fee can only be paid by a U.S. Postal Service money order.)

To get the location of the Brazilian consulate to which you must apply, contact the Brazilian embassy. Note that some consulates don't allow you to apply for a visa by mail. If you don't live near a city with a consulate, consider hiring a concierge-type service to do your legwork. Many cities have these companies, which not only help with the paperwork, but also send someone to wait in line for you.

When you apply by mail, you send your passport to a designated consulate, where your passport will be examined and the visa issued. Expediters—usually the same ones who handle expedited passport applications—can do all the work of obtaining your visa for you; however, there's always an additional cost (often at least $50 per visa).

Most visas limit you to a single trip—basically during the actual dates of your planned vacation. Other visas allow you to visit as many times as you wish for a specific period of time. Remember that requirements change, sometimes at the drop of a hat, and the burden is on you to make sure that you have the appropriate visas. Otherwise, you'll be turned away at the airport or, worse, deported after you arrive in the country. No company or travel insurer gives refunds if your travel plans are disrupted because you didn't have the correct visa.

U.S. Passport Information U.S. Department of State. ☎ 877/487-2778 ⊕ travel.state.gov.

U.S. Passport and Visa Expediters A. Briggs Passport & Visa Expeditors. ☎ 800/806-0581, 202/338-0111 ⊕ www.abriggs.com. **American Passport Express.** ☎ 800/455-5166, ⊕ www.americanpassport.com. **Passport Express.** ☎ 800/362-8196 ⊕ www. passportexpress.com. **Travel Document Systems.** ☎ 800/874-5100, 202/638-3800 ⊕ www.traveldocs.com. **Travel the World Visas.** ☎ 866/886-8472, 202/223-8822 ⊕ www.world-visa.com.

GENERAL REQUIREMENTS FOR BRAZIL	
Passport	Must be valid for 6 months after date of arrival.
Visa	Required for Americans (US$160) and Canadians (C$81.25)
Vaccinations	Needed in some areas: yellow fever and diphtheria. Recommended for all travelers but not mandatory: hepatitis A and B, typhoid, meningitis, tetanus, polio.
Driving	Driver's license with Portuguese translation or international driver's license required; CDW is compulsory on car rentals and will be included in the quoted price
Departure Tax	Approximately R$82 ($30), payable in cash only

∎ RESTROOMS

The word for "bathroom" is *banheiro*, though the term *sanitários* (toilets) is also used. *Homens* means "men" and *mulheres* means "women." Around major tourist attractions and along the main beaches in big cities, you can find public restrooms, which aren't necessarily clean.

In some smaller beach cities, there are no facilities at the beach, so be prepared to walk a bit to find a bathroom.

In other areas you may have to rely on the kindness of local restaurant and shop owners. If a smile and polite request (*"Por favor, posso usar o banheiro?"*) doesn't work, become a customer—the purchase of a drink or a knickknack might just buy you a trip to the bathroom. Rest areas with relatively clean, well-equipped bathrooms are plentiful along major highways. Still, carry a pocket-size package of tissues in case there's no toilet paper. Tip bathroom attendants with a few spare centavos.

∎ TAXES

Sales tax is included in the prices shown on goods in stores but listed separately on the bottom of your receipt. Hotel, meal, and car-rental taxes are usually tacked on in addition to the costs shown on menus and brochures. At this writing, hotel taxes are roughly 5%, meal taxes 10%, and car-rental taxes 12%.

Departure taxes on international flights from Brazil aren't always included in your ticket and can run as high as R$82 ($30); domestic flights may incur a R$22 ($8) tax. Although U.S. dollars are accepted in some airports, be prepared to pay departure taxes in reais.

∎ TIME

Brazil covers four time zones. Most of the country—including Rio and São Paulo—is three hours behind GMT (Greenwich Mean Time). From October to March (exact days vary), Brazil observes daylight saving time in most of the country, so in many areas it stays light until 8:30 pm.

∎ TIPPING

Wages can be paltry in Brazil, so a little generosity in tipping can go a long way. Tipping in dollars is not recommended—at best it's insulting; at worst, you might be targeted for a robbery. Large hotels that receive lots of international guests are the exception. Some restaurants add a 10% service charge onto the check. If there's no service charge, you can leave as much as you want, but 15% is a good amount. In deluxe hotels tip porters R$2 per bag, chambermaids R$2 per day, and bellhops R$4–R$6 for room and valet service. Tips for doormen and concierges vary, depending on the services provided. A good tip is around R$30, with the average at about R$15. For moderate and inexpensive hotels, tips tend to be minimal (salaries are so low that virtually anything is well received).

If a taxi driver helps you with your luggage, a per-bag charge of about R$1 is levied in addition to the fare. In general, you don't tip taxi drivers. If a service station attendant does anything beyond filling up the gas tank, leave him a small tip of some spare change. Tipping in bars and cafés follows the rules of restaurants, although at outdoor bars Brazilians rarely leave a gratuity if they have had only a soft drink or a beer. At airports and at train and bus stations, tip the last porter who puts your bags into the cab (R$1 a bag at airports, 50 centavos a bag at bus and train stations).

❚ VISITOR INFORMATION

EMBRATUR, Brazil's national tourism organization, doesn't have offices overseas, though its website is helpful. For information in your home country, contact the Brazilian embassy or the closest consulate, some of which have websites and staff dedicated to promoting tourism.

The official consular website in New York, ⊕ *novayork.itamaraty.gov.br/en-us*, has details about other consulates and the embassy as well as travel information and links to other sites. Cities and towns throughout Brazil have local tourist boards, and some state capitals also have state tourism offices.

Contacts Brazilian Consulate–New York. ☎ *917/777–7777* ⊕ *www.brazilny.org.* **EMBRATUR.** ☎ *61/2023–7146 in Brazil* ⊕ *www. visitbrasil.com.*

ONLINE RESOURCES

The online magazine *Brazzil* and Internet newspaper the Rio Times Online have interesting English-language articles on culture and politics. Brazil's biggest national newspaper, *Folha de S.Paulo,* also publishes its content in English and Spanish on the international version of its site. Gringoes.com is an online forum for foreigners living in or traveling to Brazil, where you'll find info about everything from security to getting a driver's license. And VivaBrazil.com provides background and travel info on Brazil's different regions as well as links that will help you arrange your trip.

All About Brazil Brazzil Magazine. ⊕ *www. brazzil.com.* **Folha de S.Paulo.** ⊕ *www1.folha. uol.com.br/internacional/en.* **Gringoes.com.** ⊕ *www.gringoes.com.* **Rio Times Online.** ⊕ *www.riotimesonline.com.* **VivaBrazil.com.** ⊕ *www.vivabrazil.com.*

INDEX

PHOTO CREDITS

Front cover: Catarina Belova / Shutterstock [Description: View of Copacabana beach, Rio de Janeiro, Brazil.] Back cover, from left to right: Filipefrazao84 | Dreamstime.com; luoman/iStockphoto; Catarina Belova / Shutterstock. Spine: Richmatts /iStockphoto. 1, Tumonis | Dreamstime.com. 2, Cicero Dias Viegas / age fotostock. 4, Ekaterinabelova | Dreamstime.com. 5 (top), Celso Pupo / Shutterstock. 5 (bottom), Marilialima | Dreamstime.com. 6 (top left), Gianluca Curti / Shutterstock. 6 (top right), Kato Inowe / Shutterstock. 6 (bottom left), HandmadePictures / Shutterstock. 6 (bottom right), Yadid Levy / age fotostock. 7 (top), John Copland / Shutterstock. 7 (bottom), Nicoletaraftu | Dreamstime.com. 8 (top left), Maxisport / Shutterstock. 8 (top right), Sfmthd | Dreamstime.com. 8 (bottom), ostill / Shutterstock. Chapter 1: Experience Rio de Janeiro and Sao Paulo: 11, Catarina Belova / Shutterstock. 13 (left), Ken Ross/viestiphoto.com. 13 (right), giulio andreini/Marka/age fotostock. 14, Raga Jose Fuste/ age fotostock. 15 (left), Degree/eStock Photo. 15 (right), Darius Koehli/age fotostock. 17 (all), Tony Morrison/South American Pictures. 25, Orange Stock/viestiphoto.com. 27, Jeffrey Dunn/viestiphoto.com. 28, Kord.com/age fotostock. 29, Bruno Ehrs/Corbis. 30, Ricardo Beliel / BrazilPhotos / Alamy. 31 (left), SuperStock/age fotostock. 31 (right), angelo cavalli/Marka/age fotostock. 32, Halaska/Mauritius/ age fotostock. 33, Gianni Muratore / Alamy. 35, Blaine Harrington/age fotostock. 37 (left), Agencia Fotosite/drr.net. 37 (right), Sue Cunningham Photographic / Alamy. Chapter 2: Rio de Janiero: 39, Celsodiniz | Dreamstime.com. Chapter 3: Side Trips from Rio: 121, Icon72 | Dreamstime.com. Chapter 4: Sao Paulo: 153, cifotart / Shutterstock. Chapter 5: Side Trips from Sao Paulo: 217, Katoton | Dreamstime.com.

Welcome To The Rio Olympics insert: 1 (top), Stephen Frink Collection / Alamy. 1 (bottom), Courtesy of Rio 2016™ Committee. 2, Fernando Maia | Rio Tur. 3, John Biever/Sports Illustrated/Getty Images. 4, J.P. Engelbrecht | Rio Tur. 5, Ian Trower/ AWL Images Ltd. 6, Epa European Pressphoto Agency b.v. / Alamy. 7, T photography / Shutterstock. 8, Filipe Frazao / Shutterstock.

About Our Writers: All photos are courtesy of the writers except for the following: Lucy Bryson, courtesy of Ademar Ribeiro.

NOTES

NOTES

NOTES

Fodor's RIO DE JANEIRO & SÃO PAULO

Publisher: Amanda D'Acierno, *Senior Vice President*

Editorial: Arabella Bowen, *Editor in Chief*; Linda Cabasin, *Editorial Director*

Design: Tina Malaney, *Associate Art Director*; Chie Ushio, *Senior Designer*

Photography: Jennifer Arnow, *Senior Photo Editor*; Mary Robnett, *Photo Researcher*

Production: Linda Schmidt, *Managing Editor*; Evangelos Vasilakis, *Associate Managing Editor*; Angela L. McLean, *Senior Production Manager*

Maps: Rebecca Baer, *Senior Map Editor*; Mark Stroud (Moon Street Cartography), David Lindroth, *Cartographers*

Sales: Jacqueline Lebow, *Sales Director*

Marketing & Publicity: Heather Dalton, *Marketing Director*; Katherine Punia, *Publicity Director*

Business & Operations: Susan Livingston, *Vice President, Strategic Business Planning*; Sue Daulton, *Vice President, Operations*

Fodors.com: Megan Bell, *Executive Director, Revenue & Business Development*; Yasmin Marinaro, *Senior Director, Marketing & Partnerships*

Copyright © 2016 by Fodor's Travel, a division of Penguin Random House LLC

Writers: Lucy Bryson, Jill Langlois, Angelica Mari, Claire Rigby

Editors: Luke Epplin, Kathryn Lane, Denise M. Leto

Production Editor: Carolyn Roth

3rd Edition

ISBN 978-1-101-87835-4

ISSN 1941–0239

SPECIAL SALES

This book is available at special discounts for bulk purchases for sales promotions or premiums. For more information, e-mail specialmarkets@penguinrandomhouse.com.

PRINTED IN THE UNITED STATES OF AMERICA

10 9 8 7 6 5 4 3 2 1

ABOUT OUR WRITERS

 Lucy Bryson is a freelance British writer based in Rio de Janeiro since 2007. She writes for a range of print and web publications and is Rio Local Expert for *USA TODAY 10 Best*. Lucy is author and editor of a Horizon Travel Press ebook about Rio Carnival, and editor of Horizon's upcoming guide to travel in the Amazon. Lucy lives in the beautiful historic neighborhood of Santa Teresa with her Brazilian partner, their British-Brazilian daughter, and their lively carioca dog. For this edition, Lucy updated the Experience, Rio de Janeiro, and Side Trips from Rio chapters and the Olympics feature.

 Jill Langlois is a Canadian freelance journalist who has been living in São Paulo since 2010. She has covered Brazil for publications like the *New York Times*, the *Los Angeles Times*, *USA Today*, *Fortune*, and *Foreign Policy*. Jill loves searching for hidden gems and new hot spots across the country with her Brazilian husband by her side. For this edition, Jill updated Travel Smart Rio de Janeiro & São Paulo.

 Angelica Mari is a Brazilian journalist based between the city of São Paulo and the mountain resort of Serra Negra. She is a Brazil correspondent for international technology and business titles and also contributes to several travel and lifestyle magazines, mostly on off-the-beaten-track destinations in the states in the southeast of Brazil. For this edition, she updated the Side Trips from São Paulo chapter.

Claire Rigby moved to Brazil in 2010 to launch and run *Time Out São Paulo* as its editor in chief, having previously been editor of Time Out's Buenos Aires magazine, and before that, its Mexico City guide. In 2014, she became a freelance journalist, and now reports from Brazil for publications including the *Guardian*, *New York Times*, *Monocle*, and *VICE News*, as well as a range of art and travel titles. For this edition, Claire updated the São Paulo chapter.